MOODY GOSPEL

MARK

COMMENTARY

MOODY GOSPEL

MARK

COMMENTARY

LOUIS BARBIERI

MOODY PRESS
CHICAGO

ISBN: 0-8024-5450-X

1 3 5 7 9 10 8 6 4 2

Printed in the United States of America

To Carol,
a faithful and devoted wife and mother,
who has been a partner with me
in the ministry all our married life

CONTENTS

NEW TESTAMENT PALESTINE

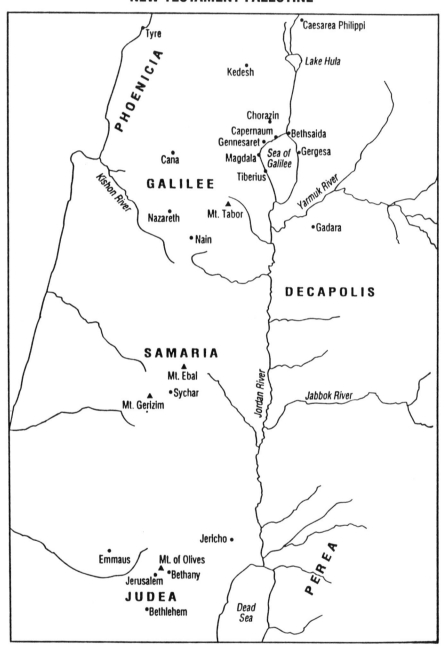

Tyre

Caesarea Philippi

PHOENICIA

Lake Hula

Kedesh

Chorazin

Capernaum
Gennesaret • Bethsaida

Cana

Magdala • Gergesa

Sea of
Galilee

GALILEE

Tiberius

Kishon River

Yarmuk River

Nazareth   Mt. Tabor

Gadara

Nain

DECAPOLIS

SAMARIA

Mt. Ebal

Sychar

Jordan River

Jabbok River

Mt. Gerizim

Jericho

PEREA

Emmaus   Mt. of Olives

Jerusalem • Bethany

JUDEA

• Bethlehem

Dead
Sea

PREFACE

The gospel of Mark has been one of my favorite books through-out my ministry career. This has been true for at least four reasons.

First, the second gospel was one of the early books that I had the privilege of translating from Greek into English when I was in semi-nary. Mark was the "text" that we used in first-year Greek, and I fell in love with Mark's vivid way of communicating his message.

Second, the picture Mark gives of the Lord is that of an active, vital Servant who moves with rapidity to accomplish His tasks. Perhaps my own Roman/Italian ancestry enables my mind to function in a fash-ion similar to Mark's readers. I enjoy reading of a Savior who moves decisively and quickly to minister among people. My own personality easily relates to that kind of a Savior.

Third, I have had the opportunity of traveling to the land of Isra-el eight times. My favorite region of the country is the area around the Sea of Galilee. Since most of Mark's gospel takes place in that region, I find it very easy to picture the stories as they occurred.

Finally, I have had the opportunity of teaching Mark a number of times in classroom situations and of preaching sermons from the pul-pit. What a thrill it is to communicate the message of the Servant who comes to serve and to give His life a ransom for many!

I have enjoyed researching the various problem texts in Mark's gospel. I am indebted to various authors whose names appear in the Bibliography. I have quoted from the works of a number of these individuals, but I have greatly benefited from the insights of many others who have challenged my thinking in various areas. It has been my goal to present what I believe Mark was trying to communicate. Some may not agree with my conclusions, but at least I have given the reader something to think about and to react to. No verse in the gospel has been overlooked.

I am indebted to my former secretary, Mrs. Delores Poulos, who typed, retyped, and again retyped my manuscript. "Dodie" is a faithful servant of the Lord who has kept me on top of things during my ministry in the Des Plaines Bible Church. I thank the Lord for her ministries to me and to that local body of believers. It is fitting that she would have the privilege of typing material about the faithful Servant of Jehovah, for she so often demonstrates that quality as she serves.

Introduction

AUTHORSHIP

Each gospel has come down through church history without any indication of authorship. Although none of the gospels names its author, each has had a fairly consistent testimony in the church. Evidence for authorship is usually of two types: external evidence, or that which comes from outside the book itself; and internal evidence, or that which is found within the pages of the book. A brief examination of each follows.

EXTERNAL EVIDENCE

The conclusion that John Mark is the author of the second gospel is the consistent traditional view of church history. Furthermore this testimony is widespread in the church. Good external evidence comes from the usual sources pointing to John Mark as the author. Papias (born between A.D. 50 and 60) appears to be the first church father to bear witness to the authorship of the second gospel as coming from the hand of Mark. Justin Martyr, Irenaeus, Clement of Rome, and Ignatius, as well as others, came to the same conclusion.[1] That John Mark did indeed write the second gospel is a valid conclusion

---

1. Norman B. Geisler and Kent Nix, *A General Introduction to the Bible* (Chicago: Moody, 1968), 193.

based on the external evidence of church history. "The evidence for the Markan authorship is early and unanimous. There seems to be no reason why tradition should assign this Gospel to a minor character like Mark rather than Peter, if he did not write it."[2]

INTERNAL EVIDENCE

Though the external evidence strongly supports the Markan authorship of this gospel, the internal evidence would have to be classified as extremely weak. In fact, there is only one brief incident in 14:50-52 that may have reference to the author. This passage states that a young man followed Jesus and the disciples to the Garden of Gethsemane. In the confusion of the events of the arrest, this young man was grabbed by one of the soldiers. He ran away into the night, leaving the sheet that had been wrapped around his body in the hands of the soldier. None of the other gospels mentions this account. The details of it undoubtedly were extremely vivid in the memory of the one to whom it happened. Is it possible that the young man was Mark and that this was his way of communicating the fact that he was there? Perhaps it is.

How these events might have related to Mark is explained in the commentary. If this young man is not Mark, there is no other internal evidence that points to the possible author. Whereas this event does not point to Mark per se, it may very well have been his signature on the book. Tenney comments, "It is difficult to resist the temptation to see here a personal reminiscence of an experience vivid to the author, but not significant to the main thread of the tale."[3]

WHO IS BEHIND THIS BOOK?

One of the principles used in determining the canonical books accepted by the churches was the test of apostleship. Was the book directly written by an apostle, or was there an apostle behind the writing of the book?[4] John Mark was not an apostle, for he is never declared to be one of the Twelve in the New Testament. Who then was the apostle behind the second gospel? There is good indication that the apostle behind the second gospel was Simon Peter. That a rela-

2. Henry C. Thiessen, *Introduction to the New Testament* (Grand Rapids: Eerdmans, 1943), 141.
3. Merrill C. Tenney, *New Testament Survey* (Grand Rapids: Eerdmans, 1961), 156.
4. Charles C. Ryrie, *Basic Theology* (Wheaton, Ill.: Victor, 1986), 108.

tionship seems to have existed between John Mark and Peter is verified both externally and internally to the gospel.

Several lines of argumentation from outside the gospel point to a
relationship between these men. (1) There is a recorded statement
from Papias, quoted by Eusebius, in which Papias cited the testimony
of an elder who was evidently an older contemporary.[5] The statement
attributed to him was: "Mark, having become the interpreter of Peter,
wrote down accurately whatever he remembered of the things said
and done by the Lord, but not however in order."[6] (2) In the first
letter Peter wrote to the Christians of Asia Minor, he concluded by
saying that Mark, his "son," was with him in "Babylon" (probably a
symbolic reference to Rome) and sent along his greeting (1 Peter
5:13). (3) The material covered in the second gospel is the same as
that mentioned by Peter in his report given to the church at Jerusalem
in Acts 10:34-43. Is it possible that Mark went along on Peter's trip
from Joppa to Caesarea? A comparison of Acts 10:23 and 11:12 could
allow for the inclusion of Mark among this group of six brethren. (4)
In the second letter of Peter, there was an awareness on Peter's part of
his imminent death (2 Peter 1:13-15). In light of that fact, Peter declared that he was taking steps to make sure his brethren would be
able to call to mind all the things he had taught. Although many believe he was referring to the two epistles he had written, could it be
that he was referring to Mark? Mark was with him in "Babylon," and
Peter could have been filling his mind with all the events of the life of
Jesus Christ that he remembered so that Mark could write them down.

As with the external evidence, several lines of internal evidence
point to a relationship between Peter and Mark that could possibly
substantiate the influence of Peter on this gospel. (1) The second gospel basically begins with the call of Peter to become a follower of the
Lord. Very little is said of the events that occurred before this (the
ministry of John the Baptist, and the baptism and temptation of Jesus),
but Peter's call is listed immediately in Mark 1:16. (2) The second gospel obviously has an eyewitness behind it. Mark makes great use of
two verb tenses: the historic present and the imperfect. He relates the
stories concerning Jesus Christ in the present tense, which pictures
them as actually occurring when in reality the events were long past.
The purpose of this literary device was to give greater vividness to

5. William L. Lane, *The Gospel of Mark*, NICNT (Grand Rapids: Eerdmans, 1974), 8.
6. Cited by Eusebius, *Hist. Eccl.* III.xxxix.15.

details. One can almost see the events happening before one's eyes as the stories are presented. There are about 150 historic presents in this gospel compared with seventy-eight in Matthew and only four in Luke. When one compares the lengths of the gospels and then notes the uses of the historical present, Mark's gospel clearly reflects attention to vivid detail. The imperfect tense conveys the picture of events occurring over a period of time, but the action occurs in the past. Both literary devices add great vividness to the stories. (3) The second gospel contains a number of things about Simon Peter that are not found in the other gospels, and some favorable details about Peter are omitted by Mark. For examples of details about Peter not found in the other gospels, see 1:36; 11:21; 13:3; 16:7. It is easy to see Peter telling these stories to Mark, including the detail that he was the one present on that particular occasion. But in Christian humility, certain stories about Peter that tend to put him in a favorable light are omitted. For example, Peter's walking on the water (Matt. 14:28-31), his capture of the fish to pay the tax (Matt. 17:24-27), his mission with John to prepare for the Passover meal (cf. Mark 14:12-16 and Luke 22:7-13), and his trip to the empty tomb with John (John 20:2-10) are not in the second gospel. "Peter's sins and weaknesses are recorded faithfully, but the praise which he received elsewhere (for example in Matt. 16:17) is omitted from Mark."[7] (4) The second gospel gives special attention to the ministry of Jesus in Galilee, especially Capernaum, which was the place of Peter's residence.

Both the external and the internal evidence point in the direction of a clear relationship between Peter and John Mark. That Peter exercised a direct control over the writing of the gospel is doubtful, as will be explained under the dating of the gospel. But there seems to be a clear connection between Peter and John Mark.

WHO WAS JOHN MARK?

John Mark has traditionally been connected with this gospel, but who was this young man? Ten direct references to him may be found in the pages of the New Testament: Acts 12:12, 25; 13:5, 13; 15:37, 39; Colossians 4:10; Philemon 24; 1 Peter 5:13; and 2 Timothy 4:11.

7. William Hendriksen, *Exposition of the Gospel According to Mark* (Grand Rapids: Baker, 1975), 13.

In the first clear reference to him in Acts 12:12, it is revealed that the Jerusalem church was meeting in his home. The implication of this statement is that Mark must have come from a fairly wealthy family if the home in which he lived was large enough to accommodate the church and was staffed by slaves. But the contention that he may have been a "spoiled rich kid" is unsubstantiated.

When Paul and Barnabas went from Jerusalem back to Antioch to continue their ministry, they took Mark along with them (Acts 12:25). When the Holy Spirit separated Paul and Barnabas for the first missionary journey, Mark went along with them as a "helper" (Acts 13:5), only to leave them for some reason in the middle of the journey and return home (Acts 13:13). The reasons for his defection are not made clear in Scripture, although it is clear that Paul thought his reasons not justified. Perhaps his early upbringing in a wealthy household made it difficult for him to deal with the conditions on the journey.

Mark became a focus of controversy when the second missionary journey was about to begin (Acts 15:37-39). Barnabas again wanted to take Mark along, but Paul was not in favor of that arrangement since Mark had "deserted them" on the first trip. Though Satan wanted to defeat the work of the Lord through this argument, he was not victorious. Instead of only one missionary team, two teams went out: Barnabas took Mark and went to Cyprus; Paul took Silas and headed overland for Asia Minor.

Perhaps it was the family relationship between Barnabas and Mark that caused Barnabas to defend Mark. Colossians 4:10 implies that they were cousins. But perhaps Barnabas also saw in Mark essential qualities of an effective servant that needed to be developed. That Mark became an effective servant cannot be denied. In fact, his life has often been pictured as a story of restoration, and Barnabas undoubtedly had a lot to do with that restoration.

After the separation of Barnabas and Paul, little is heard of Mark until near the end of the lives of Peter and Paul. Mark is with Paul in Rome at the time of the writing of Colossians (Col. 4:10) and Philemon (Philem. 24) and also with Peter in "Babylon," probably a reference to Rome, at the time of writing of 1 Peter (1 Peter 5:13). In his final letter to Timothy, Paul makes a concluding admission concerning Mark when he says, "Pick up Mark and bring him with you, for he is useful to me for service" (2 Tim. 4:11). The one who had been the point of debate and disruption had become useful again. Much of the credit for that usefulness probably should go to Barnabas, for he continued to minister in the life of Mark.

Tradition concerning this young man contains one additional fact. He was nicknamed "stump-fingered." Some believe this name was attached more to the gospel of Mark than to the man himself.[8] The gospel is "stump-fingered," or abbreviated, because it does not contain any details concerning the early life of the Lord and little following the Resurrection. It is the briefest account of the Lord's life and contains material that by and large is found in the other gospels. The conclusion of the book is rather abrupt, leaving many details up in the air. But perhaps the nickname refers to an accident that happened to Mark sometime during his life. In fact, if he was the young man in the garden who ran away from the guards, could that event have resulted in the loss of his fingers? Perhaps. Or did he simply have small hands and fingers in comparison with the rest of his frame? The truth behind his nickname will probably never be known for certain.

WHAT IS THE RELATIONSHIP OF
MARK TO MATTHEW AND LUKE?

When one compares the first three gospel accounts, one discovers a very close relationship in content and in the way the writers have expressed themselves. As a result, the first three gospels have been referred to as the Synoptic Gospels. The word "synoptic" is made up of two Greek words: the preposition *syn,* which means together, and the verb *optanomai,* which means to see. The word put together carries the idea of seeing things together or seeing them with a common view. Since the three gospels see the life of the Lord Jesus Christ in a similar manner, natural questions have arisen: Were these men aware of each other's writings, and if they were, did anyone borrow from anyone else? The whole resulting issue has been referred to as the synoptic problem, and it has been discussed by scholars for centuries.[9]

There were few attempts to deal with the literary problem presented by the Synoptics in the early church. In fact, it was not until the middle of the eighteenth century that the problem was brought forth

8. Ibid., 3.
9. See my comments in "Matthew," in *Bible Knowledge Commentary* (Wheaton, Ill.: Victor, 1983), 13-15.

by modern critical scholarship. In 1835, Karl Lachmann first called attention to the fact that the diversity of the Synoptic Gospels was more apparent than real. It was noted that if Matthew and Luke were studied and compared to Mark, the solution was very apparent. It was clear to modern scholarship that Matthew and Luke were both dependent on Mark.

This hypothesis became accepted by the scholarly world and was redefined further by other scholars. In fact, if one holds to a view other than the priority of Mark, one needs to state clearly his reasons for his departure from the vast majority of scholarship. Such a statement has been given by C. S. Mann in his departure from the established scholarly hypothesis that Mark was indeed the first gospel.[10] Mann does a thorough job of wrestling with the various issues that have been proposed by scholarship, and he concludes that "it is the view of the present writer that Mark is dependent on both Matthew and Luke, but that no absolutely certain grounds exist for determining priority between Matthew and Luke." He goes on to state,

> Although the relationships between Matthew and Luke are firmly established, there is no adequate evidence at the present moment to indicate which of the two, Matthew or Luke, first committed the traditions he knew to fixed form in writing. On balance, the advantage seems to lie with Matthew with its strongly Jewish and Palestinian emphasis.[11]

Thiessen, in his *Introduction to the New Testament,* has presented a classic overview of the whole synoptic problem.[12] Charles Dyer has wrestled with the issue of synoptic interdependence and has come to the following conclusion:

> After viewing all of the above data it is this writer's opinion that there is no evidence to postulate a tradition of literary dependence among the Gospels. The dependence is rather a parallel dependence on the actual events which occurred. The Gospels are similar because they are all recording the same events. And yet they are different because each writer under the guiding hand of Holy Spirit carefully chose the material which accorded best with the purpose of his book. Matthew based a good portion of his work on his eye witness account as a disciple. Mark

10. C. S. Mann, Mark, vol. 27 of *The Anchor Bible* (Garden City, N.Y.: Doubleday, 1986), 47-71.
11. Ibid., 56, 64.
12. Thiessen, *Introduction to the New Testament,* 101-29.

based his on the testimony of Peter, and Luke wrote after consulting several authorities which he met in his travels with Paul through Palestine and the rest of the Roman world.

One need not postulate an extensive scheme of literary dependence or hypothetical sources in order to account for the similarities and differences in the gospels. There are other options which accord with the facts given and which restore the authors to their rightful places as God's chosen servants who composed accurate accounts which are divinely inspired.[13]

Many factors were involved in the writing of each of the Synoptic Gospels.

It is clear that each author had extensive personal knowledge of the facts that he communicated. Whether that knowledge was derived through his own firsthand experience, as in the case of Matthew, or because of a close relationship with an apostle, as Mark had with Peter, or through individual study and research, as Luke did, it must be concluded that each man had to a certain extent his own awareness of facts.

Second, it cannot be disputed that there was some oral tradition involved in the communication of the biblical stories. The fact of oral tradition was well known in the Jewish community, for stories were memorized and passed from one generation to the next in a very precise manner. Everything that Jesus did and said is not recorded on the pages of the gospels. For instance, Acts 20:35 presents a statement of Jesus that is not found any place in the gospels, and Paul in 1 Corinthians 7:10 gives another quote from the Lord nowhere found within the gospel accounts.

Third, there does appear to be some written documentation concerning the stories of Jesus Christ. Luke acknowledged the fact that he researched as a good historian everything that he could find (Luke 1:1-4). That obviously entailed interviews with eyewitnesses, as well as the researching of the things that were written through any means that he could find.

But fourth, the dynamic living witness of the Spirit of God must also be brought into the equation. The process of the communication of the text is a matter of divine revelation and inspiration, and conservative scholarship cannot overlook the work of the Spirit of God in the lives of the gospel writers to communicate exactly what God wanted passed on.

13. Charles H. Dyer, "Do the Synoptics Depend on Each Other?" *Bibliotheca Sacra* 138 (July-September 1981): 244.

Perhaps the exact relationship of the synoptic writers will never be known. But it appears that the difficulties that have been mentioned are not insurmountable, and it is best to conclude that Matthew was the first gospel written (in the decade of the fifties), followed by Luke, who may have done his research while Paul was a prisoner in Caesarea. That imprisonment dates from approximately A.D. 58 to 60. Luke did accompany Paul on to Rome, where Paul was again imprisoned for two years (Acts 28:30-31). Luke's gospel, as well as the book of Acts, may have been written in this stretch of about five years. They were followed by the gospel of Mark, as will be explained in the next section.

WHEN WAS THIS GOSPEL WRITTEN?

Dates for the writing of the second gospel range from A.D. 44 to 75. The documentary theories on the writings of the Synoptic Gospels require that Mark be the earliest of the gospels. There has been a tendency in recent scholarship to move the writing of all the New Testament books to earlier times. Part of the reason for this is that one of most traumatic events after the resurrection of Jesus Christ that affected both the Jewish and the Christian communities is never mentioned in the New Testament. That traumatic event is the fall of the city of Jerusalem in A.D. 70. That fact would have been extremely significant in a number of the gospel stories, and, if it had indeed occurred, surely one or more of the gospel writers would have mentioned it.

C. S. Mann, cited earlier as rejecting the priority of Mark, places the writing of the gospel in the mid-sixties. He contends that Mark returned to Palestine with his own composition, much of which had been garnered from Peter, and that the final presentation of his document was completed before the Jewish war that broke out in A.D. 66.

> In sum, the present commentator finds himself agreeing with Weeden, Conzelmann, and Marxsen that Mark was compiled in response to a conflict and crisis situation. This writer does not believe that the crisis had to do with either Hellenistic religiosity or theological investigations about the *parousia*. He does believe that Mark is an edited and conflated version of Matthew-Luke, composed in response to a situation already fraught with danger for Christian Jews—and for Gentile Christians also —before the Jewish war broke out in A.D. 66.[14]

14. Mann, *Mark*, 83.

A quote from Irenaeus is interesting and must be evaluated when considering Mark's date:

> Matthew also issued a written Gospel among the Hebrews in their own dialect, while Peter and Paul were preaching in Rome, and laying the foundation of the church. After their departure, Mark, the disciple and interpreter of Peter, did also hand down to us in writing what had been preached by Peter. (*Against Heresies,* III, i,1)

What did Irenaeus mean by the "departure" of Peter and Paul? The word for "departure" is the word *exodus,* which is used in Scripture for physical death (cf. Luke 9:51). If that was what Irenaeus was communicating, then the writing of the second gospel did not take place until after the physical death of Peter. In what year did Peter die?

Tradition states that Peter died under the persecutions of Nero that began in A.D. 64. It is not assumed that Peter died in the first wave of those persecutions, but that his death may have occurred around A.D. 66 or 67. After his death, there was probably a movement in the church to commit to writing Peter's stories concerning Jesus. Mark, who had been prepared by Peter himself, was the natural choice to write down these accounts. Not only that, but the Holy Spirit moved him along (2 Peter 1:21) to communicate exactly the stories concerning Jesus without any errors. The actual writing, therefore, probably took place in A.D. 67 or 68.[15]

TO WHOM WAS THIS GOSPEL WRITTEN?

Mark seems to have written his gospel for a Gentile audience, and in particular he may have had Romans in view.[16] Several factors in the gospel would point to such a conclusion.

1. The second gospel has the fewest quotes and allusions to the Old Testament of all the gospels. There are only sixty-three such references in the whole gospel. A Gentile reader would not have been greatly interested in what the Old Testament had to say. In fact, he probably would not have been familiar with its contents.

2. Mark interprets the Aramaic words that are found in the gospel. For instance, in the account of the Crucifixion, Mark translates the

15. Thiessen, *Introduction to the New Testament,* 146.
16. Robert H. Gundry, *A Survey of the New Testament* (Grand Rapids: Zondervan, 1970), 81.

word *Golgotha* so that his readers would know it meant "Place of a Skull" (15:22). Also, the cry of Jesus from the cross, "Eloi, Eloi, lama sabachthani?" is translated by Mark as "My God, My God, why hast thou forsaken Me?" (15:34). He also translated such terms as *boanerges* (3:17), *talitha cum* (5:41), *corban* (7:11), *ephphatha* (7:34), and *Abba* (14:36). None of these translations would have been necessary for Jewish readers.

3. Mark explains some of the geographical locations in connection with his stories. The location of the Mount of Olives "opposite the temple" is spelled out in 13:3, which would not have been necessary for anyone familiar with the land of Israel.

4. There is not one reference in the second gospel to the Jewish law. This, of course, would be crucial to the Jew, for there were so many things of importance to the Jew that related to the law. But Mark is silent on the law.

5. Mark often explains Jewish customs. Mark 7:3 states that "Jews do not eat unless they carefully wash their hands." Such a custom would have been known and practiced by Jews. (See also 14:12 and 15:42).

6. Mark presents Jesus as the mighty worker, a man who conquers by doing. There is little emphasis in Mark's gospel on the sayings of Jesus because Romans were not concerned with what a person said. Their concern was, can a person produce? The effective service of Jesus Christ was of much greater significance to the Romans than His lineage or His claims.

WHY WAS THE SECOND GOSPEL WRITTEN?

The actual occasion that prompted the writing of this gospel is not known. Obviously there was the compulsion of the Holy Spirit working in the life of Mark to bring him to the place where he could write this book. Apart from supernatural power, however, the traditional view affirms that after the death of Peter there was a desire within the church at Rome to have the great teachings of this man written down.[17]

Whenever a great man of God dies, there is often a desire to have his teachings made available. It was my privilege to be on the faculty of the Moody Bible Institute in Chicago at the time the Lord

17. Hendriksen, *Exposition of the Gospel According to Mark,* 16.

called home Dr. William Culbertson. It was the consensus of many at that time that some of the sermons of Dr. Culbertson should be made available for all to enjoy. Therefore, a book was printed in which the keynote addresses of the Moody Founder's Week given by Dr. Culbertson were brought together in one volume. The death of Peter surely brought about a great desire on the part of many to see his recollections of the Lord committed to writing. Mark was the natural choice to do the job. Peter had spent time preparing him for the task (cf. 2 Peter 1:13-15).

From What Location Was the Gospel Written?

Although there is no direct reference to a city in the gospel, all tradition says that Mark wrote this book from the city of Rome.[18] Several lines of evidence may be presented to support this contention.

1. Mark made use of a number of Latin words, even though there were Greek equivalents. In 12:42 Jesus spoke of the poor widow who came into the temple bringing two *lepta*. A lepta was a Roman copper coin. The explanation is given that the lepta represented a Roman *quadrans*, which is translated by the English word "cent." He also mentions *modius* for bushel (4:21), *speculator* for executioner (6:27), *census* for tribute (12:14), the *Praetorium* for the palace (15:16), and *centurio* for centurion (15:39, 44, 45).

2. Roman divisions of time, as opposed to Jewish divisions, are used in this gospel. According to the Roman way of telling time there were four "watches" in the night, whereas in Jewish reckoning there were only three. This may be observed by comparing 13:35, where four watches are recorded, with Luke 12:38, which mentions only three.

3. Mark also refers to the names Alexander and Rufus in 15:21. They are listed as being the sons of Simon of Cyrene, the one who was compelled to bear the cross of Jesus Christ. Why would Mark make reference to the children of Simon of Cyrene? "Probably because they were known to the author and to his readers as personal acquaintances."[19] Paul does refer to a man named Rufus in his letter to the Romans and calls him "a choice man in the Lord" (Rom. 16:13). It is an

18. Gundry, *A Survey of the New Testament*, 81-82.
19. Tenney, *New Testament Survey*, 156.

assumption that these two men named Rufus are the same individual, but perhaps that is not an unwarranted conclusion.

WHAT ARE SOME OUTSTANDING CHARACTERISTICS OF THE SECOND GOSPEL?

1. The second gospel is first and foremost the gospel of action. Events in this gospel move rapidly. If one casts his eyes down the text, it will be noted that about two out of every three verses begin with the word "and." Teachers of English composition would not give Mark a very good grade, because he tends to run things together, but he uses that device for the purpose of action. It has been said that the second gospel presents a moving picture of the life of the Savior, whereas the other Synoptic Gospels present more of a slide show. This action is further seen in one of the key words in the gospel: "straightway," or "immediately." Rapidity of action is the thing Mark is interested in.

2. The second gospel pictures Jesus Christ as the Servant of the Lord. It is probably because of this emphasis that such a stress was placed on action and immediacy of action. When a servant is considered, one is primarily interested in his service. Can he do what he is supposed to do? Where he comes from is not one's concern. That is probably why no genealogy of the Servant is given by Mark. The Roman mind was far more concerned with the issue of performance. The point of servitude is also emphasized in the verse understood by many as being the key one in Mark: "For even the Son of Man did not come to be served, but to serve, and to give His life a ransom for many" (10:45). In some senses, this verse gives a broad outline for the gospel. The first part of the verse, the Son of Man ministering, is emphasized in 1:1–10:52. The second part of the verse, the giving of His life as a ransom for many, is seen in 11:1–15:47.

3. There is an emphasis in Mark on the miracles of Jesus. This too is in keeping with the servant character of the Lord, for as a servant His miracles are prominent. However, of the eighteen miracles Mark records, only two are unique to the second gospel. They are the healing of the deaf and dumb man (7:31-37) and the healing of the blind man at Bethsaida (8:22-26).

4. Mark emphasizes the common, familiar things of life. He gives attention to such things as boating and fishing, animals, clothing, housing, coins, and divisions of time.

5. Mark is the gospel of vivid detail. This may be seen in a number of ways. Mark's gospel gives attention to such things as the looks and gestures of the Lord (3:5; 10:16). All four gospels tell the story of the feeding of the five thousand men, not counting the women and children. But it is only in the Markan account that the vivid detail of the "green" grass and the people sitting in companies looking like "flower beds" is given (6:40; see p. 149). Mark presents a striking picture of the many-colored head coverings of the people and their sitting around in groups on the green grass. It must have been vivid to an eyewitness, and only Mark conveys that impression.

WHERE SHOULD THE SECOND GOSPEL END?

There is a problem with the ending of the second gospel. Where does the material written by Mark end? The options are that Mark's material ends at 16:8, that the gospel ends at 16:20, or that another ending should be added either after 16:8 or 16:20. The additional material has become lost over the centuries, but it was part of the early texts. The evidence for these options is of two types: external and internal. External evidence is that which is found outside of the Scripture, and internal evidence comes from within the text itself.

EXTERNAL EVIDENCE

Evidence from the Texts

The issue of textual criticism is a complicated one that cannot be discussed in detail in this book. However, the evidence to support the ending of the gospel of Mark comes down to the issue of what is the best Greek text? Simply put, the issue revolves around whether one considers the majority of the manuscript evidence to be that which supports one's conclusion or whether certain ancient texts are a better and more faithful rendering of the original Greek. When this author was in seminary, the New Testament Department of the school he attended was divided on this issue. It is obvious that good men have come to different conclusions down through the history of the church. The issue will not be resolved in this book, but simply stated it is this: The majority of the manuscripts supports the reading of Mark's gospel all the way through 16:20. The older manuscripts, which are identified as Vaticanus and Sinaiticus, support the shorter ending at v. 8. What is the best evidence? Obviously scholars have disagreed.

Evidence from Church History

When one looks at the early Fathers, it can be observed that men such as Justin Martyr, Irenaeus, and Tatian believed that the longer reading of Mark's gospel, all the way to v. 20, was part of the original manuscript. Later church Fathers, such as Eusebius of Caesarea (fourth century) and Jerome (fifth century, translator of the Vulgate), believed that the inspired text of Mark concluded at v. 8.[20] One can substantiate his view from quoting one group of historians or the other.

Evidence from Other Sources

As one checks some of the early translations of the Markan text, such as the Latin, the Syriac, and Coptic, one discovers that all of these translations included vv. 9-20 as part of Mark's gospel. However, the earliest commentary on Mark's gospel, which dates from the sixth century, stops at v. 8. How does one assess the external evidence? Clearly it is divided, and scholars have had different opinions down through the centuries.

INTERNAL EVIDENCE

As one looks at the text itself, a number of arguments can be made that spring from the text. Some of these arguments may be hard to follow at times unless one has competent ability in the original language.

Approximately one-third of the words used in vv. 9-20 are not found elsewhere in Mark's gospel. Some of those unique words do appear earlier, but they are used in a different way. Also, those who have the ability to analyze style of writing and the way a writer uses words have noted that vv. 9-20 are quite different from the earlier portion of the gospel.

It is interesting that Mary Magdalene is introduced in v. 9 as the one "from whom He had cast out seven demons." It is as though Mary needed to be introduced, yet she has just appeared in the preceding verses (cf. 15:40, 47; 16:1). Why was it necessary to mention this work of the Lord in her life at this juncture?

Also, as one reads about the postresurrection appearances of the Lord in vv. 9-20, it is a little surprising that the appearance of Jesus to the disciples in Galilee is not mentioned. The appearances recorded

20. John D. Grassmick, "Mark" in *Bible Knowledge Commentary* (Wheaton, Ill.: Victor, 1983), 193-94.

relate to things that happened around Jerusalem. But Jesus had mentioned Galilee to the disciples in 14:28, and even as recently as 16:7 the angel said that Jesus would meet the disciples in Galilee. One would expect vv. 9-20 to include at least one appearance of the Lord to the disciples in the region of Galilee.

How does one assess the internal evidence? It seems to this author that the internal evidence substantiates the claim that Mark's manuscript should conclude at v. 8.

A CONCLUDING PROBLEM

Having come to the conclusion that the gospel ends at v. 8, however, does not solve all the problems. If the gospel ends there, it certainly does have a very abrupt ending. Would Mark conclude his story with a group of trembling, astonished, and fearful women who were left speechless? That could fit with Mark's very abrupt style of writing and purpose.[21] William Lane agrees with this conclusion:

> In point of fact, the present ending of Mark is thoroughly consistent with the motifs of astonishment and fear developed throughout the Gospel. These motifs express the manner in which Mark understands the events of Jesus' life. In verse 8 the evangelist terminates his account of the good news concerning Jesus by surrounding the note by which he has characterized all aspects of Jesus' activity, his healings, miracles, teachings, the journey to Jerusalem. Astonishment and fear qualify the events of the life of Jesus. The account of the empty tomb is soul-shaking and to convey this impression Mark describes in the most meaningful language the utter amazement and overwhelming feeling of the women. With his closing comment he wished to say that "the gospel of Jesus the Messiah" (Ch. 1:1) is an event beyond human comprehension and therefore awesome and frightening. In this case, contrary to general opinion, "for they were afraid" is the phrase most appropriate to the conclusion of the Gospel. The abruptness with which Mark concluded his account corresponds to the preface of the Gospel where the evangelist begins by confronting the reader with the fact of revelation in the person of John and Jesus (Ch. 1:1-13). The ending leaves the reader confronted by the witness of the empty tomb interpreted by the word of revelation. The focus upon human inadequacy, lack of understanding and weakness throws into bold relief the action of God and its meaning.[22]

21. Mann, *Mark*, 81-82, 94.
22. Lane, *The Gospel of Mark*, 591-92.

If the gospel does end at v. 8, how can the addition of vv. 9-20 be explained? Certainly it would not have simply been lost. The gospel of Mark was probably written on a scroll, and the conclusion of the gospel would have been rolled up on the inside. It was very unusual for the last portion of any scroll to be lost. It was more common for the first portion to be removed for some reason or simply become worn out through use. Would someone have removed vv. 9-20 for an unknown reason? That too is unlikely. It is more probable that vv. 9-20 were added by a well-intentioned copyist. Perhaps over the decades, as the gospel was copied, it was felt that the ending at v. 8 was much too abrupt and not an appropriate conclusion. Thomas has concluded that "it does appear that the last twelve verses are quite old. These resurrection appearances were added to Mark's Gospel at an extremely early stage to soften the abrupt ending found at 16:8."[23]

The most common suggestion has been that Aristion, a disciple of the apostle John, was the person who made the addition, perhaps even under the authority of John. Some, while recognizing that vv. 9-20 are not Markan, nevertheless conclude that they are a part of the manuscript in the same sense that Deuteronomy 34, concerning the death of Moses, and Joshua 24, concerning Joshua's death, were added. These portions clearly were not written by Moses and Joshua, and yet over the centuries they have been considered to be part of the inspired text. Do vv. 9-20 fit the same criteria? Some feel they do. Perhaps Mark himself intended to add to the manuscript but may have died before he could do so.

The problem of the ending of Mark's gospel probably will not be solved as long as people live in physical bodies on this earth. As the evidence is assessed, however, it is the conclusion of this author that Mark's material clearly ended at v. 8. With this Thomas agrees when he says,

> Although Mark 16:9-20 has much old and good MS support, it appears that this longer reading is quite old but, still, only secondary. Even with the peculiarities of Vaticanus, the variety of family representation of 16:9-20, and the problem of the content of the longer ending, the abrupt ending at 16:8 is to be preferred.[24]

23. John Christopher Thomas, "A Reconsideration of the Ending of Mark," *JETS* 26 (December 1983): 412.
24. Ibid., 418.

It is probably not the best to consider vv. 9-20 as inspired literature. Since it is so disputed, it clearly should not be a portion of Scripture on which one should ever seek to base any doctrinal teaching. No major doctrine of Christianity rests solely on these verses. Almost every idea or historical appearance in vv. 9-20 is mentioned in other passages. The issue remains, however, and scholars will continue to debate it until the Lord's return.

OUTLINE

I. **The Introduction of Jehovah's Servant, 1:1-13**
   A. By Proclamation, 1:1-8
   B. By Identification, 1:9
   C. By Authentication, 1:10-11
   D. By Temptation, 1:12-13

II. **The Presentation of Jehovah's Servant, 1:14–3:5**
   A. By Direct Testimony, 1:14-15
   B. By Personal Enlistment, 1:16-20
   C. By Demonstrating Authority, 1:21–3:5
      1. Over demonic forces, 1:21-28
      2. Over disease, 1:29-34
      3. Over personal direction, 1:35-39
      4. Over leprosy, 1:40-45
      5. Over forgiveness of sins, 2:1-12
      6. Over men, 2:13-14
      7. Over traditions, 2:15-22
      8. Over the Sabbath, 2:23–3:5
         a. Sabbath issue questioned, 2:23-28
         b. Sabbath miracle performed, 3:1-5

III. **The Opposition to Jehovah's Servant, 3:6–8:26**
   A. The Pharisees' Conclusion, 3:6
   B. The Multitude's Confusion, 3:7-12
   C. The Servant's Decision, 3:13-19
   D. His Family's Intervention, 3:20-21
   E. The "Official" Conclusion, 3:22–4:34
      1. The accusation, 3:22
      2. The denial, 3:23-30
      3. The ramifications, 3:31-35

4. The instruction, 4:1-34
   a. A parable taught, 4:1-12
   b. A parable explained, 4:13-20
   c. Further parabolic instruction, 4:21-34

F. The Servant's Authentication in Spite of Opposition, 4:35–5:43
   1. To the apostles, 4:35-41
   2. To the region of Decapolis, 5:1-20
   3. To the "religious" leaders, 5:21-43
      a. The request, 5:21-24
      b. The interruption, 5:25-34
      c. The fulfillment, 5:35-43

G. The Rejection of Nazareth, 6:1-6

H. The Ministry to Combat Opposition, 6:7-13

I. The Civil Ruler's Opposition, 6:14-29
   1. The fear of Herod, 6:14-16
   2. The actions of Herod, 6:17-29

J. The Servant's Instruction in View of Opposition, 6:30-52
   1. The intended retreat, 6:30-32
   2. The actual reality, 6:33-44
   3. The authenticating signs, 6:45-56
      a. Walking on the water, 6:45-52
      b. Healings at Gennesaret, 6:53-56

K. The Pharisees' Continued Opposition, 7:1-23
   1. The "violation" stated, 7:1-5
   2. The servant's explanation, 7:6-13
   3. The servant's warning, 7:14-23

L. The Servant's Retreat from Opposition, 7:24–8:9
   1. To the region of Tyre, 7:24-30
   2. To the region of Decapolis, 7:31–8:9
      a. Healing of the deaf man, 7:31-37
      b. Feeding of the 4,000, 8:1-9

M. The Pharisees' Final Demand, 8:10-21
   1. Their demand, 8:10-11
   2. The servant's explanation, 8:12-13
   3. The servant's warning, 8:14-21

N. A Concluding Miracle, 8:22-26

IV. **The Instruction of Jehovah's Servant, 8:27–10:52**
A. Instruction Concerning His Person, 8:27-30

B. Instruction Concerning His Program, 8:31–9:13
   1. His coming death, 8:31-33
   2. His requirement for followers, 8:34-38
   3. His coming kingdom pictured, 9:1-10
   4. His relationship to Elijah, 9:11-13
C. Instruction Concerning the Impossible, 9:14-29
D. Instruction Concerning His Upcoming Death, 9:30-32
E. Instruction Concerning Pride, 9:33-37
F. Instruction Concerning Partisan Spirit, 9:38-50
G. Instruction Concerning Divorce, 10:1-12
H. Instruction Concerning Faith, 10:13-22
   1. Faith as a child, 10:13-16
   2. Faith for eternal life, 10:17-22
I. Instruction Concerning Wealth, 10:23-31
J. Instruction Concerning His Near Future, 10:32-34
K. Instruction Concerning Positions in the Kingdom, 10:35-45
L. Instruction Concerning Faith, 10:46-52

V. **The Rejection of Jehovah's Servant, 11:1–15:47**
   A. The Presentation of the Servant, 11:1-26
      1. The triumphal entry, 11:1-11
      2. The judgment announced, 11:12-14
      3. The cleansing of the temple, 11:15-19
      4. The judgment fulfilled, 11:20-26
   B. The Controversies with the Servant, 11:27–12:40
      1. With the religious leaders, 11:27–12:12
         a. The question of authority, 11:27-33
         b. The parable for instruction, 12:1-11
         c. The leaders' response, 12:12
      2. With the Pharisees and Herodians, 12:13-17
      3. With the Sadducees, 12:18-27
      4. With the Scribes, 12:28-34
      5. The response of the servant, 12:35-44
         a. The question of challenge, 12:35-37
         b. The warning, 12:38-40
         c. The proper illustration, 12:41-44
   C. The Predictions of the Servant, 13:1-37
      1. The questions of the disciples, 13:1-4

      2. The response of the servant, 13:5-37
         a. Coming tribulation, 13:5-23
            (1) The first half of the Tribulation, 13:5-13
            (2) The second half of the Tribulation, 13:14-23
         b. Coming triumph, 13:24-27
            (1) Return of the King, 13:24-26
            (2) Regathering of believers, 13:27
         c. Concluding teaching, 13:28-37
            (1) The fig tree, 13:28-32
            (2) The steward, 13:33-37
   D. The Preparatory Events Surrounding the Servant, 14:1-42
      1. The plot of the leaders, 14:1-2
      2. The anointing by Mary, 14:3-9
      3. The agreement with Judas, 14:10-11
      4. The Passover meal, 14:12-26
         a. Preparation, 14:12-16
         b. Participation, 14:17-21
         c. Initiation, 14:22-26
      5. The prediction of denial, 14:27-31
      6. The garden of Gethsemane, 14:32-42
   E. The Arrest and Trials of the Servant, 14:43–15:20
      1. Arrest in Gethsemane, 14:43-52
      2. Trial before the Council, 14:53-65
      3. Prediction of denial fulfilled, 14:66-72
      4. Second trial before the Council, 15:1
      5. Trial before Pilate, 15:2-15
      6. Mocking before the Roman soldiers, 15:16-20
   F. The Crucifixion of the Servant, 15:21-32
   G. The Death of the Servant, 15:33-41
   H. The Burial of the Servant, 15:42-47

VI. The Resurrection of Jehovah's Servant, 16:1-20
   A. The Revelation of the Women, 16:1-8
   B. The Appearances of the Servant, 16:9-14
      1. To Mary, 16:9-11
      2. To two disciples, 16:12-13
      3. To the eleven, 16:14
   C. The Commission of the Servant, 16:15-18
   D. The Ascension of the Servant, 16:19-20

ABBREVIATIONS

Ant.	*The Antiquities of the Jews,* by Josephus
B.J.	*Bellum Judaicum* (*History of the Jewish War*), by Josephus
JETS	*Journal of the Evangelical Theological Society*
LXX	Septuagint (ancient Greek translation of the Old Testament)
NICNT	New International Commentary of the New Testament

MARK

CHAPTER

ONE

THE SERVANT'S INTRODUCTION

The gospel of Mark has been regarded by many as their favorite account of the life of Jesus the Messiah. Some perhaps feel that way because it is the shortest account of the Savior's life and thus enables them to get a good overview of the complete story without omitting any significant details. But others have enjoyed this gospel account because of Mark's presentation of the Messiah as the Servant. The concern of the gospel is, Can the Servant perform? Mark's gospel is filled with the actions of the Servant, proving He can indeed fulfill His Word.

THE INTRODUCTION OF JEHOVAH'S SERVANT, 1:1-13

BY PROCLAMATION, 1:1-8
(cf. Matt. 3:1-12; Luke 3:1-18)

1:1   Mark begins the story of his "gospel" (*euaggelion*), or good news, by identifying the object of his presentation. His good news is clearly concerning Jesus Christ. "Jesus" (Heb., Joshua, "Jehovah is salvation") was the human name given to the Child both before and after His birth (Matt. 1:21, 25). The term "Christ" is the Greek equivalent of the Hebrew term "Messiah," meaning "the anointed one," God's chosen instrument to bring about His kingdom reign.

Mark not only stresses the humanity of Jesus Christ but also refers to Him as "the Son of God." The concept of sonship in a human realm communicates several ideas that are not implied in this relationship; i.e., sonship usually implies succession. The father comes first followed by his son. Sonship also implies an inferiority, for the father is generally considered to be superior to the son, at least while the son is a child. When the concept of sonship is applied to Jesus Christ, a different relationship is implied. The thought seems to be that sonship is emphasizing the concept of the sameness of nature: "A son is of the same nature and essence as a father; in affirming Jesus as His Son, God the Father was saying that Jesus, His Son, is deity because He is of the same essence as the Father."[1]

At the outset of his message, Mark affirms that his theme concerns the good news about a person who is both human and divine. Jesus Christ is fully man without sin, and He is fully God. This One has come as the Messiah/King of the nation of Israel.

1:2 A king would always be preceded by his ambassadors, those who went before to prepare the way. Mark indicated that Jesus the King was also preceded by His ambassador (*angelon,* lit. "messenger"). In fact, the coming of His ambassador was foretold by Old Testament prophets. Mark, in effect, said, "It was written in Isaiah the prophet that His messenger would come before Him to prepare His way." It is interesting that Mark mentioned Isaiah and then gave a quote that is more commonly associated with the prophet Malachi. "This method of quotation, namely, mentioning by name only one source when the reference is two, is not peculiar to Mark. Matthew does this also, and again with good reason."[2] The sending of the messenger who would prepare the way is directly from Malachi 3:1, with a similar idea occurring in Exodus 23:20.

1:3 However, the portion of the prophecy concerning the "voice of one crying in the wilderness" does have an echo in Isaiah 40:3. Perhaps the reason Mark identified only Isaiah was that he was the better known prophet. A. T. Robertson says, "Isaiah is mentioned as the chief of the prophets. It was common to combine quotations from the prophets in *testimonia* and *catenae* (chains of quotations)."[3] The

---

1. Paul Enns, *Moody Handbook of Theology* (Chicago: Moody, 1989), 87.
2. William Hendriksen, *Exposition of the Gospel According to Mark* (Grand Rapids: Eerdmans, 1975), 34.
3. A. T. Robertson, *Word Pictures in the New Testament* (Nashville: Broadman, 1930), 1:252.

prophecies of Malachi, although significant, were not widely known outside of the nation of Israel.

The prophecy indicates that the one who prepares the way would "make His paths straight" (*eutheias poieite tas tribous*). It was not unusual in ancient times for roads to be resurfaced to smooth out the way of an important arriving king. Mark indicated that this was a significant character whose coming had been prophesied many centuries before by Old Testament prophets.

> The blended citation functions to draw attention to three factors which are significant to the evangelist in his prologue: the herald, the Lord and the wilderness. In the verses which immediately follow, the significance of each of these elements is emphasized by Mark, who sees in the coming of John and Jesus to the wilderness the fulfillment of the promised salvation of which the prophet Isaiah had spoken.[4]

1:4   The immediate connection of John the Baptist, who was in the wilderness preaching a baptism of repentance for the forgiveness of sins, with these Old Testament prophecies shows that Mark believed John was fulfilling the role of the messenger preparing the way. John "appeared in the wilderness," not in normal intercourse with society. The specific wilderness in which John ministered is not noted, although there is a direct connection in the next verse with the Jordan River. The area immediately to the east of Jerusalem, down toward the Jordan Valley, is a dry, desert type of wilderness. Though several traditional sites in Israel today mark the place of John's ministry and Jesus' baptism, none of them can be attested to with absolute certainty. Mark's use of the wilderness is clearly to link John's ministry to the prophetic emphasis of Isaiah—the appearance of the messenger of the king in the wilderness.

John preached "a baptism of repentance" (*baptisma metanoias*) "for the forgiveness of sins." The idea of baptism was known among the Jews.

> It has been conjectured that John's baptism was derived from the Jewish practice of baptizing proselytes, or from the rites of initiation practiced at Qumran. No clear line of dependance can be shown in support of these theories. Baptism appears rather as a unique activity of this

---

4. William L. Lane, *The Gospel of Mark,* NICNT (Grand Rapids: Eerdmans, 1974), 46-47.

prophet, a prophetic sign so striking that John became known simply as "the Baptizer."[5]

The concept of baptism has not always been clearly communicated. Part of the problem is the fact that the Greek word for baptize (*baptizō*) is not really translated. It is simply transliterated, that is, English letters are assigned to the Greek letters. It is probably best to understand the idea of baptism to mean "an identification with" or "an association with." John basically was asking those who came to him in the wilderness to identify themselves with the coming Messiah by demonstrating repentance (*metanoias*).

The concept in the biblical idea of repentance is a genuine change of mind that affects the life in some way. When a person turns from the direction in which he has been going and begins to pursue a new path, the effect can lead to eternal life. John was asking the people of his day to turn from the things that they knew and to place their faith in the coming Messiah. The indication of this change of direction was to identify themselves with John and his message by submitting to water baptism. Those who came to him in saving faith would receive the "forgiveness of sins" (*aphesin hamartiōn*). John was not implying that water baptism was what removed sins; the preposition *eis* is probably best understood here as meaning "with reference to." In other words, forgiveness of sins would come about as a result of the faith expressed in repentance. The baptism would occur because one's sins had already been forgiven. "John is treating the Jewish nation as pagans who need to repent, to confess their sins, and to come back to the kingdom of God. The baptism in the Jordan was the objective challenge to the people."[6]

1:5 It is clear that the ministry of John the Baptist stirred up great excitement among the people. "All the country of Judea" may be hyperbole, but it nevertheless indicates that many were "going out to him" (*exeporeueto pros auton*) and submitting to his baptism (*ebaptizontō*). Both verbs are in the imperfect tense, picturing a continual flow of people from the countryside, as well as from the city of Jerusalem to be baptized by John. Already the vividness of detail in Mark's gospel can be seen. The picture he portrays is of constant action.

5. Ibid., 49.
6. Robertson, *Word Pictures in the New Testament,* 1:254.

Part of the people's experience involved an acknowledgment of their own sins, which they confessed before the Lord.

1:6   The appearance of John was much like that of an Old Testament prophet. He was clothed in camel's hair (Matt. 3:4), and he wore a leather belt around his waist.

> John's long, flowing garment, woven from camel's hair, reminds us somewhat of Elijah's mantle, though there is a difference in the description (cf. Matt. 3:4 with II Kings 1:8). Such rugged apparel may have been regarded as symbolic of the prophetic office. Zech. 13:4 (cf. I Sam. 28:14) seems to point in that direction. At any rate, such rough garb was fit for desert wear. It was durable and economical.[7]

His diet was the diet of the wilderness. He was able to eat "locusts" (*akridas*) and "wild honey" (*meli agrion*). Some believe that the reference to locusts is to the beetlelike insect. Many people in the world today still consider locusts to be a delicacy. It is clear from Leviticus 11:22 that the Lord permitted the Israelites to eat four different kinds of insects that could probably be categorized as locusts. Others believe that *akridas* refers to the fruit of the carob tree, which grew in the wilderness. The wild honey is found in various wilderness locations, in rocks or in crevices. The role of wild honey is seen in such biblical stories as Samson (Judg. 14:8, 9, 18) and Jonathan (1 Sam. 14:25, 26, 29). Either could be used to sustain life. It is probably not necessary to conclude that this was the totality of John's diet, but the point is to demonstrate his very simple manner of life with respect to both food and clothing. His life was quite a contrast to the average person's daily existence in society. Truly he appeared as an Old Testament prophet proclaiming the word of the Lord, and people were flocking to him.

1:7   But his preaching was not simply to draw people to himself. John clearly was the forerunner of someone far greater than he. His message was "After me One is coming who is mightier than I." John did not feel that he was worthy to stoop down and untie "the thong" (*ton himanta*) of His sandals. This is another illustration of the vivid detail that Mark adds in his account. None of the other accounts mentions "the thong" of the sandal, which was the part that held the sandal together. In this illustration, John clearly understood his role as

---

7. Hendriksen, *Exposition of the Gospel According to Mark*, 39.

the forerunner of the Messiah/Deliverer. He saw himself as a servant, for, when guests would arrive in a home, it was the responsibility of the servant to greet the master and those who came with him by helping them to remove their sandals and to wash their feet. This was a simple task, yet it was something that John did not feel worthy to do for the One who was coming.

1:8 John's message was that he baptized "with water," but the One coming after him would baptize "with the Holy Spirit." Those coming to John were identifying themselves with him and his message, but the Messiah who was coming would identify them with the Holy Spirit. The bestowal of the Holy Spirit is a thread that runs through several Old Testament passages. It was an expected feature of Messiah's coming.

Ezekiel 36:26-27 states that the Lord would give to the nation of Israel a new heart and put a new Spirit within them. This Spirit would cause them to walk in His statutes and to follow His ways. Joel 2:28ff. spoke of the outpouring of the Spirit on all mankind as part of the Day of the Lord. Though Joel's prophecy will ultimately be fulfilled at Christ's second coming, the fulfillment of the pouring out of the Spirit appears to have begun on the Day of Pentecost (Acts 2), when the Spirit of God came on the disciples and those who put their faith in Jesus Christ. It is interesting that John spoke, in the wilderness, of a mighty work of the Spirit in connection with this coming One. Isaiah described Israel's first trek through the wilderness as being a march that was done under the guidance of the Spirit of God (Isa. 63:11), and it was the Spirit who gave them rest on that occasion (v. 14). It appears that John again is speaking of a movement of the Spirit beginning in the wilderness that will come to glorious fruition as the Messiah comes to introduce His kingdom. As He does that, there will be a fresh manifestation of the Spirit in the lives of those who are His followers.

BY IDENTIFICATION, 1:9
(cf. Matt. 3:13-15; Luke 3:21a)

1:9 Mark continued to point the way to Jesus Christ by showing how Jesus became identified with John the Baptist and the message he was proclaiming at the height of his ministry. Jesus came from the northern region of Galilee, from the city of Nazareth, to the Jordan River, near the city of Jericho, where according to tradition He was baptized by John the Baptist. A normal understanding of the Greek prepositions "in" (*eis*) and "out of" (*ek*, v. 10), suggests that Jesus literally went into the water and came up out of the water. This suggests that Jesus was totally immersed in the waters of the Jordan River. Some, however, in keeping with early traditions in the church, imply that the participants went into the river and that water was sprinkled or poured over their heads. But the common Jewish method of baptism for proselytes was a total immersion in water.

Whatever the mode of the Savior's baptism, though, He was clearly identifying Himself with John and the message he was proclaiming. It is also clear that Jesus was never a proper candidate for John's baptism. All those who were identifying themselves with John through baptism were acknowledging their sinfulness and confessing their sins. Of what did Jesus Christ have to repent? What sin could He have confessed? None! Although He was baptized by John, He was not acknowledging His sinfulness. Jesus said that His baptism was necessary "to fulfill all righteousness" (Matt. 3:15), so it seems best to understand that by baptism Jesus Christ was identifying Himself with His forerunner and with the message that he was proclaiming, that people needed to repent in order to be prepared for the coming Messiah. This act of obedience to the Father's will demonstrated Jesus' righteousness and marked His entrance into His Messianic mission.

BY AUTHENTICATION, 1:10-11
(cf. Matt. 3:13-17; Luke 3:21-23a)

1:10   The most important thing about the baptism of Jesus Christ was the authentication that followed the act. Mark declared that as Jesus came out of the water "immediately" the heavens were opened and the Spirit, "like a dove," descended on Him. This is the first of some forty-two occurrences of the word "immediately" (*euthys*) in this gospel. Although its meaning may vary, it is one of the characteristic words that causes the action of the gospel to keep moving.

As soon as Jesus came out of the water, His person was authenticated. Jesus saw the heavens "opening" up (*schizomenous,* a present tense passive participle). The word literally means to "split like a garment." It is a more vivid word than Matthew and Luke use in their gospels. The opening of the heavens to provide revelation is significant, for God had not spoken through any prophet for many centuries. William Hendriksen suggests that the Spirit took the shape of a dove

> to indicate the purity, gentleness, peacefulness, and graciousness which characteristics mark the Holy Spirit, and are in popular opinion, as well as even in Scripture (Ps. 68:13; Song of Sol. 6:9; Matt. 10:16), associated with the dove. . . . The *Holy Spirit,* symbolized by a form representing a dove and resting on the Son, could very well indicate that in and by himself Jesus, Spirit-indwelt, was pure and holy; not only that but also gentle and peaceful. The sins for which he was to die were not his own but had been *imputed* to him.[8]

John 1:31-34 makes clear that John the Baptist saw this dove descend from heaven and rest on the Lord Jesus.

1:11   A second authentication that came from the opened heavens was the voice of God the Father: "Thou art My beloved Son, in Thee I am well pleased." The Father's announcement carries reminders of Psalm 2:7 and Isaiah 42:1, although neither passage is being directly quoted.

In the first phrase spoken by the Father, "Thou art My beloved Son," the verb (*ei*) is in the present tense, communicating the eternal and essential relationship that existed between the Father and the Son as expressed in Psalm 2:7. Jesus never became the Son of God, either at His baptism or at His transfiguration, or at any other time. He is always the eternal Son of God. Hence, God's statement affirms their eternal relationship.

The second phrase, "in Thee I am well pleased," contains an aorist tense verb (*eudokēsa*). The aorist tense implies a choice in the past and is a reflection of Isaiah 42:1, where the servant whom the Lord has chosen is the "one in whom [His] soul delights." This statement communicates the pleasure of the Father not only with all that the Son has done in the past but for the unique ministry into which He was about to enter. The plan of coming to earth to die for the sin of mankind as the servant of Jehovah was something that had been determined within the Godhead from eternity past, and it was something in which God took great delight.

This is one of those few passages in the New Testament in which all three members of the Godhead—Father, Son, and Holy Spirit—are

---

8. Ibid., 43-44.

brought together. Jesus, of course, was present physically on the earth, the Spirit descended in the form of a dove, and the voice of the Father came from heaven.

By Temptation, 1:12-13
(cf. Matt. 4:1-11; Luke 4:1-13)

1:12   A final incident that introduces Jehovah's servant is the temptation of Jesus Christ. Again Mark connects this event with what preceded it by the use of the word "immediately" (*euthys*). He was "impelled" (*ekballei,* a very strong word carrying the force of "to drive" in the historic present tense, used for vivid detail) to go into the wilderness. Jesus had come into the wilderness to meet John and be baptized by him, and He was driven farther into the wilderness by the Spirit of God. "This signifies that the aspect of humiliation in Jesus' mission is not yet terminated in spite of the declaration that he is the beloved Son. Jesus must remain submissive: the Spirit does not allow him to abandon the wilderness after His baptism."[9] Is there any other conclusion that can be drawn than that surely this time was a part of the will of God in the life of His Son?

1:13   He was in the wilderness for a period of "forty days," during which time He was tempted by the devil and was with the wild beasts. The number forty is a figure used elsewhere in Scripture of a time of testing. The most notable example was the period of Israel's testing in the wilderness for forty years after they had refused to enter the Promised Land. Earlier Moses had remained on Mount Sinai for forty days, and later Elijah spent the same time wandering through the wilderness to Mount Horeb.

Jesus' temptation was not in an environment conducive to normal, healthy growth. The emphasis on "wild beasts," which is unique to Mark, stresses the hostility of the environment. The wilderness was the nighttime haunt of the wolf, the jackal, the leopard, and other wild animals. Mark's readers would have been greatly impressed with the fact that Jesus was not overcome by the wild beasts. They probably witnessed many struggles between men and wild animals as "entertainment" in their Roman circuses. Yet even in a hostile environment Jesus Christ was victorious over His enemy, Satan.

---

9. Lane, *The Gospel of Mark,* 59.

The name "Satan," from the Hebrew, is used about fifty-two times in Scripture and basically means "an adversary" or "an opposer." The reality of Satan is affirmed by every New Testament writer. He was an archangel (Ezek. 28:11-19) who brought sin into the angelic realm when he said in his heart the five "I wills" recorded in Isaiah 14:12-15. The angels who followed him in his fall (cf. Rev. 12:3-4) became the demonic forces of Satan, and together they continually oppose God and those who follow Him. This was not the first time Satan opposed Jesus Christ. He used King Herod at the time of Jesus' birth in an effort to destroy Him (Matt. 2:16-18).

Mark does not give the specifics of the temptations, as Matthew and Luke do. He simply summarizes the fact that Jesus was tempted by Satan and that when the temptation was complete the angels of God came and ministered (*diēkonoun,* imperfect tense indicating action over a period of time in the past) to Him. It may be assumed that their ministry was a ministry of sustenance and encouragement, as Jesus the Son of God was victorious over His enemy. Although their ministry to Jesus was unique here, angels stand ready to minister to all those who shall be the heirs of salvation (Heb. 1:14). Whereas Satan opposes the work of God, angels are ministering spirits who support the work of the Godhead.

THE PRESENTATION OF JEHOVAH'S SERVANT, 1:14–3:5

Mark has introduced Jehovah's Servant, connected Him with His forerunner, and presented His triumph over His enemy, Satan. A clearer presentation of this Servant's authority, however, was needed.

By Direct Testimony, 1:14-15
(cf. Matt. 4:12-17; Luke 4:14-15)

1:14 Mark gives a historical reference by stating that the beginning of the ministry of Jesus Christ did not occur until after John the Baptist had been taken into custody. Mark gives no details at this point as to why John was arrested, although clarification for his arrest does come later in 6:14-29. The verb (*paradothenai*) that he uses, however, is the same verb that he uses when speaking of Jesus' betrayal by Judas in 3:19. Here the verb is in the passive voice without a stated agent. It is clear in Mark's thinking that God's purposes were being fulfilled in John's arrest, just as they would be later in the arrest of the Savior. But with John's removal from the scene, Jesus began to preach the "gospel," the good news (*euaggelion,* same word as in 1:1), of God in the region of Galilee. Mark skips an extended ministry of Jesus in Judea that probably lasted about one year (cf. John 1:19–4:45). Consequently, most of his gospel is focused on Jesus' ministry in Galilee.

1:15   The good news that Jesus was proclaiming began with the declaration that "the time is fulfilled." This expression is much like Paul's reference to "the fulness of the time" in Galatians 4:4 or "the fulness of the times" in Ephesians 1:10. However, the word that is used here for time (*kairos*) carries the idea of an opportunity or a crisis, as opposed to the more general term for time (*chronos*).

The proclamation of the Savior included the fact that "the kingdom (*basileia*) of God [was] at hand." The concept of the kingdom is one of the main themes of Scripture. In a recent book, John F. Walvoord says,

> The main concept of the kingdom is quite simple. A *kingdom* is a rule by a king (or other ruler) who exerts his authority over people and often over a territory. In the scriptural concept of kingdom, God may be king in every sense of the term without necessarily forcing recognition of this from the human race. It is, therefore, essential to examine what the Scriptures themselves have to say about the various forms of the divine kingdom.[10]

He goes on to show the variety of ways in which the term "kingdom" is used throughout all of Scripture.

In what sense was the Savior announcing the reign of God over mankind? There does not appear to be any need for an explanation in the text as to what the message was proclaiming. The nation of Israel was well instructed in the concept of the coming Messiah who would institute His reign on David's throne over the nation of Israel.

> Although doubtless our Lord said a great deal about the Kingdom of which there is no record in Scripture, we can be sure that the Biblical writers have not omitted any essential elements of His message. And, since there is no record of any formal definition in these initial announcements of the Kingdom, it is highly improbable that any was given. Obviously, such a definition would have been absolutely necessary

10. John F. Walvoord, "Biblical Kingdoms Compared and Contrasted," in *Issues in Dispensationalism* (Chicago: Moody, 1994), 75-76.

if Christ had entertained a radically novel conception of the Kingdom of God.[11]

But in what sense was the message being offered? Is it to be understood that Jesus was announcing the possibility of the institution of the literal Davidic kingdom foretold by the Old Testament prophets based on the acceptance of His message by that generation of Jews? Jesus said that the kingdom of God was "at hand," and J. Dwight Pentecost suggests that "by the term 'at hand' the announcement is being made that the kingdom is to be expected imminently. It is not a guarantee that the kingdom will be instituted immediately, but rather that all impending events have been removed so that it is now imminent."[12]

A new understanding of the kingdom is being suggested by a theological position being referred to as "progressive dispensationalism." The adherents assert that the promise concerning a kingdom has in some sense been partially fulfilled. Darrell Bock advocates this view: "The kingdom, at least in some form, is present; the promise, at least in some way, is anticipated as imminent. And yet after lengthy teaching by Jesus about the kingdom, Acts 1 suggests that this kingdom is still expected by the disciples in a certain form that relates to Israel."[13] The fact of the institution of a messianic Davidic kingdom on the earth was clearly within the expectations of the nation. That kingdom was the focus of many Old Testament prophecies (cf. 2 Sam. 7:8-17; Isa. 11:1-9; Jer. 23:4-6; Zech. 9:9-10; 14:9). However, did not the offer of that kingdom necessitate an affirmative response?

The very fact that there was a second aspect to the good news concerning repentance and believing in the gospel implies that there was an element of question concerning the actual institution of this kingdom. The second aspect was necessary because the teaching of Jesus' day had degenerated into an understanding that when Messiah came He would bring in His kingdom and all Jews would automatically be a part of His reign. They would be allowed entrance simply because they were the offspring of Abraham. The second aspect of Jesus' message, however, implied that there first needed to be a change in their thinking—to "repent" (*metanoeō*). As was noted in the com-

11. Alva J. McClain, *The Greatness of the Kingdom* (Grand Rapids: Zondervan, 1959), 276.
12. J. Dwight Pentecost, *Things to Come* (Findlay, Ohio: Dunham, 1958), 449-50.
13. Darrell L. Bock, "The Reign of the Lord Jesus Christ," in *Dispensationalism, Israel and the Church* (Grand Rapids: Zondervan, 1992), 45.

ments under 1:4, repentance carries the idea of turning away from an existing object of faith. In the message of the Savior, this turning away from one object is tied directly to the placing of one's trust in another object. Jesus also said they needed to "believe [*pisteuō*] in the gospel." They needed to turn away from what they were trusting in—their confidence in their physical relationship to Abraham—to a belief in the good news concerning Jesus as the Messiah, the Son of God. *He* is the good news.

Although there are two facets in the concept of repentance, there is only one act, for as one turns away from one position, one also turns immediately to the second. It is significant that the term "repentance" is found many times in the gospels and the book of Acts, but as the message of Jesus Christ went out to regions where He was unknown, the concept of repentance is emphasized less and less. Many individuals knew nothing of Jesus. They had no reason to repent or turn away from any view concerning Him. They simply needed to put their trust in the message of Jesus Christ, the Savior and Lord who died for them.

By Personal Enlistment, 1:16-20
(cf. Matt. 4:18-22; Luke 5:1-11)

1:16 The freshwater "Sea of Galilee," located in the northern portion of Israel, is approximately eight miles wide and thirteen miles long. Its harp shape gave it the name in ancient times of the Sea of Chinnereth, but in more recent times the name was changed again to the Sea of Tiberius, after the regional capital, which was built there by Herod Antipas to honor the Roman emperor. The sea is approximately six hundred feet below sea level, although a visitor to its coast would never know it. Here Jesus encountered two brothers, "Simon and Andrew." This was not their first meeting. Approximately one year earlier Andrew and an unnamed disciple, probably John, had been invited to come and see where Jesus lived, and they became His spiritual followers (John 1:35-42). Andrew went out and found his brother, Simon, and brought him to Jesus as well. Evidently the men did not immediately become His disciples. But on this occasion, approximately one year later, Jesus met them again as they were in the process of casting their nets (*amphiballontas*) into the sea. A. T. Robertson says that this word refers "literally [to] casting on both sides, now on one side, now on the other."[14] Thus, they were actively involved in their fishing profession as Jesus came on the scene.

1:17 As Jesus encountered these two men He exerted His authority by saying, "Follow Me, and I will make you become fishers of men." It was a practice of the time for men to follow a learned rabbi and to be taught by him. John the Baptist had his followers, as did the leading Pharisees and other rabbis. Usually it was the students who sought out the rabbi. However, here it was the other way around. There was something dynamic in the power of this One as He appeared to men who were busy in their occupations of life and laid down the challenge for them to follow Him:

> The immediate function of those called to be fishers of men is to accompany Jesus as witness to the proclamation of the nearness of the kingdom and the necessity for men to turn to God through radical repentance. Their ultimate function will be to confront men with God's decisive action, which to faith has the character of salvation, but to unbelief has the character of judgment. In specifically calling Simon and Andrew to be fishers, there is reflection upon the unpreparedness of the people for the critical moment which has come.[15]

Jesus was choosing His followers for a task that was greater than had ever been attempted.

1:18 Mark stated that "they immediately [*euthys*] left their nets and followed Him." The inherent authority of Jesus necessitated obedience. "In the Gospels the verb 'follow' (*akoloutheō*), when referring to *individuals,* expresses the call and response of discipleship. Later events (cf. vv. 29-31) show that their response meant not a repudiation of their homes but rather giving Jesus their full allegiance (cf. 10:28)."[16]

1:19 As Jesus walked on farther He saw two other men, James and John, the sons of Zebedee, who also were fishermen by trade, possibly partners with Peter and Andrew (cf. Luke 5:7). John may have been a follower of John the Baptist and met Jesus previously. His older brother, James, apparently was not present when the incidents recorded in John 1 occurred. It is thought by many scholars, based on their

---

14. Robertson, *Word Pictures in the New Testament,* 1:257.
15. Lane, *The Gospel of Mark,* 68.
16. John D. Grassmick, "Mark," in *Bible Knowledge Commentary* (Wheaton, Ill.: Victor, 1983), 108.

understanding of John 19:25, that the mother of James and John was Salome, a sister of Mary, the mother of Jesus. If that is true, Jesus was the cousin of James and John. On this occasion, Jesus found them in the process of mending their nets as they were preparing for another round of fishing.

1:20   Again the inherent authority of Jesus was evident as He enlisted James and John to follow Him. Although the command given to Andrew and Peter is not repeated in this verse, it may be inferred that the very same words were spoken to James and John. They followed so quickly (again the Greek word *euthys* is used) that they left their father, Zebedee, in the boat. The stress in Mark's account clearly emphasizes Jesus' sovereign authority and the radical obedience of these men. It was clear that they were leaving a well-established and significant business in order to follow Jesus Christ, for not only did they leave their father in the boat but the hired servants who were with him. James and John would one day inherit the whole operation, and yet the authority of Jesus Christ was such that they left it to follow Him. This is not to imply that

> these four fishermen completely forsook all their wealth when they followed Jesus. James and John left their boats and the business in the hands of their father and the hired help (Mark 1:20). Since they were partners, Zebedee may have managed the affairs of Peter and Andrew also. Or possibly Peter had a manager who looked after the business. He continued to maintain a house in Capernaum, which seems to have served as apostolic headquarters. This presupposes some kind of income.[17]

By Demonstrating Authority, 1:21-3:5

As Jesus Christ began His ministry, the question on the mind of everyone hearing Him was, "Can this man produce?" They were basically asking if He had the power to accomplish what He said He would do. In the sections in Mark's gospel that follow, various realms are presented in which the authority of the Servant is seen. And it is clearly demonstrated that the Servant can produce.

17. Howard F. Vos, *Mark* (Grand Rapids: Zondervan, 1978), 20.

OVER DEMONIC FORCES, 1:21-28
(cf. Luke 4:31-37)

1:21 Capernaum was one of the more prominent cities on the northern shore of the Sea of Galilee at the time of Jesus. Ruins at Capernaum have been excavated, and the remains of a large synagogue dating approximately from the third century stand at the site. This area was strategically located not only because it was on the shore of the sea but also because the primary routes traveling to the east and west went through Capernaum. Merchants from Damascus would bring their silks and spices from the East and return home with dried fish from the sea and fruits from the nearby plains of Gennesaret. When the Sabbath day came, Jesus, according to His regular custom, "entered the synagogue," which was a place of assembly, instruction, and worship.[18] He was recognized as a rabbi and was given the privilege of teaching. The Jewish custom was to grant the opportunity to teach to "any competent Israelite who was invited by the officers. Hence the synagogue supplied invaluable opportunities to the first preachers of the Gospel."[19]

1:22 Those who heard His teaching reacted as never before. They were astonished at the manner of His teaching, for He taught as one who had inherent authority (*exousia*).

> The term [*exousia*] is found nine times in Mark—six with reference to Jesus (1:22, 27; 2:10; 11:28, 29, 33), twice of the apostles (3:15; 6:7), and once in the simile of the man who "gave authority over his house to his servants" (13:34), which doubtless is an allusion to the disciples of Jesus. In the three instances where Jesus is not the subject, *exousia* connotes the conferring of his authority on the disciples. Thus every occurrence of *exousia* in Mark reflects either directly or indirectly the authority of Jesus.[20]

The issue of authority (on what does one base his statements?) is always a paramount factor. Jesus did not teach as their scribes had taught in the past. Their teaching basically was relegated to quoting older or greater rabbis and utilizing the authority of their predeces-

18. For an interesting discussion on the synagogue during New Testament times, see Hendriksen, *Exposition of the Gospel According to Mark,* 74-76.

19. Henry Barclay Swete, *The Gospel According to St. Mark* (Grand Rapids: Eerdmans, 1956), 18.

20. James R. Edwards, "The Authority of Jesus in the Gospel of Mark," *JETS* 37 (June 1994): 220.

sors. Jesus taught as one who possessed His own authority and who did not depend on what others had previously stated.

1:23   As He was teaching in the synagogue a man was present with "an unclean spirit" (*pneumati akathartō*). The spirit world basically consists of angelic beings who worship and serve God (cf. Ps. 103:20; Rev. 22:9; Heb. 1:6; Rev. 5:8-13) and angelic beings who followed Satan in his fall and who now serve him (Rev. 12:3-4; Eph. 6:11-12). The latter group has become known as demons (cf. v. 34). The demon within the man was present and undetectable, but he reacted to the authoritative teaching that was being proclaimed by crying out.

> The inbreaking of God's kingdom in Jesus first begins, according to Mark, not in the human arena but in the cosmic arena, in order to bind "the strongman" (3:27) who exercises power over the natural order. Indeed, as supernatural powers themselves the demons recognize the mission and authority of Jesus before humanity does (1:24; 3:11; 5:7).[21]

1:24   What the demon-possessed man said reflected a knowledge of several things. First, he clearly knew the identity of Jesus. The fact that the demon refers to Him as "Jesus of Nazareth" was not necessarily done to imply disdain or to point out the Messiah's lowly state (in the minds of most Jews) as coming from a despicable village. The Lord used the term of Himself in a respectful way in Acts 22:8. The form of address the demon used was simply the common designation by which Jesus was known at this time. He also called Him "the Holy One of God" or the One empowered by God (cf. 3:11, 5:7).

> Jesus was "holy" not only in the sense of being sinless in himself, filled with virtue, and the cause of virtue in others, but specifically also in this sense, that he had been anointed, hence set apart, separated, for the performance of the most exalted task (Isa. 61:1-3; Luke 4:18, 19; 19:10; John 3:16; 10:36; II Cor. 5:21).[22]

It is also clear that the demon knew some things about Jesus' ministry. James 2:19 implies that the demons do have a knowledge of God, but that knowledge does not lead them to salvation. Rather, it simply causes them to be frightened. This demon knew that Jesus would one day be his Destroyer/Judge. "Have You come to destroy us?" he asked.

21. Ibid., 221.
22. Hendriksen, *Exposition of the Gospel According to Mark,* 66.

His word for "destroy" (*apolesai*) does not mean to annihilate, but it carried the idea of ruin. The demon clearly recognized the Lord of glory and understood something of his ultimate doom.

It should be noted that in his two comments the demon used the plural pronouns "we" and "us." This could imply that more than one demon possessed this man in the synagogue, or it could mean that the demon was aware of the significance of Jesus not only for Himself but for the entire demonic realm. Whereas the men in the synagogue were amazed at His teaching, the demons were aware that His presence spelled their ultimate destruction.

1:25   The Lord Jesus was not about to accept such an acknowledgment from a thoroughly corrupt demon. He therefore rebuked the spirit, telling him to "be quiet" (*phimōthēti*, lit., "be muzzled") and to "come out of" the man. The Lord had the authority to silence all creatures and to direct their movements. "In contrast to contemporary exorcists, who identified themselves by name or by relationship to some deity or power, who pronounced some spell or performed some magical action, Jesus utters only a few direct words, through which his absolute authority over the demonic power that had held the man captive was demonstrated."[23]

1:26   The demon left the man but, in the process, threw him to the ground and caused him to go "into convulsions." Luke in his account (4:35) states that the demon did him no harm. This Greek word *sparazan* is used elsewhere (cf. Matt. 17:15) of epileptic convulsions. Medical writers used the word for the rotating of the stomach. The demon utilized the human vocal cords of the man one last time as he screamed "with a loud voice" and finally left him. The demonic world responds immediately to the direct commands of the Lord, for they recognize His authority.

1:27   Those in the crowd "were all amazed" (*ethambēthēsan hapantes*) and actually began to debate among themselves. They could not understand what was happening. First, they were astonished that Jesus Christ taught with His own authority (v. 22). This was amplified when they saw that "even the unclean spirits . . . obey Him." Certainly these individuals had seen exorcisms in the past, and yet those were never done in the authority of the one commanding the spirits. This was unique. "There had been no technique, no spells or incantations, no symbolic act. There had been only the word. There was no category

23. Lane, *The Gospel of Mark*, 74-75.

familiar to them which explained the sovereign authority with which Jesus spoke and acted."[24] Jesus Christ by His own authority gave directions to the demons and they obeyed. "The cornerstone of Jesus' public ministry is set. In both his word and work Jesus is endowed with the sovereign authority of God."[25]

1:28   It was to be expected that "the news about Him" would spread throughout all the districts of Galilee. An event of this magnitude could never be confined simply to the city of Capernaum. It is therefore not surprising that in the ensuing stories Jesus was usually mobbed by crowds.

OVER DISEASE, 1:29-34
(cf. Matt. 8:14-17; Luke 4:38-41)

1:29   As they left the synagogue, they went "immediately" (*euthys*) to the house of Simon Peter, which he evidently shared with his brother, Andrew. Archaeological digs in Capernaum have identified a house in the immediate vicinity of the third century synagogue that is called the house of St. Peter. It is well within the prescribed limit that Jews could walk on the Sabbath day. This house became the home of Jesus in Galilee and was the center of His ministry in this northern region.

1:30   As they entered the house, they discovered that Simon Peter's "mother-in-law was lying sick with a fever." There are not many references in Scripture concerning the marital status of the apostles. This makes clear, however, that Peter was married, for here information about the physical condition of his mother-in-law is noted. It may be assumed that Peter was already a married man when he began to follow Jesus. Paul states that Peter's wife traveled with him in his ministry (1 Cor. 9:5). The fact that Peter's mother-in-law was ill was quickly communicated to Jesus. Luke 4:38 implies that Jesus was asked to intervene in her behalf.

1:31   Jesus went to the woman, and Luke states that He "stood over her" (Luke 4:39) as a physician would do, and then He rebuked the fever. Mark and Matthew (Matt. 8:15) say that He took her by the hand and restored her to physical health. The fever left her, He lifted her up, and she immediately began to wait on them. There is actually a double miracle here, for Jesus not only healed her of her physical

24. Ibid., 76.
25. Edwards, "The Authority of Jesus in the Gospel of Mark," 222.

illness but gave her the power to get up and immediately work. Often after one has recovered from a fever, it takes awhile to find the strength to resume normal tasks. She however was not only cured of her fever but was enabled to immediately wait on those who had come in from the synagogue services.

> Not only was the woman's temperature normal but such a surge of new strength was coursing through her entire being that she insisted on getting up. In fact, she actually got up and started to perform the duties of a busy hostess. She began to wait on all those present: Jesus, Peter, Andrew, James, John, and perhaps even on her daughter if she too was present, as is probable. Or, "mother" may have ably been assisting "daughter" in performing this act of hospitality.[26]

1:32   After the sun had set and the Sabbath was over, suddenly many people appeared outside Peter's home. Reports about the healing of the demon-possessed man (cf. v. 28) and perhaps even the healing of Peter's mother-in-law had rapidly spread. As a result, many came "bringing" (*epheron,* imperfect tense picturing action that continued to happen over a period of time) their loved ones and friends who were ill or who were possessed by demons. It would not have been possible for them to travel until the Sabbath had concluded at sunset, but now people could travel and carry burdens once again. Much activity was involved here.

1:33   Mark, again using hyperbole (cf. v. 5), stated that "the whole city had gathered at the door." The size of the town of Capernaum at this time has been estimated at several thousand. It was a prominent city in the region. Even if only a small percentage of the town had converged on Peter's and Andrew's home, the place would have been crowded. The vivid detail given by Mark implies that the place was quickly mobbed by people: "Mark alone mentions this vivid detail. He is seeing with Peter's eyes again. Peter no doubt watched the beautiful scene with pride and gratitude as Jesus stood in the door and healed the great crowds in the glory of that sunset. He loved to tell it afterwards."[27]

1:34   Jesus "healed many who were ill with various diseases," and those who were demon possessed were also set free. Jesus, however, did not allow the testimony of the demons to be given, even though

26. Hendriksen, *Exposition of the Gospel According to Mark,* 69.
27. Robertson, *Word Pictures in the New Testament,* 1:263.

they knew who He was. Mark noted that "He was not permitting the demons to speak" (*ouk ēphien lalein ta daimonia,* imperfect tense giving a vivid picture of Jesus silencing the demons as they tried to speak over a period of time). The Savior did not need the testimony of demons. Mark maintained a clear distinction between physical disease and demonic possession. Clearly the authority of the Savior was demonstrated in the realms of both.

OVER PERSONAL DIRECTION, 1:35-39
(cf. Matt. 4:23-25; Luke 4:42-44)
1:35 Even after an extremely strenuous day, Mark reveals that "in the early morning" (*prōi*), in fact, "while it was still dark," Jesus rose and went to a place where He could be alone to pray. Mark's time notation (*prōi*) refers to the last watch of the night, which occurred between 3:00 and 6:00 A.M. Those who have been involved in public ministry realize the importance of getting away for a period of private reflective thought and for communication with God. Even the Savior needed that. Mark records that Jesus "was praying" (*proseucheto,* imperfect tense implying that His prayers continued over a period of time). The content of His prayer is not revealed. Perhaps in light of the sudden rush of acceptance following the miracles on the previous day, Jesus needed to be certain that His priorities concerning His future ministry were in line with His heavenly Father's. This is the first of three occasions where the gospel of Mark records that Jesus prayed. Later He would pray after the feeding of the 5,000 (cf. 6:46) and at the conclusion of His ministry, in the Garden of Gethsemane (cf. 14:32-42).
1:36 Simon Peter and his companions are pictured as actively hunting for Him. The verb Mark uses for "hunted" (*katedioxen*) is a combination of the verb *diōkō* and the preposition *kata.* When put together the two words carry the idea of "to hunt something down to the very end." Peter and those with him kept up the search until they found Jesus. In Mark's gospel Peter always seems to be at the forefront of the movements of the disciples. This is a good indication that Mark's information concerning the stories surrounding the Lord Jesus Christ did indeed come from Simon Peter.
1:37 When they found the Lord, they said to Him, "Everyone is looking for You." Most assuredly everyone was looking for Him. Since Jesus was performing miracles and casting out demons, there were always those who were looking to be restored to physical health and

to be free from demons. The purpose of the extensive hunt was to find Jesus and bring Him back to Capernaum. Luke, in his account of this same event (cf. 4:42), implies that the people wanted to keep Jesus Christ in their city. Who would not want to keep Jesus present if He could satisfy all physical ills?

1:38 But Christ's primary ministry was not to bring physical healing to individuals. He came to bring spiritual salvation, and His authority was such that He was able to direct His own personal steps. Rather than going back to Capernaum to minister to the multitudes there, He instructed the disciples that they all needed to go to other towns that He might "preach there also." His statement "Let us go somewhere else" included the disciples. Though He said nothing about performing miracles in these other places, it is clear that that did happen. But His primary emphasis was on preaching the good news. He came not just from Nazareth but from heaven to spread the message of the coming kingdom and the necessity for people to repent in order to be prepared for that kingdom.

1:39 Jesus and the disciples traveled "throughout all Galilee." The news about Him had circulated throughout "all the surrounding district of Galilee" (cf. v. 28). He made synagogues the center of His preaching ministry. This showed that His ministry was primarily, although not exclusively, to Jews. As He went preaching He also cast out demons as a demonstration of His authority.

> Preaching and the expulsion of demons are related facets of this ministry, the means by which the power of Satan is overcome. In this connection it may be significant that there is no reference to acts of healing in the summary statement. Healing is an aspect of the redemption but it demonstrates Jesus' confrontation with Satan less graphically than the restoration to wholeness of those who have been possessed by demons.[28]

OVER LEPROSY, 1:40-45
(cf. Matt. 8:2-4; Luke 5:12-16)

1:40 In the process of dealing with various illnesses, Mark records that a leper came to Jesus, falling before Him and beseeching Him to make him clean. Leprosy was a dreaded disease at that time, probably much as AIDS is feared in our modern culture.

28. Lane, *The Gospel of Mark,* 83.

> Leprologists who have examined the biblical data in Lev. 13–14 feel certain that the biblical term "leprosy" is a collective noun designating a wide variety of chronic skin diseases, one of which may have been interpreted in the modern sense of the word. Nevertheless, any man who was identified as a leper was reduced to a most pitiful state of existence. In addition to the physical ravages of the disease, his cultic impurity was graphically described in the Levitical provision: "The leper who has the disease shall wear torn clothes and let the hair of his head hang loose, and he shall cover his upper lip and cry, 'Unclean, unclean.' He shall remain unclean as long as he has the disease; he is unclean; he shall dwell alone in a habitation without the camp." (Lev. 13:45f.)[29]

The modern terminology for leprosy is Hansen's Disease. Whether or not the biblical designation of leprosy is that exact disease cannot be conclusively determined. The biblical disease is clearly some kind of a skin condition that could be noted by doctors or other individuals.

To be infected with leprosy was like a death sentence, for the disease made one unclean. A leper could not move freely through society. A provision could be made, however, for a leper to attend a synagogue service as long as a screen was provided to separate the leper from the congregation at large. That this leper came to Jesus was a bold move on his part.

> This man must have heard enough about Christ's deeds of power coupled with sympathy to understand that here was someone who could be hopefully approached. Of course, he did not know whether the help he craved would be given to him . . . a man "full of leprosy" (Luke 5:12). But there was nothing wrong with asking.[30]

The humility of the leper, however, was seen as he fell to his knees and said to Jesus, "You can make me clean." He was certain of the power of Jesus to heal him. The only question was of Jesus' willingness to demonstrate His mercy on this man.

1:41 Jesus was "moved with compassion" (*splagchnisthesis*) toward the leper. This aorist passive particle is found only in Mark's account. It probably should be translated "gripped with compassion," showing the immediate reaction of Jesus Christ when confronted by human

---

29. Ibid., 84-85.
30. Hendriksen, *Exposition of the Gospel According to Mark,* 78.

need. In fact, Jesus demonstrated an unheard of act of compassion when He reached out His hand and touched the leper. That would never have been done by anyone in that culture, for to touch a leper would make one unclean. Lepers were avoided at all costs, yet Jesus touched him and said, "I am willing; be cleansed."

The tenses of these verbs present some interesting observations. "I am willing," the verb *thelō*, is in the present tense. The Savior's will is always active and ready to assist a need. The verb "be cleansed" (*katharistheti*) is in the aorist tense. That tense implies an immediate, radical healing that took place in the life of this individual. This man who formerly was known by his friends and relatives as a leper would now be known to them as a completely healthy individual.

1:42 "Immediately" (*euthys*) the man was cleansed of his leprosy. Truly this was a miracle that had not been observed in the lifetime of any of the individuals watching the Savior. In fact, as one reads the pages of Scripture, in all recorded time only two individuals are known to have been healed of leprosy. The sister of Moses, Miriam, was struck with leprosy in Numbers 12 when she questioned whether the Lord had spoken only through Moses. It was through the intervention of Moses that Miriam was healed. The second individual was the Syrian captain Naaman (2 Kings 5). Naaman, a Gentile, came to Elisha and was told to wash in the River Jordan seven times. When he washed, he was cleansed of his leprosy. These are the only recorded cases of healing from the dreaded disease, and yet a specific portion of Scripture instructs a person who has been cleansed of leprosy to offer the appropriate sacrifices (cf. Lev. 14:1-32).

1:43 Jesus gave a stern warning (*embrimēsamenos*) to the healed leper. Only Mark uses this word in the story. "It is a strong word for the snorting of a horse and expresses powerful emotion as Jesus stood here face to face with leprosy, itself a symbol of sin and all its train of evils."[31]

> But the idea of anger is not inherent in the word; see Jo. xi.33, 38, where it is used of our Lord's attitude towards Himself; rather it indicates depth and strength of feeling expressed in tone and manner. A close parallel to the present passage is to be found in Mt. ix.30. In neither case can we discover any occasion for displeasure with the subject of the verb.[32]

31. Robertson, *Word Pictures in the New Testament,* 1:265.
32. Swete, *The Gospel According to St. Mark,* 30.

Surely the stern warning that Jesus gave to the man as He sent him away had something to do with the scriptural requirement mentioned in the next verse. One who had been cleansed certainly should offer the appropriate Levitical sacrifices.

1:44 Jesus said to him, "See that you say nothing to anyone; but go, show yourself to the priest." It was important that this man go to Jerusalem and follow the cleansing that Moses commanded. By so doing he would become a testimony to the religious leaders that something unique was happening in their midst. It would necessitate a complete investigation of Jesus' claims. Such a dramatic healing implied that a prophet was present in their midst. The instructions from Leviticus 14 declare that one who had been cleansed of leprosy was to offer two birds. One was to be killed as a symbol for purification and the other was to be released as a symbol of the individual's freedom. The offering also involved washing with water as well as other offerings that were to be given in worship and thanksgiving to God for the cleansing. The ritual was extended and elaborate, and surely was one that had rarely been used, if ever, by a priest.

Jesus said to the man that his presentation of himself was to be "a testimony" to the priests. One can only speculate as to the commotion this man caused when he showed up at the temple in Jerusalem claiming to have been cleansed from leprosy. Probably the priest on duty that day had long forgotten the ritual concerning the cleansing from leprosy. Perhaps he had to consult several other priests, if not the actual text in Leviticus, to see what should be done. This man's testimony was a positive piece of evidence that something radically new was happening in Israel. The formal certification by the priests that this man had been healed from leprosy was also necessary before he would be allowed back into the normal channels of society.

1:45 However, the man who had been cleansed immediately went out and began to tell others of his cleansing. This is not to say that he did not also go and present himself to the priest. But he was so excited about his cleansing that he wanted to tell others. Consequently, the crowds so thronged around Jesus that He "could no longer publicly enter a city." He had to stay in the "unpopulated areas." But people were still "coming [*ērchonto,* imperfect tense vividly describing the multitudes of people continuing to come out to Jesus over an extended period of time] to Him" from all locations. No doubt that would happen even in today's world if one appeared with the ability to cure disease, especially dreaded diseases such as AIDS or cancer. One can only imagine what kinds of crowds would be attracted to such an individual. Clearly this was a demonstration of the Savior's authority.

HOMILETICAL SUGGESTIONS

An introductory chapter provides many opportunities to introduce various ideas. It can be effective at the beginning of a book such as Mark to present various people. Mark himself can be introduced, although not directly springing from the text. It is also possible to introduce John the Baptist, who comes on the scene at the' outset of the book. Of course, the major character being introduced by Mark in his gospel is the Lord Jesus Christ.

The Lord Jesus Christ can be presented in His identification with John in baptism. The authenticating voice that came from heaven clearly identified this One as the beloved Son with whom the Father was pleased. He was also authenticated by the fact that He successfully met His opponent, Satan, in the temptations and was victorious over him. Another good preaching point from this chapter is the recognition of the men who began to follow Jesus Christ. Excellent character studies of various individuals such as Simon Peter, Andrew, James, and John can be made here. Perhaps the best authenticating point in the chapter is to present the power of Jesus being demonstrated in various realms. Of special interest is the account of the healing of the leper. The uniqueness of that miracle is critical to the gospel, for only two other miracles are recorded. Truly the fact that Jesus Christ could heal a leper and use him as His "calling card" is a significant event that needs to be presented.

MARK

CHAPTER

TWO

THE SERVANT'S AUTHORITY

OVER FORGIVENESS OF SINS, 2:1-12
(cf. Matt. 9:1-8; Luke 5:17-26)

2:1 Jesus returned to the city of Capernaum after "several days" in the unpopulated areas. In fact, the city of Capernaum became His "home" and the center of His ministry in Galilee. In all probability Jesus returned to the home of Simon Peter, although some believe He may have been with family members there (cf. 3:31-32). Some believe that a follower of Jesus may have turned his home over to the Lord for His use while in Capernaum. But it seems best to conclude that this was Peter's and Andrew's home, where Jesus had earlier performed miracles (cf. 1:29-34).

2:2 So many "were gathered together" that it was impossible for others to enter the room, "another graphic Markan detail seen through Peter's eyes. The double compound negative in the Greek intensifies the negative. This house door apparently opened into the street, not into a court as in the larger houses. The house was packed inside and there was a jam outside."[1] William Hendriksen pictures this scene in this manner:

> In view of the amazement caused by Christ's words and works (1:21-34, 38-45) we can understand why it was that the house was filled. No

---

1. A. T. Robertson, *Word Pictures in the New Testament* (Nashville: Broadman, 1930), 1:266.

doubt friends and disciples of Jesus were present in goodly numbers, with genuine interest in the truth. Also, there must have been many "rubbernecks" burning with curiosity to hear what Jesus would say and especially what he would do. Last but not least, there were straitlaced rabbis—Pharisees and doctors of the law (Luke 5:17)—filled with envy, deeply disturbed about the large crowds Jesus was attracting. These "important" people had come from every village not only in Galilee but even in Judea and Jerusalem! Result: not even near the doorway was there any room left.[2]

In the midst of this commotion Jesus sat and spoke (*elalei,* imperfect tense giving vivid detail of action extending over a period of time in the past) the Word of God to those who would listen.

2:3 But into this crowd suddenly "came" (*erchontai,* a vivid use of the historic present tense) a group of men carrying on a pallet one who had been paralyzed. Mark's gospel includes a picturesque detail not given by the other synoptic writers. Mark indicates that this pallet was born by four individuals. Whether they were friends or relatives is not known. "It is impossible to say anything definite about the nature of the man's affliction beyond the fact that he was unable to walk. The determination of those who brought him to Jesus suggests that his condition was wretched."[3]

2:4 The crowd had so thronged the house in which Jesus was teaching that it was impossible for the men to enter carrying the paralytic on his pallet. This was not, however, going to keep them from getting their relative/friend to the Savior. Their plan was an ingenious one and very possible, considering the type of construction used in the building of houses at that time. Most homes had flat roofs, and most also had outside staircases leading up to the roof. The four went there carrying their friend, opened up the roof tiles, dug through the thatch, creating a hole, and through it they let their friend down into the room, still on his pallet.

> *They let down the bed* (*chalōsi ton krabatton*), historical present again, aorist tense in Luke 5:19 (*kathēkan*). The verb means to lower from a higher place as from a boat. Probably the four men had a rope fastened to each corner of the pallet or poor man's bed (*krabatton,* Latin *graba-*

2. William Hendriksen, *Exposition of the Gospel According to Mark* (Grand Rapids: Baker, 1975), 86-87.

3. William L. Lane, *The Gospel of Mark,* NICNT (Grand Rapids: Eerdmans, 1974), 93.

tus. So one of Mark's Latin words). Matthew (9:2) has *klinē,* general term for bed. Luke has *klinidion* (little bed or couch).[4]

This must have caused a great deal of commotion in the room, as dust and debris obviously started to fall on those inside. One also thinks of the home owner, probably Simon Peter, and what his reaction must have been.

2:5   As Jesus saw "their faith" (plural), He said to the man on the stretcher, "My son, your sins are forgiven." It is interesting that the Savior recognized the faith not only of the paralyzed man but of his friends who brought him to Jesus. But, whereas the four individuals carrying the pallet seem to be the objects in view in most of the previous verbs, there is no reason to exclude the man on the pallet as one who also had faith in Jesus to heal him. R. A. Cole cites this story as "a veritable sermon on the text of James ii. 26, showing that faith, unless it manifests its reality by action, is unreal and self-deceptive."[5]

Evidently the physical infirmity that brought about the paralysis of this individual had something to do with sin. Not all sickness is the direct result of sin, but it is clear that some illness does come about directly because of sin in one's life. The Lord Jesus knew the difference. When He said, "Your sins are forgiven (*aphientai,* aorist tense indicating an accomplished fact), He also placed the verb first in His sentence (lit., "Forgiven are your sins"), thus placing the emphasis on forgiveness. This man's sins were at that very moment permanently forgiven.

Not only for the paralytic was this pronouncement of pardon an inestimable blessing, it was also a source of gladness for his benefactors. They must have rejoiced in his joy. More even, it was a lesson for the entire audience. All were made aware of the fact that *this* Physician regarded spiritual blessings above material, and claimed to possess "authority"—that is, *the right* and *the power*—to heal not only the body but also the soul.[6]

2:6   At this point in Mark's gospel he introduces the scribes. They will be mentioned many times throughout the remainder of the gospel. In only one passage is the reference favorable (cf. 12:28-34). The

4. Robertson, *Word Pictures in the New Testament,* 1:267.
5. R. A. Cole, *The Gospel According to Mark* (Grand Rapids: Eerdmans, 1979), 66.
6. Hendriksen, *Exposition of the Gospel According to Mark,* 89.

scribes were men formerly schooled in the written law of God and its oral interpretations. They were admitted to their closed order only after they were deemed fully qualified and had been set apart by the laying on of hands. They considered themselves to be the guardians of the teaching office and challenged anyone who refused to submit to their interpretations. They communicated nothing verbally here, but their minds were racing, and their faces probably gave away their displeasure with Jesus' statement. They had heard clearly what Jesus said and knew its implications.

2:7　In their reasoning they concluded that Jesus' comment was blasphemy. Forgiveness of sins, according to their interpretation of Scripture, is something only God can do. "The Messiah would exterminate the godless in Israel, crush demonic power and protect his people from the reign of sin, but the forgiveness of sins was never attributed to him."[7] But Jesus was claiming to forgive this man's sins. If He was speaking the truth and this man's sins had been forgiven, then the only proper conclusion would have to be that He was God. Their conclusion, however, was that Jesus was guilty of blasphemy (*blasphē-mei*), which means "injurious speech or slander." There actually is nothing wrong with their logic. The only problem is that they failed to accept the possibility that this One could indeed be God.

2:8　Jesus in His own spirit knew "immediately" (*euthys*) what they were thinking:

> The recognition was in the sphere of human spirit, and was not attained through the senses; there was not even the guidance of external circumstances, such as may have enabled Him to 'see the faith' of the friends of the paralytic. He read their thoughts by His own consciousness, without visible or audible indications to suggest them to Him.[8]

His question brought their secret thoughts out into the open, for He asked them why indeed they were reasoning about these things. His questioning of them was a commonly used rabbinical device, for rabbis loved to debate issues back and forth with their students. Jesus was simply debating with the religious leaders their thinking, which was falsely accusing Him of blasphemy. They were the true sinful ones in

7. Lane, *The Gospel of Mark*, 95.
8. Henry Barclay Swete, *The Gospel According to St. Mark* (Grand Rapids: Eerdmans, 1956), 36.

this story, for they had come there that very day with the specific purpose of finding accusations that they might use to destroy Him.

2:9 His comment exposed the controversy raging in their hearts and made very clear what had happened in this situation. He asked them which would be the easier thing to say, "Your sins are forgiven," or to say, "Arise, and take up your pallet and walk"? It is obvious that anyone could make either statement. What Jesus was asking was which was the easier statement to make in the situation for the purposes of verification. Clearly it would be easier to say, "Your sins are forgiven," because no one would be able to judge whether or not that had actually taken place. But if one says, "Arise, and take up your pallet and walk," and the person continues to lie on his pallet sick, the speaker is clearly an imposter.

2:10 Jesus clearly wanted His hearers to understand who He was, so for the first time in Mark's gospel He used the term "Son of Man." This term is used again in v. 28, then twelve times after Peter's confession concerning His person in 8:29 (see 8:31, 38; 9:9, 12, 31; 10:33, 45; 13:26; 14:21 [twice], 41, 62).

> The origin of the term *Son of Man* is Daniel 7:13 where He is pictured as triumphantly delivering the kingdom to the Father. The position of the Son of Man at the right hand of the Father relates to Psalm 110:1 and the One who is Lord. Matthew 26:63-64 indicates the term is basically synonymous with Son of God. The term emphasizes various themes: authority (Mark 2:10); glorification (Matt. 25:31); humiliation (Matt. 8:20); suffering and death (Mark 10:45); relationship with the Holy Spirit (Matt. 12:32); salvation (Luke 19:10).[9]

Some question Jesus' use of the title "Son of Man" in the presence of unbelievers so early in His ministry. That, plus the awkward change of address in the verse, which seems at first to be addressed to the scribes and then abruptly speaks to the paralytic, have caused some to conclude that "Son of Man" might have been an editorial comment by Mark.

> He inserted it into the narrative to explain the significance of this event for his readers: that Jesus as the risen Son of Man **has authority** (*exousian,* the right and power) **on earth to forgive sins,** something the

9. Paul Enns, *Moody Handbook of Theology* (Chicago: Moody, 1989), 87.

scribes did not fully recognize. Only here in the Gospels is the forgiveness of sins attributed to the Son of Man.[10]

The use of *exousia* here contrasts with *dynatai* in v. 7. There the scribes ask: "Who can forgive sins but God alone?" The shift from *dynatai* to *exousia* means that the Son of Man not only has the power but the right to forgive sins. "The authority of Jesus has become the central issue. The question here is whether Jesus exercises divine authority on earth (v. 10), and whether therefore Jesus stands in the place of God (v. 7c)."[11]

That Jesus claimed the ability to forgive sins meant that He claimed to be God (Pss. 65:3; 78:38; 130:4; Isa. 43:25).

The statement by Mark "He said to the paralytic" is another illustration of the historical present. It is a vivid way for the readers to see the event actually taking place before their eyes.

2:11 "Rise, take up your pallet and go home" was the direction of the Savior. That statement could be immediately verified one way or the other. "His power to forgive, no less effective because of its invisibility, will be proved by the healing the paralytic. The power to forgive and the power to heal are one."[12] Either the paralytic would obey and get up, pick up his pallet, and go home, or he would continue to lie there sick. His getting up (which he does in the next verse) would demonstrate that truly Jesus Christ not only had the authority to heal but obviously had the authority to forgive his sins. "The [pallet] without its burden could easily be carried by one man if in good health. That the paralytic could do this was proof of his complete recovery."[13] If he remained prostrate, Jesus would be proven a fake, and neither statement would have any validity. Such a blasphemer would be worthy of death.

2:12 The paralytic responded "immediately" (*euthys*) to the Savior's command. He got up, picked up his pallet, and with the crowd giving way went out of the room before them all. The result was amazement (*existasthai,* from which the English word "ecstasy" comes), and the people glorified God saying, "We have never seen

10. John D. Grassmick, "Mark," in *Bible Knowledge Commentary* (Wheaton, Ill.: Victor, 1983), 113.

11. James R. Edwards, "The Authority of Jesus in the Gospel of Mark," *JETS* 37 (June 1994): 222.

12. Ibid., 223.

13. Swete, *The Gospel According to St. Mark*, 38.

anything like this." Truly the miraculous work of Jesus Christ was far beyond their ability to comprehend and demonstrated His authority in the situation. "Jesus had acted with the power of God and claimed equality with God and had made good his claim. They all marveled at the *paradoxes* (*paradoxa,* Luke 5:26) of that day. For it all, they glorified God."[14]

> The point of this incident now becomes clear. The scribes held that a man could not be healed until all his sins had been forgiven. The paralytic had been obviously healed; no one could deny it. But according to the rabbinical saying, that meant that his sins must first have been forgiven. How then could these religious leaders deny Jesus' power to forgive sins?[15]

James Edwards summarizes this miracle well:

> Jesus presents himself as one who confidently stands in the place of God. In answer to the question, "Who except God alone?" (v. 7), hearers and readers are invited to supply the name of Jesus. The exclamation of the crowd gives voice to the uniqueness to the event: "We have never seen anything like this" (2:12). It was this very conviction in fact that led the early fathers to the acknowledgement that, in the claim to forgive sins in Mark 2:10 and elsewhere, Jesus was the *Logos* of God.[16]

OVER MEN, 2:13-14
(cf. Matt. 9:9; Luke 5:27-28)

2:13   Jesus left the house of Peter probably to get away from the multitude that had gathered there. He went out along the shore of the Sea of Galilee, a walk that our Savior surely loved. Multitudes continued to come (*ērcheto*) to Him and throng about Him. Everywhere He went He "was teaching" (*edidasken*). Both main verbs are imperfect tenses implying activity that lasted over a period of time as people continued to come to Jesus and then went on their way.

2:14   As He was walking along (present participle picturing the action as occurring) He saw a man, Levi, the son of Alphaeus, sitting in his "tax office" (*telōnion,* lit. "a toll gate"), probably strategically located on the main road between Damascus and the Mediterranean Sea.

14. Robertson, *Word Pictures in the New Testament,* 1:269.
15. Ralph Earle, *Mark, The Gospel of Action* (Chicago: Moody, 1970), 24-25.
16. Edwards, "The Authority of Jesus in the Gospel of Mark," 223.

When Jesus said to him, "Follow [*akolouthei,* present tense command] Me!" Levi immediately rose, left everything, and followed the Lord Jesus. This was truly a monumental decision on Levi's part, for he was involved in a very lucrative profession. A tax gatherer obtained his position by purchasing it from the Roman government. He then could charge whatever he wanted in order to recoup his investment plus earn his living. Tax gatherers were usually looked on with disfavor by the Jewish people, for they considered them to be compromisers with the Romans.

> They acquired the reputation of being *extortionists.* In addition, Jewish publicans were regarded by other Jews as being *traitors,* unfaithful to their own people and to their own religion. Were they not in the service of the foreign oppressors, ultimately in the service of the pagan Roman emperor? Were they not filling his coffers?[17]

Levi (Matthew) is declared in the text to be "the son of Alphaeus." One other of the twelve disciples is said to be a son of Alphaeus—a man named James (cf. 3:18). It is doubtful that this James and Matthew were brothers, for Matthew is mentioned in this same verse and is not connected with James. The other brothers in the list—James and John, and Simon and Andrew—are grouped together. Their fathers simply happened to have the same name.

Levi came to be known as Matthew (cf. Matt. 9:9; 10:3). Whether he changed his name or had been given both names cannot be determined from the text. He may very well have known the other disciples who were following Jesus. As a tax gatherer, he would have had dealings with the fishermen, for even fish were subject to taxation. But Levi left it all and followed Jesus. Clearly the inherent authority of the Savior was demonstrated in a man leaving everything in order to personally commit himself to One like this. Howard Vos adds that "whether or not he had any spiritual preparation in having heard John the Baptist or Jesus' message from another, we cannot determine. Certainly he was familiar with all the stir that had centered around Jesus and His message in previous weeks."[18]

17. Hendriksen, *Exposition of the Gospel According to Mark,* 94.
18. Howard F. Vos, *Mark* (Grand Rapids: Zondervan, 1978), 27.

OVER TRADITIONS, 2:15-22
(cf. Matt. 9:10-17; Luke 5:29-39)

2:15 As Levi decided to follow the Lord Jesus he wanted to give a final dinner to say good-bye to his friends, as well as to introduce them to Jesus. Luke 5:29-39 clearly indicates that this banquet occurred in Levi's home. Jesus, therefore, "was reclining" at dinner with many "tax-gatherers and sinners," along with the disciples who were following Him.

> Tax-collectors and sinners! As the Pharisees saw it, a "sinner" was one who refused to subject himself to *the Pharisaic interpretation* of God's holy law, the Torah. In that sense even Jesus himself and his disciples were sinners, that is, sinners as the Pharisees understood the term; for in several respects—not rinsing the hands before every meal, not observing various man-made sabbath regulations, based on sophistical reasoning—neither the Master nor his followers conducted themselves in accordance with the rabbinic interpretation of the law.[19]

Often when a person comes to faith in Jesus Christ, most of his friends are at that time unsaved. It is only after a period of time that a new Christian discovers he has lost most of his unsaved friends. Levi wanted to introduce these people to the Lord Jesus as soon as he began to follow Him.

2:16 Mark reported that some scribes who belonged to the party of the Pharisees were observing this dinner banquet. Perhaps the leper's showing up at the temple, demonstrating himself as one having been cleansed, prompted their investigation of this Jesus who was supposedly healing individuals. They observed Him eating with sinners and tax gatherers, but it is doubtful they were participants in the meal. They would never have broken bread with individuals who failed to keep the law and their traditions. It is possible they may even have refrained from entering the house, observing the banquet through open windows. They were seriously questioning why Jesus would be eating with such people if He were indeed a holy man. Their questions were not, however, directed toward Jesus. They raised their points of controversy with His disciples instead. It is probable that their question was raised as the banquet was breaking up and the guests were departing from the house.

19. Hendriksen, *Exposition of the Gospel According to Mark*, 95.

2:17   When Jesus heard their questioning of His disciples, He responded with a traditional proverb that it is not those who are healthy who need a physician but those who are sick. It is rare for a healthy person to go to a physician. Many individuals never think about a doctor when they are well. It is only when one becomes sick that the help of a physician is sought. That was exactly the kind of people Jesus was dealing with. Jesus was not interested in dealing with people such as these scribes, who already considered themselves to be righteous. They would never acknowledge that they were sinners in need of repentance (cf. 1:15).

> There are three kinds of "patients" whom Jesus cannot heal of their sin sickness: (1) those who do not know about Him; (2) those who know about Him but refuse to trust Him; and (3) those who will not admit that they need Him. The scribes and Pharisees were in that third category, as are all self-righteous sinners today. Unless we admit that we are sinners, deserving of God's judgment, we cannot be saved. Jesus saves only sinners (Luke 19:10).[20]

Jesus was interested in reaching out only to those who acknowledged their sinfulness and were willing to turn from it.

2:18   Not only did these scribes, who were Pharisees, come questioning Jesus, but some of John's disciples along with other Pharisees came and asked Jesus a question. It was common for John's disciples and for Pharisees to "fast" (*nēsteuontes,* imperfect tense picturing the action as going on over an extended period of time). The Pharisees made a great display of fasting, following that practice at least twice a week on Mondays and Thursdays. They thought it made them far more spiritual. The law of God required only one time in the entire year when Jews were to fast—the Day of Atonement (cf. Lev. 16:29-34; 23:26-32; Num. 29:7-11). With the passing of time, however, the idea of fasting began to multiply until it had reached the twice-a-week formula that was followed in the days of Jesus. So they asked Jesus about the issue of fasting. If "John's disciples and the Pharisees" fasted, why did His disciples not fast? Hendriksen maintains that

> there was no justification for this question. Had these men been better students of Scripture they would have known *a.* that, as has been indicated, the only fast that could by any stretch of the imagination be de-

---

20. Warren W. Wiersbe, *Be Diligent* (Wheaton, Ill.: Victor, 1987), 25.

rived from the law of God was the one on the day of atonement, and *b.*
that according to the teaching of Isa. 58:6, 7, and Zech. 7:1-10 it was not
a literal fast but love, both vertical and horizontal, which God demanded.[21]

2:19   The response of the Savior was taken from a common custom
of their time and from a metaphor that John the Baptist had previously
used (cf. John 3:29). When one was celebrating a festive occasion such
as a wedding, the attendants at that wedding, the associates of the
bridegroom, did not fast, did they? Indeed not! The wedding feast was
something that one looked forward to. Jesus Christ was here picturing
Himself as a bridegroom at a feast. "Bridegroom's attendants fasting
while the feast is in progress! How absurd, says Jesus as it were. Disciples of the Lord mourning while their Master is performing works of
mercy and while words of life and beauty are dropping from his lips,
how utterly incongruous!"[22] The time for rejoicing was now, while He
was with His disciples.

2:20   Jesus did indicate, however, that this joyous situation would
change. There would come a time when He would be "taken away
[*aparthē,* implying a violent removal, cf. Isa. 53:8] from them." This is
the first indication in Mark's gospel that something was going to happen to Christ. When He was finally taken away from them, then "in
that day" they would fast. These words of the Lord constituted a
prophecy, not a command. But it is interesting that a fast before Easter
specifically connected with this saying of the Lord Jesus did develop at
the end of the second century. However, it is better to understand in
this context that the contrast Jesus gives between joy and sorrow is the
imagery He had in mind, rather than the institution of a formal fast
following His death.

2:21   Jesus continued to instruct His hearers in an attempt to explain His relationship to their existing religious systems. He introduced two parables taken from their daily lives, both of which are
given in the same order in the other synoptic accounts. These parables provide additional information in answer to the question of v. 18.
In modern times, little thought is given to materials that are shrunken
or unshrunken. But it was a common problem in Jesus' day. If one
was trying to patch a garment, one would not patch it with a brand
new piece of cloth. The repaired garment would then not be able to

21. Hendriksen, *Exposition of the Gospel According to Mark,* 100.
22. Ibid.

be washed else the patch would shrink and pull away from the garment. A "worse tear" would probably result.

2:22   A second parable common to them was that of wineskins. When new wine was placed into animal skins, the process of fermentation caused expansion to occur. New wineskins have elasticity and are able to stretch as the expansion occurs. But once the wineskins have expanded, they retain that size and cannot expand further. If one were to fill an old wineskin with new wine, the skins would burst because of the pressure, and all the wine would be lost.

In these two parables, that of the patched garment and the old wineskins, Jesus was trying to show that He had not come to be a reformer of Judaism. He was not there to patch up an old system. He was coming into the world to present truths that had previously not been revealed. His program would include the establishment of a new body, the body of Jesus Christ, the church. This is something unrevealed in the pages of the Old Testament. J. Dwight Pentecost summarizes these parables:

> To the Pharisees He said one cannot make an old garment acceptable by superimposing something new on it. And to John's disciples He said that what He was offering could not be superimposed on Pharisaism so as to reform it. What He offered also could not be contained in the old system. Rather, what He was introducing had to be entirely separated from the old. The incident closed with Christ's words that if men would taste His wine, that is, if they would accept what He was offering them, they would not want the old. However, the Pharisees, having tasted the old, were satisfied with it; they had no desire for what He was offering them.[23]

OVER THE SABBATH, 2:23–3:5

Sabbath Issue Questioned, 2:23-28 (cf. Matt. 12:1-8; Luke 6:1-5)
2:23   As Jesus and His disciples passed "through the grainfields on the Sabbath," His disciples began to pluck the heads of the grain in their hands and eat it, for Matthew reports that they were hungry (cf. Matt. 12:1). Their actions were not considered theft at that time. The corners of the fields were left for the poor to gather, and it was also permissible for anyone to go into a field and take what he could eat. A

---

23. J. Dwight Pentecost, *The Words & Works of Jesus Christ* (Grand Rapids: Zondervan, 1981), 157.

person could not carry anything from a field, but, as long as he ate what he had picked, that was not contrary to the Law (cf. Deut. 23:24-25). Jesus and the disciples were probably in a wheat or barley field. The primary issue was that their actions were taking place on the Sabbath.

2:24   The Pharisees began to question Jesus, for

> among the scribes it was assumed that a teacher was responsible for the behavior of his disciples. For this reason the Pharisees addressed their protest directly to Jesus. They raised a question of *halakha,* of what is legally permitted or prohibited, perhaps with the intention of satisfying the legal requirement of a warning prior to prosecution for Sabbath violation.[24]

They were not questioning the legality of their eating or that they had traveled farther than a Sabbath day's journey. They were complaining about the disciples' actions on the Sabbath. Luke in his gospel reports that the disciples "were picking and eating the heads of grain, rubbing them in their hands" (6:1). The Pharisees' argument was that when the disciples picked the grain they were harvesting. When they rubbed the kernels of grain between their palms in order to get rid of the chaff, they were threshing. As they tossed the grain in their hands so that the chaff would be blown away, they were winnowing. In other words, the Pharisees were saying that the disciples were working on the Sabbath, and that was not lawful. It is clear from Exodus 34:21 that harvesting was a work that was never to be undertaken on the Sabbath.

2:25   Jesus' defense of His disciples' actions was an appeal to Scripture. He reminded the Pharisees of an incident that happened in the time of King David when he was fleeing from Saul (cf. 1 Sam. 21:1-6). Since they were the keepers of the Law, they should have been familiar with this story. In the process of his flight, David and the companions fleeing with him became hungry. The Lord was clearly drawing a comparison between David and his men and the greater Son of David and His disciples.

2:26   David came to Nob where the tabernacle had been set up and there asked the priest for something to eat. The priest informed him

24. Lane, *The Gospel of Mark,* 115.

that the only food available was the consecrated bread that was set apart only for the priests to eat. This would have been the bread from the Table of the Bread in the holy place of the tabernacle (cf. Ex. 25:23-30) that was changed in the tabernacle every Sabbath day. By Mosaic Law only the priests were permitted to eat that bread (cf. Lev. 24:5-9). Nevertheless, the bread was given to David and his companions for them to eat. Why? Because the greater principle of necessity dictated that the human need for food transcended the Law.

> The point is this: if David had a right to ignore a *divinely ordained ceremonial provision* when necessity demanded this, then would not David's exalted Antitype, namely, Jesus, God's Anointed in a far more eminent sense, have a right, under similar conditions of need, to set aside *a totally unwarranted, man-made sabbath regulation?* After all, to a considerable extent the rabbinical sabbath regulations amounted to misapplications of God's holy law. That was true also in the present case.[25]

The fact that Mark says this occurred "in the time of Abiathar" should not be construed as an error of history. The high priest actually was Ahimelech, Abiathar's father, but Abiathar became a much more prominent figure in Israel's history. Mark was simply following the customary Jewish way of attempting to place a historical event into an Old Testament time frame. Mark's readers did not have manuscripts with chapters and verses to refer to. But they did have a time frame of history based on key people. Abiathar was a much better known historical figure than his father. It is also possible that both Ahimelech and Abiathar were present when David came to Nob. Also, shortly after this historical event, Ahimelech was killed and Abiathar escaped to King David, and he thereafter became the high priest. It is not possible to speak with any degree of absolute authority on this problem, but either of these suggestions help to explain this apparent problem in Mark's gospel. It is clear that this event did occur in the lifetime of Abiathar.

2:27   Mark alone of the synoptic writers records that Jesus concluded His remarks by saying that "the Sabbath was made for man, and not man for the Sabbath." The religious leaders of that time had so corrupted the rules and regulations surrounding Sabbath observance that

---

25. Hendriksen, *Exposition of the Gospel According to Mark*, 106.

they had made the Sabbath into something far less than God intended it to be. The Sabbath rest was to be a blessing to people, not a curse with so many rules and regulations that one could not find time to truly worship and have fellowship with God. The religious leaders "had thus quite forgotten that in origin the sabbath was God's merciful provision for man. Man was certainly not created simply to exemplify and observe an immutable theological principle of sabbath keeping, as certain of the extremists were quite ready to uphold."[26]

2:28   Jesus' final statement demonstrated His authority for He, as the "Son of Man," is "Lord" over the Sabbath. As the Son of Man He was the One with whom the Father was well pleased (cf. 1:11), and He had been sent into the world by the Father to preach (cf. 1:38). As the Lord, He is able to command what should transpire on any given day. "As sovereign Lord he possesses the authority to lay down principles governing that day. Therefore no one has any right to find fault with him when he allows his disciples to satisfy their hunger by picking and eating heads of grain!"[27] Even that basic necessity for food that caused the disciples to go into the fields was not in violation of the laws concerning that day. Jesus is the One with authority, and His authority is to be exercised every day of the week. "His lordship over other things extended 'even' to the Sabbath. Lordship implies administration, rule, authority to regulate, and even to set aside regulations imposed by the Pharisees. He was not claiming freedom to violate the sabbath law, but ability to interpret it."[28]

HOMILETICAL SUGGESTIONS

This chapter continues to point out realms in which the authority of the Lord Jesus Christ is clearly seen. The power to forgive sins is something that is attributed rightly only to God. Yet that is what Christ was claiming in the first story. There is no doubt that those observing this event clearly understood what Christ was claiming.

The interesting analogies that Jesus Christ gave, sewing unshrunken material onto that which had already been shrunken or to place new wine into an old wineskin, are subjects for continued study. These illustrations were given to show the relationship of Jesus Christ

26. Cole, *The Gospel According to Mark*, 74.
27. Hendriksen, *Exposition of the Gospel According to Mark*, 109.
28. Vos, *Mark*, 30.

to the religious system of the time. It is clear that Jesus Christ was not a reformer of Judaism but that His ministry instituted various elements that were new.

The relationship of the Lord to the Sabbath question is also a great study throughout the gospels. Christ clearly is Lord of the Sabbath and as such has the right to declare what actions are acceptable or unacceptable for people. God's purpose in giving the Sabbath was never to be a binding destructive force. The Sabbath was meant for mankind's good.

MARK
CHAPTER
THREE

THE SERVANT'S CONTROVERSY

Sabbath Miracle Performed, 3:1-5 (cf. Matt. 12:9-13; Luke 6:6-10)
3:1   Since it was the Sabbath, Jesus naturally was heading toward the synagogue. The city is not specified in the account, but it is natural in the flow of the gospel to assume that the city probably was Capernaum.

> In view of the fact that Mark and Luke relate this story in close connection with that of the choosing of The Twelve and the ascent up the mountain (Mark 3:13-19; Luke 6:12-49), a "mountain" or "hill" probably not far removed from Capernaum (Luke 7:1; cf. Matt. 8:5), it is at least possible that a synagogue somewhere in the vicinity of what was now Jesus' headquarters is meant. But we cannot be sure.[1]

As He entered the synagogue, he saw a man "with a withered hand." When one understands the way the Jewish culture viewed people who were not perfectly whole physically, it is clear that this man should not have been there. Normally, people who were physically impaired, whether by birth defect or by disease or injury, were ostracized from the community (as the text seems to imply here by the use of the perfect passive participle *exērammenēn*). Such a deformity was viewed as an indication that the individual was a terrible sinner. An interesting observation is that only the physician Luke records that it

1. William Hendriksen, *Exposition of the Gospel According to Mark* (Grand Rapids: Baker, 1975), 114.

was the man's *right* hand that was withered (6:6). The very fact that this man was conspicuously seated in the synagogue implies that he was a "plant." Perhaps the religious leaders had put him there to see what Jesus would do.

3:2   That "they were [all] watching" (*pareteroun*, imperfect tense giving a vivid picture of continual looking by the religious leaders) Him to see what He would do further implies that this man was a plant. The parallel account in the gospel of Luke (6:7) uses the same verb in the middle voice, accentuating the personal interest of those who were watching Jesus in these proceedings. They were hoping that Jesus would try to heal this man so that they would have something to accuse Him of. Although there was clearly a difference of opinion between the pharisaical disciples of Shammai and the followers of Hillel as to what was permissible on the Sabbath day, it was clear that these people were looking for something that they could use to bring an accusation against Jesus.

3:3   The Savior was never concerned by the threats of men. If there was something to be done, He would do it, regardless of the outcome. Consequently, He called forth the man with the withered hand so that everyone could see what He was going to do. Perhaps bringing him out into the open was also done in order to elicit the sympathy of the audience for the physical condition of this handicapped man. Certainly he was someone in need of assistance.

3:4   But before He helped the man, He turned to His accusers all around Him and asked a very significant question: "Is it lawful on the Sabbath to do good or to do harm, to save a life or to kill?" The answer to that question was that of course it was lawful to do good and save a life. If anyone had the opportunity of doing a good deed on the Sabbath day, he would have done it with delight, thinking that it might be something to gain him favor in the sight of God. Jesus rightly addressed His question to the religious leaders, for they were the ones who were always claiming to know what was permitted or not in any given situation. Therefore they should have been the ones who would know what was right and what was wrong. Jesus was giving them an opportunity to express their expert opinion. But they, of course, would not answer the question; they simply "kept silent" (*esiopon*, imperfect tense giving a vivid sense of their continuing silence). It is somewhat ironic that these religious leaders, who were always so interested in doing what was right, were actually in the process of doing harm on the Sabbath. They were plotting at this very moment how they might kill Jesus, and this was occurring on the day that was set aside for the worship of Jehovah.

3:5   Jesus looked around (*periblepsamenos,* aorist tense indicating a completed action) at all these accusers "with anger." Mark has a great deal to say about the looks as well as the words of Jesus. This is the only clear reference in Scripture that Jesus Christ became angry. His momentary anger at the hardness of their hearts brought continual grief (*syllypoumenos,* present tense) in His own heart. "Mark alone gives this point. The anger was tempered by grief. . . . Jesus is the Man of Sorrows and this present participle brings out the continuous state of grief whereas the momentary angry look is expressed by the aorist participle above."[2] He was grieved that people could be so heartless in their dealing with a fellow man. Their heart condition was hardened like the hard substance that forms to knit together a broken bone (*pōrōsei,* used as a medical term).

He told the man simply, "Stretch out your hand." The man immediately obeyed, and his healing was instantaneous and complete. Jesus had done nothing to violate the Sabbath. He did not even touch the man but simply spoke the words. His accusers were left with no accusations to level against Him. But the Savior's authority was clearly seen. The day of the week on which that authority was exercised was truly significant.

THE OPPOSITION TO JEHOVAH'S SERVANT, 3:6–8:26

In the preceding section, Mark presented the Servant of Jehovah working in many different areas to demonstrate His authority. With such a clear demonstration, the only issue that needed to be settled was, Would the people accept that authority? At this point in the gospel, Mark began to demonstrate that a negative conclusion was going to be reached—he shows the opposition that was developing to Jehovah's Servant.

THE PHARISEES' CONCLUSION, 3:6
(cf. Matt. 12:14; Luke 6:11)

3:6   One would think that the religious leaders could not help but fall at Jesus' feet and worship, but the exact opposite was the case. The

2. A. T. Robertson, *Word Pictures in the New Testament* (Nashville: Broadman, 1930), 1:276.

Pharisees went out and "immediately [*euthys*] began taking counsel [*symboulion edidoun,* imperfect tense implying something that occurred over a period of time] with the Herodians" about "how they might destroy Him." Their interaction must have been intense as they tried to find accusations they could use against Jesus Christ. They not only failed to do good on the Sabbath, but they actively began to plan how they might do away with this man—a truly evil act.

This is the first mention of the Herodians in Mark's gospel. This combination of Herodians and Pharisees was unusual, especially when one understands the Herodians. They were followers of Herod the Great. They thought that the former ruler of the nation of Israel was a man to be emulated, and they favored his progressive administration and change. "When in Rome do as the Romans do," would have been the motto of the Herodians. How was it possible that a group holding to those principles could get together with the Pharisees? The Pharisees were the religious purists of the nation of Israel. They were for all of the conservative elements of their faith. But one thing that seems to be able to draw former enemies together is a new common enemy, and Jesus Christ was a common enemy for both the Pharisees and the Herodians.

> Undoubtedly they lent their support to the Pharisees because they saw Jesus as a threat to the peace and stability of the tetrarchy. The history of Herodian Galilee is marked by popular uprisings under the leadership of quasi-messianic figures, and they may have envisioned that Jesus posed this kind of peril to the land.[3]

It was clear that the Pharisees had concluded that Jesus was not a man to be followed, and they were now out to do everything they could to destroy Him.

THE MULTITUDE'S CONFUSION, 3:7-12
(cf. Matt. 12:15-21)

3:7   In response to the conclusion of the religious leaders, Jesus departed from the city of Capernaum. Taking His disciples with Him, He "withdrew to the sea." Matthew 12:15 implies that Jesus was aware of the plot to kill Him. Henry Swete believes that "Jesus withdrew

---

3. William L. Lane, *The Gospel of Mark,* NICNT (Grand Rapids: Eerdmans, 1974), 125.

from the town to the seashore because He was aware of the plot. He and His [disciples] would be safer on the open beach, surrounded by crowds of followers, than in the narrow streets of Capernaum."[4] Of course, wherever Jesus went multitudes of people followed Him. And now people from Judea, as well as from Galilee, were present in the crowd.

3:8   The attraction of the Savior was so great that people came all the way from Jerusalem and even from Idumea, the area to the southeast of the Dead Sea, formerly known as Edom. Individuals from the eastern side of the Jordan River, as well as from the seacoasts of Tyre and Sidon, were now following Jesus. The only area Mark did not mention was Samaria.

> The several districts enumerated are important in the general scheme of the Gospel. In the course of the narrative Jesus is active in all of the places specified in Ch. 3:7f. with the exception of Idumea. His entrance into Galilee is reported in Ch. 1:14. He visits the Transjordan in Ch. 5:1, the regions of Tyre and Sidon in Ch. 7:24, 31, the territories of Judea and Transjordan in Ch. 10:1 and enters Jerusalem in Ch. 11:11.[5]

Multitudes of people were coming to Him, for they were hearing (*akouontes,* present participle) "all that He was doing." The multitude could not comprehend how the One who was doing all of these miraculous things could not be the promised Messiah. Surely they were confused since the religious leaders were failing to recognize Him.

3:9   The press of the crowd around the Savior was always intense. In fact, Jesus instructed His disciples that a small boat (*ploiarion*) should be kept ready for them to leave should the press of the crowd become so strong that He would need to get away quickly. This fact is recorded only by Mark and probably is another illustration of Peter's inside information.

> It was but one of the instances in which it was proved that the prior life and training of His fisherfolk disciples was by no means wasted, though they had forsaken it to follow Him. Frequently He used their skill and strength to cross the sea by boat, although they had to learn that, even in the sphere where they felt most at home, Christ was still Lord (cf. iv. 41).[6]

4. Henry Barclay Swete, *The Gospel According to St. Mark* (Grand Rapids: Eerdmans, 1956), 54.
5. Lane, *The Gospel of Mark,* 129.
6. R. A. Cole, *The Gospel According to Mark* (Grand Rapids: Eerdmans, 1979), 78.

3:10   The reason for the boat was His growing popularity. Because Jesus was healing many who were brought to Him, news of His ability spread, and He was being pressed by people who had many afflictions. Their persistence around Him was actually becoming dangerous. They were not hostile, but they were eager "to touch Him," thinking they might be cured. Even if they were not cured merely by touching, they would have gained His attention and He then could heal them. The sudden moves of some of the people may have had the potential of causing Jesus to fall into the sea.

3:11   Not only was the Savior dealing with physical infirmities, but people possessed with unclean spirits were coming to Him also. As previously seen (cf. 1:23-26), the spirits knew who Jesus was. "These spirits are called 'unclean' because they are morally and spiritually filthy, evil in themselves, and because they urge those whom they inhabit to commit evil."[7] As these individuals came in touch (*hotan* with an imperfect verb implying repeated action) with Jesus, the unclean spirits would cry out, giving testimony, "You are the Son of God!" Although the religious leaders failed to understand who Jesus Christ was, the demonic creatures clearly understood His person. This notation is not simply an expression of Mark's theology; the demons recognized the true character of Jesus Christ as God's Son.

3:12   Testimony from such a wicked source, however, was not something that Jesus needed. "In Scripture God has ordained that only those who have experienced divine grace shall witness or testify of Christ and His saving power. He does not employ either evil spirits or the unfallen ones (angels) as witnesses."[8] The demons had the potential of further confusing the people, so the Savior commanded them to keep quiet and to stop their testimony.

THE SERVANT'S DECISION, 3:13-19
(cf. Luke 6:12-16)

3:13   It came time for Jesus to get away from the multitudes. "He went up" into one of the mountains (*anabainei eis to oros,* historic present tense to add vivid detail to the story) in the Galilee region. The reader can picture Jesus in the process of ascending the mountain. Neither of the gospels gives the name of the specific mountain.

---

7. Hendriksen, *Exposition of the Gospel According to Mark,* 121.
8. Howard F. Vos, *Mark* (Grand Rapids: Zondervan, 1978), 33-34.

As He went He "summoned" or called (*proskaleitai,* again a present tense) "those whom He . . . wanted" to follow Him. This special group was handpicked by Jesus and followed Him throughout the remainder of His time on earth.

> Luke states that Jesus "continued all night in prayer, to God." It was a crisis in the ministry of Christ. This select group up in the hills probably respected the long agony of Jesus though they did not comprehend his motive. They formed a sort of spiritual body-guard around the Master during his night vigil in the mountain.[9]

3:14   The Savior "appointed twelve" men. Why Jesus chose twelve cannot be determined conclusively. There were twelve tribes in the nation Israel, and perhaps that number of appointed followers carried special significance for the Jews. He chose the Twelve that, first of all, "they might be with Him." What a privilege these men had to go wherever Jesus went throughout the land, to sit at His feet, and to learn from Him. Clearly His first reason for choosing this group was for the purpose of giving them specific instructions that they would need later on for ministry. "This underscores the fact that a call to preach presupposes a call to prepare. And the most important preparation is being with Jesus and learning from Him. Along with this must come formal education and learning all we can from others."[10] Second, He appointed them "that He might send them out." There were two purposes in sending forth the disciples, for two infinitives follow in the text—one in v. 14 and one in v. 15. Jesus sent them "to preach" (*kēryssein,* "to herald"; related to *kēryx,* "a herald"). One person can accomplish a great deal but twelve people going out with the same message can cover a much greater area and speak to a much larger group of people. Jesus sent His disciples out preaching the same message that He had proclaimed from the beginning of His ministry (cf. 1:14-15).

3:15   The second infinitive demonstrating His purpose in sending them forth was that they might have the power "to cast out demons" (*ekballein ta daimonia*). The ability to demonstrate "authority" (*exousian,* the right and the power) over demons showed that truly they were going with the authority of God, for only God has greater au-

9. Robertson, *Word Pictures in the New Testament,* 1:278-79.
10. Ralph Earle, *Mark, the Gospel of Action* (Chicago: Moody, 1970), 35-36.

thority than demonic forces. These twelve men went out with specific authority from God.

3:16 The listing of the twelve apostles appears in four New Testament passages. In addition to this account in Mark, the listings are found in Matthew 10:2-5; Luke 6:14-16; and Acts 1:13. A comparison of the four lists of Jesus' chosen apostles as given by Matthew, Mark, Luke, and Acts is instructive.

Matthew 10:2ff.	Mark 3:16ff.	Luke 6:14ff.	Acts 1:13ff.
1. Simon Peter	1. Simon Peter	1. Simon Peter	1. Simon Peter
2. Andrew	2. James, son of Zebedee	2. Andrew	2. James
3. James, son of Zebedee	3. John	3. James	3. John
4. John	4. Andrew	4. John	4. Andrew
5. Philip	5. Philip	5. Philip	5. Philip
6. Bartholomew	6. Bartholomew	6. Bartholomew	6. Thomas
7. Thomas	7. Matthew	7. Matthew	7. Bartholomew
8. Matthew	8. Thomas	8. Thomas	8. Matthew
9. James, son of Alphaeus	9. James, son of Alphaeus	9. James, son of Alphaeus	9. James, son of Alphaeus
10. Thaddaeus	10. Thaddaeus	10. Simon the Zealot	10. Simon the Zealot
11. Simon the Zealot	11. Simon the Zealot	11. Judas, son of James	11. Judas, son of James
12. Judas Iscariot	12. Judas Iscariot	12. Judas Iscariot	

The first four names in the four lists begin with Simon Peter and include the same people but not in the same order each time. In like manner, the second four names beginning with Philip are the same in each of the four lists, although not in the same order. In the third group each list begins with James, the son of Alphaeus, and the first three groups conclude with Judas Iscariot. All four [lists] have Simon the Zealot. [But] Matthew and Mark [mention] Thaddaeus, while Luke and Acts have Judas, son of James. By elimination, Thaddaeus must be the same person as Judas, son of James; and thus the four lists are harmonized.[11]

Simon was a fisherman by trade and resided in the village of Bethsaida (John 1:44), although he later had a home in Capernaum (Mark 1:21, 29). Simon was brought to the Lord Jesus by his brother, Andrew, as recorded in John 1:41. When Jesus saw Simon for the first

11. J. Dwight Pentecost, *The Words & Works of Jesus Christ* (Grand Rapids: Zondervan, 1981), 170-71.

time He said, "'You are Simon the son of John; you shall be called Cephas' (which translated means Peter)" (John 1:42). The mention of Peter in Mark's list is the first time the name "Peter" occurs in his gospel. He uses it an additional eighteen times. Jesus saw in this individual the strength of character that would be evidenced later as Peter stood firm in the face of opposition to the risen Lord Jesus Christ. On the Day of Pentecost he publicly proclaimed the risen Lord as Messiah, and 3,000 people became part of the church, the body of Christ. He was true to the name Jesus gave him, for "Peter" is the Greek word that means "a rock."

3:17   James and his brother, John, the sons of Zebedee, are next mentioned in the text. John 1:35-40 seems to indicate that the unnamed follower of John the Baptist was this John. John the Baptist had pointed both Andrew and John to Jesus. In Mark 1:19 Jesus called them to follow Him. They, as did Peter, left a lucrative fishing business when they began to follow the Lord Jesus.

Mark alone adds the notation that to these brothers Jesus gave the Hebrew nickname "Boanerges," which translated means "Sons of Thunder." Why Mark records this fact is not clear. The words literally mean "sons of tumult" in Syriac. That certainly does not seem to coincide with the normal picture of John as the apostle of love. Yet the fiery temperament of both James and John is evident when they suggested to the Lord in Luke 9:54 that they ought to call down fire on the rejecting Samaritans. Also, in Mark 9:38 John's displeasure with some disciples was displayed when he commanded them to stop their work because they were not part of the apostolic group. James became the first apostolic martyr (Acts 12:1-2). Did his martyrdom occur because of his thunderous witness? John concluded his writings with the book of the Revelation, which is filled with many thunderous predictions. These men indeed proved to be sons of thunder.

3:18   Andrew (from *anēr,* meaning "a man") is next named in the list. He was a fisherman with his brother Simon Peter and was one of only two apostles who had a Greek name. The other was Philip (*Philippos,* fond of horses). Both Andrew and Philip may also have had Hebrew names. According to John 1:40, Andrew was a follower of John the Baptist. He was also the one to whom the young boy came with his five loaves and fishes at the feeding of the 5,000 (cf. John 6:8-9). And he was the one to whom Greeks came with the request, "Sir, we wish to see Jesus" (John 12:21). He was evidently a very approachable individual.

Philip is next mentioned because he also was of the same town of Peter and Andrew—Bethsaida (John 1:44). After Jesus called Philip, Philip immediately found his friend, Nathaniel, and brought him to Jesus (vv. 43-47). The apostle Philip and Philip the deacon (Acts 6) are not the same individual and should not be confused.

Next, Mark names Bartholomew, which means "son of Tolmai." The only mention of Bartholomew in the whole New Testament is in the four listings of the apostles, plus some references in John 1 and 21. His connection to Philip has led many Bible scholars to believe that Bartholomew and Nathaniel are one and the same. When Philip told Nathaniel that he had found the Messiah, Jesus of Nazareth, Nathaniel replied, "Can any good thing come out of Nazareth?" (John 1:46). When Jesus saw him, He said of Nathaniel, "Behold, an Israelite indeed, in whom is no guile!" (v. 47).

Mark then names Matthew, or Levi the tax collector, as he was previously called in 2:14, where he was called to follow Jesus. Why Mark fails to underscore that connection is not certain, for he evidently was a very wealthy man who left everything behind to follow Jesus. Matthew is a beautiful Hebrew name meaning "the gift of God." Matthew has been faithful to his name, for he has given the church a beautiful gift in the account of the Lord's life in the first gospel.

Next Thomas's name appears. He is called Didymus (John 11:16), or "the twin." Thomas is known by an adjective often put in front of his name—"doubting" Thomas. He was not present when Jesus first appeared following His resurrection, and he wanted to be certain that Jesus had risen from the dead. When Jesus did appear to the group eight days later and Thomas finally saw his Lord, he proclaimed, "My Lord and my God!" Whereas that famous incident concerning Thomas is often recounted, it is rarely mentioned that in John 11:16 he courageously said, "Let us also go, that we may die with Him." He made this exhortation on the east side of the Jordan when Jesus made clear that He was going to Bethany to raise Lazarus from the dead.

James, the son of Alphaeus, is an inconspicuous figure in Scripture. He is thought to be the same individual who in 15:40 is called "James, the less," which probably means that he was either a short man or younger in age than the other apostles. If this identification is correct, James's mother's name was Mary, one of the women who accompanied Jesus and stood near the cross. He is the "son of Alphaeus," as is also stated about Levi (cf. 2:14). If this is the same Alphaeus, Levi (Matthew) and James were brothers. This would have made three sets of brothers among the Twelve (Peter and Andrew, James and John, Levi and James). However, it is doubtful that Mark was referring to the same Alphaeus, otherwise he would have identified them as brothers as he did the others.

Thaddaeus is declared to be another apostle that Jesus chose. The name "Thaddaeus" appears in the listings of Matthew and Mark but not in the lists in Luke and Acts. Instead, Luke and Acts mention "Judas the son of James," and there is also a reference to "Judas not Iscariot" in John 14:22. Is it possible that this Judas and Thaddaeus are one and the same? Many believe that to be the case. Perhaps the betrayal of Jesus Christ by Judas Iscariot caused Judas to change his name, or perhaps he used a second given name. Beyond these speculations nothing is known from the Scriptures about Thaddaeus.

Simon the Zealot is next presented in the list. The terminology used for him (*Kananaion*) comes from the Hebrew word that means to be jealous or zealous. Luke (Luke 6:15; Acts 1:13) calls him "Simon who was called the Zealot" (*Simōn ho zēlōtēs*). Although some texts translate Mark's designation as "the Canaanean," the term really has nothing to do with racial (Canaanite) or geographic (Cana) origins. It was a term used of a group of Jewish extremists who were organized for one specific purpose—the overthrow of the Roman government by whatever means possible. They even believed that murder might be necessary to advance their cause. The Jewish historian Josephus referred to them as "dagger men." It is amazing that a man such as Simon—and an individual such as Matthew the tax collector—could be part of an apostolic group. Those two disciples must have had some interesting discussions as they considered being followers of Jesus of Nazareth, for they were poles apart in their political ideology. Lane, however, gives another possible interpretation of what being a zealot might have meant:

> The designation marks Simon as one who was jealous for the honor of God. He may have sought to pattern his life after the patriarch Phinehas whose indignation at Israelite idolatry turned aside God's wrath from Israel: "he was jealous with my jealousy among them . . . and made atonement for the people of God" (Num. 25:10-13). Phinehas' zeal for God had been honored in Scripture (Ps. 106:30f.) and invited emulation.[12]

12. Lane, *The Gospel of Mark,* 136.

3:19   The final apostle named is Judas Iscariot, who, as Mark notes, ultimately betrayed the Savior. Iscariot (Heb. *ish-keristra*) literally translated means "a man of Kerioth." There was a town in the southern part of Judah named Kerioth. If that identification is correct, it seems that Judas was the only one of the twelve apostles who was not a Galilean. He was a Judean, which perhaps accounts for the fact that he was entrusted with the treasury purse of the apostolic band (John 12:6). Perhaps he was considered to be a little better than the others, being a "cultured" Judean and not an "unsophisticated" Galilean. The infamy of this man, of course, is that he betrayed the Savior.

> What caused this privileged disciple to become Christ's betrayer? Was it injured pride, disappointed ambition, deeply entrenched greed, fear of being put out of the synagogue (John 9:22)? No doubt all of these were involved, but could not the most basic reason have been this, that between the utterly selfish heart of Judas and the infinitely unselfish and outgoing heart of Jesus there was a chasm so immense that either Judas must implore the Lord to bestow upon him the grace of regeneration and complete renewal, a request which the traitor wickedly refused to make, or else he must offer his help to get rid of Jesus? See also Luke 22:22; Acts 2:23; 4:28. One thing is certain: The shocking tragedy of Judas' life is proof not of Christ's impotence but of the traitor's impenitence! Woe to that man![13]

HIS FAMILY'S INTERVENTION, 3:20-21

From a harmony of the gospels, it is apparent that Jesus preached the Sermon on the Mount (Matthew 5–7) and participated in the events described in Luke 7:1–8:3 before the event occurred that is recorded here. It is probable that Mark did not record that famous sermon because of his emphasis on the *works* of Jesus rather than on His *words*.

3:20   Mark states simply that Jesus "came home." Though it is uncertain exactly what Mark meant here, it is probably best to conclude that "home" meant the city of Capernaum, specifically the house of Simon Peter and Andrew (as recorded in 1:29ff.). It is doubtful that Jesus ever owned His own home while He ministered on this earth, for, when a Scribe said he would follow Jesus wherever He went, Jesus responded, "The foxes have holes, and the birds of the air have

13. Hendriksen, *Exposition of the Gospel According to Mark*, 128.

nests; but the Son of Man has nowhere to lay His head" (Matt. 8:19-20).

So Jesus treated the home of Simon Peter as His own, and as He returned to that city and to that home once again, a "multitude gathered" outside the house. The verbs that Mark uses in this verse concerning Jesus' coming and the multitudes gathering are both present tense verbs, giving a vivid picture of the event. "Again" there were so many people that it was impossible for Jesus and those with Him to even take time for a meal. Certainly by the use of the word "again" Mark is reminding his readers of the previous occasion when the crowd jammed around Peter's house to such an extent that access into and out of the home was virtually impossible (cf. 1:32-34; 2:1ff.). Jesus was so involved in the needs of people that His time was completely occupied with ministry needs.

3:21   Only Mark's gospel records that this failure to take time to eat brought concern to "His own people." This term basically means "those from his side," and although it is a fairly ambiguous expression it probably refers to Jesus' extended family members. Jesus' immediate family lived in the area of Nazareth, but other family members could have lived closer. Perhaps it was these who began to be concerned for Him. They went "to take custody of Him; for they were saying, 'He has lost his senses.'"

> The Marcan term describes one who is ecstatic in the sense of psychic derangement. Reflection on Jesus' eschatological sense of mission, his urgent drive to minister, his failure properly to eat and sleep undoubtedly led the family to their conviction, but it reveals both misunderstanding and unbelief.[14]

Their primary concern of course was what people would think of the family name.

THE "OFFICIAL" CONCLUSION, 3:22–4:34

THE ACCUSATION, 3:22
(cf. Matt. 12:22-24)

3:22   It was obvious now that Jesus was someone whose claims had to be investigated. Scribes, who were the keepers of the Law and the

---

14. Lane, *The Gospel of Mark*, 139.

traditions, came all the way from the city of Jerusalem to investigate what He was doing and teaching.

> It is possible that they were official emissaries from the Great Sanhedrin who came to examine Jesus' miracles and to determine whether Capernaum should be declared a "seduced city," the prey of an apostate preacher. Such a declaration required a thorough investigation made on the spot by official envoys in order to determine the extent of defection and to distinguish between the instigators, the apostates and the innocent.[15]

Mark correctly notes that they "came down from Jerusalem," for anyone who leaves Jerusalem (at approximately 2,400 feet above sea level) descends. By the time they arrived at the shores of the Sea of Galilee (approximately 600 feet below sea level), they had descended 3,000 feet. Their conclusion, which they repeatedly offered (*elegon,* imperfect tense), was that Jesus was "possessed by Beelzebul." Baalzebub, the lord of the carrion-fly, was the Baal worshiped at Ekron centuries earlier.

> The reason for the change in spelling is not clear. It may have amounted to no more than an accident of popular pronunciation. Another explanation is that there is a play on words, for *-zebul* resembles *zebel*: dung. Thus, those who despised the Baal of Ekron were able, by means of a slight change in pronunciation, to heap scorn upon him by conveying the thought that he was nothing but a "lord of dung."[16]

King Ahaziah of Israel sent messengers to inquire of this Baal whether he would recover from his fall (2 Kings 1:2, 3, 6). God told him that, because of his idolatrous disloyalty, he would die. Clearly "Beelzebul" was used as an epithet for Satan. Thus, the scribes' conclusion was that Jesus Christ was demonically possessed. They furthermore thought that His ability to cast out demons, which Jesus had just done in Matthew's account (cf. Matt. 12:22), was done by the power of the ruler of the demons, that is, Satan himself.

15. Ibid., 141.
16. Hendriksen, *Exposition of the Gospel According to Mark,* 135 n.

THE DENIAL, 3:23-30
(cf. Matt. 12:25-37)

3:23 Jesus called all the scribes to Himself and "began speaking to them in parables." This is the first time Mark states that Jesus used parables. The word "parable" is made up of two Greek words. The first, *para,* is a preposition that means "alongside." The second word is *ballō,* which literally means "to throw." Putting these concepts together, a parable is an idea that is thrown alongside for the purpose of illustrating a truth. Since at least two levels are involved in parables, they usually need to be given an interpretation.[17]

Jesus defended Himself by means of parables at this point in His ministry. It was rare for the Savior to defend Himself, but the charge that He was empowered by the ruler of the demons was indeed one that needed to be addressed. Jesus' question was, "How can Satan cast out Satan?" If he were doing that, would Satan not be destroying his own realm? It is interesting that Jesus does not use the proper name Beelzebul but the true name of the one by whose power they were accusing Him of working, Satan (*satanas*).

3:24 If, indeed, Satan were casting out Satan, would not his "kingdom be divided against itself"? The term "kingdom" here would probably have been understood by the people to mean "nation." If a nation is divided against itself, truly that nation would never be able to stand. The nation of Israel was in many ways a divided nation. There were so many sects within Judaism that it was virtually impossible for the nation to come together on anything. Ironically, the one thing that did bring them together, however, was their hatred for Jesus Christ and their determination that they had to get rid of Him.

3:25 Jesus carried the analogy of kingdom division a step further by saying, "If a house is divided against itself, that house will not be able to stand." The term "house" usually carried the idea of posterity. If a family was divided against itself, that family would not be able to remain powerful for very long. Throughout the history of the nation of Israel the Southern Kingdom, or Judah, had only one ruling family—the family of King David. But the Northern Kingdom, or Israel, was ruled by nine different dynasties, many of which lasted only a very brief period of time. The Northern Kingdom lasted only until 722 B.C., when the capital, Samaria, was destroyed by the Assyrians. Jerusalem

---

17. For an extensive discussion of Jesus' use of parables, see Lane, *The Gospel of Mark,* 149-51.

and the Southern Kingdom remained until 586 B.C., when the city fell to the Babylonians.

3:26 To bring the statement to a conclusion, Jesus applied everything He had said directly to Satan himself. If Satan would rise up against himself and work against himself by releasing those he already possessed, how would he be able to survive? His kingdom would not stand; it would quickly be destroyed. But the evidence indicated that the exact opposite was the case: Satan was not in the process of being defeated; his kingdom was powerful; his demons were very active, not only in their influence on men but in their confrontations with the Lord Jesus Christ.

3:27 But Jesus suggested that He was more powerful than Satan. He used an analogy they all would have understood. No one would be able to enter into a strong man's home and take away property from that home unless he was strong enough to bind the strong man first. Once the strong man was bound, the intruder would be able to "plunder" (*diarpasai,* "thoroughly ransack") his home. If indeed Jesus Christ were casting out Satan's demons, does that not imply that Jesus had greater power and authority than Satan? Satan is "the strong man" in this analogy, but Jesus was even stronger.

> The expulsion of demons is nothing less than a forceful attack on the lordship of Satan. Jesus' ability to cast out demons means that one stronger than Satan has come to restrain his activity and to release the enslaved. The heart of Jesus' mission is to confront Satan and to crush him on all fields, and in the fulfillment of his task he is conscious of being the agent of irresistible power.[18]

3:28 The consequences of the conclusion of the scribes carried serious ramifications. For the first time in Mark's gospel, Jesus uses a significant introductory phrase. Literally Jesus says, "Amen, I tell you" (*amēn legō ymin*). "Amen," a transliteration from the Hebrew, refers in general to truth and faithfulness. "In the New Testament the word Amen, an adverbial accusative, combines the ideas of truthfulness and solemnity."[19] Such an introduction conveys that what Jesus is about to say is of great importance. A comparison of the parallel account in Matthew 12:23-37 affirms the significance of the Savior's pronounce-

---

18. Ibid., 143.
19. Hendriksen, *Exposition of the Gospel According to Mark,* 137.

ment. He said that all sin that is acknowledged as such will be forgiven to any man, even "blasphemies" (*blasphēmiai,* an expression of defiant hostility against God) can be forgiven. Jesus clearly says in Matthew 12:32 that it was entirely possible that they might have misunderstood the Son of Man. Jesus Christ looked very much like any other man who walked on the face of this earth. Therefore, blasphemy against the Son of Man would "be forgiven."

3:29 But blasphemy "against the Holy Spirit" would never be forgiven. The one who commits blasphemy against the Holy Spirit "is guilty of an eternal sin." These scribes were religious leaders who should have recognized and understood the power of God at work. It was their responsibility to be aware of true demonstrations of God's power. Even though they might have misunderstood Jesus Christ, they never should have misunderstood the power He was demonstrating as He was casting out demons.

3:30 Their conclusion, which they were continually "saying" (*elegon,* imperfect tense), was that Jesus had "an unclean spirit" and therefore He was working by the power of Satan. That conclusion was unforgivable, especially coming from religious leaders who should have known better. Of course, any individual could turn in saving faith and acknowledge who Jesus Christ truly was. It was not too late for them to change their minds. But if they persisted in their conclusion concerning the person of Christ, their sin would have serious consequences, both personal and national. Their persistence in unbelief and rejection would lead eventually to the rejection of their King and the postponement of His kingdom. Bible scholars are divided in their convictions with regard to whether or not this sin of the blasphemy of the Holy Spirit can be repeated in the modern-day world. But the conclusion of Charles Ryrie seems best:

> Speaking against the Spirit was not merely a sin of the tongue. The Pharisees had not sinned only with their words. It was a sin of the heart expressed in words. Furthermore, theirs was a sin committed to His face. To commit this particular sin required the personal and visible presence of Christ on earth; to commit it today, therefore, would be impossible. But to show wickedness of heart is unpardonable in any day if one dies persisting in his or her rejection of Christ. A person's eternal destiny is determined in this life, but no sin is unpardonable as long as a person has breath.[20]

20. Charles C. Ryrie, *Basic Theology* (Wheaton, Ill.: Victor, 1986), 352.

THE RAMIFICATIONS, 3:31-35
(cf. Matt. 12:46-50; Luke 8:19-21)

3:31 As Jesus was involved in the process of discussing these things with the religious leaders, suddenly "His mother and His brothers arrived." This is the only time in Mark's gospel that Jesus' mother appears. He is called "the son of Mary" in 6:3, but no other mention of Mary is given. Perhaps "His own people" (v. 21) had communicated to Mary and the family their concern over Jesus' erratic behavior. Because of that Mary and some of Jesus' brothers had traveled the twenty-five miles or so from Nazareth to Capernaum to meet with Him. Since no mention is made of His earthly father, Joseph, it is assumed by most scholars that by this time Joseph had died. Mary and her unnamed sons stood outside the house and "sent word" in to Jesus because they were not able to enter the crowded building. Perhaps they overheard the discussion going on inside relating to the issue of whether or not Jesus was demon possessed. Their concern for Him was a genuine concern any family member might have for a loved one.

3:32 Unfortunately "a multitude was sitting around" Jesus, and word had to be passed to Him that "His mother and His brothers [were] outside looking for [Him]." The implication of this statement is that His family had some kind of a claim on Jesus, a hold over Him that took precedent over other matters. "At the present moment the relatives of Jesus were forfeiting their claim to consideration by opposing His work (Mt. x.35). Here again His knowledge of the unspoken purposes of men appears; for He could hardly have been informed of the nature of their errand."[21]

3:33 Jesus' answer to them took the form of a question: "Who are My mother and My brothers?" This rhetorical question was not uttered by the Savior to repudiate family values. Jesus respected His mother, and even when He hung on the cross He was concerned about her future. He committed her care to the disciple whom He loved by saying to John, "Behold, your mother!" (John 19:27). God established the family at the time of creation. But other relationships are important also.

3:34-35 He looked around the room at those who were sitting before Him. The fact that the Savior took time to look around the room is another of those vivid details distinctive of Mark's gospel. One can

21. Swete, *The Gospel According to St. Mark,* 70.

almost see Peter filling Mark in on this detail. Jesus simply said, "Behold, My mother and My brothers! For whoever does the will of God, he is My brother and sister and mother." Jesus was asserting that the issue of simple physical relationship was not the proper access to Him. The relationship that counts is one of obedience, for doing God's will is what brings one into a personal relationship with Jesus Christ. It is doing the will of the heavenly Father that gives evidence that one is properly related to Jesus Christ through faith.

> Rather than recognizing blood ties as constituting a true relationship, He pointed to His disciples, that is, those who by faith had accepted His person. He said, "For whoever does the will of my Father in heaven is my brother and sister and mother" (Matt. 12:50). This relationship was instituted not by natural birth but as a result of a supernatural birth. These were related to Him by faith in His person. The nation of Israel claimed a relationship to Messiah when He should come because of a common relationship to Abraham. But Christ rejected blood ties as constituting a true spiritual relationship. The only ones whom He would accept as being spiritually related to Him were those who were related to Him by faith. In that multitude there were those who claimed a relationship to Abraham as a basis for entrance into the kingdom. Christ said the kingdom must be entered by faith in His person, not by the accident of physical birth.[22]

HOMILETICAL SUGGESTIONS

The opposition to the Lord Jesus Christ that Mark presents in this chapter is instructive to trace. The joining together of the Herodians and the Pharisees is an interesting development. Later in Mark's gospel other groups united themselves in an attempt to trick the Savior (cf. 11:27-33; 12:13-17; 12:18-27).

Of significant note in this chapter and a subject for much study is the listing of the twelve apostles. These men present fascinating character studies, for almost all of them can be researched in other passages. Truly a study of the Twelve is rewarding.

The official conclusion of the religious leaders that Jesus did not work by the power of God but by the power of Satan is most significant. In order to adequately deal with this passage, a comparative study of Matthew 12:23-37 is imperative. This section, commonly

---

22. Pentecost, *The Words & Works of Jesus Christ,* 210.

known as the unpardonable sin, causes much confusion among Christians. One would do well to have strong convictions as one preaches on this passage of Scripture. The context seems to necessitate Jesus Christ's being present on earth working miracles by the power of the Spirit. Therefore it is not possible for a believer today to commit "the unpardonable sin." Any sin committed today can be forgiven if the unbeliever will turn in saving faith or the believer in confession to the Lord Jesus Christ.

MARK

CHAPTER

FOUR

THE SERVANT'S PARABLES

THE INSTRUCTION, 4:1-34

A Parable Taught, 4:1-12 (cf. Matt. 13:1-17; Luke 8:4-10)

4:1   Jesus continued His ministry among the people by teaching them at the seaside, which had become a common occurrence in His ministry (cf. 2:13; 3:7-9). The multitude "gathered" around (*synagetai,* present tense graphically picturing this scene) Him was so great that Jesus was not able to communicate effectively with them. So He simply "got into a boat" (cf. 3:9) that was maneuvered out into the sea and there anchored. As Jesus sat in the boat, the crowd, which was even greater than on former occasions, gathered on the shore. With the natural terrain sloping to the sea, everyone was probably able to see Jesus, and as He spoke they also were able to hear.

4:2   "He was teaching [*edidasken,* imperfect tense implying a repeated action] them many things," and He continued to use the parabolic method in His instruction. Though this raised questions later, Jesus had reasons for using parables "in His teaching":

> A parable is a literary device and is used to teach by means of transference. In order to make it possible to discover truth in an unknown realm, something familiar is transferred from the known realm to the unknown realm. A simple figure of speech in the form of a *metaphor* may be used: "I am the gate" (John 10:9). The figure may be a *simile*

such as "Be shrewd as snakes and as innocent as doves" (Matt. 10:16). The figure may be more complex, consisting of a *parable* which is a narrative and which conveys one principal point of parallelism even though there may be other incidental parallelisms. Sometimes there is an *allegory,* which is a narrative in which there are many intended parallelisms. Our Lord used parables frequently, but employed allegories only on rare occasions (such as in John 10 where He used the whole analogy of the relationship between a shepherd and sheep). While an allegory may or may not be true to life, a parable is always true to life. (Italics added)[1]

4:3 He arrested their attention by saying, "Listen to this!" Mark's gospel alone records this introductory word (*akouete*), which is translated "listen." "With this call Jesus involves his hearers in the situation he describes and leads them to form a judgment upon it. He also warns them that there may be more to the parable than appears upon its surface; there can be a superficial hearing which misses the point."[2] It is possible that, at the very moment of speaking, He pointed to someone in an adjacent field who was doing what He was describing in His parable—a sower who was sowing seed. That would have been a common figure that everyone hearing Him would have witnessed or performed himself on many occasions.

4:4 As a sower sowed his seed in a field, the seed would fall on different kinds of soil. One of the greatest problems a farmer in Israel had was getting all the rocks out of his field. The rocks were dug out and piled in rows. Those rows often turned into roads or footpaths that passed through the fields. As seed was sown, some of the seed would fall on "the road," "not of course that the sower deliberately sowed the pathway, but that he partly missed his aim, as in such rapid work must needs happen; or he had not time to distinguish nicely between the pathway and the rest of the field."[3] Since there was no soil and the ground was hard, it would be easy for "the birds," which would be present in abundance at the time of sowing, to come and eat up the seeds.

4:5 Some of the other seeds would fall "on the rocky ground." It was virtually impossible at that time to get all the rocks out of a field.

---

1. J. Dwight Pentecost, *The Words & Works of Jesus Christ* (Grand Rapids: Zondervan, 1981), 211-12.

2. William L. Lane, *The Gospel of Mark,* NICNT (Grand Rapids: Eerdmans, 1974), 153.

3. Henry Barclay Swete, *The Gospel According to St. Mark* (Grand Rapids: Eerdmans, 1951), 72.

But because there was some soil in that area, the seeds would imme-diately spring up. Henry Swete proposes a slightly different alternative to the translation of the word "rocky." He suggests that

> the word implies not a stone-strewn surface, as the English versions except R.V. suggest, but rock thinly coated with soil and here and there cropping up through the earth—a characteristic feature in the corn-lands of Galilee, still to be noted by the traveller among the hills which slope down to the Lake.[4]

Whichever view one takes of the word here, the outcome is still the same. The seeds apparently have only one way to grow, and that is upward, since they are unable to penetrate deeply into the earth.

4:6   Since the soil was shallow, there would be little moisture, and as soon as the sun rose the ground would dry out. The plants that had sprung from those seeds would wither away quickly. The problem with these plants was that they lacked a sufficient root system, and life could not be sustained.

4:7   "Other seed fell among the thorns." It was impossible to re-move all the weeds and thorns from the fields, especially along the edges. The thorns grew up and choked some of the crop, because they have the tendency to grow faster and higher. As a result, there would once again be no yield from the sowing.

4:8   Some seeds, however, did fall "into the good soil," and as these seeds grew and increased they "yielded a crop" (*edidou karpon*, im-perfect tense verb picturing the yield from the crop as continuing to come). The crop that followed produced varying amounts, "thirty, six-ty, and a hundredfold" increase. "Most of the field consisted of good soil and most of the seed landed on good soil, where it had varying degrees of yield according to the fertility of the soil. It is important to recognize that the seed was of equally good quality; problems of ger-minations and fruit bearing lay in the soil."[5]

> The climax of the parable strongly emphasizes the glorious character of the harvest, the thirtyfold, the sixtyfold and hundredfold yield, the last of which would be an unusually large harvest. Since this is seen against the background of many obstacles, it is clear that the emphasis does not fall on the enormity of the waste, but on the enormity and splendor of

4. Ibid., 72-73.
5. Howard F. Vos, *Mark* (Grand Rapids: Zondervan, 1978), 40.

the harvest. The harvest is a common figure for the consummation of the Kingdom of God and in the parable there is a significant reflection on the future, eschatological aspect of the Kingdom: it shall be glorious in character.[6]

4:9 Jesus responded to the multitude with an earnest admonition, for He encouraged them to listen very carefully to what He had said. Everyone could hear His words with their ears, but understanding occurs in the heart. His message was one of great importance to them because they were considering whether they would commit themselves to Jesus and become His followers. Thus, this parable ends as it began, with a solemn call to pay close attention to the Savior's words, for it was meant to be more than just a nice story told with pleasant and common word pictures.

4:10 "As soon as" they were able to get away from the multitude, His followers and the Twelve gathered around Him. Only the Marcan account notes that this discussion with Jesus occurred when they were "alone." This probably was a vivid recollection of the apostle Peter, communicated to Mark. They began to ask "Him about the parables." Why was Jesus speaking in parables? And what was the meaning of the parable He had just given them?

4:11 The response of the Savior made clear that He spoke in parables that He might reveal the truth to those who were His followers. He said they were having the privilege of being given "the mystery" (*mystērion*—singular in Mark, plural in Matthew and Luke) concerning the "kingdom of God." The term "mystery" implies a previously unrevealed truth that now is revealed in such a way that the instructed may know. It may only be known because God has chosen to reveal it. The concept of the kingdom was not something foreign to these Jewish followers of Jesus Christ. The kingdom promised to David is described in many passages of the Old Testament and could not be considered a "mystery." But not everything about God's kingdom program had been revealed, and Jesus was going to communicate those things to His disciples. On the other hand, unbelievers would not receive explanations of the parables. Those who were on the outside would simply receive the parabolic truth. With regard to the expression "those who are outside," Robertson says,

6. Lane, *The Gospel of Mark,* 154.

Peculiar to Mark, those outside our circle [were] the uninitiated, the hostile group like the scribes and Pharisees, who were charging Jesus with being in league with Beelzebub.... Without the key the parables are hard to understand, for parables veil the truth of the kingdom being stated in terms of another realm. Without a spiritual truth and insight they are unintelligible and are often today perverted. The parables are thus a condemnation on the willfully blind and hostile, while a guide and blessing to the enlightened.[7]

4:12   It is clear that this parabolic teaching carried an aspect of judgment, similar to the kind of message Isaiah the prophet was commissioned to carry to the people (cf. Isaiah 6). Though Isaiah was told to speak the Word of God, the people would hear but would not truly perceive. Whereas they would seek comprehension, they would not really understand. This may seem like a harsh judgment, but the historical context gives clues to understanding, for the scene is one of hostility and unbelief. These individuals had seen Jesus Christ and had heard Him preach and teach. But instead of responding in faith, they were reacting negatively toward the Savior. They were even concluding that He worked by the power of Satan (cf. 3:22-30). To those individuals He would not reveal His truth. The parables themselves became judgmental, for although the instruction was parabolic the truth had been communicated.

When Jesus explained a parable to His followers, the parable contained truth for those whose hearts were open to Him. There was still time for anyone to come to Jesus in saving faith and to begin to follow Him. Individuals who were "outside" could come "inside" by acknowledging the true character of Jesus.

Jesus' audiences were not denied the opportunity to believe in Him. But after they persistently closed their minds to His message (cf. 1:15), they were excluded from further understanding of it by His use of parables. Yet even the parables, which veiled the truth, were meant to provoke thought, enlighten, and ultimately reveal it (cf. 12:12). They uniquely preserved people's freedom to believe, while demonstrating that such a decision is effected by God's enabling (cf. 4:11a).[8]

7. A. T. Robertson, *Word Pictures in the New Testament* (Nashville: Broadman, 1930), 1:285-86.
8. John D. Grassmick, "Mark," in *Bible Knowledge Commentary* (Wheaton, Ill.: Victor, 1983), 119.

A Parable Explained, 4:13-20 (cf. Matt. 13:18-23; Luke 8:11-15)

4:13 As Jesus began to explain the parable, He asked a rhetorical question of His followers because He saw that they did not understand it: "Do you not understand this parable?" Mark's gospel alone records these words of the Savior. The question implies that they perhaps should have had spiritual ears to understand, and could be construed as a mild rebuke. If they could not understand a simple parable, how would they understand the more complicated parables? R. A. Cole implies that "the Lord gives gentle warning that this parable is, as it were, the 'Parable of the Parables', for it describes the reaction of His hearers to the whole system of parabolic teaching. It is not only the easiest of the parables, it is the key to them all."[9]

4:14 The sower in this parable was pictured as the one who was sowing "the word." In the parallel account in the gospel of Matthew (Matt. 13:37), the one pictured as sowing the seed was the Son of Man Himself. Jesus Christ was the One sowing the truth, which He equated here with "the word." Mark probably does not clearly identify the sower because his emphasis seems to be on the kinds of soils. Mark emphasizes the response of the seed to the soils, or the response of the various types of individuals who receive the word.

4:15 As the word was sown, it received four different responses in individuals. The word that was sown "beside the road" was sown on individuals unprepared for the truth. "Immediately Satan," the Adversary, would come and snatch away the word. Jesus always presented Satan as a real person whose goal was to do whatever he could to thwart the work of God. This does not excuse the individual, however, for Mark does not present their opportunity as occurring only one time. "When they hear" implies that they had several opportunities, but each time the seed found hard soil and was "immediately" (*euthys*) snatched away.

4:16 "In a similar way" the truth sown "on the rocky places" corresponded to individuals who, when they heard the word, immediately received it with great joy. As the word was proclaimed, it was recognized as being truth and was accompanied by a corresponding joyful response of heart. But the penetration of the seed is superficial. The impact of the word does not seem to make a true change.

4:17 The seed nevertheless germinates because there is life in the seed. But the plants that sprang forth had no potential for the develop-

9. R. A. Cole, *The Gospel According to Mark* (Grand Rapids: Eerdmans, 1979), 92.

ment of firm roots. Because of the profession of the word, however, "affliction" (*thlipsis*) and "persecution" (*diōgmos*) also developed. As soon as persecution begins, it has an impact similar to that of the hot sun on a rootless plant. Since there would be nothing to fall back on, the plant would quickly (*euthys*) "fall away" (*skandalizontai,* lit., "to take offense at, to fall away").

4:18   A third response to the seed occurred when it was "sown among the thorns." That kind of soil would not be classified as ideal for sowing. The soil itself contains too many elements detrimental to the seed. But, again, because there is life in the seed, there will be a response. When the word is heard it springs forth into life.

4:19   Unfortunately thorns arise to choke out the truth so that fruit never develops. The thorns that arise are "the worries of the world" or the age (*aiōnos*), including the "deceitfulness of riches, and the desires [*epithymiai*] for other things," unfortunately the wrong things. The word *epithymiai* can be used of desiring high and holy things (cf. Luke 22:15; Phil. 1:23). These same enemies of the truth are present in the world today. Many clamor after riches and desire to accumulate possessions. Unfortunately these sometimes keep an individual from responding to the truth in such a way that fruit develops in his life.

4:20   But there was soil on which the seed sown produced fruit. The seed also fell into hearts that were prepared, and as it sprang forth into life it was able to grow and develop. The final result was fruit, which seems to be the mark of genuine believers in Scripture (cf. Matt. 3:10; Luke 3:8; John 15:1-8; Rom. 7:4; Gal. 5:22-23; Col. 1:6; Heb. 13:15; James 3:17-18). The production of fruit was not the same in every case. There was a thirtyfold response, a sixtyfold response, and a hundredfold response. Matthew has the response in descending order: hundredfold, sixtyfold, thirtyfold (Matt. 13:23). Each writer is employing his own style, and there is no essential difference in the two accounts. The parable seems to be teaching the reason that not everyone responded positively to the presentation of Jesus the Messiah: the seed, or the truth, did not always fall on hearts that were prepared.

> This parable describes the various responses to Christ's message as He preached it and responses to the gospel during this present age as the message of Christ is preached. It is important to note that most hearers did not receive the truth, even when Christ proclaimed it. Modern servants of Christ should not conclude that if they enjoyed greater power of the Holy Spirit they would necessarily sweep the masses into the

kingdom. But of course such an observation should not be used as an excuse for laxness or low expectation of success in the work of God.[10]

Further Parabolic Instruction, 4:21-34 (cf. Matt. 13:31-32, 53; Luke 8:16-18)
4:21   Jesus continued His parabolic instruction by using other common objects that all understood. A lamp, a peck-measure (bushel), a bed, and a lampstand were objects found in every Israeli home. The specific purpose of a lamp is to give light. One does not light a lamp and then place it under a bushel, for to do so would diminish the light or even put it out. Nor does one light a lamp and hide it under one's "bed" (*klinēn,* perhaps better translated "dining couch"), for to do so might set it on fire. The way Jesus' question is stated, the expected answer is "No!" Rather, one takes a lamp and puts it on a lampstand so that the light will be able to shine out into the entire room. Jesus' second question was so worded as to demand the positive answer "Yes!"
4:22   Jesus implies that the same thing is true of the gospel message. He proclaimed His message that it might "be revealed," not that it would remain "secret."

> The period of hiddenness is merely a prelude to the period of manifestation, when apparent obscurity and weakness will be exchanged for messianic glory and power. Like the parable of the sower, the parable of the lamp views the mission of Jesus in comprehensive terms and has a distinctive eschatological perspective from which the disciples were to find reassurance and insight concerning the nature of the coming of the Kingdom of God.[11]

Much of Jesus' instruction became the content of the apostles' sermons after the Savior's resurrection and ascension. They did not understand much of what He said until the Holy Spirit empowered them (cf. John 14:25-26, 16:12-15).
4:23   Jesus' repeated admonition (see v. 9) was that, if a person has ears to hear, he can hear. Obviously people have ears, but not all individuals truly hear what is being proclaimed. Jesus' admonition warned those listening to Him to be careful listeners to His words. They were not unimportant; indeed, His words were life.

10. Vos, *Mark,* 41.
11. Lane, *The Gospel of Mark,* 166-67.

4:24 Jesus was continually "saying" (*elegen,* imperfect tense stressing repetition) to His followers the truth contained in this verse. It is a principle of Scripture that a person is judged by the light he is given. The truth that one receives is what he is held accountable for. Mark says that a person should be careful "what" he listens to. Luke 8:18 says that a person should be careful "how" he listens. Both ideas are important. Those who respond positively to the truth they are given will always be given more.

4:25 It is the delight of God to give additional revelation to the person who responds positively to the light he has received. But the individual who has the truth and who turns away from it may find himself coming under the judgment of God, and even the truth he knows might "be taken away from him." It is impossible to stand still when scriptural truth is presented. A person must either advance or decline. Swete says,

> Here the sense is: 'for the appropriation of any measure of Divine truth implies a capacity for receiving more; and each gift, if assimilated, is the forerunner of another'; . . . But the converse is also true: 'incapacity for receiving truth leads to a loss of truth already in some sense possessed.'[12]

4:26 As Jesus continued the instruction concerning the rule (the kingdom) of God over a person's life, He said that God's rule was "like a man who casts seed upon the soil." This parable (vv. 26-29) is unique to Mark's gospel. Jesus had just talked about a sower who sowed the seed that fell on four different kinds of soil. Perhaps the Savior was concerned that the mostly negative response to the sowing would be a discouragement to His disciples. He wanted them to know that God's truth does accomplish its goal. Therefore He used another illustration of the sowing of seed. The tense of the verb for "casts" (*balē*) is an aorist subjunctive, which implies that the Savior was viewing this as an individual act of sowing.

4:27 The man casts his seed on the ground during the day, then "goes to bed at night and gets up" day by day. The verbs for going to bed and getting up are present subjunctives picturing the process of retiring and rising over a period of many days, thus allowing time for the seed to actually sprout and begin to grow. One of the characteris-

---

12. Swete, *The Gospel According to St. Mark,* 83.

tics of a sower/farmer is that he must learn patience. How the seed sprouts is something that the farmer "does not know," for he does not give life to the seed. The life is in the seed. The farmer's job is simply to sow it.

> All the farmer can do is trust. To be sure, he can cover the seed, root up weeds, loosen the soil, add fertilizer, and perhaps even channel water to his plot. All these things are important. But he cannot cause the seed to sprout and grow. . . . The rest he must leave entirely to the seed, ultimately to the One who created the seed, who knows it thoroughly, and activates it. The farmer must trust and pray. He must wait patiently.[13]

4:28 The Lord notes that the soil produces crops "by itself" (*automatē*), automatically, spontaneously. This word is found only one additional time in the New Testament. In Acts 12:10 an iron gate opened "by itself" for Peter and the angel. In both cases, no visible human cause can explain the action. But the sower does ultimately reap a harvest. The crop gets to that point in stages: "first the blade, then the head," and finally "the mature grain in the head." All this takes time, but the seed does grow. It is the sower's responsibility to wait patiently for the maturation process to occur.

4:29 Once the seed is mature, it is time to bring out the sickle and harvest the crop. All of this happens by the marvelous provision of God, not by the strife and effort of man. So it is with the coming of God's kingdom rule on this earth through the person of His Son. Man's efforts do not bring in the kingdom, but people need to wait patiently for God to accomplish His goal for history.

> The total organic situation must be appreciated: emphasis falls not merely on the harvest which is assured, but upon the seed and its growth as well. The seed which is sown is the authoritative proclamation of Jesus, which does not prove barren. The proclamation of the gospel is the pledge of the ultimate manifestation of the Kingdom; it mysteriously, but irresistibly, brings it near. The parable thus depicts the coming of the Kingdom in comprehensive terms while emphasizing the sovereign initiative of God in the establishment of his rule.[14]

13. William Hendriksen, *Exposition of the Gospel According to Mark* (Grand Rapids: Baker, 1975), 167.
14. Lane, *The Gospel of Mark*, 170.

4:30   So how is the "kingdom of God" to be pictured? "By what parable shall we present it?" Jesus asks. The double question is repeated in a different form and context in Luke 13:18ff. Matthew, in 13:31, introduces the same parable without either question. In all probability, Jesus repeated these parables many times with different audiences over the period of His ministry. How He varied the introductions may be reflected by the various gospel renderings. Surely Jesus always took His audiences into consideration.

4:31   The kingdom is pictured here "like a mustard seed." The mustard was the smallest of all of the seeds known in the land of Israel. In Jewish thinking, "small as a grain of mustard" was proverbial for anything that was minute in its beginning (cf. Matt. 17:20; Luke 17:6). Although it is known today that the mustard seed is not the smallest of all the plant seeds, it would be unfair to conclude that Jesus Christ was in error here. He simply was using this as the proverbial statement of the time. Further, it should be noted that Jesus does not use the superlative degree. Rather, He uses the comparative. It probably would be better to translate "smaller than all the seeds" as "one of the smaller seeds." Though it was a tiny seed when it was sown, it grew to be an incredibly large plant, often more than ten feet tall. Little is said about the seed's growing. The emphasis, rather, is the contrast in size between its beginning and its end.

4:32   The tiny mustard seed "becomes larger" than other plants. It becomes so large that it is able to sustain "the birds of the air" on its branches. In fact, the birds could even build nests "under its shade." The Savior's language reflects a number of Old Testament passages (cf. Ps. 104:12; Ezek. 17:23, 31:6; Dan. 4:12, 21). Jesus was teaching that the kingdom of God, which the disciples would come to understand after His rejection, would begin with a small group of individuals but would grow into a very large number.

The apostolic band numbered twelve, one of whom betrayed the Lord. But following the resurrection of the Savior and His ascension back to heaven, the followers of Jesus began to grow rapidly as God's rule in the hearts of people continued to increase. The rule of God, or His reign in people's hearts, was like the mustard seed, which, though it began small, grew into something that provided great benefit, pleasure, and sustenance for others. The birds coming to "nest" (*kataskēnoun,* "to tent or camp down") in the branches may illustrate peoples from many ethnic backgrounds finding blessing under God's rule. Although birds had appeared earlier to picture Satan's destructive work (cf. 4:4, 15), their presence here does not indicate judgment but blessing. Hendriksen summarizes the parables of Jesus in this manner:

> In the parable of The Sower (vs. 3-9, 13-20) the emphasis was on *human responsibility;* in that of The Seed Growing in Secret (vs. 26-29), on *divine sovereignty.* When these two co-operate—man working out his own salvation because God is working within him (Phil. 2:12, 13)—, *abundant growth* results, as shown in the parable of The Mustard Seed.[15]

4:33   Mark's summary declares that Jesus taught with many parables, and He continued to communicate the truth as His hearers "were able to hear it" (*kathōs ēdunanto akouein,* imperfect tense implying that over a period of time Jesus continued to teach the people). Only Mark makes this statement. "Jesus used parables now largely, but there was a limit even to the use of them to these men. He gave the mystery of the kingdom in this veiled parabolic form which was the only feasible form at this stage. But even so they did not understand what they heard."[16]

4:34   His speaking did not occur without parabolic instruction. Though He spoke in parables to the masses, "He was explaining" [*epeluen,* imperfect tense implying this continued over a period time] everything privately to His own disciples. The verb "to explain" (*epiluō*) is used only here and in Acts 19:39, where the town clerk said that the issue that was being contested with Paul and his followers should "be settled in the lawful assembly." The idea of the word is to give additional explanation or to make something clearer to the point of revelation. That is exactly what Jesus did with His disciples. Thus, the purpose of the parables was fulfilled. The Savior was able to clearly instruct those who were His followers, but at the same time the parables made it possible to conceal the truth from people who were turning from Him (cf. Matt. 13:10, 36). God always reveals His truth clearly to those who seek Him, but those who turn from Him will find even the truth that they understand to be taken away.

15. Hendriksen, *Exposition of the Gospel According to Mark,* 171-72.
16. Robertson, *Word Pictures in the New Testament,* 1:290.

Whereas the parables of Jesus were obviously a key part of His teaching ministry, it should be noted that Mark records only these three.

> We are not surprised that this evangelist does not reveal nearly as many parables as do Matthew and Luke. . . . Mark was writing for Romans, people who were interested in action, power, conquest. To them he pictures Jesus as an active, energetic, swiftly moving, conquering King, a Victor over the destructive forces of nature, over disease, demons, death, and moral-spiritual darkness, the One and only Deliverer. So having related these three parables, Mark now quickly turns to an awe-inspiring *action* account.[17]

THE SERVANT'S AUTHENTICATION
IN SPITE OF OPPOSITION, 4:35–5:43

TO THE APOSTLES, 4:35-41
(cf. Matt. 8:18, 23-27; Luke 8:22-25)

4:35   As Jesus came to the end of a full day of ministry, He said to His disciples, "Let us go over to the other side" of the Sea of Galilee. Such a journey would be a distance of only five miles, but it would have taken them to a region where Jesus was unknown. The intent of the Lord was to get away from the crowds who were constantly thronging about Him. Unless one has been in a public ministry where people are constantly desiring one's attention, it is hard to understand the drain such contact can produce. Jesus and the disciples needed to get away from the press of people. Since the Lord was thoroughly human as well as thoroughly divine, He needed periods of rest and relaxation. "It had been a busy day. The blasphemous accusation, the visit of the mother and brothers and possibly sisters, to take him home, leaving the crowded house for the sea, the first parables by the sea, then more in the house, and now out of the house and over the sea."[18]

4:36   They left the multitude as the disciples provided a boat for themselves and for Jesus to leave the area. Mark says that "they took Him along with them, just as He was." There was no time to go back and secure extra clothing or provisions. They quickly found a boat and departed. Earlier in this chapter Jesus had taught the multitudes

---

17. Hendriksen, *Exposition of the Gospel According to Mark*, 174.
18. Robertson, *Word Pictures in the New Testament*, 1:291.

from a boat near the edge of the seashore (cf. 4:1ff.). Since some of the disciples were fishermen, they had a number of contacts that would enable them to secure a vessel for the journey. Mark's gospel is the only one that indicates that "other boats" (*alla ploia*) were with them as they departed. Thus, there was even a crowd around Jesus on the lake! Whether these other boats stayed with the apostles or fell behind, or possibly even got separated in the storm, is not revealed in the story.

4:37 As the apostles started across the sea, there was no problem with the weather. But as the little boat sailed on, "a fierce gale" suddenly arose. The storm became so strong that "waves were breaking over" the bow. The text literally says that the waves were causing the boat to be filling up with water. Though some translations imply that the boat was "full of water," a boat full of water usually sinks. Nevertheless, the storm was so strong that the waves were causing a serious problem for the disciples.

A quickly rising, fierce storm with strong winds is not uncommon on the Sea of Galilee. One can leave the western shore and encounter a violent storm before reaching the eastern side.

> The Sea of Galilee, surrounded by high mountains, is like a basin. Sudden violent storms on the sea were well known. Violent winds from the southwest enter the basin from the southern cleft and create a situation in which storm and calm succeed one another rapidly. Since the wind is nearly always stronger in the afternoon than in the morning or evening, fishing was done at night. But when a storm arises in the evening, it is all the more dangerous. Such a storm struck as a fierce gust of wind came upon the lake, driving the waves over the side of the boat, which was being swamped with water.[19]

4:38 Jesus was not bothered by the storm, however. The long day of physical exertion and the demands of the multitude had surely brought great physical exhaustion. As soon as He got into the boat and they departed from shore, He retreated to the stern, where He quickly fell asleep on a "cushion" (*proskephalaion*), a vivid detail recorded only by Mark. The increasing storm did not even cause Him to awaken. It was not until the disciples roused Him (*egeirousin auton*, present tense to picture the action) and spoke to Him that He finally

19. Lane, *The Gospel of Mark*, 175.

woke up. Their concern was that they were "perishing" (*apollymetha,* a present tense verb), also a detail noted only by Mark.

By this time they had done everything possible to save themselves and their ship. Since the boat was filling with water, they had undoubtedly been bailing as quickly as they could. In fact, their admonition to the Lord implied a rebuke, for He was sleeping and they needed His help to bail water to keep from going down. That He was sound asleep was taken by them to imply that He was unconcerned about their condition. "The Lord's sleep was not only the sleep of weariness: it was also the rest of faith, for there is a rest of faith as well as a watch of faith (Is. xxx. 15). Faith and fear are mutual exclusives in the Bible: it was the disciples' idea that they were perishing, not the Lord's."[20]

It is interesting that the presence of the Lord in the boat did not prevent the difficult situation from developing. So also the presence of Jesus Christ in one's life does not mean that one will always sail on smooth seas. "Many people have the idea that storms come to their lives only when they have disobeyed God, but this is not always the case. Jonah ended up in a storm because of his disobedience, but the disciples got into a storm because of their *obedience* to the Lord."[21]

4:39   When Jesus awoke, "He rebuked the wind and [spoke] to the sea."

> Christ was here demonstrating the same authority He had when He created the world by the word of His mouth. The authority that brought the world into existence can control the elements within nature. One day all nature will be subject to His authority and control by His power. Christ was demonstrating through this miracle that He is the Lord of creation and one day all creation will be in subjection to Him.[22]

Only Mark records the fact that Jesus spoke directly to the wind and said, "Hush," or, "Stop your noise" (*Siōpa*). Jesus the Creator was simply commanding the wind that He had created to stop making its noise. To the sea Jesus literally said, "Be muzzled" (*pephimōso*). One can picture what happens when a muzzle is placed over a mouth. A muzzle effectively stops the undesired action. The sea He had fashioned He simply muzzled to bring about absolute peace. It was as

20. Cole, *The Gospel According to Mark,* 96.
21. Warren W. Wiersbe, *Be Diligent* (Wheaton, Ill.: Victor, 1987), 46.
22. Pentecost, *The Words & Works of Jesus Christ,* 221.

though He were placing His hand over the sea. Immediately "the wind died down and it became perfectly calm." One can comprehend a double miracle here. Those who have been on a lake when a storm occurs may have seen the winds stop blowing as quickly as they started. But the action of the wind on the water normally causes the water to continue to agitate until it has an opportunity to calm down on its own. Jesus immediately brought a great calm (*galēnē megalē*) both to the wind and to the sea simply by His spoken word. The Creator who fashioned all of these things can command them, and they immediately obey.

4:40   The Savior did not stop with the physical elements. The greatest danger in the story was not the wind and the waves. The greater problem that Jesus was dealing with was the disciples' unbelief. Jesus turned and rebuked them (this is the first of a series of rebukes in Mark's gospel: cf. 7:18; 8:17f., 21, 32f.; 9:19) and asked, "Why are you so timid?" Why was it that after months of following Him they still had "no faith"? Jesus had not said to them that they were going into the middle of the lake to drown. Jesus' original command to them was, "Let us go over to the other side." The Master of the universe was not going to drown in the midst of the sea. Where, indeed, was their faith?

4:41   The disciples were, however, "very much afraid" (*ephobēthēsan phobon megan,* lit., "they feared a great fear"). Their reverential awe was far greater than their previous fear of the elements of nature. They realized they were standing in the presence of majestic power. They had never seen One command the physical elements and bring about immediate obedience. They were amazed that "even the wind and the sea" obeyed Him.

> This miracle came home to the Apostles above any that they had witnessed. It touched them personally: they had been delivered by it from imminent peril. It appealed to them as men used to the navigation of the Lake. Thus it threw a new and awful light on the Person with Whom they daily associated.[23]

HOMILETICAL SUGGESTIONS

Parabolic instruction makes up a large portion of chapter 4. It helps in dealing with parables to remember that the story was given

23. Swete, *The Gospel According to St. Mark,* 90-91.

for the purpose of revealing truth, not to make the truth unknowable. Sometimes the truth is clearly revealed in the surrounding context, whereas other times the interpreter is left to make an educated suggestion based on the nature of the illustration itself. One should try to understand the totality of the passage before one begins to deal with the parts. The suggestions made in the commentary should point to the main idea Jesus was communicating through these parables. He was trying to show why individuals responded the way they did to the presentation of His person.

The concluding story in this chapter—Jesus crossing the sea with the disciples and the violent storm that arose—has many interesting facets. The authority of Jesus over the realm of nature and the immediate response of the creation to the authority of the Savior is clearly presented. The fearful reaction of the disciples showed that they had never encountered an individual like Jesus Christ. Never had anyone commanded the elements and produced immediate obedience. Jesus Christ was clearly more than an earthly man.

MARK

CHAPTER

FIVE

THE SERVANT'S AUTHENTICATION

THE SERVANT'S AUTHENTICATION
IN SPITE OF OPPOSITION, 4:35–5:43

TO THE REGION OF DECAPOLIS, 5:1-20
(cf. Matt. 8:28-34; Luke 8:26-39)

5:1 In 4:35 Jesus had said to the disciples, "Let us go over to the other side." As chapter 5 begins they arrive on the other side of the sea in a region called by Mark "the country of the Gerasenes." This region was largely populated by Gentiles, although Jews were there as well. Scholars debate the precise location of this region, for whereas Mark and Luke (in 8:26) refer to the region as "the country of the Gerasenes," Matthew (in 8:28) calls it the "country of the Gadarenes." A town known as Gerasa was located at least thirty miles to the southeast of the Sea of Galilee, and a larger city by the name of Gadara, situated a few miles southeast of the Sea, was the capital of the entire district. Henry Swete notes that perhaps "the neighbourhood of the lakeside Gerasa might perhaps be loosely described as Gadarene territory."[1] This incident probably occurred in the area where the modern village of Kersa is located. This is the only area along the eastern shore of the Sea of Galilee where there is a fairly steep slope, which

---

1. Henry Barclay Swete, *The Gospel According to St. Mark* (Grand Rapids: Eerdmans, 1956), 92.

would enable the ensuing story to take place, as well as numerous caves in nearby hillsides.

5:2   As soon as Jesus got out of the boat, He was "immediately" (*euthys*) met by a man who was possessed by "an unclean spirit" (*en pneumati akathartō*). It is clear that "unclean" means "evil" (cf. Luke 7:21, 8:2, with 4:33, 36). These unclean spirits were morally filthy. They were evil in themselves and a true source of harm and evil toward those over whom they exercised control. In the account of this event in Matthew 8:28, this demon-possessed individual was exceedingly violent and would not permit anyone to pass along that road without opposition. Consequently, most travelers avoided the road through this area.

Another interesting difference occurs in the synoptic accounts. Matthew, in 8:28, notes that there were two demon-possessed individuals. Mark's account, along with that of Luke's (8:26-37), focuses on one demon-possessed man, but neither account says "only one." The differences in the accounts actually give greater evidence for authenticity. Each of these writers was writing his own story and used the facts significant to him. The fact that Matthew mentions two, whereas Mark and Luke mention only one, does not imply that there is a mistake here. Probably two men were present, but Mark and Luke mention the more prominent and/or more violent one of the two. From all three accounts it is clear that the man was demon possessed, although each states it uniquely.

5:3   The effects of the demon possession on the individual in Mark's account demonstrated his pitiable state. Here was a man who because of the impact of the demon in his life was not able to dwell with his own family. Instead, his life was relegated to dwelling in a graveyard, probably the abandoned burial chambers carved in the cliffs or natural caves. It was not uncommon for people to find refuge in tombs. The resting place of the dead actually could provide shelter for the living as well. There are a number of cavelike tombs near Kersa on the eastern side of the Sea of Galilee. Another effect of the demon in this man was his incredible power, for Mark states that no one was able to bind him, not even with a chain.

> The people of the town undoubtedly felt that the man was mad, for his appearance and behavior conformed to the proper diagnosis of insanity. In accordance with the practice of the day they had attempted to bind him by chains to protect themselves from his violence. When this

proved to be futile, they had driven him off to wander restlessly in the wild hill country and to dwell in the subterranean caves which served as tombs and dwellings for the poorest people of the district. . . . The attitude and actions of the people of the town were an added cruelty based on popular misunderstanding. But ultimate responsibility for the wretchedness of the man and the brutal treatment he had endured rested with the demons who had taken possession of the center of his personality.[2]

5:4   The townspeople had often tried to bind this man by placing his hands in chains and his feet in shackles. But because of his incredible power he had been able to break the shackles, which probably were made of wood, and to work free of the chains by tearing them apart. The main verbs here are written in the perfect tense indicating actions that had been attempted in the past, not at the moment when Jesus approached him. He was so strong that no one was able "to subdue him" (*damasai,* "to tame as a lion," imperfect tense picturing an action that had been attempted on repeated occasions).

5:5   The people of the region were constantly aware of his presence, for Mark notes that both "night and day" his shrieks could be heard as he gashed "himself with stones" (*katakoptōn heauton lithois*).

> The verb for cutting himself occurs only here in the N.T., though an old verb. It means to *cut down* (perfective use of *kata-*). We say *cut up,* gash, hack to pieces. Perhaps he was scarred all over with such gashes during his moments of wild frenzy night and day in the tombs and on the mountains.[3]

The effects of demon possession as they are pictured in the life of this individual show a pitiful condition. Demonic possession is something that does great harm to a man. What had happened to the image of God in which this man had been created? The demon was doing everything he possibly could to pervert and destroy that image in the life of this individual.

5:6   When this demon saw Jesus coming, perhaps even seeing Him in the boat, he ran to Him so that they met when Jesus disembarked (cf. v. 2). He "bowed down before Him." Swete adds that "the onrush

---

2. William L. Lane, *The Gospel of Mark,* NICNT (Grand Rapids: Eerdmans, 1974), 182.

3. A. T. Robertson, *Word Pictures in the New Testament* (Nashville: Broadman, 1930), 1:295.

of the naked yelling maniac must have tried the newly recovered confidence of the Twelve. We can imagine their surprise when, on approaching, he threw himself on his knees."[4] This act of bowing was not necessarily an act of genuine worship. The same verb (*prosekunē-sen*) is used of the Roman soldiers (15:19) who mockingly "worshiped" Jesus Christ. It may simply have been the act of an inferior recognizing a superior in his presence and bowing before him.

5:7   He cried out "with a loud voice" and said, "What do I have to do with You, Jesus, Son of the Most High God?" It is interesting that the demon recognized Jesus, even calling Him by His personal name. Do all of the demons know Jesus, or had one of the disciples inadvertently called out His name? The text does not say clearly. More important, though, the demon was fully aware of Jesus' divine origin, for he calls Him the Son of the Most High God. That statement acknowledged who truly is the One with the greatest authority, the Most High God, but it also recognized that Jesus is the Son of that God. William Lane suggests that "the full address is not a confession of Jesus' dignity but a desperate attempt to gain control over him or to render him harmless, in accordance with the common assumption of the period that the use of the precise name of an adversary gave one mastery over him."[5]

He continued by saying, "I implore You by God, do not torment me!" This literally is the form of a vow. By saying "I implore you," he was literally trying to place Jesus under a vow, asking that Jesus would not torment him (*mē me basanisēs,* a word meaning to test metals, which came to mean "to test by torture"). It certainly seems that the demon realized that he was a creature who will be dealt with by God, that he was under His authority, and that his ultimate end was going to be torment and separation from God.

5:8   This verse actually explains why the individual had come running to Jesus. It appears that as soon as Jesus got out of the boat and assessed the situation, He realized that here was a man possessed by a demon. Mark declared that "He had been saying" (*elegen,* an imperfect indicating repeated past action) to this individual, "Come out of the man, you unclean spirit!" As soon as Jesus realized the man's condition He began immediately and continuously to exorcise the demon. That was what had produced the demon's cry and his interaction

4. Swete, *The Gospel According to St. Mark,* 94.
5. Lane, *The Gospel of Mark,* 183-84.

with Jesus. But it was not his wish to return to the Abyss. In Matthew 8:29 the demon implies that Jesus had come too early, literally, "before the time."

5:9   Mark notes that Jesus continued His discussion by "asking" (*epērōta,* imperfect tense carrying on the narrative of conversation) the demon, "What is your name?" The exact reason that Jesus inquired of the demon is not stated in the text. R. A. Cole suggests that Jesus may have asked his name "in order to make apparent to all the man's need, and perhaps to bring home to the man's own clouded mind the awful plight in which he stood."[6]

His response is interesting: "My name is Legion; for we are many." The name "Legion" (*Legiōn*) is a Latin word, but like other military and governmental terms, it had entered the language and is found in Hellenistic Greek and in Aramaic. A Roman legion at maximum strength consisted of at least six thousand men. Usually, though, the legions were not fully manned. However, a legion surely implied several thousand men. In this particular case there probably was a very large number of demons in this individual, perhaps all working under the control of the one who was their spokesperson. That may account for the switching back and forth between "my" and "we." "The meaning here is undoubtedly figurative: a very large number. It is also possible that the term 'Legion' conjured up the vision of an army of occupation, cruelty, and destruction."[7] It is also clear from other passages (cf. Matt. 12:45; Mark 16:9; Luke 8:2) that more than one demon could at times occupy and enslave a person.

5:10   The demon continued to speak to Jesus, and he begged Him (*parekalei autou,* imperfect implying many repetitions) that they not be sent out of that country, or that particular region. Surely the demons felt "at home" in this area of skeletons and death. In the parallel passage in Luke 8:31 the demon entreats Him not to make them depart into "the abyss." It appears that demons need to possess something and do not wish to be disembodied spirits, for once disembodied the only alternative for them is to go into the Abyss. The Abyss is a place of evil spirits that is opened during the time of the Tribulation (Rev. 9:1-12). The demons' desire was that they not have to leave the area and be confined to the Abyss.

6. R. A. Cole, *The Gospel According to Mark* (Grand Rapids: Eerdmans, 1979), 98.

7. William Hendriksen, *Exposition of the Gospel According to Mark* (Grand Rapids: Baker, 1975), 192.

5:11   At this point in the story it is explained that there was a large "herd of swine feeding" nearby. The presence of a herd of pigs brings up several questions. Who were the owners? Were they Gentiles, as many believe, since this was a predominantly Gentile region, or were they Jews? If they were Jews, why would Jews be keeping a herd of swine, since swine were unclean animals according to Mosaic Law? None of the answers to these questions is found in the story, but perhaps the context provides suggestions as to the best view to follow.

5:12   The demons were begging (*parekalesan,* imperfect implying repetitions) the Lord to permit them to enter into the swine. Why the demons asked such a question is not specified. Some think that, since they were unclean spirits and the pigs were unclean animals, the demons believed their request might be looked on with favor by the Savior. Others maintain that perhaps Satan encouraged the demons to go into the swine and bring them to their death in order to destroy any possible ministry Jesus could have in that region. The latter view is questionable. At any rate, their request was that they be permitted to enter the swine. It is noteworthy that apart from Christ's permission they would not have been able to do so.

5:13   Jesus "gave them permission," and as they entered into the swine the whole herd "rushed down the steep bank into the sea," where "they were drowned" (*epnigonto,* imperfect of "to choke," picturing the scene graphically) in the water. Hendriksen describes this scene as follows:

> In answer to their request (v. 12) Jesus *gave* them permission. So they *came out of* the man and *went into* the pigs. Result: the herd . . . *rushed* pell-mell *down* the cliff. . . . Here Mark suddenly changes the tense of the verb. So far he has briefly stated four incidents, four summary facts: *gave, came out of, went into, rushed down.* It is as if he, in very rapid succession, showed us four snapshots. Then we are shown a slow-motion movie: one by one we see the (approximately) 2,000 pigs choking to death in the sea, until all have drowned.[8]

Only Mark's gospel records that there were about two thousand pigs in this herd. One can only imagine what the scene must have been like as the squeals of the animals resounded horrendously while they were drowning in the Sea of Galilee. Why did Jesus permit the de-

8. Ibid., 193. He explains in a footnote that the first four verbs are all aorist and the final verb an imperfect.

mons to enter into the swine, only to bring about their destruction? Lane suggests that

> Jesus allowed the demons to enter the swine to indicate beyond ques-
> tion that their real purpose was the total destruction of their host. While
> this point may have been obscured in the case of the man, there was
> the blatant evidence in the instance of the swine. Their intention was
> no different with regard to the man whom they had possessed.[9]

5:14   Those who were keeping the herd realized that they were in a serious predicament. They were probably not the owners but were simply keeping the animals for others. Now the pigs were gone. How would they explain what happened to them? Somehow the blame would have to be shifted from them to the true reason for the death of these animals. They quickly "ran away and reported" what had happened in the city and, Mark adds, "out in the country." The result was that many people came out to see the aftereffects of the event. In the sequence of the events in Mark's gospel, this response of the people probably occurred the next day. Jesus and the disciples had crossed the sea in the evening (cf. 4:35). If the deliverance of the man occurred as soon as Jesus got out of the boat (cf. 5:2), it is doubtful that the news could have circulated throughout the city and the region until the next day.

5:15   How surprised the residents were when "they came [*erchon-tai*, present tense picturing vivid action] to Jesus," and sitting quietly beside Him was the formerly demon-possessed man. They all knew him well. They had seen him before, running around shrieking without clothing. But now this same man was sitting peacefully beside Jesus Christ, in his right mind, fully clothed. There could be no doubt that this was the same man, for Mark adds a phrase to emphasize that this was "the very man who had had the 'legion.'" No one could dispute it! That, of course, brought great fear (*ephobēthēsan*, aorist tense picturing this emotion as a whole). What kind of an explanation was there for this?

5:16   The story of what had happened was repeated many different times by various witnesses. The herdsmen probably took the owners to the very brink of the hill, showed them how the animals had run down the slope and how they had drowned in the sea. The position-

9. Lane, *The Gospel of Mark*, 186.

ing of the phrase "and all about the swine," which Mark alone records, shows that the impact of this event on the pigs was of greater concern to them than its impact on the man. Nevertheless, the story of the change in the demon-possessed man was repeated as well. This incident surely was retold again and again in the hearing of those who were present. One would think that they would respond with great joy and appreciation over the healing of this man whose condition had been so bleak. Why did they not return to their homes and bring out to Jesus others who were sick or demon possessed?

5:17   Rather, they began to ask Him "to depart from their region." They seemed not to question Him about their financial loss. Could that be a clue that perhaps the herd was owned by some Jewish investors who, knowing that they were doing something contrary to the Law, would not debate that point with Jesus? Certainly if these owners were Gentiles they might have asked Jesus about their financial loss. Would Jews actually get involved in the raising of pigs?

Potentially there was a large market for pork products in the Gentile region of Decapolis, and not every Jew living at the time of the Savior was a firm follower of his religion. It is this author's conclusion that the herd was owned by Jewish individuals who were more concerned for their hogs than they were about the Healer. Their financial loss was far more important to them than the benefits given to the man who had been useless to society but who now was restored. Their asking Jesus to leave the region implied that they wanted Him out of town before He could bring about more loss to them.

> The saddest thing in the whole story is that the Lord listened to their request, and left them: there are times when the worst possible thing for us is that the Lord grants our prayer.... Gerasa... desired only to be left alone by this frightening supernatural Christ: and it was to be her judgment that the Lord left her, to return no more, for there is no biblical evidence for any later ministry by Christ in this part.[10]

5:18   Jesus Christ never pushed Himself on anyone. So "He was getting into the boat" to depart from their shores when the man He had delivered came to Him and began begging (*parekalei*, imperfect tense implying continuous action over a period of time) Him "that he might accompany Him." The formerly demon-possessed man used

---

10. Cole, *The Gospel According to Mark*, 99-100.

the same form of entreaty that the demon had used previously with Jesus (cf. v. 10). The demon had continuously begged Jesus that he not be required to leave the country. The healed man now continuously begged Jesus to allow him to leave. He wanted to go with Jesus and be like one of the apostles.

5:19   But Jesus did not grant his wish. He realized the greater need was for the man to return back to his own home and to report "what great things" God had done for him and how God had had mercy on him. Here was a man who had been deprived of his family for a long time. Now he could return to them to be a testimony of what God had done in his life. Jesus' statement, however, "Go home to your people," may well have included a circle much wider than the man's family, for his actions in the next verse demonstrate that he saw his task as reaching out to the whole region.

5:20   The text indicates that he did indeed become a great testifier for Jesus Christ in the region of the Decapolis. The Decapolis was a league of ten cities, nine of which (Philadelphia, Gerasa, Pella, Damascus, Kanata, Dion, Abila, Gadara, and Hippos) were east of the Sea of Galilee and the Jordan River. One city, Scythopolis, was just west of the Jordan.

> These ten cities, at one time deprived of their freedom by the Maccabees, had by the Romans been delivered from their yoke and had even been given a considerable measure of home rule. Though required to render tribute and military service to Rome, they had been allowed to form an association for commercial progress and for mutual defense against any encroachment from . . . either Jews or Arabs. They had their own army, courts, and coinage. Throughout this region there was a scattering of Jews, but by and large this was definitely Gentile territory; a fact to which, for example, many Greek amphitheaters bore witness.[11]

Since this was Gentile territory, there would be no one in that area testifying of the Messiah. Many people were accompanying Jesus as He returned; no one would remain to bear witness of Christ on the east side of the Sea of Galilee. Though Jesus placed no restrictions on this man (cf. 1:44), He asked him to remain in a region where there was no testimony and to tell of the "great things Jesus had done for him." He became a faithful witness for Jesus, which shows that in his own mind he made the proper connection between "the Lord" (v. 19)

11. Hendriksen, *Exposition of the Gospel According to Mark,* 198.

and "Jesus." He faithfully proclaimed his testimony throughout the whole region of Decapolis, and the result was that "everyone marveled" (*ethaumazon,* imperfect tense indicating a state that continued over a period of time).

TO THE "RELIGIOUS" LEADERS, 5:21-43
(cf. Matt. 9:18-26; Luke 8:40-56)

The Request, 5:21-24

5:21 Scripture does not always give all the details that relate to the biblical stories. As was pointed out (cf. v. 14), it is unlikely that Jesus and the disciples crossed the Sea of Galilee late in the day only to get back in the boat and return that same evening. How much time passed and exactly how these stories related to each other is not always clear. But the crowd on the eastern shore probably asked Jesus to leave the day following the miracle. Therefore He departed from them and sailed across the sea to the western side. The crowd on the east side was happy to see Him depart, but as He arrived on the west side "a great multitude gathered" and welcomed Him openly. It seems clear from Matthew's gospel (9:1) that Jesus and the disciples returned to the city of Capernaum, where many miracles had previously occurred (cf. 1:21-34; 2:1-13; 3:1-6, 20-35).

5:22 At this point "one of the synagogue officials [*arxisunagōgōn*] named Jairus came up" to Jesus. The synagogue official occupied an important position in a town. He was responsible for the administrative, not the priestly, details of the synagogue, including such things as appointing those who would say prayers and those who would be privileged to read Scripture in the services. In a small synagogue there would usually be one official, but a larger one could have several (cf. Luke 13:14; Acts 13:15). The person who held this position was usually looked on with honor. Often he was a leading citizen of the community. All these factors communicate a great deal about Jairus. Yet when he came up to Jesus he "fell at His feet." Swete says that "his dignity was forgotten in the presence of a great sorrow; he recognised his inferiority to the Prophet who had the power to heal."[12]

5:23 He kept begging Jesus (*parakalei,* imperfect tense indicating repeated action) "earnestly," saying that his little girl was at the point of death. Although some might not consider a child of twelve (cf. v. 42)

---

12. Swete, *The Gospel According to St. Mark,* 101.

to be "little," Jairus's expression shows how precious and dear she was in his eyes. She would probably always be his "little girl." Literally she was "at death's door," and he wanted Jesus to "come and lay [His] hands on her" that she might be brought back to physical health. This was apparently the pattern that Jairus had observed before in Jesus' healing. He surely would have been present on that day when Jesus entered the synagogue in Capernaum and encountered the man with a withered hand (3:1ff.). On that particular occasion, Jesus healed a man with a horrible infirmity with but a spoken word. Jairus believed that if only Jesus would come to his house and lay hands on his daughter, she too would get well.

5:24   Mark does not indicate the Savior's response but simply states that Jesus "went" (*apēlthen,* aorist tense summarizing the departure) with Jairus. Since those surrounding Him had heard the exchange between the two men, "a great multitude of people was following" along (*ēkolouthei,* imperfect indicating a continuous action). Perhaps they were anxious to see Jesus perform another of His famous miracles. They crowded around (*synethlibon,* imperfect emphasizing the continuous activity of the crowd), "pressing in on Him" and actually keeping Him from rapidly arriving at the home of Jairus. Luke 8:42 implies that the crowd's pressing on Him made it difficult even to breathe.

The Interruption, 5:25-34

5:25   A woman who had been suffering a physical infirmity for a period of twelve years was part of the multitude that day. The participle describing her condition (*ousa,* "being") is in the present tense, indicating that she was at that moment suffering with the condition. Her problem is described as "a hemorrhage." Scholars debate the exact nature of her illness, but it probably involved some kind of uterine discharge.

> There are those who believe that the drain was constant. Another view would be that throughout the twelve years an excessive loss of blood, occurring periodically, had made it impossible for her ever to feel strong and healthy, and that at this particular moment she was again suffering as a result of loss of blood.[13]

Not only was the physical problem a source of irritation and pain, it made the woman ceremonially unclean, as Leviticus 15:25ff. suggests.

13. Hendriksen, *Exposition of the Gospel According to Mark,* 204.

This woman was not allowed to have the normal relationships that others could sustain in society.

5:26 Mark includes the detail that she "had endured much at the hands of many physicians, and had spent all [her money]." Unfortunately she had not gotten better but had simply grown worse. Various remedies for her physical problem are described in ancient writings such as the Talmud. Those remedies would be laughed at by the modern medical community, for they truly had elements of quackery in them. One remedy consisted of drinking a goblet of wine containing powder compounded from rubber, alum, and garden crocuses. Another consisted of a dose of Persian onions. Other physicians prescribed sudden shock or carrying the ashes of an ostrich egg in a certain cloth. Matthew 9:20ff. makes no mention of her experience with doctors, and when Dr. Luke reported on this woman's condition (Luke 8:43ff.), he simply noted that she "had a hemorrhage for twelve years, and could not be healed by anyone." Perhaps Luke's professional sensitivity kept him from commenting on how other doctors from his time had treated this woman.

5:27 This woman's condition truly was to be pitied, for she had come to the end of herself. But then she heard about Jesus. Exactly what it was that she heard is not stated in the text. Surely she heard that He had performed miracles of healing. Perhaps that fact stirred within her the hope that she too could be healed. Because of her condition it is not surprising that she did not come out into the open. Her uncleanness would not have permitted her to confront Jesus directly. She merely devised the plan that she would come up behind Jesus and "touch His garments" (v. 28). Matthew and Luke make clear that what she touched was one of the tassels (*kraspedou*, "fringe"; cf. Matt. 9:20; Luke 8:44) of His garment (cf. Num. 15:38; Deut. 22:12). "The Law required every Jew to attach to the corners of his quadrangular covering tassels, which according to later usage consisted of three threads of white wool twisted together with a cord of blue."[14] Having devised this plan she proceeded to carry it out.

5:28 Her thinking was revealed by Mark. She had been saying to herself (*elegen*, imperfect tense indicating she had been saying this over and over), "If I just touch His garments, I shall get well." Perhaps she had heard of others who had been healed in a similar fashion (cf. Mark 3:10). Her intention was simply to reach out and touch the Sav-

---

14. Swete, *The Gospel According to St. Mark*, 103.

ior, not to stop Him. Since He was on His way to take care of the daughter of Jairus, she did not mean to delay Him. "If I can just touch Him, I shall get well," she kept repeating to herself as she approached Him from behind.

5:29 The Lord did, indeed, reward her faith, for "immediately" (*euthys*) upon touching His garments, her hemorrhaging stopped. She knew she had been "healed of [the] affliction" (*tēs mastigos,* "the plague") that she had carried for twelve years. The object of faith is always the thing that is key, and the object of her faith was Jesus Christ. This was a vivid moment of joy for her.

5:30 Jesus knew "immediately" (*euthys*) that "power" had gone out from Him. "[He] was not ignorant of the fact that someone had touched him, and this not accidentally but purposefully, and not just with a finger but with faith. He knew that it was to that faith that the power within him and proceeding from him had responded."[15] This was not some mysterious, miraculous kind of healing, and He wanted to make that very clear. So Jesus suddenly stopped, "turned around . . . and said, 'Who touched My garments?'"

5:31 The question was viewed as almost humorous by the disciples. It would seem funny, with the crush of people, many reaching out to touch Jesus, for Him to suddenly stop, turn around, and say, "Who touched Me?" The disciples probably thought, *Everyone has been touching You, Lord.* Luke 8:45 makes clear that the response given by the disciples recorded in this verse was repeated to the Savior by Peter. Surely that fact had been communicated to Mark, but perhaps it had also been suggested by Peter that the quote be given anonymously, for all the disciples agreed with Peter's comment. In fact, the Lord's question seemed pointless, "since he had been jostled and touched by a host of individuals. Their impatience with the Lord reflects an awareness that their immediate mission was to assist a girl who was dying, and delay could be fatal. It also betrays that they had no understanding of what had taken place."[16]

5:32 But Jesus "looked around" (*perieblepeto,* imperfect tense indicating that Jesus kept looking around). His eyes moved from person to person in the group. His purpose was to allow "the woman who had done this" to come forward so that there could be clarification as to what really had happened on this occasion. When His eyes caught

---

15. Hendriksen, *Exposition of the Gospel According to Mark,* 207.

16. Lane, *The Gospel of Mark,* 193.

the woman's, she came forward. She could not have removed herself very far from Jesus because of the crowd.

5:33 The woman came forward in fear and with great trembling. It was not normal for a woman in that culture to speak in public. She "fell down before" Jesus in an act of worship "and told Him the whole truth." It was entirely possible that part of her fear was caused by the fact that by Levitical law her uncleanness could have made Him unclean as well. How would Jesus respond to her?

5:34 His response must have been a tremendous encouragement. He used a word that is used only in this particular passage in the New Testament. Jesus called the woman "Daughter" (*Thygatēr*). The implication is that a very special relationship had started between Jesus and this woman. She was now viewed by Him as one of His children. He wanted to clarify for her that it was not some kind of magical, mystical touch that had brought about her healing, so He said, "Your faith has made you well."

> It was *the grasp of her faith* rather than her hand that had secured the healing she sought. Her touch had brought together two elements—faith and Jesus—and that had made it effective. Power had gone forth from Jesus to the woman for the precise reason that she sought healing *from Him.* The woman's faith that Jesus could make her well expressed an appropriate decision with respect to his person.[17]

He further said to her, "Go in peace, and be healed of your affliction." This statement indicated that this woman not only received physical healing but spiritual healing as well. She truly had become a follower of Jesus Christ. One of the first things that happens when a person comes to faith in Christ is that a relationship of peace is established between that person and God. In fact, it is only through personal faith in the Lord Jesus that one can have peace with God.

> Although none of the evangelists report the woman's reaction to these gracious words of the Savior, is it unrealistic to affirm that her soul was flooded not only with relief but also with boundless gratitude, the kind of emotion experienced by the inspired composer of Ps. 116 (see especially vs. 12-19)? Jesus had healed her. He had imparted to her a double blessing: restoring her body and causing her soul to testify, so that faith

17. Ibid., 193-94.

concealed had become faith revealed. Now she was able to be, and undoubtedly had become, a blessing to others, to the glory of God.[18]

Later tradition embellished the Gospel account, seeking to answer the questions asked by generations of people. In the Greek tradition the anonymous woman was given the name Berenice, while in the Coptic and Latin tradition she received the related name Veronica. Eusebius states that she was from Caesarea Philippi, and that by the door of her home there was erected on a high stone a copper statue of a woman kneeling, her hands outstretched before her, entreating one purported to resemble Jesus. At the feet of the male figure a "strange sort of herb" is said to grow on the column which possessed medicinal powers against a wide variety of diseases. In this way the evangelical tradition was embellished. What was not appreciated was that the woman had experienced an aspect of salvation in anticipation of the more radical healing to be experienced by the daughter of Jairus. From Mark's perspective, the entire incident is a call for radical faith.[19]

The Fulfillment, 5:35-43

5:35   It was while Jesus was in the process of speaking to the woman that a group came from the house of Jairus with news. The commotion of the group's arrival quickly diverted the attention of the crowd away from the woman. They were not very diplomatic in conveying their sorrowful news, for they simply reported to Jairus that his daughter "has died" (*apethanen,* aorist tense indicating an accomplished fact). They also suggested that Jairus should not "trouble the Teacher anymore." It was as though there was nothing more that could be done. The girl was dead. Their remark shows "that the power of raising the dead was not yet generally attributed to Jesus; only one instance, so far as we know, had occurred, and that not in the Lake district ([Lk.] vii.11ff.)."[20] If Jesus had not taken so much time in dealing with the woman with her problem, perhaps He could have arrived in time to do something for the child. But now there was no reason to further trouble the Teacher. He need not take one step more toward the house of Jairus.

5:36   Jesus, however, completely ignored the words that were spoken by the delegation. The verb *parakousas* actually implies this. In-

18. Hendriksen, *Exposition of the Gospel According to Mark,* 210.

19. Lane, *The Gospel of Mark,* 194.

20. Swete, *The Gospel According to St. Mark,* 106.

stead of listening to them, He spoke (*legei,* present tense picturing vividly the action as occurring) two commands to Jairus. These commands were given in the present tense, which carries the idea of "Stop fearing" (*Mē phobou*) and "Keep on believing" (*monon pisteue*). Jairus had demonstrated great faith in coming to Jesus in view of the opposition of many of the religious leaders. Surely Jairus believed that Jesus could do something for his daughter while she was alive. Why should he now think that there was nothing the Savior could do for her in death?

5:37 At this point Jesus dismissed the large following of people, taking along with Him to the household of Jairus only three of His disciples—Peter, James, and John. These three were privileged to observe what followed. They also were privileged to observe a later event in the life of Jesus, when He was transfigured before them (cf. 9:1-9), and they were privileged to be closer to Jesus as He prayed in the Garden of Gethsemane (cf. 14:32-42). For this reason these three disciples have often been referred as "the inner circle."

> That Peter was among the three does not surprise us, in view of Matt. 16:16-19. It is entirely possible that John's spiritual affinity with his Master—that he was "the disciple whom Jesus loved" (John 13:23; 19:26; 20:2; 21:7, 20)—accounted for his inclusion in this innermost circle. But what about James, John's brother? Was it not considerate of the Lord to grant to him, who was going to be the first of The Twelve to seal his testimony with his blood (Acts 12:2), the privilege of being included among the three most intimate witnesses?
>
> These are considerations that may well be taken into account in attempting to answer the question, "Why these three?" Nevertheless, it must be frankly admitted that the answer to this question has not been revealed.[21]

5:38 When Jesus, the disciples, and Jairus arrived (present tense verb *erxontai,* to make the action vivid) at Jairus's home, a large commotion had already been started, and a group of people were there "weeping and wailing" (*klaiontas kai alalazontas,* the latter an onomatopoeic word picturing the monotonous wail of the mourners). It was a common practice in Middle Eastern cultures for intense wailing to take place at the time of an individual's death. "Since even the poorest man was required by common custom to hire a minimum of

21. Hendriksen, *Exposition of the Gospel According to Mark,* 212-13.

two flute players and one professional mourner in the event of his wife's death, it is probable that one who held the rank of synagogue-ruler would be expected to hire a large number of professional mourners."[22] It was clear that in the minds of these people this little girl had truly died. According to their custom, burial had to follow within twenty-four hours of death, so this was their opportunity to mourn. Perhaps since Jairus was an important official in their community, their mourning was even greater.

5:39 When Jesus entered, He turned to those who were weeping and told them (*legei*, present tense, "He was saying," picturing action taking place) to stop. He said, "The child has not died, but is asleep." There are some who have construed the words of Jesus to imply that the little girl had not truly died but was simply in a coma. But this idea was disputed by those who knew the facts and understood that she really was dead (cf. Luke 8:53). Furthermore, Luke 8:55 states that "her spirit returned" to her, indicating that there had been a separation of spirit and body. Others have interpreted the words to imply that death is likened to a state of sleep—one simply rests until the time of the resurrection. But it is probable that Jesus meant to convey another meaning by using this particular figure. Perhaps He was trying to say that the girl's condition was simply a temporary one, much like sleep. The concept of the soul's sleeping between the time of death and the resurrection is not affirmed anywhere in Scripture. Jesus was simply using a figure, for when one's life is removed, one's body appears to be asleep. "Jesus undoubtedly meant that she was not dead to stay dead, though some hold that the child was not really dead. It is a beautiful word (she is *sleeping, katheudei*) that Jesus uses of death."[23]

5:40 All three synoptic gospel writers note that the reaction of the people was laughter (*kategelōn,* imperfect tense, indicating that they continued to laugh at His suggestion). Their repeated laughter at such a solemn occasion was a clear indication that most of these people were insincere. They had only come there because it had been reported to them that someone had died, and they were there to do a job. Obviously in front of a group like this Jesus would not be able to perform any kind of miraculous work. He therefore put them all out of the room. "In this case some pressure was needed, for it was the interest of these paid mourners to remain. There is a sternness mani-

22. Lane, *The Gospel of Mark,* 196.
23. Robertson, *Word Pictures in the New Testament,* 1:302.

fested in their ejection that finds a counterpart on other occasions when our Lord is confronted with levity or greed."[24] He simply "took along" (*paralambanei,* present tense picturing the action occurring) Jairus, his wife, and his three companions, and they went into the room. The purpose of having these people along was to provide adequate witnesses to what transpired. According to the law of Moses, it was necessary to have two or three witnesses (Deut. 17:6).

5:41   As Jesus came to the little girl, all three synoptics note that He took her "by the hand" and spoke to her. Jairus's request (cf. v. 23) was that Jesus would come to his home, place His hands on his daughter, and restore her to health. His words to her in the original Aramaic are preserved only by Mark's account: *"Talitha kum!"* Those words were not a magical formula. There is no evidence that later Christian healers used any of Jesus' spoken words to perform their miraculous healings. The presence of the Aramaic expression probably reflects a faithfulness to the tradition that these were the words Jesus actually spoke. Cole notes that "if, as tradition has it and internal evidence confirms, Peter was Mark's informant, then it is obvious that the scene made such an impression upon the apostle that the Lord's actual words were remembered long after."[25]

Mark translated the Aramaic expression so that His largely Gentile audience would understand exactly what Jesus had said. The translation is, "Little girl, I say to you, arise!" *Talitha* is probably an affectionate term for the little girl, and *kum* simply means to get up. The addition of the phrase "I say [*legō,* present tense] to you" is there for the purpose of showing the authority of the Lord Jesus Christ. As God, He is the One who calls people forth in resurrection. Someday Jesus Christ will call all people from the grave. His authority to do this was demonstrated here as He said, "I say to you, arise."

5:42   "Immediately [*euthys*] the girl arose [*anestē,* aorist tense indicating a complete act] and began to walk" around (*periepatei,* imperfect tense indicating an act that continued over time) the room. Only Mark notes that she was twelve years old. It is interesting that the age of the little girl and the length of time the woman suffered the physical infirmity are exactly the same in these stories. That surely was not coincidental. The people in the room "were completely astounded"

24. Swete, *The Gospel According to St. Mark,* 108.
25. Cole, *The Gospel According to Mark,* 105.

(*exestēsan euthys ekstasei,* lit. "astonished immediately with great astonishment"; cf. Mark 2:12; Matt. 12:23) by what had happened.

> A moment ago [the girl] was a corpse, pale and lifeless. Now she is walking around, filled with life, health, and vigor. Therefore the astonishment of the overjoyed parents and of the three disciples as well knows no bounds. And in this astonishment all others who saw her afterwards must have joined.[26]

5:43   But Jesus issued two directives. First, He ordered them (*diesteilato,* an aorist middle that carries the idea of "to forbid") that they should not make known what had happened. Jesus was thronged by many people in this northern Galilee area, and He did not want this miracle to attract additional people to Him for the wrong reasons. The news about Him was circulating, and the Savior's message was being proclaimed. His message was not simply a message of the giving of life or the healing of physical bodies. Therefore, He did everything He could to keep those facets of His ministry from becoming primary. His second directive simply displayed His compassion for the little girl. He encouraged her parents to give her something to eat. She had been ill for some time and probably had not been able to consume food. Now she was completely restored to health and she needed food in order to strengthen her body. The compassion of the Savior is clearly seen as He authenticated Himself in this particular incident by giving life back to this little girl. Swete notes that in this concern of the Lord

> we have fresh evidence of the sympathetic tenderness of the Lord, and His attention to small details in which the safety or comfort of others was involved. In the excitement of the moment the necessity of maintaining the life which had been restored might have been overlooked. But life restored by miracle must be supported by ordinary means; the miracle has no place where human care or labour will suffice.[27]

HOMILETICAL SUGGESTIONS

This chapter contains two main incidents in the life of Jesus Christ, and each of them has many interesting ramifications to explore.

26. Hendriksen, *Exposition of the Gospel According to Mark,* 214.
27. Swete, *The Gospel According to St. Mark,* 110.

The story of Jesus dealing with the demon-possessed man prompts many questions. What is the nature of demon possession, and what does it do to a man? Who actually owned the herd of swine? Why did the herd owners have such disregard for the condition of the man? Also, the contrast between the people of the area of the Gerasenes and those who welcomed him back to Capernaum is truly remarkable.

The story of Jairus is a wonderful story of faith. Here is a man who clearly demonstrated faith in Jesus Christ, and even with an interruption that brought about another miracle, his faith in the Lord remained firm.

A number of parallels exist in the stories, for there is the reoccurring theme of illness and death, and the twelve years found in both stories. Some interesting contrasts occur. Three positive responses to the Savior are interspersed with two negative reactions. The interchange between the positive and the negative swings back and forth like the pendulum of a clock. First, there is the positive response to the Savior by the demon-possessed man. This is followed by the negative reaction of the people of the region who asked Jesus to leave. Then the woman with the issue of blood responds positively as she reaches out and touches His garment. This is followed by the negative reaction of the people who come from Jairus's home, telling him to no longer bother the Savior, and the scoffing laughter of the professional mourners. Finally, the pendulum swings back to the positive as Jairus and his wife respond in faith following the raising of their daughter from the dead.

MARK

C H A P T E R

SIX

THE SERVANT'S RESPONSE
TO OPPOSITION

THE REJECTION OF NAZARETH, 6:1-6
(cf. Matt. 13:54-58)

Some scholars believe that the event recorded here parallels the account in Luke 4:16-30. But it is probably better to understand that the Lukan account occurred about one year earlier, at the beginning of Jesus' Galilean ministry. At that time He was rejected and thrown out of the synagogue in Nazareth. "There is no real reason for identifying this visit to Nazareth with that recorded in Luke 4:16-30 at the beginning of the Galilean Ministry. He was rejected both times, but it is not incongruous that Jesus should give Nazareth a second chance."[1]

6:1   Jesus left the city of Capernaum and took the one-day walk of about twenty-five miles that brought Him back to His hometown, Nazareth. It was in Nazareth that Jesus had spent most of the first thirty years of His life. After going through Galilee and performing miracles, calling disciples, and preaching, He returned to attempt to minister again in "His home town" (*patrida* means "fatherland," "the place where one has been brought up"). Although Mark never refers directly to "Nazareth" in this context, he has previously noted that Nazareth was the village from which Jesus came (cf. 1:9, 24). This time as He came to the city He was accompanied by those disciples whom He

---

1. A. T. Robertson, *Word Pictures in the New Testament* (Nashville: Broadman, 1930), 1:305.

had called and who were following Him. "It was not a private visit to His family; He came as a Rabbi, surrounded by His scholars."[2]

6:2 When the Sabbath day came, Jesus naturally found His way to the synagogue. As a visiting rabbi with quite a growing reputation, He would certainly have been asked to speak. As "He began to teach in the synagogue," those who heard Him "were astonished" (*exeplēssonto,* imperfect tense indicating something that continued over a period of time). They marveled at the apparent "wisdom" (*sophia*) Jesus was displaying. They wondered what was the source of this man's wisdom. He had never attended the rabbinic schools of the time and, moreover, spoke as one who had His own authority. He did not quote others or use their authority in His messages. Where did He get these ideas? Furthermore, they wondered how He was able to bring to pass (*ginomenai,* present tense participle implying that such things were continually being wrought) the mighty "miracles" (*dynameis*) that they had heard about. "They felt that there was some hocus-pocus about it somehow and somewhere. They do not deny the wisdom of his words, nor the wonder of his works, but the townsmen knew Jesus and they had never suspected that he possessed such gifts and graces."[3]

6:3 They knew this man. He was their "carpenter" (*tektōn*). The Greek word *tektōn* was originally used of a man who worked with wood but later was used of any artisan or craftsman who worked in metal or stone. Apparently with the death of Joseph, Jesus had taken over the business and became "the carpenter of Nazareth." They had seen His hands perform work with wood as He worked among them for many years.

> It is worthy of note that here in Mark, Jesus himself is called "the carpenter," whereas in Matt. 13:55 he is called "the son of the carpenter." This cannot rightfully be called a discrepancy, since he may well have been called both. In times ancient and even comparatively recent a son would often, as to chosen occupation, follow in the footsteps of his father.[4]

---

2. Henry Barclay Swete, *The Gospel According to St. Mark* (Grand Rapids: Eerdmans, 1956), 111.

3. Robertson, *Word Pictures in the New Testament,* 1:305.

4. William Hendriksen, *Exposition of the Gospel According to Mark* (Grand Rapids: Baker, 1975), 222.

They acknowledged that He was "the son of Mary," but this was actually a derogatory comment, for a Jewish man was never identified with his mother, even if his father had died. "Rumors to the effect that Jesus was illegitimate appear to have circulated in his own lifetime and may lie behind this reference as well."[5] Or perhaps that comment was a reflection on the miraculous story surrounding His conception. Since that event had occurred in Nazareth, many of the people still living could remember some of the details of Mary and Joseph's engagement.

The brothers and sisters of Jesus are mentioned here as well. These were the children of the union of Joseph and Mary following His birth. Although some believe that Mary remained a virgin all of her life, the normal reading of the biblical texts seems to imply otherwise. Once the Savior was born, Mary and Joseph began to enjoy the normal relationships of a husband and wife, which in the process of time led to children. Named in the text are James, Joses, Judas, and Simon, and unnamed "sisters" are mentioned. That means that He had at least two sisters.

Though four brothers of Jesus were named, only James and Judas became prominent in the history of the church. James apparently became the head of the church at Jerusalem and served as moderator when the Jerusalem council met (cf. Acts 12:17; 15:13-29). It is also thought by many that he wrote the New Testament book of James. Judas was probably the one who wrote the New Testament book of Jude. Nothing is known about Joses and Simon other than that their names are given in the other list of "the Lord's brothers" (cf. Matt. 13:55). His sisters are never named and may be presumed to have been living with their husbands in Nazareth.

In effect what these people were saying was "We know this Jesus. He is common. He is one of us." As a result they stumbled over Him. They "took offense" (*eskandalizonto,* a graphic imperfect demonstrating their continued refusal to accept Jesus as legitimate) at the Savior.

6:4 This prompted Jesus to repeat a proverb well known at that time: "A prophet is not without honor except in his home town and among his own relatives and in his own household" (cf. Matt. 13:57). John reported (cf. John 4:44) that Jesus had made a similar comment earlier in His ministry when He returned to Galilee. He was picturing

5. William L. Lane, *The Gospel According to Mark,* NICNT (Grand Rapids: Eerdmans, 1974), 203.

Himself as an Old Testament prophet whose words were often rejected by those who were closest to Him. "Jesus' observation involves a
claim to the prophetic office and shows clearly the main function of a
prophet—that of proclaiming rather than predicting truth."[6]

The problem that the people were dealing with here was the
problem of familiarity. Jesus was familiar to them, and as a result they
did not listen to Him. They did not become His followers. The most
tragic aspect seems to be that those closest to Him, His own family,
disbelieved His messianic claims (cf. John 7:1-5). But at least some of
His family members later became His followers.

6:5   The unbelief of the city of Nazareth was so great that Jesus
could not perform miracles there. This does not mean that the power
of Jesus was lacking. He could have performed any miracle He wanted
to in that situation. But He never forced Himself on anyone, nor did
He force His miraculous acts on any city.

> It is not Mark's intention to stress Jesus' *inability* when he states that he
> could perform no miracles at Nazareth. His purpose is rather to indi-
> cate that Jesus was not free to exercise his power *in these circum-
> stances.* The performance of miracles in the absence of faith could have
> resulted only in the aggravation of human guilt and the hardening of
> men's hearts against God. The power of God which Jesus possessed
> could be materialized in a genuinely salutary fashion only when there
> was the receptivity of faith.[7]

Since they did not believe in Him, He did not demonstrate His power
among them except for healing "a few sick people" who came to Him
so that He could lay hands on them and heal them (*etherapeusen,*
aorist tense indicating a completed fact, not a continuous action).

6:6   The unbelief of the city of Nazareth caused the Lord Jesus to
wonder (*ethaumasen,* aorist tense summing up His emotion on this
occasion). It is mentioned only twice in the New Testament that Jesus
wondered or that He was amazed. The only other occurrence is with
reference to the Roman centurion and his faith (Matt. 8:10). Instead of
remaining in the city of Nazareth, He departed because of their unbelief and went around (*periēgen,* imperfect tense picturing the action
continuing over a period of time) to the villages of Galilee teaching.

---

6. Howard F. Vos, *Mark* (Grand Rapids: Zondervan, 1978), 55.
7. Lane, *The Gospel According to Mark,* 204.

THE MINISTRY TO COMBAT OPPOSITION, 6:7-13
(cf. Matt. 9:35–11:1; Luke 9:1-9)

6:7   Jesus had called twelve men to be with Him and that He might send them out to preach (3:14). The time had now arrived for the apostles to begin a ministry on their own. Consequently Jesus "summoned [*proskaleitai*, present tense picturing the action] the twelve [*tous dōdeka*]," who clearly by now were a recognized group, "and began to send them out [*apostellein*, present tense infinitive] in pairs." This verb is related to the noun "apostle," which literally means "one who is sent with the authority of another." Jesus sent out the Twelve "in pairs" (*duo duo*, "two by two," a Hebraism that also appears in some Greek writings). He gave them "authority over the unclean spirits." The verb "giving" (*edidou*) is in the imperfect tense, which "means he kept on giving them all through the tour, a continuous power (authority) over unclean spirits singled out by Mark as representing 'all manner of diseases and all manner of sickness' (Matt. 10:1), 'to cure diseases' (*iasthai*, Luke 9:1), healing power. They were to preach and to heal (Luke 9:1; Matt. 10:7)."[8] As they preached and cast out demonic spirits, they were demonstrating the authority of God.

6:8   Jesus' instruction to the apostles seemed a little strange at first. He told them that "they should take nothing for their journey, except a mere staff," which they probably already had in their possession. Every traveler and pilgrim carried a walking stick. But they were not to secure food or a traveling bag (*pēran*, a leather bag like a knapsack to carry provisions), nor were they even to take "money in their belt." The belt girding their body (*zōnēn*) provided pockets in which they could conceal their money. But Jesus told them that their pockets should be empty as they went.

6:9   They were told "to wear sandals" for the journey, but no extra pair was to be carried, nor were they to take with them "two tunics." The second tunic was often carried by a man at this time to provide a covering should he be required to spend the night out in the open. These instructions were given to the apostles only for this specific journey. The implication of what He told them was that they should not make elaborate preparations but should depend on Him to provide for them.

8. Robertson, *Word Pictures in the New Testament,* 308.

The specific terms of the commission demanded of the disciples a rigorous commitment to total dependence upon God for food and shelter. While the minimum requirements for the journey—staff and sandals—were permitted, they were to take nothing else. Bread, the beggar's bag, the smallest coin in the belt, or a second tunic to keep out the night chill were all excluded.[9]

6:10   He instructed them that whenever they entered a town they were to secure lodging in a home. Once that lodging was secured, they were to remain in that home until they were finished with their ministry in that city. This would keep the apostles from looking around for better accommodations and better provisions.

> They must not be so fastidious that whenever some small detail is not to their liking in one home, they immediately leave and enter another where the facilities seemed to be more desirable and the food more palatable. The spread of the gospel has the priority over personal likes and dislikes.[10]

It would also keep them from spreading gossip from one home to another as they ministered. It was clear that Jesus was telling them that accommodations would be provided for them if they would trust in Him.

6:11   If they found rejection as they went from town to town, they should not be surprised. Everyone did not always accept Jesus as He proclaimed His message; therefore, the message concerning Jesus as Messiah from the mouths of His disciples would undoubtedly also find opposition. But Jesus instructed that they should "shake off the dust from the soles of [their] feet for a testimony against them." It was a common practice for Jews leaving Gentile territory to pause and shake off the dust from their feet. Such an action was symbolic, showing that they did not want to carry any part of non-Judaism with them. To do so might contaminate their own country or their own home, thus making it "unclean." The disciples' actions, however, would show that when the message of Jesus Christ was rejected the issue was not a personal one. The people were not rejecting the messengers but the Messenger, the Lord Himself. Consequently the rejecting town would be considered as "Gentile territory," that is, unclean, and the

9. Lane, *The Gospel According to Mark*, 207-8.
10. Hendriksen, *Exposition of the Gospel According to Mark*, 230.

disciples would be free to move on to other locations. Their actions would be a testimony against those who rejected the word. "The action . . . was not to be performed in a contemptuous or vindictive spirit, but with a view to its moral effect: either it would lead to reflexion and possibly repentance, or at least it would justify God's future judgment (cf. Mt. x.15, [Lk.] x.12)."[11] Perhaps that testimony led some to repent and turn in faith to Jesus the Messiah.

6:12   Mark declares that the disciples "went out and preached" (*exelthontes akēruxan,* an aorist tense summarizing their preaching as an accomplished fact regarded as a whole). Their message was the same message that John the Baptist and Jesus had proclaimed, a message of repentance (*metanoōsin*). People needed to change their minds. The fact that the infinitive "to repent" is in the present tense implies that repentance is not simply a one-time act that followed their preaching. Once a person comes to an understanding of the Christian life, his life should be constantly characterized by repentance. These people were steeped in the traditions of their day, and they needed to look beyond those traditions to the true understanding of what God wanted from mankind.

6:13   As they preached they also demonstrated their authority by "casting out" (*exeballon,* imperfect tense implying that they continued to do this over a period of time) demons. Mark adds the notation that they anointed with oil (*ēleiphon elaiō,* also imperfect implying a continuous thing) many sick people, bringing about healing. Mark is the only gospel to mention anointing with oil for the purpose of healing. The only other occurrence of this in the New Testament is James 5:14. There is medicinal value in oil (cf. Luke 10:34), but whether the healing actually came from the oil or simply was an expression of God's grace could be debated. The anointing with oil was clearly an attempt to show that God was indeed pouring out His blessing on these people.

> That oil did at times serve as a symbol of the invigorating presence and power of the Spirit is very clear from Zech. 4:1-6. Matt. 25:2-4 also deserves consideration in this connection. In the light of Exod. 25:37 and Zech. 4:1-6 examine also Isa. 11:2; Rev. 1:4, 12. Now if that is true, then anointing the sick with oil meant, "Look to *God* for healing, not to us." It meant, "His Spirit is able to heal both body and soul."[12]

11. Swete, *The Gospel According to St. Mark,* 118.
12. Hendriksen, *Exposition of the Gospel According to Mark,* 232.

THE CIVIL RULER'S OPPOSITION, 6:14-29
(cf. Matt. 14:1-12; Luke 9:7-9)

THE FEAR OF HEROD, 6:14-16

6:14 News of the expanding ministry of the Twelve throughout Galilee, as well as that of Jesus Christ, eventually found its way into the palace of the ruler. "The [king's] court, even if located at Tiberius, could regard with indifference the preaching of a local prophet, so long as it was limited to the Jewish lake-side towns; but when it was systematically carried into every part of the country, suspicion was aroused."[13] Mark's reference to Herod as a "King" was probably an act of courtesy, for he technically was only a tetrarch, a ruler of a fourth part of an empire. When Herod the Great died, his territory was divided among four of his sons. This "Herod," whose given name was Antipas, ruled the regions of Galilee and Perea. Although he was only a tetrarch, it was customary to refer to all native rulers in the east as "kings," and Mark was writing for Romans who would understand it in that manner. William Lane suggests that "Mark's use of the royal title may reflect local custom, or it may be a point of irony. Herod had modeled his court after the imperial pattern, and it is possible that the irony of designating him by a title he coveted, but failed to secure, would have been appreciated in Rome where his sentence had been sealed."[14]

As the miraculous ministry of Jesus was becoming better known, some conclusions had to be drawn as to who this man really was. Some of the conclusions are stated in this account. One was that this was "John the Baptist [who had] risen from the dead." Just as Elijah was thought by some to have reappeared in John, so now some thought that John was reappearing in Jesus. Although John the Baptist had performed no miracles (cf. John 10:41), perhaps some thought that following his death he had received some kind of miraculous power and had come back to life to perform miracles. "Even Herod had theological insight enough to see that, once granted a resurrection, any other miracle is not only possible but logical."[15]

6:15 Others, however, were saying that this was the prophet Elijah, who had come back. It is not surprising that Elijah would be chosen

---

13. Swete, *The Gospel According to St. Mark,* 119-20.

14. Lane, *The Gospel According to Mark,* 211.

15. R. A. Cole, *The Gospel According to Mark* (Grand Rapids: Eerdmans, 1979), 110.

because of the prophecies that say Elijah must come before the Messiah appears (cf. Mal. 3:1; 4:5-6). John the Baptist had denied that he was Elijah (cf. John 1:21), so perhaps it was Jesus who was fulfilling the ancient prophecies. A third possibility was that Jesus was simply "a prophet, like one of the prophets" from olden times. Earlier Jesus had used the designation "prophet" of Himself (cf. v. 4). This was an acknowledgment that Jesus came with great power and authority.

6:16   The conclusion of Herod, however, agreed with the first alternative offered. Although Herod probably did not believe in resurrection, he clearly knew that John the Baptist was dead. He had issued the order that resulted in his beheading (*apekephalisa*). No doubt Herod could still picture that head on the platter. But when he learned of the ministry of Jesus Christ, his guilty conscience concluded that this must be John risen from the dead. This provides Mark with the opportunity to explain what had happened to John the Baptist. Although the death of John had occurred previously, no record of it had been given in Mark's gospel. Mark knew that the statement about his beheading required an explanation.

THE ACTIONS OF HEROD, 6:17-29
The story of John the Baptist's death is fully recorded by Mark. Matthew's account is not nearly as complete, and Luke briefly mentions the fact of his death. The difference in the three accounts is noted by Hendriksen when he says,

> To be sure, each Gospel has a beauty of its own. All are fully inspired. It would be rash to praise one Gospel above another. Matthew's reserve is as consonant with that evangelist's aim as is Mark's love for vivid detail, reflecting undoubtedly the preaching of an eye witness, effervescent Peter. But God be praised for having given the church, in his wisdom, not only Matthew, Luke, and John, but also the man who as a story-teller is unsurpassed among the four, namely, John Mark![16]

6:17   Mark begins by indicating that Herod "had John arrested." Since most of John the Baptist's ministry occurred in the wilderness of Perea, he came under the jurisdiction of Herod. According to the Jewish historian Josephus, Herod had John placed in the fortress palace of Machaerus, in the Judean wilderness near the northeastern shore of

16. Hendriksen, *Exposition of the Gospel According to Mark,* 236.

the Dead Sea. The reason for imprisonment was the preaching of John
against Herod because of his marital situation. From historical records
it is clear that Herod was married to the daughter of the Arab king of
Petra, Aretas IV. However, on one of his trips to Rome, when he was
seeking to gain greater favors from Caesar, he stayed in the home of
his half brother, Philip (not the same Philip as mentioned in Luke 3:1).
Philip was married to Herodias, a granddaughter of Herod the Great
through Aristobulus, and they had a daughter by the name of Salome.
Herod fell in love with his niece, Herodias, and persuaded her to return with him to Israel. She divorced Philip, he divorced his wife, and
they became husband and wife. Such a marital relationship was totally
contrary to the Law of Moses, and John the Baptist fearlessly de-
nounced Herod for this. The Mosaic Law could not be set aside by the
king, for its statutes applied equally to all in Israel.

6:18   John the Baptist had been preaching (*elegen,* aorist tense
summarizing his message as a completed fact) against Herod, reminding him that it was "not lawful for [him] to have [his] brother's wife."
Both Leviticus 18:16 and 20:21 make clear that a man was not to "uncover the nakedness of his brother's wife." To "uncover the nakedness" was an idiom that carried the idea of entering into sexual
relationship. Such an act is declared to be "abhorrent," or an impure
deed. The Levirate law enabled a man to marry a brother's wife only
after the brother was deceased. In light of the revelation in the New
Testament in Romans 7:2-3, it might also be concluded that the relationship of Herod and Herodias was adulterous. There is also a clear
reference in Leviticus 18:13 that expressly forbids the marriage of a
nephew to his aunt, though nothing is said in the Old Testament of
the marriage of an uncle to his niece. Some rabbis permitted such
marriages, but others prohibited them. Nevertheless, John the Baptist
viewed this marriage between Herod and Herodias as something that
was not permitted by the Mosaic Law.

6:19   Whereas Herod was upset with John's preaching, Herodias
was infuriated. The Greek verb *eveichen* carries the idea of "bearing a
grudge," and the imperfect tense indicates that this attitude continued
over a period of time. She became so angry with John the Baptist that
she "wanted to put him to death" (*ēthelen,* also imperfect showing a
continual wish) and would have done so but Herod had locked him
away in prison. Perhaps he thought that by removing him from society
he could silence the impact of his preaching. It is interesting, as many
scholars have noted, that the principal characters in this story, Herod

and Herodias, are much like an earlier duo in the history of the nation of Israel, Ahab and Jezebel. Perhaps the mention of Elijah in the context has something to do with creating that parallel. Both stories feature a weak king who vacillates and a very strong woman who seeks to carry out her plans.

6:20   According to Mark's rendering, Herod was actually very "afraid" (*ephobeito,* imperfect tense showing a continual state of fear) of John the Baptist. He knew he was a "righteous and a holy man" and, therefore, innocent of any wrong. He did everything he could to protect him and keep him safe (*syneterei,* also imperfect tense). In fact, it seems as though he even enjoyed times of sitting with John and "listening to him" (*hedeos autou ekouen,* another imperfect). But he was confused (*polla eporei,* "perplexed"; imperfect tense) by what John was telling him. He did not want to recognize his own sin and repent. He was also afraid of Herodias and surely knew of her hatred for "the Baptizer." He was a very confused man. He probably greatly admired John for his courage to stand up and speak his mind. Most of those gathered around Herod were flatterers, simply telling him what he wanted to hear. Surely he had a sense of guilt, realizing that he had divorced his own wife, stolen away his brother's wife, and arrested and imprisoned an innocent man.

6:21   The occasion finally arose that allowed Herodias to carry out her plan to do away with John. Herod was hosting a birthday party for himself at which a number of influential people were present. According to Mark, this birthday celebration had a very select guest list. First of all, present on this occasion were "his lords" (*tois megistasin),* which refers to the chief men of civil life. Second, "military commanders" (*tois chiliarchois)* were present, who represented military commanders of at least a thousand men. These were the chief military officers of Galilee and Perea. Finally, present on that occasion were "the leading men of Galilee" (*tois protois tes Galilaias),* the men of social prominence and importance. Clearly, a very special group of people was gathered at this banquet. Banquets of this kind were lively, and certainly the wine must have been flowing (cf. Est. 1:1-12).

6:22   When the banquet was reaching its peak, "the daughter of Herodias," Salome, "came in and danced" for the assembled guests. Such an event was totally unheard of in Jewish circles. A Jewish mother would never have encouraged a daughter to dance in a sensuous way in front of a group of men. That was the kind of thing a slave girl might do but never a princess. Therefore the statement that "the daughter of Herodias" came in and danced before this audience has caused some to reject the whole story. Lane, however, notes that

> the final objection, that it is wholly improbable that a Herodian princess would debase herself by dancing before the company of men assembled by the tetrarch, loses its force when consideration is given to the moral depravity of Antipas and Herodias. It is clear from the Marcan narrative that there was calculation on Herodias' part to achieve her will; the dancing of her daughter was a crucial element in her plan, and was probably arranged by Herodias herself.[17]

The dance of Salome greatly "pleased Herod and his dinner guests." Perhaps some of their pleasure stemmed from the fact that she was not a "professional" dancer but only a young, inexperienced "princess." It led the king to say to "the girl" (*korasiō*, meaning a young girl of marriageable age, probably a teenager), "Ask me for whatever you want and I will give it to you."

6:23   This phrase became a promise that he repeated with an oath. He even promised her "up to half of [his] kingdom." Herod, of course, did not have a kingdom that he could give away. This proverbial statement should probably be understood as hyperbole, for Herod was simply saying that he wanted to be very extravagant in his dealings with her, for she pleased him so much (cf. Est. 5:3 and 7:2 where a similar phrase may be found).

6:24   Salome left the banquet room and asked her mother what she should ask for. This implies that Herodias had not told Salome her complete plan in advance. She had probably instructed the girl to dance in such a way as to win Herod's approval. The opportunity was now here, and Herodias immediately responded by encouraging her daughter to ask for "the head of John the Baptist." This must have been something that Salome agreed with, for she expresses no shock or regret. Perhaps her mother had poisoned her thinking concerning John. Or perhaps she also relished the power she was holding over her stepfather.

6:25   She "immediately" (*euthys*) returned to the king and said that she wanted the head of John the Baptist "right away" (*exautēs*, "in this selfsame hour," meaning as quickly as possible). She further added that she wanted the head "on a platter" (*epi pinaki*, "a plate or a

---

17. Lane, *The Gospel According to Mark*, 217.

dish"). Perhaps the luxurious banquet had many platters of food sitting around, and her request was for the head of John to be delivered on one of those platters.

6:26   This greatly saddened the king. Surely he was distressed because he admired John and did not want to kill him. He also must have realized that his wife had tricked him. He did not want to see John executed, but he had taken an oath. However, there were some ways he could have gotten out of his predicament. Hendriksen points out that he could have said "to Salome, 'I promised to favor you with a *gift;* I did not promise to commit a *crime.*' Or else, 'I promised *you,* not your mother, a gift.' Best of all would have been the way of escape pointed out in Lev. 5:4-6."[18] But he saw no way to save face before his dinner guests, so he did not refuse the request.

6:27   Instead he immediately sent "an executioner" (*spekoulatora*) and commanded that the head of John the Baptist be brought back.

> The designation for the guardsman charged with the execution transliterates the Latin form *speculator.* The *speculatores* were a well-known division of the imperial guard at Rome. These soldiers served as a police force, and in the pages of Tacitus tend to figure in moments of military intrigue. The use of the Latin term for the guardsman ordered to execute John is appropriate to the context, and offers further illustration of Herod's attempt to pattern his court after the imperial administration.[19]

That individual went and carried out the sentence. The close proximity of prison to the location of the banquet probably implies that this event took place in the palace at Machaerus in the Judean wilderness.

6:28   The head of John the Baptist was brought and given to the girl. Her callousness is obvious as she immediately brought the "treasure" to her mother. "One wonders whether even Herod's callous courtiers were used to such a banquet dish as this. Rash oaths are condemned by the Lord in Matthew v. 34: rash oaths brought Jephthah into agony (Jdg. xi. 31ff.) and nearly undid Saul (I Sa. xiv. 38ff.)."[20]

6:29   Matthew 11:2 implies that even though he was in prison, John had some contact with "his disciples." It is not surprising that following his death they were permitted to properly bury his decapitated

18. Hendriksen, *Exposition of the Gospel According to Mark,* 241.
19. Lane, *The Gospel According to Mark,* 222.
20. Cole, *The Gospel According to Mark,* 112.

body. It is clear from Matthew 14:12 that after they performed the burial they came and reported this news to Jesus. This is the last recorded mention of the disciples of John in this gospel. What happened to them? It is clear that many of John's followers had become disciples of Jesus and that that was what John wanted them to do (cf. John 3:22-36). Paul later encountered those who considered themselves to be followers of John the Baptist (cf. Acts 18:24-25; 19:1-5). These individuals only knew about the baptism of John. In both cases Paul introduced them more fully to the person of Jesus as the Messiah, and they became believers in Him.

THE SERVANT'S INSTRUCTION
IN VIEW OF OPPOSITION, 6:30-52

THE INTENDED RETREAT, 6:30-32
(cf. Matt. 14:13-14; Luke 9:10-11; John 6:1-3)

6:30 Mark's gospel now returns to the story that had been interrupted by the details concerning the death of John the Baptist at the hands of King Herod. The twelve apostles "gathered together [*synagontai,* present tense to picture the action] with Jesus" and reported to Him what "they had done" (*epoiēsan,* aorist) and what they had "taught" (*edidaxan,* also aorist summing up their actions and their teachings as a completed fact). The exact location of the meeting is not given nor is the time factor. It is not known how long their mission lasted. It appears that there must have been some prearranged time and location for the twelve men to return, which may have coincided with the arrival of John's disciples, leading in turn to the course the Lord undertook. Many believe that they returned to the city of Capernaum, and it was there that this report occurred.

6:31 Jesus realized that they had been actively involved in ministry and needed to get away. Moreover, even as they were discussing all that had happened, they were constantly being interrupted by people who were "coming and going." The press of the crowd was so great that "they did not even have time to eat" (*oude phagein eukairoun,* imperfect tense indicating constant activity). This further lends support to the idea that they met in a town where Jesus was well known. Every time He came to Capernaum He attracted large crowds. Therefore, Jesus suggested to the Twelve that they depart "to a lonely place and rest a while." The middle voice used with these verbs implies that the disciples needed to refresh themselves. Literally they needed to rest up.

6:32   Jesus and the disciples departed by boat "to a lonely place" where they could talk more freely about what had happened in their ministries. "Periodic reference to 'the boat,' rather than 'a boat,' leads to the conclusion that it was one available to the apostolic company virtually on demand and presumably belonged to the partnership of Peter, Andrew, James, and John."[21] While Mark did not specify the location, the parallel passage in Luke 9:10 implies that their withdrawal was to the northeastern side of the Sea of Galilee near the area where the Jordan River empties into the sea. That area was known as Bethsaida Julias.

THE ACTUAL REALITY, 6:33-44
(cf. Matt. 14:15-21; Luke 9:12-17; John 6:6-13)

6:33   The intent of the Savior was to take the disciples to an isolated location where they could rest. But many people recognized where they were headed and went around the shore on foot in order to arrive there before Jesus and His disciples. The distance would be no more than four or five miles, and if there was little wind they could easily have arrived before the boat. As the people ran they also went into the cities of that area and informed people what was happening. The news spread rapidly that Jesus and the disciples were back in their area.

6:34   By the time the disciples and the Lord actually arrived, a large crowd had already gathered on the shore. One can understand how disappointment might have set in, for this had been anticipated as an opportunity to get away. But Jesus did not view the crowd as an inconvenience. Instead He saw them as opportunity for ministry. Mark reports that "He felt compassion for them." In fact, He saw them as sheep who did not possess a shepherd.

> No animal is as dependent as is a sheep. Without someone to guide it, it wanders, is lost, becomes food for wolves, etc. Without someone to graze it, it starves. Jesus knows that people are like that: their leaders fail to give them reliable guidance. They do not supply their souls with nourishing food. The minds of the would-be guides are too occupied

21. Vos, *Mark,* 59.

with legalistic niceties about sabbath restrictions, fasts, phylacteries, tassels, etc., to be concerned about souls."[22]

Jesus, of course, is the true shepherd (John 10:1-21), and as the true shepherd He was concerned about the needs of the sheep. That was why "He began to teach [*didaskein,* present tense infinitive stressing a continuous activity] them many things," and His teaching continued throughout most of that day.

6:35   As it began to get late, the disciples became concerned. They came to Jesus and reminded Him that they were in a desolate area and that it was getting "quite late" in the day. There is a notation in the gospel of John (cf. 6:4) that this event occurred during the time of year when the Jewish Passover Feast would be observed. That would mean that this event occurred in the spring. It also implied that the setting of the sun probably would have occurred somewhere around 6:00 P.M. The disciples probably were becoming very concerned as the late afternoon hour approached. Perhaps their comment to Jesus may have occurred several hours before sunset.

6:36   Their solution was to send the people away so that they might go into surrounding villages to secure food for themselves. Bethsaida Julias was not far away, and other smaller towns might also have been able to provide some food. It is ironic that Jesus had earlier sent the disciples out to the multitudes, but now, when the multitudes came to the disciples, they tried to send them away.

6:37   Jesus' answer probably startled the disciples: "You give them something to eat!" The emphasis in the statement is on "you." Their immediate reaction to His command was that He intended for them to go and purchase food for the people to eat. Philip made the calculation (John 6:7) that it would cost two hundred denarii to purchase enough bread for each person to be provided with "something" to eat, that is, just "a bite." A denarius was the amount of money a common laborer would make for one day's labor. Two hundred denarii, therefore, would be the equivalent of more than eight months of work. It is unlikely that the disciples actually had that much money, if indeed there was some place they could have purchased the food.

6:38   Jesus then asked the disciples to determine what their resources were. He encouraged them to look around and see "how many loaves" of bread they actually had. The disciples must have scur-

---

22. Hendriksen, *Exposition of the Gospel According to Mark,* 250.

ried through the crowd and even gone back to the boat to see if they had brought any food with them. As a result of their search, Andrew located a boy who had a grand total of five loaves and two fish (John 6:8-9). The actual loaves were reported by John to be the small barley type, the common food of the poor. They were made of the coarsest and cheapest barley flour. The fish are not identified, but they were probably either smoked or pickled.

6:39   Jesus then began to issue commands. He brought order out of chaos when He told the assembled crowd to sit in groups. The words "by groups" "could be rendered 'table company by table company' (*symposia symposia,* lit., 'drinking or eating parties')."[23] Mark alone notes that they reclined by groups on the "green" grass. The reference to green grass in this verse helps date this event as occurring in the springtime and confirms the comment in John 6:4 (see v. 35 above). That is the normal time of year, following the winter and spring rains, when the grass in the Galilee region greens up. Once again Mark adds a vivid detail to the story.

6:40   Mark records also that "they reclined in companies of hundreds and of fifties." The expression that Mark used here for "companies" (*prasiai prasiai*) is unique. Literally the term refers to garden plots. Mark's statement pictures these people reclining "garden plot by garden plot" in the green grass. Such a scene is truly quite vivid. The people, probably attired in brightly colored clothing, sitting together in groups of hundreds and fifties as the apostles served the food, looked like garden plots all in bloom dotting the green landscape.

> The purpose of the arrangement was probably to prevent a dangerous scramble for the food, or at any rate, confusion and disorder (cf. I Cor. xiv.33, 40), and to secure an easy and rapid distribution: twelve men could serve fifty to one hundred companies in a comparatively short time. Incidentally the division into companies made the counting of the multitude a simple matter, and accounts for the same number being given by the four evangelists.[24]

6:41   Jesus Christ "took the five loaves and the two fish" in His hands and looked upward "toward heaven" to provide a blessing. The

---

23. John D. Grassmick, "Mark," in *Bible Knowledge Commentary* (Wheaton, Ill.: Victor, 1983), 130.
24. Swete, *The Gospel According to St. Mark,* 133-34.

blessing was one of thanksgiving for God's provisions. After "He blessed the food," He began to break the loaves and kept on breaking them and the fish into baskets that were given (*edidou,* imperfect tense indicating a repeated action) to the disciples. After all, Jesus had said to the disciples, "You give them something to eat!" (v. 37). The disciples became the ones who carried the provision to the crowd. The miracle occurred in the hands of the Lord as He multiplied the loaves and the fish.

As the disciples passed the baskets among the people, they were emptied. What were the disciples to do at that point? They were to return to the Lord, where there was the provision of food. Jesus by this miracle was teaching the apostles that they would be the ones to provide nourishment and strength to God's people following His departure. But that provision always comes from the Lord Himself.

> The miracle took place before the multitude, but there is no indication in the Marcan text that they had any realization of what was taking place. . . . The messianic meal remained hidden from the thousands. The event is intended to be revelatory to the disciples alone. They are the ones who prompt the action, who bring the loaves and fish, who distribute the meal and who gather the fragments. In contrast to their usually passive stance Jesus actively involved them in the total proceedings.[25]

6:42   It is clear that all who were present on this occasion "ate and were satisfied" (*ephagon . . . exortasthēsan,* aorist tense summarizing the satisfaction as a completed event). According to the estimate of the disciples, eight months' worth of wages would have been necessary to provide a small amount of food for each person. When the Savior, however, provides the food, there is abundance.

6:43   There was such abundance that, when the meal was over and they picked up the extra scraps, there were "twelve . . . baskets" (*kophinōn*) full of broken pieces of bread and of fish. The word *kophinōn* is used in all four accounts. It was a stout wicker-type basket common among the poorer class of Jews. Swete suggests that perhaps these baskets were "those in which the Apostles had carried what they needed for their recent circuit of Galilee."[26] Some have suggested that this turned out to be the "tip" for the servers, the twelve apostles. Perhaps it became their food for the next day.

25. Lane, *The Gospel According to Mark,* 232.
26. Swete, *The Gospel According to St. Mark,* 135.

6:44 Mark adds the final comment that the number of men who were fed on that occasion were 5,000. The number was probably a rough calculation based on the number of companies that were there. Matthew in his gospel adds the notation women and children were also present (Matt. 14:21). This miracle of the feeding of the 5,000 men, plus women and children, is the only miracle other than the resurrection that is recorded in all four gospels. Truly this was a significant miracle of the Savior. But in light of the comment that Jesus will make in 6:52, it appears that His disciples failed to understand its meaning.

THE AUTHENTICATING SIGNS, 6:45-56

Walking on the Water, 6:45-52 (cf. Matt. 14:22-33; John 6:14-21)

6:45 Mark states that "immediately" (*euthys*) following the miracle of the feeding of the 5,000, Jesus "made His disciples get into the boat and go ahead of Him to the other side to Bethsaida." The urgency in this statement is not revealed in Mark's gospel. But when one reads the parallel account in John 6:14-15, it becomes clear why He sent the disciples away. As a result of the feeding of the multitudes, the people concluded that Jesus truly was the Prophet who was to come into the world. They intended, according to John 6:15, to take Him by force and make Him the King. What a subtle temptation this would have been, especially for the disciples who had just returned from a victorious preaching mission. With the sudden adulation of the crowd, who knows what might have happened? But the time was not right. This was one year before Jesus would present Himself as the rightful King of the nation of Israel. This was also the wrong place. This was Galilee, not Jerusalem. Therefore Jesus put the disciples in a boat and told them to go toward Bethsaida. But Mark's statement causes some confusion. Probably the best solution is to conclude that, although Bethsaida Julius was on the eastern side of the Jordan River in that area, the region of Bethsaida spread across the western side of the Jordan along the Sea of Galilee back toward Capernaum. Jesus encouraged the disciples to head their boat in that direction while He dispersed (*apoluei,* present tense picturing Jesus persuading the crowds to go away) the multitude and sent them away.

6:46 After Jesus had bid the multitude farewell, He departed to a mountain to pray.

The evangelist speaks of Jesus' withdrawal to a solitary place for prayer after the excitement of the sabbath activity in Capernaum (Ch. 1:35-39), after the miracle of the loaves (Ch. 6:45f.), and following the Last Supper (Ch. 14:26-42). In each case it is night and Jesus finds himself in a moment of crisis prompted by the enthusiasm of the crowds or the impending passion. On this occasion it was the threat inherent in irresponsible excitement which prompted Jesus to retreat from the people.[27]

There truly was temptation here for the Savior to go His own way and in His own power try to accomplish His role as Messiah/King. But the timing was not right, and Jesus retreated to a mountain to pray.

6:47 When it was evening the boat with the disciples in it "was in the midst" of the Sea of Galilee, and Jesus was alone on the land. Only Mark notes that He spent some time alone on the shore of the Sea. The fact that this occurred near the time of Passover probably means that there was a near-full moon, and the disciples rowing on the Sea were probably clearly visible. They apparently had not made much progress.

6:48 They were "straining at the oars" because a northerly wind was blowing against them, driving them off course. They had rowed for many hours, yet had gone a very short distance. Finally, at "the fourth watch of the night," sometime between 3:00 and 6:00 A.M., Jesus decided to join them, as He had implied in v. 45, by walking out to them on the water. This, of course, would be no problem for the Creator of the universe. The One who had created water could walk on it, if He so chose.

> The reader is left to complete the picture; the Lord must be imagined as walking on a seething sea, not upon a smooth surface . . . now on the crest of a wave, now hidden out of sight. It was the darkest hour of the night, and the moon probably had set; only the outline of a human form could be seen appearing from time to time, and approaching the boat.[28]

Mark alone makes the interesting statement that "He intended to pass by them." That should not be understood as implying that the Savior was simply going to bypass the boat and keep going. Rather, He in-

27. Lane, *The Gospel According to Mark,* 235.
28. Swete, *The Gospel According to St. Mark,* 138.

tended to "pass by" in the sense of an Old Testament appearance of Jehovah, a theophany. Such language is used with the theophanies in the Septuagint. His purpose in doing so was simply to reassure them of His presence. He had sent them out in the boat, and He was aware of their circumstances.

6:49   The disciples, however, all "saw Him" and were greatly frightened. The text literally says that "they cried up" (*anekraxan*), implying that a great shriek of terror went up. They did not conclude that it was Jesus. They came to the conclusion that surely this "was a ghost," a phantasm (*phantasma*). There was popular belief among the Jews in spirits or ghosts based perhaps on passages such as Job 4:15ff.; 20:8. Apparently people other than Herod Antipas (cf. v. 14), including the Twelve, held superstitious beliefs.

6:50   Mark explains that when "they all saw Him" at the same time, they were truly "frightened" (*etaraxthēsan*). The verb that Mark uses here for "frightened" is very descriptive. It was used in Matthew 2:3 to describe Herod the Great's horror when he learned about the birth of the "King of the Jews." If the verb is found in the active voice, it can mean "to shake," "stir up," or "trouble." When it is used in the passive, as it is here, it carries the idea of being terrified or frightened. But Jesus immediately spoke words of encouragement to them.

He was saying (*legei,* present tense picturing a most vivid scene), "Take courage; it is I, do not be afraid." The verbs here are imperatives and should have been obeyed because of who spoke them. The statement "It is I" could be understood to mean that Jesus was identifying Himself to them. "It is I—Jesus!" It is also possible that the statement "It is I" (lit. "I am"), could have been an echo of the Old Testament formula of God's self-revelation, "I am who I am" (cf. Ex. 3:14). It should be noted that in the parallel account of this story recorded in Matthew 14:22-33, it is revealed that Peter got out of the boat and walked on the water to meet the Lord. If Mark got his material about Jesus from Simon Peter, would he not have known of Peter's walking on the water? Perhaps that part of the story was purposefully omitted so that Peter was not made to either look good because he walked on the water or to look bad because he later sank.

6:51   Mark declares that, as soon as Jesus "got into the boat" with the disciples, the wind that they had been battling for some time immediately stopped. Whether this is a further indication of His sovereignty or simply a fact that coincided with His entering the boat cannot be conclusively determined. Regardless of the reason, the disciples "were greatly astonished" (*existanto,* an imperfect tense indicating their astonishment extended over a period of time). Matthew 14:33 notes that when they were all in the boat the disciples worshiped Him, saying, "You are certainly God's Son!"

6:52 Mark says they were greatly astonished because they failed to gain "insight from the [previous] incident of the loaves [and the fish]." Indeed, their hearts "were hardened." Truly these miracles coming in such close proximity should have reminded the disciples again of the true character of the Lord Jesus. He is the Son of God who has power over creation, for both of these events were "nature" miracles. He can create food; He can walk on water. "Somehow the miracles connected with the multiplication of food failed to impress the Twelve (cf. viii. 17ff.); perhaps their administration of the food diverted their thoughts from the work wrought by the Lord."[29] But a heart that is not open to Him can become hardened if one is not careful. The heart in Scripture seems to be the fulcrum of people's feelings and faith, as well as the place from which words and actions spring. It is the root of a person's intellectual, emotional, and volitional life.

> When Mark says that the hearts of these disciples were "hardened," this probably means that the obtuseness of The Twelve, their inability to draw the necessary conclusions from the miracles of Jesus, was the result of sinful neglect to ponder and meditate on these marvelous works and on the nature of the One who performed them.[30]

Healings at Gennesaret, 6:53-56 (cf. Matt. 14:34-36)

6:53 According to v. 45, Jesus made the disciples get into a boat and depart immediately for "the other side to Bethsaida," while He sent the multitude away and then went to the mountain to pray. After He joined them in the boat, Mark continues his narrative by telling of another experience that happened after they had crossed over and landed at Gennesaret. Many scholars believe that the storm had driven them off course and they had not been able to land at Bethsaida or even at Capernaum. Gennesaret was located on the shore of the Sea of Galilee in the plain that bore its name. The Plain of Gennesaret was a very fertile area approximately two miles wide and four miles long that extended to the northwest from the Sea. It was over this plain that

29. Ibid., 139-40.

30. Hendriksen, *Exposition of the Gospel According to Mark,* 263.

the storms of the Sea of Galilee were often generated. The disciples came to Gennesaret and anchored there.

6:54   If Jesus and the disciples had been seeking a place of solitude and rest, Gennesaret would not prove to be that. "Immediately" (*euthys*) as they came out of the boat, people from that region "recognized" (*epignontes,* "a full knowledge") Jesus. They knew Him from their previous experiences with Him. Perhaps some of these people had even been present at the recent feeding of the 5,000.

6:55   The result was that they began to run around (*periedramon*) throughout the entire region and brought to Jesus on pallets those who were sick. The verb action in this verse pictures the frenzied activity of people carrying their sick friends to the various places they thought Jesus might be. If they could not find Him in one location, they tried another.

6:56   Wherever Jesus "entered" (*eiseporeueto,* imperfect tense picturing continuous activity), in villages or in different cities or in the countryside, He was constantly encountering sick people in the marketplaces. They simply were asking that they might reach out and touch "the fringe of his cloak" (*kraspedou*). The fringe of the cloak referred to the blue-banded fringe that the Law required all male Jews to have on the corners of their outer garments (cf. Num. 15:38). Since Jesus obeyed the Law in all of its aspects, He surely would have worn this tassel as part of His garments. Perhaps the word had reached this region concerning the healing of the woman with the issue of blood (cf. 5:25ff.; Matt. 9:20ff.). Faith is always honored, and those who "touched" (*hepsanto,* aorist tense indicating a completed act) the fringe of His cloak were healed (*esōzonto,* imperfect tense indicating healing for all who touched) because of their faith in the person of Jesus. "As with the woman with the issue of blood, so here, healing power flowed from His person in response to faith; there was nothing magical in His clothing."[31]

HOMILETICAL SUGGESTIONS

This chapter contains many interesting preaching points. The unbelief of the citizens of Nazareth has always been amazing to this author. How could these people, who had spent a great deal of time with Jesus Christ, not believe in Him? Surely the danger of allowing

31. Vos, *Mark,* 63.

things to become so familiar that their significance is lost is clear in this story.

A rewarding study is the sending out of the Twelve. The parallel accounts from the other gospels as noted in the commentary have interesting points of comparison.

The story of what happened to John the Baptist brings out some clear analogies to Elijah in his role as the forerunner of the Messiah. As the one who came in the spirit and power of Elijah, John the Baptist encountered an oppressive king with an extremely powerful wife who was out to do to him whatever she could. The sad story of the Baptist's death is a classic case of a righteous man coming to an untimely end.

The feeding of the 5,000 is a significant miracle since it is the only miracle other than the Resurrection that is recorded in all four gospels. The way John's gospel follows that event with the fact that the people were ready to make Him King (cf. John 6:14-15) points up what a significant event that miracle was in the eyes of the people.

That Jesus walked on the water is not surprising since God has authority over all creation. The fact that Mark omits Peter's walking on the water is a surprise, but Peter probably instructed Mark not to communicate that part of the story.

The continued impact of the Savior's ministry to deal with the physical needs of people concludes this chapter. The frenzy of activity, as people did their best to bring those who were ill to Him, cannot be missed. But His primary purpose in coming into the world was not to provide physical healing but to bring spiritual salvation for all mankind.

MARK

CHAPTER
SEVEN

THE SERVANT'S REJECTION
BY THE PHARISEES

THE PHARISEES' CONTINUED OPPOSITION, 7:1-23
(cf. Matt. 15:1-20)

The material that Mark presents in this section is not directly connected with the preceding narrative. The way Mark 6 as well as Matt. 14 ends, Jesus was pictured as being actively engaged in healing the sick in the plain of Gennesaret. From a comparison with the other gospels, it appears that He and the disciples left there and proceeded to Capernaum, where He then delivered the discourse on the bread of life (John 6:22-71). It may have been in connection with that discourse, or shortly thereafter, that the events described here in Mark 7:1-23 occurred.

THE "VIOLATION" STATED, 7:1-5

7:1 Mark reveals that a delegation of Pharisees and religious leaders "had come from Jerusalem" to investigate what Jesus of Nazareth was doing (cf. 3:22-30). Some believe that the Pharisees were local Galileans and that only the scribes had come down from Jerusalem. The parallel passage in Matthew 15, however, implies that both groups were from Jerusalem. In this encounter, a delegation of Pharisees, along with some scribes, confronted Jesus concerning a problem.

The scribes were a group of professional students and defenders of the law, both scriptural and traditional.

157

It is proper to speak of the *profession* of the scribes, and the *sect* of the Pharisees. The *scribes* were the law specialists. They studied, interpreted, and taught the law, that is, the Old Testament. More exactly they transmitted to their own generation the traditions which from generation to generation had been handed down with respect to the interpretation and application of the law, traditions that had their origin in the teaching of the venerable rabbis of long ago. . . . Naturally many scribes were also Pharisees.[1]

They are also referred to in Scripture as "lawyers" because they were entrusted with administrating the law as judges. These individuals had probably traveled to Galilee at the request of the Sanhedrin to discover charges that could be used against Jesus.

7:2 They would, of course, be quick to point out any violation of the Law or traditions they could connect with Jesus or His disciples. In this instance, they had seen some of the disciples (no names are given) "eating their bread with impure hands." The Greek word for impure or unclean (*koinais*) "meant what was common to everybody, like the Koiné Greek. But in later Greek it came also to mean as here what is vulgar or profane. So Peter [uses it] in Acts 10:14 [to mean] 'common and unclean.' The next step was ceremonially unclean."[2] Mark quickly explained for his predominantly Gentile readers that "impure hands" meant "unwashed" hands. The issue here was not one of personal hygiene but one of ceremonial washings that were extremely important to the strict Pharisees.

They attacked Him, not personally, but through His disciples (verse 2), as in ii. 24 they had attacked His disciples for eating corn and in ii.18 they had criticized the failure of the disciples to fast. They here attack them on a point of ritual, not one of faith, and a point of ritual drawn not directly from the law, but from the body of explanatory tradition that was growing up round the law, later to form the Mishnah and Gemara, the modern Jewish Talmud.[3]

7:3 Mark continues with a detailed explanation for his Gentile readers as to the nature of ceremonial washings. As one would expect, there is no explanation of this tradition at all in Matthew's gospel.

1. William Hendriksen, *Exposition of the Gospel According to Mark* (Grand Rapids: Baker, 1975), 271.
2. A. T. Robertson, *Word Pictures in the New Testament* (Nashville: Broadman, 1930), 1:321.
3. R. A. Cole, *The Gospel According to Mark* (Grand Rapids: Eerdmans, 1979), 118.

Mark tried to help his readers understand that the Pharisees and all other Jewish people normally would not eat a meal unless they first very carefully washed their hands. The Greek text here says "with the fist" (*pygmē*), implying careful washing of one's hands for ceremonial cleansing. Though not part of the Mosaic Law, it was a tradition that had been passed down by the elders of the nation.

7:4   Mark further explained that this practice not only was followed when strict Jews sat down to eat a meal but was something observed whenever they returned from the marketplace. Any trip to the market would inevitably bring about ceremonial defilement because of the mixing of humanity, for not every Jew strictly observed the traditions of the elders and there was the possibility that one might come in contact with a Gentile. Therefore, when they came home, they would immediately "cleanse themselves." Mark adds that there were "many other things" that the Jews practiced involving cleansing, such as the meticulous "washing of cups and pitchers and copper pots."

> It is probable that a tone of irony is intended, however, when [Mark] makes a sweeping reference to the oral tradition ("and many other things there are, which they have received to hold") and concludes his catalogue with reference to the "washing of cups and pots and copper vessels." There may be here a certain justifiable impatience with the mass of detail which was later codified in the Mishnah tractate *Kelim* (Vessels), but it has the effect of exposing the oral law to ridicule. Mark's final remark serves to broaden the issue from the washing of hands to cultic cleansing per se.[4]

7:5   Mark returns to his story at this point and presents the actual violation the Pharisees brought up. They asked Jesus, "Why do Your disciples not walk according to the tradition of the elders . . . ?" since some of them ate their bread with hands that had not been ceremonially cleansed. Although they did not accuse Jesus of doing this Himself, they were in effect saying that He, as the head of this group of individuals, was responsible for their actions. They had levied the same accusation against Him in 2:23-24. A failure to observe the traditions of the elders was considered to be a significant breach of authority, and Jesus was held accountable. He accepted their challenge, for in His answer He never mentions the disciples.

4. William L. Lane, *The Gospel of Mark,* NICNT (Grand Rapids: Eerdmans, 1974), 247.

THE SERVANT'S EXPLANATION, 7:6-13

7:6   Although Jesus did not attempt to defend His disciples, He did take the offensive against the religious leaders by using scriptural arguments from Isaiah and Moses. First, He quoted from Isaiah 29:13: "This people honors Me with their lips, but their heart is far away from Me." When Jesus said that Isaiah rightly called these individuals hypocrites, He

> did not necessarily mean that Isaiah was thinking of the Pharisees and scribes of Jesus' day. He probably meant that what the prophet wrote concerning the people of his own day was still relevant, for both then and now those condemned were honoring God with their lips, while their hearts were far removed from him. History was repeating itself.[5]

This is the only time in Mark that the term "hypocrite" (*hypokritōn*) appears, although the related word "hypocrisy" appears in 12:15. Literally "hypocrite" refers to one who speaks from behind a mask. It was used with reference to actors on the Greek stage, who often wore exaggerated masks portraying an emotion, and yet one never saw the face of the actor behind the mask. The mask enabled the actor to be something he was not. His own emotions could be concealed by the mask. He might be heartbroken in his personal life but portrayed someone who was filled with joy. Jesus said these religious leaders were hypocrites because they were seeking to honor God with their lips and yet their hearts were far away from Him.

7:7   The illustration Jesus used to support His charge of hypocrisy was with regard to their worship. It was vain, or empty, for them to seek to worship God when they were seeking to substitute the ideas of mere men for clearly stated doctrines.

> History reveals that the Jewish religious leaders came to honor their traditions far above the Word of God. Rabbi Eleazer said, "He who expounds the Scriptures in opposition to the tradition has no share in the world to come." The *Mishna*, a collection of Jewish traditions in the *Talmud*, records, "It is a greater offense to teach anything contrary to the voice of the Rabbis than to contradict Scripture itself." But before we criticize our Jewish friends, perhaps we should examine what influ-

---

5. Hendriksen, *Exposition of the Gospel According to Mark*, 274-75.

ence "the church fathers" are having in our own Christian churches. We also may be guilty of replacing God's truth with man's traditions.[6]

7:8   Jesus accused the religious leaders of "neglecting the [clear] commandment of God" in order to "hold to the traditions of men." He made a clear contrast here between God's commandment and man's traditions. Surely if one had to choose between commandments and traditions, one would accept the commandments over the traditions. Yet the Jews had devised their own system of many elaborate traditions to carry out what they considered to be the commands of Torah. They had divided the Torah into 613 separate decrees, 365 of them prohibitions and 248 of them positive declarations.

> Then, in connection with each decree, by drawing arbitrary distinctions between what they considered "permitted" and "not permitted," they had attempted to regulate every detail of the conduct of the Jews: their sabbaths, travel, meals, fasts, ablutions, trade, relation towards outsiders, etc., etc. . . . Thus, having an eye only for the multiplicity of the decrees and of their myriad applications to concrete life situations, they had piled up precept upon precept (cf. Isa. 28:10, 13) until at last, by most of these scribes and Pharisees, the unity and purpose of God's holy law—see Deut. 6:4; then Lev. 19:18; Mic. 6:8; cf. Mark 12:28-34— had suffered a total eclipse.[7]

7:9   Jesus pointed out that they had a clever way of setting aside "the commandment of God in order to keep [their] traditions." The irony is that they were trying to honor God with their lips, but by their decisions they were making themselves into God. Their traditions were being set above His law.

7:10   To substantiate His statement, Jesus gave an illustration with reference to the fifth commandment and the position of the elders on the sanctity of an oath. He quoted a clear commandment in which Moses stated God's word both in the positive and in the negative. The positive statement comes from Exodus 20:12, where God gave as one of the Ten Commandments "Honor your father and your mother." This same idea was repeated in Exodus 21:17, where it was given in the negative: "He who speaks evil of father or mother, let him be put to death." One cannot argue with a clear commandment given in

---

6. Warren W. Wiersbe, *Be Diligent* (Wheaton, Ill.: Victor, 1987), 71-72.

7. Hendriksen, *Exposition of the Gospel According to Mark,* 275-76.

Scripture. As to the meaning of the commandment, to honor father and mother meant more than simply to obey them. "To honor implies to love, to regard highly, to show the spirit of respect and consideration. This honor is to be shown to *both* of the parents, for as far as the child is concerned they are equal in authority."[8] The seriousness of an offense against one's parent is indicated by the fact that the death penalty was decreed for anyone who cursed his parents or treated them with contempt.

7:11 But Jesus said that the religious leaders of His day had figured out a way to get around this commandment. All a man had to do was to turn to his father or mother and say that anything of his, even if it might have been of financial help to the parents, had been declared "Corban," or devoted to God. Mark explained this term for his Gentile readers, using the Greek word *dōron,* which meant "a gift." No matter what the situation might be, all a man had to say was that the thing was "Corban."

7:12 In effect, what that did was no longer permit the father or the mother to benefit in any way from that particular thing. Thus one can see how easy it would be to deprive one's parents of possible financial aid, for declaring something to be Corban did not necessarily mean that one had to give it up. It was entirely possible that the thing devoted to God could still be retained by the individual.

> Should the son regret his action and seek to alleviate the harsh vow which would deprive his parents of all the help they might normally expect from him, he would be told by the scribes to whose arbitration the case was submitted that his vow was valid and must be honored. Jesus' statement that the scribes do not allow him to do "anything" for his parents is not extreme. The renunciation of all profitability extended beyond financial support to such practical kindness as assistance in the performance of religious duties or the provision of care in sickness.[9]

These religious leaders had devised a very clever scheme that they felt was in keeping with Numbers 30:1-2, which stated that a man needed to make certain he kept vows that he made to the Lord. But the making of one vow could in effect set aside a clear commandment of God.

7:13 Therefore Jesus attacked the religious leaders directly by telling them that they were "invalidating [*akyrountes,* used in the papyri

8. Ibid., 277.
9. Lane, *The Gospel of Mark,* 251.

for annulling contracts] the word of God" through the traditions they were handing down. This tradition of devoting something to God through the use of the "Corban" vow actually did away with a clear commandment. The religious leaders were guilty of many other similar things, but this in Jesus' thinking was a classic illustration of how they were invalidating the word of God through their traditions. No wonder He called them "hypocrites"! They were not properly honoring God, but that is exactly what their position as Pharisees and scribes demanded.

THE SERVANT'S WARNING, 7:14-23

7:14   Although Jesus had temporarily diverted the question of the Pharisees to deal with their own problem of hypocrisy, He now returned to the matter of the true source of defilement. He called the multitude who were with Him and began to speak to them. This does not mean that the Pharisees and scribes were not still in the crowd listening, but the Savior's remarks were basically addressed to the larger group of people. He encouraged them to listen and to understand. His opening words, "Listen to Me, all of you, and understand," almost sound like the opening words of an Old Testament prophet's address. It is clear that what He was about to say was important, and the people would do well to listen.

7:15   The issue of defilement had nothing to do with external materials that might come into contact with a person's body. It was the religious leaders' contention that unwashed hands will defile the food and then the partaker's body. But Jesus said that nothing entering from the outside defiles a person. Although the logical effect of what the Savior has just said would abrogate all the Levitical distinctions between clean and unclean meats, "it was not understood even by the Apostles until long afterwards, Acts x.14ff.; for the time the Lord was content to drop the seed and leave it to germinate."[10] Defilement starts from within a person and proceeds outward. Whereas Jesus contradicted the rabbinic view of His time, He certainly presented a biblical view of defilement (cf. Jer. 17:9-10; Eccl. 9:3).

7:16   Although this verse is in the majority of the manuscripts, it does not appear in the most ancient. It probably was a scribal addition similar to the statements that appear in 4:9 and 4:23, which conclude

10. Henry Barclay Swete, *The Gospel According to St. Mark* (Grand Rapids: Eerdmans, 1956), 150.

parabolic instruction with this call to hearing. Perhaps some scribe thought the repetition of the phrase here would conclude Jesus' instruction.

7:17 Jesus then left the multitude and entered a house, a fact that is recorded by Mark alone. Although the specific city in which this event occurred is not mentioned, the best possibility seems to be Capernaum, and the house would be that of Simon Peter. Once again His disciples came and "questioned Him about the parable" that He had just presented in v. 15. Matthew's account (Matt. 15:15) indicates that it was Peter who raised the question with Jesus.

7:18 The Savior responded to the disciples with a rebuke concerning their comprehension: "Are you so lacking in understanding also?"

> Their lack of understanding . . . indicates that in spite of their privileged relationship to Jesus they are not fundamentally different from the crowd. The failure of the disciples to understand Jesus' mighty acts and teaching is particularly emphasized in this section of the Gospel (Chs. 6:52; 7:18; 8:14-21) and is traced to hardness of heart.[11]

Jesus said, "Do you not understand that whatever goes into the man from outside cannot defile him . . . ?" That was one of the greatest emphases of the religious teachers of the time. They taught that people were morally defiled because something unclean came in contact with their bodies. The disciples, with their hard and fast distinctions between things "clean" and "unclean," were the product of their Pharisaic training.

7:19 Jesus pointed out that things coming into the body from outside never touch the heart. Instead, all foods brought into a person's body simply go "into his stomach." Then, in the process of time, as the food passes through the digestive system, the waste products are eliminated. The food, whether it was ceremonially clean or unclean, never really touches a man's heart, which is the true source of defilement. The heart was considered to be the center of human personality and determined a person's activity or inactivity (cf. Isa. 29:13).

Mark adds an editorial comment for his Roman readers, who perhaps did not rightly understand the significance of the Jewish distinctions of clean and unclean foods: by His statement Jesus "declared all foods clean." Mark wrote this many years after the event took place.

11. Lane, *The Gospel of Mark*, 255.

In fact, Mark's gospel was written years after Peter's vision on the rooftop in Joppa (Acts 10:9-16). In that vision a sheet was let down from heaven holding all kinds of animals, and Peter was told to kill and eat. He refused at first because he said those things were unholy and unclean. But a voice from heaven said, "What God has cleansed, no longer consider unholy" (Acts 10:15). That story was communicated from Peter to Mark, and Mark saw Jesus' teaching here to be its theological foundation.

Although Jesus' words did not formally break down the Levitical distinctions between clean and unclean animals at that time, He was pointing out that defilement really does not come from what one eats. If a Jew ate something that he was not supposed to eat, he would have been defiled. But the defilement would not have occurred because of the food itself but because of his personal disobedience to the expressed will of God in the prohibition of the Law.

7:20 What truly defiles a person is that which comes from within. Jesus did not introduce a new idea here; He simply amplified on what He had said in vv. 15b and 19. As a man speaks and acts, his true character is seen.

7:21 It is out of the heart of the person that all kinds of evil comes. The expression "evil thoughts" (*hoi dialogismoi hoi kakoi*) appears before the verb in this verse, thus placing great emphasis on that particular expression. "The commission of any sin is preceded by a deliberation, however rapid, in the mind of the sinner."[12] Evil thoughts are pictured as the basic idea in the twelve words that follow in the text. Matthew in his account did not give all twelve words as Mark does. Why Matthew abbreviated the list is uncertain. The first six that appear are in the plural, and the last six are singular.

The plural nouns describe various wicked acts. Jesus says that evil thoughts produce "fornications" (*porneiai*), a broad term that describes all kinds of illicit sexual activities of the unmarried. The next three plural expressions given are "thefts" (*klopai*), "murders" (*phonoi*), and "adulteries" (*moicheiai*). Interestingly enough, these three acts occur side by side in the Ten Commandments, as well as in Hosea 4:2.

7:22 The term for "adulteries" specifically speaks of sexual unfaithfulness within the marriage bond. Next Jesus lists "deeds of coveting" (*pleonexiai*), which is basically an expression of greed, an insatiable

12. Swete, *The Gospel According to St. Mark,* 153.

desire to have what belongs to someone else, or a craze for more and more. The final plural word here is "wickedness" (*ponēriai*), which is translated in other versions by the word "malice."

Jesus then presented six singular nouns that seem to picture internal attitudes: "deceit" (*dolos*), a fishing term that implies the idea of ensnaring someone; "sensuality" (*aselgeia*) or lewdness, stressing lack of self-control; "envy" (*ophthalmos ponēros*), literally "an evil eye," an expression for stinginess or a displeasure in someone else's blessings; "slander" (*blasphēmia*), the defamation of another person; "pride" (*hyperēphania*) or boastfully exalting oneself over others, the major problem of the Pharisees; and, finally, "foolishness" (*aphrosynē*) or folly, which implies moral and spiritual insensitivity.

7:23   Jesus said that all these evil things proceed from within and are what bring defilement to a person. This section began with the religious leaders criticizing Jesus' disciples over a matter of defilement that came about from an external source. Jesus not only pointed out their hypocrisy but truly clarified that the source of defilement is not external things but what comes from within a person's heart.

> The Pharisees were concerned about external contamination. They scrupulously observed traditional rituals to rid themselves of that uncleanness and did not deal with the uncleanness that came from within. If a man is himself righteous, he need concern himself only with external contamination; but if a man is himself unrighteous, he certainly needs more than ceremonial cleansing. The Pharisees' concept led them to reject Jesus, who offered them a righteousness from God. They sensed no need of such a righteousness and insisted that ceremonial cleansings were sufficient, thinking they were essentially clean within.[13]

THE SERVANT'S RETREAT FROM OPPOSITION, 7:24–8:9

TO THE REGION OF TYRE, 7:24-30
(cf. Matt. 15:21-28)

7:24   From the city of Capernaum Jesus "went away to the region of Tyre." Some of the better manuscripts add the words "and Sidon" at this point. The region of Tyre and Sidon was in the area of ancient Phoenicia, which is the coastline of modern Lebanon. In the time of David and Solomon, an alliance existed between Israel and Tyre.

---

13. J. Dwight Pentecost, *The Words & Works of Jesus Christ* (Grand Rapids: Zondervan, 1981), 243.

Building materials for the temple were supplied by Tyre in exchange for food (cf. 1 Kings 5).

This was the third time that Jesus departed from the northern shore of Galilee and went into Gentile territory. On the first departure He healed the demon-possessed man in the country of the Gerasenes (5:1-20), and on the second departure He fed the 5,000 men (6:30-44). It is not without significance that immediately after discussing the matter of ceremonial cleanliness and that which defiles, He departed from the land of Israel and went out among the Gentiles. "Phoenicians had sought Him in Galilee (iii.8), but He had no mission to their country; His purpose in entering it was retirement and not public work."[14] He entered into a house with the intent of keeping His presence there a secret. Jesus had been trying to get time alone with His disciples to instruct them. But in every place He turned He was constantly thronged by people. In this Gentile location Jesus and the disciples hoped their presence would escape notice.

7:25 But word of the arrival of Jesus and His disciples quickly circulated. Many from the vicinity of Tyre and Sidon had already been blessed by the ministry of Jesus (cf. 3:8). According to Luke (Luke 6:17), when He preached the Sermon on the Mount, some of those present were from these cities. When news reached a certain woman whose daughter was possessed by a demon, she "immediately" (*euthys*) sought out the Savior and "fell at His feet." The fact of demonic possession and an understanding of its consequences were not limited to Jews or to the land of Israel.

7:26 Mark made clear that this woman was not a Jew. She "was a Gentile," probably a Greek (*Hellēnis*), "of the Syrophoenician [*Syrophoinikissa*] race." The emphasis here was on the fact that the area of Phoenicia was under the ruling control of Syria at this time. The woman persisted as "she kept asking" (*ērōta,* imperfect tense emphasizing her continual repetition) Jesus "to cast the demon out of her daughter."

7:27 Jesus' response to her, however, was that He needed to satisfy the children first and that He could not "take the children's bread and throw it to the dogs." Jesus' statement must be understood using

> the background provided by the OT and later Judaism where the people of Israel are designated as the children of God. Understood in this

14. Swete, *The Gospel According to St. Mark,* 156.

light, Jesus acknowledges the privileges of Israel and affirms that the time has not yet come for blessings to be extended to the Gentiles. "Let the children first be fed" has reference to God's election of Israel and his appointment that the gospel be proclaimed "to the Jew first and (then) to the Greek" (Rom. 1:16; 2:9f.; Acts 3:26; 13:46).[15]

It is doubtful, however, that this woman would have truly understood the Old Testament background and the fact that Jesus' ministry was directed primarily to the nation of Israel. It is best to see this statement in light of all that was going on. Jesus and the disciples had probably entered a home in order to eat a meal. Since the woman interrupted their meal, Jesus simply used an analogy that would have been easy for her to understand. The disciples sitting at the table with Him would have been "the children" who were being satisfied by the meal they were eating. It would be inappropriate for Jesus to stop what He was doing in order to feed the dogs. Literally His word for "dogs" does not speak of the wild dogs that roamed in packs but of domesticated house dogs, the puppies that might be in a home under the table.

7:28   The woman immediately saw herself in this story. She did not dispute the fact that she was not an invited guest, but she saw herself as one of the "puppies" in the room. She addressed the Savior as "Lord" (*Kyrie*). This is the only time in Mark's gospel that Jesus Christ is addressed as Lord. She reminded Him that even the puppies in the room were able to catch the little scraps that would fall off the table around the children. She drew a delightful picture. She was not asking Jesus to interrupt what He was doing. She was simply putting herself in the place of a "little puppy" and asking for a small blessing that might fall from the table. "Instead of resenting Christ's words about giving the children's bread to the dogs (Gentiles) in v. 27, she instantly turned it to the advantage of her plea for her little daughter."[16]

7:29   Jesus marveled at her answer, for it was an answer of true humility. She recognized her position as well as His. Perhaps she did understand that His ministry was primarily to Israel. "It is true that according to Matthew, Jesus said, 'O woman, great is your *faith*,' whereas in Mark he is represented as praising her for her *statement*,

15. Lane, *The Gospel of Mark,* 261.
16. Robertson, *Word Pictures in the New Testament,* 1:326.

her *word*. However, since by means of this *word* she revealed her *faith* there is no essential difference."[17]

7:30   A further indication of her faith is seen in the fact that she went home. When she arrived there she found her daughter lying on a bed completely released from the demon who had possessed her. The demon had "departed" (*exelēlythos*, a perfect active participle expressing a state of completion). This miracle occurred at a distance, with no spoken command from the Savior. Similar miracles at a distance occurred when Jesus healed the nobleman's son at Capernaum (John 4:46) and when He healed the centurion's servant (Luke 7:6).

TO THE REGION OF DECAPOLIS, 7:31–8:9
(cf. Matt. 15:29-31)

Healing of the Deaf Man, 7:31-37

7:31   Mark explains that Jesus left "the region of Tyre, and came through Sidon to the Sea of Galilee, within the region of Decapolis." That simple statement involved a considerable amount of traveling. Jesus and His disciples would have gone north from Tyre, approximately twenty miles, to the city of Sidon. Although their precise route is not given, they probably traveled to the east through Philip's territory around Mount Hermon and then came down on the eastern side of the Sea of Galilee into the area of the ten Greek cities of Decapolis. It appears that Jesus was purposefully avoiding the northern shore of the Sea of Galilee. His reasons were probably to avoid the multitudes who were at that time seeking to make Him king. He also was trying to avoid additional controversy with the religious leaders. Finally He was seeking to avoid any contact with Herod Antipas whose feelings toward Jesus at this time were clearly hostile (cf. 6:14-16). Exactly how far and how long Jesus and the disciples were involved in this journey are not revealed.

7:32   As He came into the region of Decapolis, "they brought to Him [*pherousin autō*, present tense verb to dramatically picture the action] one who was deaf and [who] spoke with [great] difficulty [*mogilalon*]."

> Mark's use of an extremely rare word to describe the man's speech defect is almost certainly an allusion to Isa. 35:5f. which celebrates God

---

17. Hendriksen, *Exposition of the Gospel According to Mark*, 301.

169

as the one who comes in order to unstop the ears of the deaf and to provide song for the man of inarticulate speech. The fulfillment of the prophecy was expected in the Days of the Messiah in the exegetical tradition of the rabbis. By means of the biblical allusion Mark provides his readers with a sign that the promised intervention of God took place in the ministry of Jesus.[18]

It is common for a person who is deaf to have a difficult time with his speech. This man probably had not been born deaf, but through some illness he had become deaf. "They entreated" (*parakalousin,* also present tense for vivid detail) Jesus "to lay His hand upon him" to bring about his healing. They had probably seen Jesus heal others in this way (cf. 6:5). The miracle that follows is recorded only in Mark's gospel.

7:33 Jesus took the man away "from the multitude" to be alone with him. It is possible that Jesus did this in order not to make the man a public spectacle. It is also possible that He did it simply because it is difficult for a person who is deaf to follow instructions in a crowd. Jesus was able to communicate with him on a one-to-one basis, and that surely helped to put the man at ease. The first thing Jesus did was to "put His fingers into [the man's] ears." Mark also declares that Jesus spat on the ground, probably to catch the attention of the deaf man, then reached out and touched the man's tongue. These hand gestures and symbols probably communicated to the man that He was about to do something to affect his ears and tongue, both of which Jesus had touched.

7:34 Jesus' next action was to look up to heaven. This attitude of prayer probably communicated to the deaf man that his help was going to come from above, so Jesus was taking a moment to pray to His heavenly Father. He also gave "a deep sigh," perhaps a sigh of compassion as Jesus felt the burden of the man. There could possibly have been a deep spiritual battle going on here between the forces of God and the forces of Satan. The reason for the man's deafness and dumbness is not given in the text, but it is possible that it could have been satanic. Then Jesus spoke to the man. Mark states the actual Aramaic word that Jesus communicated: *"Ephphatha!"* Does the fact that Jesus spoke to the man in Aramaic indicate that although he was in Gentile territory this man might have been Jewish? That is a possibility. But

18. Lane, *The Gospel of Mark,* 266.

also, the word "ephphatha" would have been an easy word for someone to lip-read. Mark explains for his Gentile audience that "Ephphatha!" meant "Be opened!"

7:35 The ears of the deaf man were opened and immediately (*eutheōs*) "the impediment [*desmos*, literally "the bond"] of his tongue was removed" so that he was able to "begin speaking plainly" (*elalei orthōs*, imperfect tense indicating that he was continuing to speak over a period of time). When Jesus performed a miracle in a person's life, the results were dramatic and immediate. "The recounting of these various vivid details shows that the story of an eye-witness (probably Peter) is being transmitted here by Mark."[19]

7:36 It was not the intent of the Lord Jesus to begin an extended ministry of healing in this Gentile region, where He apparently intended to stay for a while. Therefore He gave orders that the details of this miracle not be told (*diesteilato*, imperfect tense implying that Jesus repeated this request over and over) to anyone. But "the more He ordered them" to be quiet, "the more widely" the message continued to be proclaimed (*perissoteron ekēryssen*, imperfect tense verb picturing a continual telling of the story). This was good news; in fact, this was great news, and it was hard to keep it quiet.

7:37 The people "were utterly astonished," saying that Jesus had "done all things well."

> The parallelism with Genesis i may have been unnoticed by the original audience, but can hardly have escaped unseen by the early Church. All God's creative works are perfect, and so is the manifestation of His Son's power. Not only God saw that it was good (Gn. i.4), but even, on this occasion, man also.[20]

The remarkable achievement of the Savior was that He was able to make both deaf people hear and dumb people speak. The words "deaf" and "dumb" appear in the plural in the text. The implication could be that more than the one miracle occurred here in this Gentile region and that Mark was aware of that fact.

> It is of interest to note that following His challenging of the traditions of the Pharisees Jesus had in this chapter healed a Gentile woman's daughter, traveled through Gentile territory, and healed a man in Decapolis,

19. Hendriksen, *Exposition of the Gospel According to Mark*, 305.
20. Cole, *The Gospel According to Mark*, 125.

which was also predominantly Gentile. Perhaps Mark has grouped
these events together to underscore Jesus' contest with the Pharisees
and His willingness to do things that overly legalistic Pharisees would
not do.[21]

HOMILETICAL SUGGESTIONS

The controversy of Jesus with the Pharisees and scribes carries
many parallels with religious systems of our day. The emphasis of
these religious leaders was on external defilements, whereas Jesus'
emphasis was that defilement basically comes from within, from man's
sinful nature. There is a tendency to equate spirituality with external
things such as attendance at meetings and Bible studies, ways that one
dresses, and activities one avoids. These things fail to deal with the
true issue—the heart. A person would do well to look within and to
make certain that he or she is truly walking in a way that is pleasing to
the Lord, with nothing standing between himself and God.

The chapter concludes with two incidents in which Jesus Christ
dealt with people outside of the land of Israel. It is a joy to see that,
whereas Jesus came primarily with a ministry for the nation of Israel,
He did have an impact on Gentile peoples as well. The story of the
Syrophoenician woman has always been a blessing. She truly saw herself in relationship to the Lord Jesus Christ, and He rewarded her faith
by granting her request. The man He dealt with in the region of Decapolis also received healing as Jesus dealt with him in a unique way.

21. Howard F. Vos, *Mark* (Grand Rapids: Zondervan, 1978), 69.

MARK

CHAPTER

EIGHT

THE SERVANT'S REJECTION
OF THE PHARISEES

Feeding of the 4,000, 8:1-9 (cf. Matt. 15:32-38)

8:1   Again "a great multitude" was thronging around Jesus Christ. Perhaps the miracle of the healing of the deaf and dumb man had brought them.

> There is no mention of any traveling that took place between the preceding event (7:31-37) and this one (8:1-10), though there may have been. But since the "uninhabited region" mentioned in 8:4 can easily have been Decapolis near the eastern shore of the Sea of Galilee (7:31), the conclusion that Jesus is still, or is again, in or near the same place where he healed the man who was deaf and who spoke with difficulty is reasonable.[1]

Wherever Jesus went He attracted large crowds (cf. 7:33, "the multitude"). On this particular occasion it became obvious that there was a need for food. The people "had nothing to eat," so Jesus called His disciples and spoke (*lelei,* present tense to vividly portray the scene) to them.

8:2   Jesus had "compassion" (*splagchnizomai,* "my heart goes out") for the people, for they had been with Him for some time, many for as long as three days. The fact that some were there for that length of

---

1. William Hendriksen, *Exposition of the Gospel According to Mark* (Grand Rapids: Baker, 1975), 310.

time implies that they had sat under Jesus' teaching ministry. Whatever food they might have brought along was now gone, and there
was nothing for them to eat. Jesus was concerned for their physical
needs.

> This audience had proved their right sense of spiritual values by three
> days of eager listening to the Lord's preaching. It is not just that they
> were hungry, but that they were hungry in God's service: and so theirs
> was to be an experience of 'seek ye first the kingdom of God,' . . . 'and
> all these things shall be added unto you' (Matt. vi. 33). Like the Lord
> Himself, in their hunger to know and do God's will, they had scarcely
> been conscious of physical hunger up to this moment (Jn. iv. 32-34).[2]

8:3   His concern extended to the possible consequences of sending
them away to their homes hungry. Mark alone records that many of
them had come from great distances. "Gamala, Hippos, Gadara were
perhaps the nearest centres of population. The towns and villages of
the Decapolis were fewer, and at longer distances from each other
than those of the populous western shore."[3] Jesus was concerned that
they would not make it back to their homes before fainting (*eklythē-
sontai,* future indicative passive verb carrying the idea of having one's
strength be loosened or relaxed) on the way. The fact that some had
come from great distances could imply that this crowd was composed
of both Jewish and Gentile people.

8:4   The disciples realized that Jesus was thinking again of feeding
the multitude. Their answer to Him seems somewhat surprising when
one considers that they had already been through an experience
where Jesus had fed 5,000 men, plus the women and children. Although some scholars believe that this story is simply a distortion of
the miracle that had occurred earlier (cf. 6:30-44), there is ample evidence that this miracle is a unique event. It is true that only Matthew
(Matt. 15:32-39) and Mark record this particular miracle, but the differences in the two stories, plus the fact that Jesus later refers to both
miracles (cf. 8:19-20), implies that this was a unique event. Surely the
disciples remembered that the Master had fed a large group on a previous occasion, but it seems that they were slow of hearing and slow
to learn. They acknowledged that this was a "desolate place" and that
it would be very difficult to find food.

2. R. A. Cole, *The Gospel According to Mark* (Grand Rapids: Eerdmans, 1979), 127.
3. Henry Barclay Swete, *The Gospel According to St. Mark* (Grand Rapids: Eerdmans, 1956), 164.

This region to the east or southeast of the Sea of Galilee was a desolate place, a veritable wilderness. The scene of the feeding of the *five* thousand was somewhat more favorable, for in that case food could be purchased from the surrounding farms and in the nearby villages (6:36), but that was not the case here. Apart from Jesus and his power to perform miracles, the present terrain was worthless as a source of needed food supply.[4]

The disciples simply referred the matter back to the Savior.

8:5 It is interesting that Jesus did not rebuke His disciples for their lack of memory. He did, however, ask them to look around to see how much food they actually possessed. He had asked the identical question in 6:38. Perhaps some of the disciples at this point began to remember what had happened previously. The Lord must have wanted them to look at their resources to clearly fix in their minds the total inadequacy of their supply. They discovered that they had only seven loaves of bread available to them. Such a small number would cause the magnitude of this miracle to stand out clearly.

8:6 As in the previous miracle, Jesus brought order to the situation. This time, however, He told "the multitude to sit down on the ground," not the "green grass" as in 6:39. It was clearly later in the year when this miracle occurred. Jesus then took the material that was available, "the seven loaves," and gave thanks to His Heavenly Father for the provision. He "broke" (*eklasen*, aorist tense emphasizing the fact) the bread and continued to give (*edidou*, imperfect tense picturing the continuous action over a period of time) it to the disciples "to serve" (*paratithōsin*, "to set before," present tense picturing the action as continuing) to the multitude. Once again the miracle of creation occurred in the hands of the Creator. But Jesus did utilize His disciples as the conveyors of the food to the multitudes.

8:7 Mark also explains that there were "a few small fish." The fact that he mentioned the fish last does not necessarily mean that they were not served until after the bread was distributed (cf. Matt. 15:34ff.). But Mark does make a special notation that Jesus blessed the fish separately.

The pronouncement of blessing over bread is the normal Jewish practice for beginning a meal, but the blessing of God's Name prior to the distribution of the fish seems to have been intended to teach the peo-

4. Hendriksen, *Exposition of the Gospel According to Mark*, 311.

ple to thank God for their daily food. The offering of praise and thanksgiving acknowledges that the multiplied food is the gracious provision
of God.[5]

After blessing the fish, Jesus ordered them to be served also. As in the
earlier miracle, the provision of bread and fish was made available to
all.

8:8   "They ate and were [completely] satisfied." Not only was there
ample food for each person, but they filled up "seven large baskets"
(*hepta spyridas*) with the leftovers. In the previous miracle the twelve
baskets were the smaller wicker-type baskets (*kophinōn*, 6:43), which
probably were a type of knapsack carried by each apostle. The basket
used here, however, was a very large basket, one capable of actually
holding a man. This was the kind of basket used in Acts 9:25 to lower
Saul through an opening in the wall so that he might escape from
Damascus. Therefore, the seven large baskets of leftovers that were
picked up here probably amounted to more food than the twelve baskets on the previous occasion.

> The seven wicker baskets [that were] borrowed (it is unlikely that the
> peripatetic preachers carried such around with them) pin the story to
> history as surely as does the unusual 'four thousand' for the crowd,
> which could in no sense be used metaphorically for any large number
> as, say, 'ten thousand' could have been.[6]

8:9   Mark declares that 4,000 were fed at this point. The number
was probably ascertained, as before, by the orderly division of the
crowd, although no mention is made in this account of the people
sitting in companies of fifties and one hundreds (cf. 6:40). Matthew
adds that there were also women and children present (Matt. 15:38).
After feeding this multitude Jesus "sent them away." There does not
appear to be any expectation of messianic blessing in this gathering.
Perhaps that implies that the majority of the people were Gentiles.
William Lane remarks that, when considering the composition of this
multitude,

> it has been common since the time of Augustine to assign the first feed-
> ing to the nourishment of Israel and the second to the Gentiles. There

---

5. William L. Lane, *The Gospel of Mark*, NICNT (Grand Rapids: Eerdmans, 1974), 274.
6. Cole, *The Gospel According to Mark*, 127-28.

can be no doubt of the Gentile associations of the Decapolis and of Mark's interest in the apostolic mission to the Gentiles. . . . In view of the mixed population of the area, however, it is probable that both Jews and Gentiles sat down together in meal fellowship on this occasion, and this prefigured Jesus' intention for the Church. This seems to be a more realistic approach to the historical situation than the desire to find an exclusively Gentile audience in Ch. 8:1-9.[7]

THE PHARISEES' FINAL DEMAND, 8:10-21

THEIR DEMAND, 8:10-11
(cf. Matt. 15:39–16:1)

8:10   Jesus and the disciples "immediately" (*euthys*) got into a boat and came across the sea to "the district of Dalmanutha," an unknown location. Many believe that the district of Dalmanutha was on the western side of the Sea of Galilee near modern-day Tiberias. Matthew's account says that they got into a boat and came to "the region of Magadan" (Matt. 15:39), which is thought to be another form of Magdala, a city clearly on the western shore of the Sea of Galilee at the southern end of the Plain of Gennesaret.

8:11   As soon as Jesus and the disciples got out of the boat they were met by the Pharisees, who probably were still seething at His earlier denunciation of them concerning the matter of cleanliness (cf. 7:1-23). Matthew notes that they were joined by Sadducees (Matt. 16:1), the only mention of this group interacting with Jesus during His Galilean ministry. Henry Swete notes that

> as the aristocratic and priestly party they resided principally at Jerusalem and in its neighbourhood. Some were possibly connected with the court of Herod . . . residing at Tiberias. Their association with the Pharisees on this occasion indicates the extent to which the hostility of the latter was now carried.[8]

They "began to argue with [Jesus], seeking from Him a sign from heaven, to test Him." The sign from heaven they were seeking was some kind of miraculous display that would prove His claims beyond a doubt. Perhaps they had heard about the miraculous multiplication that had just taken place in Decapolis. But was that a genuine miracle?

7. Lane, *The Gospel of Mark*, 274-75.
8. Swete, *The Gospel According to St. Mark*, 167.

After all, what He had provided was *earthly* bread, not "bread from heaven," as Moses had done. Let Him then produce "a sign from *heaven.*" Yes, let him do what Moses had done (Exod. 16; cf. John 6:32). Or, like Joshua, let him cause the sun and the moon to stand still (Josh. 10:12-14). Let him repeat what Samuel had done (I Sam. 7:10), or Elijah (I Kings 18:30-40; cf. James 5:17, 18). As if, had he done any of these things, or anything of similar sensational nature, they would not have ascribed also such a sign to Beelzebul as its source! See Luke 16:31.[9]

By asking the Lord to produce a sign, the religious leaders in effect were saying that they had rejected all of His previous miracles as spurious. But they were also testing, or tempting, Jesus. They truly hoped that He would attempt before their eyes some mighty deed and that He would fail completely, thus being discredited publicly.

THE SERVANT'S EXPLANATION, 8:12-13
(cf. Matt. 16:2-4)

8:12   When Jesus heard the request of the religious leaders, He sighed deeply in His spirit (*anastenaxas tō pneumati*). The compounded verb that Mark gives here for "sighing deeply" is the only usage of this word in the New Testament. The noncompounded form of the same verb appears in 7:34. But the preposition *ana* greatly intensifies the meaning. Swete says "the sigh seemed to come, as we say, from the bottom of the heart; the Lord's human spirit was stirred to its depths."[10]

He asked a rhetorical question: "Why does this generation seek for a sign?"

Jesus had filled the land with "infallible proofs" (cf. Acts 1:3) of the fact that he was indeed the One who had been sent by the Father, as predicted by the prophets. These signs had been of various kinds: restoration of the handicapped, healing of the sick, cleansing of the lepers, stilling of the waves, feeding of the hungry, and even raising of the dead. Asking for still another sign was clearly an insult. It implied that the miracles already performed were insufficient as credentials.[11]

That generation should have accepted all the miracles that the Savior had performed and not have looked for something in the spectacular

9. Hendriksen, *Exposition of the Gospel According to Mark*, 314-15.
10. Swete, *The Gospel According to St. Mark*, 168.
11. Hendriksen, *Exposition of the Gospel According to Mark*, 315.

realm, such as the Messiah suddenly descending from the pinnacle of the temple in a spectacular display (cf. Matt. 4:5-7). No such spectacular sign would be given to this generation. R. A. Cole says that

> a literal translation of verse 12b would be 'Amen I say to you, if a sign will be given. . . .' This has, in Semitic speech, the full force of an oath, as even a double 'Amen' had to a Jew (cf. Jn. i. 51, etc.). It was a firm refusal on the Lord's part to take a line of action that He had decisively rejected at the temptation (Mt. iv. 6)—that of compelling men's allegiance by a spectacular sign.[12]

It is noteworthy that Matthew, in writing his gospel to Jews, adds that the only sign they would receive was the sign of Jonah the prophet (Matt. 16:4). The sign of Jonah the prophet is understood generally as being a reference to death, burial, and resurrection. Of course, by the time they saw that sign it would be too late. In order to see the sign of resurrection they would have already crucified their Messiah. Mark, writing to a predominantly Gentile audience, did not mention that ancient Jewish prophet, for their interest in the Old Testament would have been minimal.

8:13   Not only did Jesus refuse to give the religious leaders a sign, but He and the disciples abruptly departed from them. His rapid departure demonstrated His indignation. There was no possibility that any good would come of His conversation with these leaders. Therefore He and His disciples departed by the sea and went over to "the other side" of the lake.

THE SERVANT'S WARNING, 8:14-21
(cf. Matt. 16:5-12)

8:14   The rapid departure of Jesus and the disciples resulted in their forgetting to take along provisions with them. As they started across the sea, they had only "one loaf" of bread (*hena arton*) with them. That fact is recorded only by Mark, and it becomes significant in the following story. One loaf of bread would not begin to satisfy the hunger of thirteen men. Perhaps they each thought there was still a sufficient supply left over from the recent miracle in Decapolis.

8:15   Jesus communicated (*diestelleto*, imperfect tense showing that this was a repeated charge) to His disciples a solemn warning. He

12. Cole, *The Gospel According to Mark,* 129.

encouraged them, using present tense imperatives to "watch out" for (*horate*), to "beware of" (*blepete*) the "leaven of the Pharisees and the leaven of Herod." Leaven is a reference to yeast, which, when put in flour, causes it to rise. Once yeast has been placed into ingredients, the process cannot be stopped, but it will permeate the whole loaf of bread. Although leaven does not always refer to evil in Scripture, it is a fitting description of evil. By this figure Jesus was warning the disciples about the teachings of the Pharisees and the teachings of Herod and his followers. Jesus had just come from a meeting with Pharisees and Sadducees, and, though Herod was not formally a Sadducee, the worldliness of the Herodian family and especially of the court of Antipas was not far removed from the temper of the Sadducean aristocrats. Perhaps that is why Jesus referred to Herod here rather than the Sadducees as a group. The Pharisees were hypocritical and very proud, with a legalistic spirit surrounding their laws and traditions. The Herodians on the other hand were very worldly and had an intense interest in political power. Jesus warned His disciples to be careful of both attitudes.

8:16 The disciples began to reason among themselves (*dielogizonto pros allēlous,* an imperfect tense indicating that they kept their discussion going for some time). However, they completely missed the intention of Jesus' words. As soon as He mentioned "leaven," they began to discuss with one another the fact that they had failed to bring bread with them. They probably were quick to assign blame, pointing fingers, and saying, "But I thought you were bringing the bread."

> The dispute among the disciples, which indicated how completely they were absorbed in their temporal preoccupations, was the immediate occasion for Jesus' sharp condemnation of the lack of understanding in men whose privileged position should have led them to perceive the truth of his person and the importance of hearing his word.[13]

8:17 Jesus was aware of their discussion and immediately brought to their attention the fact that He was not talking merely about bread. In the next few verses He asked six questions that must have been a strong rebuke to the disciples. That they had failed to bring along bread was irrelevant. He asked them, "Do you not yet see or understand?" They should have been able to put two and two together, but

13. Lane, *The Gospel of Mark,* 281.

they were not using their heads. "Do you have a hardened heart?" "'Hardened' is here used not in the sense of obstinacy and resulting imperviousness that marked the Pharisees, but of spiritual sluggishness."[14] Surely those words must have been stinging rebukes to the disciples.

8:18 Jesus picked up the words of the prophet Ezekiel, for he was addressed as one who lived in the midst of a rebellious people who did not have eyes that could see or ears that could hear (Ezek. 12:2). Such a description was not to be true of the Twelve, even though Jesus had said previously (cf. 4:11ff.) that it would be true of the crowds. These disciples were walking in the presence of the Lord of glory, but they failed to see what He was doing and hear the words that He was saying. Not only that, but their memory was often not good.

8:19 Jesus took them back to the incident that had occurred only recently when He had fed 5,000 men, plus the women and children, from five loaves of bread and two fish (6:38-44). He asked them if they remembered "how many baskets [*kophinous*] full of broken pieces" they had picked up following that miracle. Their recollection was correct in saying that they had picked up twelve small baskets full of food.

8:20 Jesus then referred to the incident that had only just happened, when He had fed 4,000 men, plus the women and children, with the seven loaves (8:1-9). Jesus asked, "How many large baskets [*spyridōn*] full of broken pieces" were picked up on that occasion? "Seven," they responded. They could remember the facts of the story, but they did not always properly understand the significance of the facts.

> The argument is basically as follows: if five bread-cakes more than sufficed for five thousand people, and seven bread-cakes more than sufficed for four thousand—facts which the disciples here and now reaffirmed—, then would not Jesus be able to feed himself and The Twelve with *one* (8:14) bread-cake? In fact, would he not be able, even without any bread-cake, to provide all that was necessary?[15]

8:21 He concluded by saying, "Do you not yet understand?" Mark's account left the Twelve to ponder the matter themselves and to come

---

14. Hendriksen, *Exposition of the Gospel According to Mark,* 320.
15. Ibid.

to a conclusion. As one reads the parallel account in Matthew 16:11-12 it appears that they were beginning to understand that Jesus was not simply speaking about bread, but He was speaking of the teachings of these different groups.

A CONCLUDING MIRACLE, 8:22-26

8:22   The disciples and Jesus "came" (*erchontai,* present tense to picture dramatically the scene) across the Sea of Galilee to the city of Bethsaida. This probably is a reference to the area of Bethsaida Julius on the eastern side of the sea near the area where Jesus had performed the miracle of the feeding of the 5,000 (cf. 6:33ff.). Jesus had rebuked this region for its lack of faith (cf. Matt. 11:20-24). However, there were individuals there who recognized Jesus. When they realized He was in their midst, "they brought [*pherousin,* also present tense to make the scene vivid] a blind man to Him" and begged Him to touch him. This is "the first mention in [Mark] of blindness as an infirmity for which a cure was sought from Christ: a second case occurs in x.46ff."[16] Although their statement was that they simply wanted Jesus to touch him, surely the intent in their desire was that His touch would bring healing, as it had done on previous occasions (cf. 1:41; 5:41; 6:5; 7:32). Although Jesus is reported to have healed a number of blind men during the course of His ministry (cf. Matt. 9:27; 11:5; 12:22; 15:30; 21:14; John 9:1ff.), this particular incident is recorded only by Mark.

8:23   Jesus took "the blind man by the hand" and led him "out of the village [*kōmēs*]." Luke says that Bethsaida was a "city" (*polin,* Luke 9:10).

> For a long time Bethsaida had been a mere village. Then Philip the tetrarch (Lk. 3:1) enlarged and beautified it. It now became a city, and in honor of Julia, the daughter of Emperor Augustus, was named Bethsaida Julias. However, having been a "village" for so long a time, it is not surprising that the designation "village" continued for some time to be applied to it.[17]

This miracle is similar to the healing of the deaf and dumb man in 7:31-37, for there Jesus also led the man who was in need away

16. Swete, *The Gospel According to St. Mark,* 173.
17. Hendriksen, *Exposition of the Gospel According to Mark,* 321.

from the crowd. Jesus wanted to get with this man one on one. By so doing Jesus was establishing communication with a person who probably had learned to be passive in his society. Perhaps He brought him out of the village because of the previous words of condemnation against Bethsaida (cf. Matt. 11:21). Another possibility is that He did not want to be besieged with people in need of healing at this time. Jesus spit on the man's eyes and laid His hands on him. This also was similar to the way He had dealt with the deaf and dumb man (7:31-37). His actions probably communicated to the man that something was going to be done to his eyes. Jesus then asked a question, "Do you see anything?" This was obviously asked to invoke a response from the man, thus involving him in his own cure.

8:24   The man "looked up and said, 'I see [*Blepō,* present tense] men,'" but "'I am seeing [*horō,* also present tense] them like trees, walking about.'" The use of present tense verbs pictures the action as actually taking place before his eyes. The fact that he knew what trees and men looked like implies that this man at one time could see. "Persons blind from birth do not have an exact idea of objects and cannot properly visualize a tree. On the other hand, optical images become modified as blindness continues, and the visualization of men under the form of trees indicates that the man had been blind for a long period of time."[18]

8:25   Jesus laid His hands on the man's eyes a second time. When that happened the man looked steadfastly, or steadily (*dieblepsen,* aorist tense indicating a completed action), and he was completely "restored" (*apekatestē,* also an aorist indicating that the restoration was complete). He then kept on looking (*eneblepen,* an imperfect tense communicating that he continued looking). He was able to see all things clearly, even things that were at a distance. This miracle is unique because the healing occurred in stages. Did the Savior not have the power to heal the man completely the first time? The answer obviously is yes. But since the miracle occurred in stages and the stages were initiated by the Savior, there must be a reason.

> Was it, perhaps, because especially *this* person was in need of understanding the inestimable nature of the blessing that was being bestowed upon him? The reason cannot have been initial lack of power on the part of Jesus. Surely, he who was able instantly to raise the dead

18. Lane, *The Gospel of Mark,* 285.

was also able to impart instant recovery to this blind man. For a reason known to the Healer the present restoration occurred in two stages.[19]

Perhaps the best explanation for the two stages is that Jesus was trying to show the disciples that their faith, like this man's sight, was becoming clearer as they walked with Him. They had just come from a ride across the sea during which He had warned them and asked them if they were still without understanding. Their knowledge of the person of Jesus Christ was becoming clearer all the time, as was this man's sight.

8:26 Jesus told the man to go home and not even return to Bethsaida to give a testimony to them. This may imply that the man was not from Bethsaida. At any rate, the day of opportunity for Bethsaida had passed, and they had failed to accept Jesus as the Christ.

> Should he not give another opportunity to the people in Bethsaida? Perhaps they would believe if they heard how Jesus had restored his sight. No, Bethsaida had been given adequate evidence, but still had refused to believe. It is a dangerous thing for anybody to reject the message of God and to harden his or her heart in unbelief.[20]

Further testimony to them would be useless. Instead, Jesus told him to return to his own family and present himself as a witness of Jesus' work in his life. "Is there a touch of love there? Must there not have been wife or children at home, to whom the man's healing would mean everything? and was the Lord desirous that theirs should be the first joy?"[21]

THE INSTRUCTION OF JEHOVAH'S SERVANT, 8:27–10:52

INSTRUCTION CONCERNING HIS PERSON, 8:27-30 (cf. Matt. 16:13-20; Luke 9:18-21)

8:27 Not only did Jesus send the man away from Bethsaida, but He and His disciples headed for the "villages of Caesarea Philippi," an area about twenty-five miles north of the Sea of Galilee. Caesarea Philippi was built on a spur of Mount Hermon in Iturea by a son of Herod

---

19. Hendriksen, *Exposition of the Gospel According to Mark,* 323.
20. Warren W. Wiersbe, *Be Diligent* (Wheaton, Ill.: Victor, 1987), 80-81.
21. Cole, *The Gospel According to Mark,* 133.

the Great, Philip, to honor Augustus Caesar. In order to differentiate that city from Caesarea on the seacoast built by his father, he added to Caesarea his own name. Thus it became known as Caesarea Philippi.

The region is a beautiful one, situated near the foot of snow-capped Mount Hermon in the area where one of the sources of the River Jordan is found.

> The old name of the town—Paneas, now Banias—marked it as sacred to the worship of Pan; its second name connected it with the worship of the Emperor, in whose honour a temple had been erected close to the old shrine of Pan (Joseph. *ant.* xv.10.3). The population was chiefly Gentile . . . yet, as this context shews, not exclusively so, especially in the suburbs, to which the Lord seems to have confined Himself.[22]

As they traveled toward the region, Jesus began to question (*epērōta,* imperfect tense implying that the questioning continued over a period of time) His disciples. The previous miracle had implied that their knowledge was coming in stages. Jesus was inquiring as to exactly where the disciples were in their understanding of His person. "They knew the various popular opinions about Jesus of which Herod Antipas had heard (Mark 3:21, 31). It was time that the disciples reveal how much they had been influenced by their environment as well as the direct instruction of Jesus."[23] He therefore questioned them, saying, "Who do people say that I am?" According to Matthew (Matt. 16:13) Jesus used the designation "Son of Man" for Himself. Mark and Luke (Luke 9:18) simply use the personal pronoun "I." But Jesus often referred to Himself as "the Son of Man."

8:28 The responses of the disciples were similar to those given previously (cf. 6:14-16). Again the suggestions of John the Baptist, Elijah, or one of the prophets were all flattering suggestions. Matthew adds "Jeremiah" as a possibility. Some believe that Jeremiah was added because of the denunciatory character of some of the Lord's teaching. Also Jeremiah occupied the first place in the order traditionally assigned to the "Latter Prophets." Finally, both Jeremiah and Jesus were rejected by their own people. However, all the suggestions of the disciples were wrong.

22. Swete, *The Gospel According to St. Mark,* 176.
23. A. T. Robertson, *Word Pictures in the New Testament* (Nashville: Broadman, 1930), 1:334.

8:29   Jesus sought to confront the issue with them by specifically asking what *their* opinion was. The emphasis in the Savior's question is on the "you" in contrast to other men in general: "Who do *you* say that I am?" All the synoptic writers state that Peter acted as spokesman for the group. He would later function in the same capacity for the Twelve (cf. 9:5; 10:28; 11:21; 14:29). He responded with words all agreed with: "Thou art the Christ" (*Christos*), which is the same as "Messiah" in Hebrew. Both words carry the idea of the "one anointed by God." Matthew gives the full confession, stating that Peter added that Jesus was also "the Son of the living God" (Matt. 16:16). Luke's language is similar to Matthew's: "The Christ of God" (cf. Luke 9:20). Mark simply presented the shortest version with an emphasis on the messiahship of Jesus Christ.

Matthew also records that Jesus went on to pronounce a great blessing on Peter: "Blessed are you, Simon Bar-jona, because flesh and blood did not reveal this to you, but My Father who is in heaven. And I say to you that you are Peter and upon this rock I will build My church; and the gates of Hades shall not overpower it" (Matt. 16:17-18). Mark did not give any of this information concerning Peter or the blessing pronounced on him. If Peter told Mark of these particular words of the Savior, he must have encouraged Mark not to use them. Why would he do so?

> The answer may very well be that, to him, the most vivid recollection was the Lord's stern rebuke which followed: or he may have shrunk from introducing into his preaching that blessing which must seem to aggrandize himself. But whatever the reason, it is surely a good commentary on later Roman claims that, by Church tradition, the one place where the Petrine promises were most certainly not preached was the very city of Rome, where we have good reason to believe Peter was an *episcopos,* or elder-bishop, before his death, possibly in the same persecution as that in which Paul died.[24]

Not boasting of special words of praise may be viewed as normal Christian humility. Peter did not want to appear to be promoting himself; he wanted to glorify his Savior. "Peter's confession recognized that Jesus was the appointed agent of God whose coming marks the fulfillment of the divine promise and the realization of Israel's hopes.

24. Cole, *The Gospel According to Mark,* 135-36.

Of the deeper and more costly dimensions of messiahship, however, he had no intimation."[25]

8:30   Jesus warned His disciples that they should not tell anyone about this disclosure of His messiahship. There is speculation as to why Jesus said that at this point. It probably related to the fact that the concept of the Messiah had become quite perverted in Israel from what it was intended to be in the Old Testament. "We cannot be fully sure what the Twelve meant by a declaration of messiahship. In the century or two before the birth of Christ Jews had come to attach political aspirations to the messianic concept and Old Testament references to a suffering servant (e.g., Isa. 53) were largely ignored."[26] The role of the Messiah had been relegated to a political position. When the Messiah came He would institute a political kingdom and overthrow Israel's enemies. The concept of a suffering Messiah who would come to redeem His people had virtually been lost. Perhaps Jesus encouraged the disciples to say nothing about His messiahship until He would have an opportunity of explaining the true concept. "The disciples as yet had no way of knowing what conception Jesus had of His messianic vocation and it was imperative that they should not be allowed to fill the content of the term with their own dreams."[27]

It is significant that this identification of Jesus as the Messiah occurred at this juncture in Mark's gospel. To this point there had been many questions and discussions concerning the person of Jesus Christ. That now is clear. From this point on Jesus began to explain to His disciples what that would mean, for it would ultimately lead to His death and resurrection. All of this was completely in keeping with the will of God for Him.

Instruction Concerning His Program, 8:31–9:13

HIS COMING DEATH, 8:31-33
(cf. Matt. 16:21-23; Luke 9:22)
8:31   It is interesting that, immediately following the testimony concerning His person as Messiah, Jesus "began to teach" His disciples of His coming death. This is the first of three predictions that Jesus made concerning His death in the gospel of Mark (cf. 9:31 and 10:33-34). He

25. Lane, *The Gospel of Mark,* 291.
26. Howard F. Vos, *Mark* (Grand Rapids: Zondervan, 1978), 75.
27. Lane, *The Gospel of Mark,* 292.

explained that the "Son of Man" must suffer many things and be killed. This identification is the common title Jesus used for Himself throughout the Gospels, and it is never used of anyone but Jesus. It is probably a reference to the Son of Man in Daniel 7:13-14, who is the One entrusted by God with sovereign rule, glory, and power. But in Daniel's prophecy the idea of suffering never occurs. That was the issue Jesus was trying to clarify for His followers. The Son of Man must suffer and die as Isaiah predicted in his servant song (Isa. 52:13–53:12).

> The statement that the Son of Man *must* suffer many things points to the overruling purpose of God and reflects Jesus' conviction that the intention revealed in Scripture attains its fulfillment in the shame of the crucifixion as well as in the triumph of the resurrection. The disciples may behold in Jesus' submission to the divine will the perfect human response to the regal claims of God.[28]

The Son of Man would "be rejected [*apodokimasthēnai,* literally means "to fail to pass the scrutiny"] by the elders and the chief priests and the scribes." These individuals were the ones who constituted the Sanhedrin in Jerusalem. Although Jesus does not mention Jerusalem as being the place where all these events would occur, the listing of these three groups of people points clearly to that city. These groups would be the ones to officially condemn the Son of Man and bring about His death. But that would not be the end of Him, for Jesus clearly said that after three days He would rise again. One wonders if the disciples actually heard that part of His statement.

8:32   This was the first time that Jesus plainly stated (*elalei,* imperfect tense showing He repeated this teaching over and over) the matter of His coming death. Mark alone mentions this fact and uses a word for "plainly" (*parrēsia*) that means "open," that is, speech that conceals nothing. This was a brand-new revelation to the disciples. It was not in keeping with their understanding of what the Messiah would do. It is therefore not surprising that Peter took Jesus aside and began to rebuke Him. "To Peter such frankness seemed to be indiscreet; such premonitions of failure were at variance with all his conceptions of the Christ. The Master had manifested a momentary weakness; it was his duty as senior of the Twelve to remonstrate."[29] The idea of the

---

28. Ibid., 301.

29. Swete, *The Gospel According to St. Mark,* 180.

Messiah's dying did not fit at all with Peter's convictions and hopes. His reaction is understandable but nevertheless presumptuous. The Lord could not allow Peter's words and actions to stand.

8:33   Mark alone notes that Jesus turned around and looked at all of His disciples. They were probably standing there in complete agreement with Peter's rebuke of the Savior. But Jesus rebuked Peter as the spokesman for the Twelve in the presence of the full group by telling him to get away from Him. The fact that He referred to him as Satan does not mean that Peter and Satan were one and the same. It was simply to imply that Peter was acting as Satan's spokesman at this point. Peter was actually encouraging the Lord to follow the route that Satan had suggested earlier: that He could have the glory without the cross (cf. Matt. 4:8-9). "The avoidance of the cross had been a temptation faced and overcome by the Lord in the wilderness: and for Peter to suggest it here was to think in human terms, and not in divine terms."[30] Peter clearly was setting his mind on the things of man and man's interests, not on the interests and will of God. Jesus clearly knew the difference.

HIS REQUIREMENT FOR FOLLOWERS, 8:34-38
(cf. Matt. 16:24-28; Luke 9:23-27)
8:34   Jesus summoned not only His disciples but the multitude that was apparently not far away. "Mark alone notes the unexpected presence of a crowd up here near Caesarea Philippi in heathen territory."[31] It was hard for Jesus and the disciples to ever get away from people. Having just pictured for His apostolic band the fact that He was going to be killed, He turned to the disciples to point out the true cost of discipleship. The fact that He spoke to a large crowd shows these conditions for following Him are relevant for all believers, not just for the Twelve alone. His statements are clear: "If anyone wishes to come after Me, let him deny himself, and take up his cross, and follow Me."

What must a true disciple do? He must first of all "deny himself" (*aparnēsasthō heauton,* aorist imperative indicating a decisive act that is viewed as a completed thing), then "take up his cross" (*aratō ton stauron autou,* also an aorist imperative). A denial of self does not mean a denial of one's personality. It simply means a denial of self-

30. Cole, *The Gospel According to Mark,* 137.
31. Robertson, *Word Pictures in the New Testament,* 1:336.

centeredness. It is a removal of the individual from the throne of his life and the placing of Jesus Christ on that throne.

> The central thought in self-denial is a disowning of any claim that may be urged by the self, a sustained willingness to say 'No' to oneself in order to be able to say 'Yes' to God. This involves a radical denunciation of all self-idolatry and of every attempt to establish one's own life in accordance with the dictates of the self.[32]

Taking up one's cross was not a Jewish metaphor, but it was a figure that would have been common to Mark's readers. Every condemned criminal was required to carry his cross or his crosspiece to his place of execution. By making a criminal carry his cross, the Roman government was showing that they had authority over that individual. When Jesus Christ said a disciple must take up his cross in a decisive act, He was teaching that one must come to the realization of who is the authority in one's life. Once that decisive act of putting Christ on the throne has occurred, then the disciple is to "follow" (*akoloutheitō*, present tense indicating continuous action) Him. "To 'come behind' Jesus means to attach oneself to him as his disciple. The figure is based on the fact that Christ's 'followers'—not only The Twelve but also many others—often accompanied the Master, frequently literally *came on behind* him."[33] He then will reveal His will afresh daily, and the disciple is to follow that will.

8:35 In vv. 35-38 the Lord gave four statements to elaborate on v. 34. Each begins with the same Greek preposition—"for" (*gar*). What person would not wish to save his life? Yet, if he seeks the wrong things in life, he will lose it. But if a person loses his life for the cause of Jesus Christ and for the gospel, he will save it. An individual who truly understands the person of Jesus Christ and the need of the lost will live his life to proclaim the "good news," the gospel. Mark's account alone adds this notation about losing one's life for Jesus Christ and for the sake of the gospel. This emphasis on the gospel is characteristic of Mark (cf. 1:1, 15; 10:29). "Note that Christ lays claim to such absolute devotion. This proves that he regards himself as Lord of all and that the evangelist was fully aware of this!"[34] When one loses himself to the gospel, he finds eternal life.

32. Lane, *The Gospel of Mark*, 307.
33. Hendriksen, *Exposition of the Gospel According to Mark*, 329.
34. Ibid., 331.

8:36 In a rhetorical question Jesus asked, "For what does it profit a man to gain the whole world, and forfeit his soul?" Surely there is much to be gained in this world. Riches, wealth, power, prestige have been things many have tried to gain. But what if a person should gain everything this world has to offer? What would that profit him? The answer that is expected is that it would profit him nothing, for whatever one would gain in this life cannot be taken with him beyond the grave. Perhaps in His rhetorical question here and in the following verse, Jesus may have been thinking about the men who trust in their riches in Psalm 49:5-9.

8:37 Jesus asked a second rhetorical question: "For what shall a man give in exchange for his soul?" The answer is that there is nothing that one can give in exchange for one's soul. The soul is a precious thing that is of eternal consequence and must be guarded carefully. "When a man has forfeited eternal life, he experiences absolute loss, even though he may have won the approval of the whole world with his denial of Jesus and the gospel."[35]

8:38 In a final statement Jesus reflected on His return to this earth in power and glory. This may be the earliest announcement made by Jesus of His return in glory (see Matt. 10:32-33) for judgment. He truly is the Son of Man, who will come back to this earth as the Judge of all people. When that occurs, those who have been ashamed of Him and His words will find that He will be ashamed of them. "To be ashamed of Jesus means to be so proud that one wants to have nothing to do with him. Thus, for example, Heb. 2:11 states, 'He is not ashamed (i.e., not too proud) to call them brothers.'"[36] Such individuals have not committed themselves to Him as Savior. They are indeed classic examples of those who live in an "adulterous and sinful generation." To be adulterous carries the idea of being unfaithful. Old Testament prophets decried Israel as being an adulterous nation for their unfaithfulness to Jehovah. They not only were adulterous but were definitely sinful, for they completely missed the goal of serving and glorifying God. Therefore He will reject them, and they will be cast out when He comes in the glory of the Father with the holy angels to exercise judgment (cf. Matt. 24:29-31; 25:10-13, 31ff.).

35. Lane, *The Gospel of Mark,* 309.
36. Hendriksen, *Exposition of the Gospel According to Mark,* 332.

HOMILETICAL SUGGESTIONS

The miracle of the feeding of the 4,000, coupled with Jesus' teaching on leaven, present some interesting observations. The fact that He met the needs of a large group of people in a Gentile region is also significant for Mark's gospel, which was primarily directed to Gentiles. The Savior had significant ministry among Gentiles as well as among Jews. Jesus Christ was quick to use that event to instruct His disciples about the teachings of the religious leaders and to warn them to be careful with their own instruction.

The healing of the blind man at Bethsaida is unique in the gospel accounts because the miracle occurred in two stages. The fact that Jesus Christ did not immediately bring healing to this individual must be significant. A lesson was clearly being taught. It appears that Jesus was trying to help the disciples understand that their comprehension of His person was coming in stages. Immediately following that miracle, Jesus asked them that great question: "Who do people say that I am?" The responses are interesting and show that the disciples themselves were growing in their understanding of His person. The fact that Peter's great confession is recorded with no indication of the Lord's words of blessing on Peter is most interesting. How Peter could immediately take the Savior aside and rebuke him following the great statement concerning His person is remarkable. Yet Jesus Christ continued to minister to His disciples, teaching them the true cost of discipleship, as a disciple must deny himself, take up his cross, and follow Him.

MARK

CHAPTER

NINE

THE SERVANT'S GLORY

HIS COMING KINGDOM PICTURED, 9:1-10
(cf. Matt. 16:28–17:9; Luke 9:27-36)

9:1   Jesus had just mentioned His return in glory to serve as Judge. Perhaps the prospect of seeing the Son of Man in glory excited the hopes of the Twelve. Now Jesus said there was to be a display of His glory on this earth for some of those who were hearing Him speak at that moment. The true glory of His kingdom would be seen even though the nation was about to reject and crucify Him. That was why Jesus said that some were standing there who would not die until they saw the kingdom of God come in its power.

> The immediate sequel to Jesus' solemn promise is the account of the transfiguration (Ch. 9:2-8). This indicates that Mark understood Jesus' statement to refer to this moment of transcendent glory conceived as an enthronement and an anticipation of the glory which is to come. . . . The transfiguration was a momentary, but real (and witnessed) manifestation of Jesus' sovereign power which pointed beyond itself to the parousia, when He will come "with power and glory" (Ch. 13:26).[1]

9:2   The story continues "six days later" when "Jesus took" (*paralambanei,* present tense, which pictures the story as occurring) Peter, James, and John with Him "up to a high mountain."

---

1. William L. Lane, *The Gospel of Mark,* NICNT (Grand Rapids: Eerdmans, 1974), 313-14.

There need be no theological reason for the precise *six days* of Matthew (xvii. 1) and Mark, though attempts have been made to connect them with the 'six days' of God's working in Genesis followed by His sabbath rest. This is just one of the irrelevancies of the memory of any eyewitness, assuring us that the story of the Christ is penned to history, firmly set in place and time, though we may not always be able to reconstruct these from the scanty data given.[2]

Various locations have been suggested by scholars concerning the high mountain into which Jesus took His disciples. Many believe that it was Mount Tabor located about ten miles southwest of the Sea of Galilee. A beautiful church commemorating the Transfiguration sits on the top of this mountain. Others believe that the immediate connection of the previous section with Caesarea Philippi more accurately pictures this event as occurring on some peak of Mount Hermon. Regardless of where it took place, it happened, and the three disciples were there to observe it.

Why the Lord chose Peter, James, and John is unclear from the text. It is true that they had previously shared the experience of the raising of Jairus's daughter (cf. 5:37), and they would later on be allowed to go farther with Him at His time of prayer in the Garden of Gethsemane (cf. 14:33ff.). There is never any indication as to why God chose these three men, but it is clearly not a matter of favoritism. "If such a question has any answer, it may be that these three had shown themselves especially spiritually responsive to what illumination they had already been given (cf. Peter's declaration in Mk. viii. 29)."[3]

Jesus being "transfigured [*metemorphōthē*] before them" was an event clearly designed to be the demonstration of kingdom glory that Jesus spoke of in v. 1. The Greek word for transfigured is similar in its meaning to the English word "metamorphosis," the concept being that of a change of form (*meta* = "change," *morphe* = "form"), which takes place from within. "The word *transfigured* describes a change on the outside that comes from the inside. It is the opposite of 'masquerade,' which is an outward change that does not come from within. Jesus allowed His glory to radiate through His whole being, and the mountaintop became a holy of holies!"[4] Jesus was transfigured

2. R. A. Cole, *The Gospel According to Mark* (Grand Rapids: Eerdmans, 1979), 141.
3. Ibid.
4. Warren W. Wiersbe, *Be Diligent* (Wheaton, Ill.: Victor, 1987), 88.

from the inside out—that is, His true glory was allowed to radiate from within.

> The theory that the transfiguration is a misplaced account of a resurrection appearance of the Lord continues to find support in spite of the solid objections which have been marshalled against such an interpretation. It is necessary to recognize in the narrative the presence of details which ground the event in history: the precise time reference (Ch. 9:2), the designation "Rabbi" and the proposal of verse 5. Mark clearly believed that he was reporting a factual event which had primary significance for the disciples as a disclosure of Jesus' transcendent sonship.[5]

9:3   As a result, "His garments became radiant," or gleaming (*stilbonta,* a word found only here in the New Testament and that carries the idea of sparkling, glistening), "and exceedingly white." Mark alone adds a comment, evidently learned through Peter, that the whiteness was purer than any "launderer [*gnapheus,* old word for one who carded wool] on earth" could ever hope to achieve. Concerning the use of the Greek word *gnapheus,* William Hendriksen says, "In the present instance of its use the emphasis falls on cleaning, making white; hence, a bleacher. Another rendering that deserves consideration would be, '. . . as white as no laundryman on earth could make them.'"[6]

9:4   Appearing with Jesus on the Mount of Transfiguration were Elijah and Moses. Both Matthew (Matt. 17:3) and Luke (Luke 9:30) reverse the order of these two visitors, listing Moses first. It seems strange that, if both Matthew and Luke copied from Mark's gospel, they would reverse the order. Elijah had recently been in the disciples' thoughts and discussions (cf. 8:28). Moses, however, was a complete surprise to them.

The two visitors "were talking with Jesus." Luke's account (Luke 9:31) explains that they were talking about His "departure" (*exodon*). The word "departure" is used in other New Testament passages to speak of death.

> We receive the distinct impression that for Elijah and Moses this speaking with an exalted being like Jesus Christ was not something unusual.

5. Lane, *The Gospel of Mark,* 316.
6. William Hendriksen, *Exposition of the Gospel According to Mark* (Grand Rapids: Baker, 1975), 339.

These two messengers from heaven were filled with reverence, of course, as they stood there on the Mount of Transfiguration, "talking with" Jesus. But it was a reverence which excluded any earthly fear and alarm. Does not the description offered to us here in Mark 9:4 and parallel passages shed some light on the character of heavenly fellowship?[7]

The appearance of Elijah and Moses on the Mount of Transfiguration probably occurred to bring together the Prophets and the Law:

Moses appears as the representative of the old covenant and the promise, now shortly to be fulfilled in the death of Jesus, and Elijah as the appointed restorer of all things (Chs. 1:2f.; 9:11). The stress on Elijah's presence at the transfiguration indicates that the fulfillment of "all things" has arrived (Ch. 9:12). The transfiguration is the prelude to the passion, and Elijah is there to testify to the ultimate importance of the impending events in an historical sequence which culminates in consummation. The presence of Elijah and Moses thus has eschatological significance in the specific sense that they proclaim the coming of the end."[8]

9:5   Peter was not to be outdone on this occasion. Even though he was not directly addressed, he spoke out, "Rabbi, it is good for us to be here; and let us make three tabernacles, one for You, and one for Moses, and one for Elijah." Although the text says he "answered and said," the word for answering (*apokritheis*) has broad meanings. Here it may simply mean that Peter reacted or responded to the situation. Also it is interesting to compare the synoptics as to Peter's form of address. Here in Mark he called Jesus "Rabbi" (*Rabbi*). In Matthew he addressed Jesus as "Lord" (*Kyrie,* 17:4). Luke's form of address is "Master" (*Epistata,* 9:33). "Clearly, in the present passages these three terms must be considered synonyms: all aim to do justice to the exalted character of the Savior. Each evangelist offers his own translation of the Aramaic word which Peter must have used."[9]

There is much discussion about Peter's comment. "Why did Peter say anything? Luke says that he spoke, 'not knowing what he said,' as an excuse for the inappropriateness of his remarks. Perhaps Peter

---

7. Ibid., 340.
8. Lane, *The Gospel of Mark,* 319.
9. Hendriksen, *Exposition of the Gospel According to Mark,* 340.

felt embarrassed at having been asleep (Luke 9:32) and the feast of
tabernacles or booths (*skēnai*) was near."[10] Is it possible that Peter
envisioned the manifestation of the glory as the coming of the kingdom and fulfillment of the Jewish Feast of Tabernacles (cf. Zech.
14:16)? To celebrate that feast, the Jews would leave their homes annually in the Fall and live in tents for eight days. The purpose of the
Feast of Tabernacles was to cause the Jew to look backward and remember that he had wandered in the wilderness for a period of time.
But it also looked forward to anticipation of blessing in the land,
which many extended to enjoying the blessings of the Millennium under Messiah. Peter may very well have thought that the kingdom had
come, so he was suggesting that they enjoy it.

9:6   Mark's comment, written many years after the event, shares the
reason Peter spoke up. He really "did not know what to answer," and
he was terrified at the whole situation.

> Under such circumstances it is generally best not to say anything. This,
> however, would hardly have been in character for loquacious Simon,
> especially for a Simon just awakened out of sleep, and, like James and
> John, filled with fear. But before we begin to criticize this apostle too
> severely, would it not be in order to take to heart the warning of James
> 1:19?[11]

9:7   Peter's proposal would have put Jesus, Elijah, and Moses on the
same level. But a cloud suddenly formed, overshadowing all the people on the mountain, and a voice coming from the cloud said, "This is
My beloved Son, listen to Him!" As on a previous occasion, when Jesus
came up out of the water following His baptism (cf. 1:11; Matt. 3:17;
Luke 3:22), the authenticating voice of God spoke from heaven identifying this One as His beloved Son. "The Greek *agapētos, beloved,* almost certainly has the connotation of 'only begotten' here, as the
Hebrew *yachîd* would have had."[12] It is because Jesus is God's only
Son that the disciples are exhorted to "listen [*akouete,* present tense
imperative carrying the idea of something that is habitual] to Him"
and to obey Him. This command probably reminded the disciples of
Deuteronomy 18:15 and connected Jesus with "the Prophet" God had
promised to raise up.

10. A. T. Robertson, *Word Pictures in the New Testament* (Nashville: Broadman, 1930), 1:339.
11. Hendriksen, *Exposition of the Gospel According to Mark,* 340-41.
12. Cole, *The Gospel According to Mark,* 144.

9:8 When the disciples looked around, they "saw no one . . . except Jesus." Mark graphically describes their sudden glance around the mountain only to discover that Moses and Elijah were gone. If Moses and Elijah represented the Law and the Prophets, it is significant that they were no longer present. It is reminiscent of what the writer of the book of Hebrews says: "God, after He spoke long ago to the fathers in the prophets in many portions and in many ways, in these last days has spoken to us in His Son" (Heb. 1:1-2a). Jesus is the final form of God's revelation. He is the One who is to be listened to.

But how was this event a taste of the kingdom of God (cf. v. 1)? Several significant factors are involved here. First, this event does take place on the earth, and when Jesus Christ rules in power and glory from David's throne, that kingdom will also take place on the earth. Second, the Lord is in His glory. Again, when He rules from David's throne He will also be in His glory. Third, all the necessary people who will be part of Jesus' kingdom are represented here: the saints in physical bodies are represented by Peter, James, and John; the saints who have passed through death but who will be resurrected in order to share in Jesus' kingdom are represented by Moses; and the group of people in Jesus' kingdom who never tasted death—those saints who will be caught up at the rapture of the church (1 Thess. 4:13-18)—are represented by Elijah. Perhaps that is why this was a taste of the kingdom of God.

9:9 It is clear that what happened on this mountain was not a subjective vision. They truly saw Jesus glorified, a fact Peter was certain of (cf. 2 Peter 1:16-18). But as they came down from the mountain, Jesus gave orders to the disciples that they were "not to relate . . . what they had seen" until after the Son of Man rose from the dead. That meant that the disciples would have to keep this event quiet only for a short period of time. Then they were free—in fact they were required—to proclaim the story. This is the only instance in the Gospels when a limit was placed on the silence of the disciples.

9:10 "They seized" (*ekratēsan,* aorist verb meaning to take hold of something and to hang on) on this "statement" (*logon*), and yet they continued to discuss among themselves "what rising from the dead might mean." "The [*logos*] in this case is not the fact of the Transfiguration, but the Lord's saying, especially what He had said about rising from the dead; they discussed this among themselves, not venturing to ask Him the meaning."[13] They were still wrestling with the concept of the Messiah's dying and rising from the dead. Hendriksen suggests that

> perhaps their questions were somewhat along this line: "Peter, what do you think he meant by this?" "John, do you think he was referring to the resurrection at the last day?" "James, why is the Master going to die at all if he is going to rise again?" Another question may have been, "Was he referring to a physical resurrection?" But these are merely guesses.[14]

HIS RELATIONSHIP TO ELIJAH, 9:11-13
(cf. Matt. 17:10-13)

9:11   The appearance of Elijah on the Mount of Transfiguration may have prompted the question that was on the minds of the disciples. "The three have been reflecting upon the vision, and it has revived and given fresh point to an old perplexity. How was Elijah's appearance at the Transfiguration to be reconciled with the official doctrine of his return?"[15] They were also wrestling with the concept of Elijah's coming. And if indeed Jesus was the Messiah, where was Elijah? Did Elijah's presence on the Mount of Transfiguration satisfy the Old Testament prophecies? Their question was, Why did the scribes say that Elijah must come first? The disciples had on many occasions listened to scribal teaching that was based on Malachi 4:5-6. "But even though on the one hand the Tishbite obviously has not as yet reappeared upon the scene of history, restoring everything, yet on the other hand Jesus, the Messiah, not only has already arrived but even declares that he is about to die. How is this possible?"[16]

9:12   Jesus reaffirmed that Elijah must come and prepare the way for the Messiah. The scribes were right on this point. But He tried to help them understand the conflict that existed in their thinking between the coming of Elijah and the suffering of Messiah. Many at that time had connected Elijah's coming with the inception of Messiah's kingdom. Jesus said there was a misunderstanding by many about the suffering of the Son of Man and how He would "be treated with con-

13. Henry Barclay Swete, *The Gospel According to St. Mark* (Grand Rapids: Eerdmans, 1956), 192.
14. Hendriksen, *Exposition of the Gospel According to Mark,* 342.
15. Swete, *The Gospel According to St. Mark,* 193.
16. Hendriksen, *Exposition of the Gospel According to Mark,* 343.

tempt." Even though Elijah had come, His suffering was necessary, and this too had been predicted. While Jesus did not quote any specific Old Testament prophecy, could He have been thinking of passages such as Psalm 22:1-18; 69:1-21; Isaiah 52:13–53:12?

> The response to the disciples' question concerning Elijah by a further question concerning the rejection of the Son of Man has a deeper intention, however. Basic to Jesus' understanding of Elijah's function is the restoration through repentance promised in Mal. 4:6, and fulfilled in the prophetic ministry of John the Baptist. Verse 12b serves as a warning that the sufferings of John and his shameful rejection do not disqualify him from fulfilling the role of Elijah nor do Jesus' sufferings discredit him as the transcendent Son of Man.[17]

9:13 Jesus stated that Elijah had already come, adding, "And they did to him whatever they wished, just as it is written of him." It was clear in the thinking of Jesus that the ministry of John the Baptist fulfilled the prophecy concerning the coming of Elijah. Mark alone notes that John's persecution had been foretold. "In this case Scripture had foretold the future not by prophecy but by a type."[18] Just as Ahab and Jezebel made life miserable for Elijah in Old Testament times, Herod Antipas and his wife, Herodias, had made life miserable for John the Baptist. John found his Jezebel in Herodias.

> This very fact—that it was written, hence divinely planned—is filled with comfort. It shows that without in any way erasing human responsibility and guilt, these murderous intentions and (in the case of the Baptist and Jesus) deeds happen in accordance with the divine decree. In the end, therefore, God always triumphs. His truth is victorious.[19]

But John the Baptist was Elijah, as Jesus said in the gospel of Matthew, only if the nation had believed (Matt. 11:14). The coming of Elijah is seen by some as again occurring before Christ comes the second time in power and glory. They believe that the appearance of the two witnesses in Revelation 11:3-12, one of whom demonstrates the characteristics of Elijah, will completely fulfill the prophecy before the coming of Jesus Christ in glory.

17. Lane, *The Gospel of Mark*, 326.
18. Swete, *The Gospel According to St. Mark*, 194.
19. Hendriksen, *Exposition of the Gospel According to Mark*, 343-44.

INSTRUCTION CONCERNING THE IMPOSSIBLE, 9:14-29
(cf. Matt. 17:14-20; Luke 9:37-48a)

9:14   When Jesus and the three disciples came down from the mountain, they encountered a large crowd surrounding the other nine disciples. Mark alone records that the disciples were in the midst of an argument with some scribes. The exact nature of the argument is not revealed, but it concerned the disciples' failure to cast a demon out of a boy (v. 18). "It was just like the professional scribes to take keen interest in the failure of the nine disciples to cure this poor boy. They gleefully nagged and quizzed them. Jesus and the three find them at it when they arrive in the plain."[20]

9:15   "Immediately" (*euthys*) when the crowd saw Jesus, "they were amazed [*exethambēthēsan,* an intensive verb implying great amazement], and began running up to greet Him." Some speculate that the amazement came because there was some kind of an afterglow from the Transfiguration surrounding the person of Jesus. That, however, would be contrary to the command He had just given His disciples that they should not talk about what they had just witnessed until after His resurrection (cf. v. 9). It is more probable that it was simply the sudden appearance of Jesus at this juncture. The crowd and the disciples did not know He was near and were surprised that He was suddenly there. Their next impulse was to run "to greet" (*ēspazonto,* imperfect tense picturing an action that continued for a while) Him.

9:16   He asked the disciples what the discussion was all about. "The Lord's first questioning words were not words of ignorance; they were designed to draw the attention of the crowd away from the humiliated disciples, and to Himself, as verse 19 makes explicit."[21] What was the debate that was taking place with the religious leaders? It is interesting that there was no response from either the disciples or the scribes. "For the scribes the 'fun' they were having suddenly ends. So embarrassed are they that they do not know what to say. So the arguing and jeering suddenly stops. Not even one of the law-experts was anxious to answer Christ's question."[22]

20. Robertson, *Word Pictures in the New Testament,* 1:340.
21. Cole, *The Gospel According to Mark,* 145.
22. Hendriksen, *Exposition of the Gospel According to Mark,* 345.

9:17 One from the crowd stepped forward and addressed the Lord as "Teacher" (*Didaskale*), a very respectful form of address. The speaker had brought his son (his "only child," cf. Luke 9:38) to Jesus that the boy might be healed. His intention was to come to Jesus, but when he found the nine disciples, he went ahead with his request. This was reasonable, for Jesus had previously given His disciples authority over unclean spirits (cf. 6:7). According to the father, his son was possessed by a demonic spirit that caused him to be mute. In light of v. 25, it appears that the demon made the boy deaf as well as mute. This, therefore, was a difficult case.

9:18 The man proceeded to explain to Jesus that the demon at times would seize his son, causing him to fall to the ground. At such times he also would foam at his mouth, grind his teeth, and stiffen his body. Each of the verbs Mark uses adds graphic detail and presents a truly pitiable condition. The picture given by the father is characteristic of epileptic seizures, but it must be noted that epilepsy and demonic possession are not identical. Since Jesus was not available, the boy was brought to the disciples. "In Jesus' absence the disciples stood in his place and were regarded as he is. It was therefore legitimate to expect that they possessed the power of their master."[23] However, they were not able to accomplish the exorcism.

9:19 Jesus' words were probably addressed to the nine disciples who failed in their attempt to cast out the demon. He addressed them as an "unbelieving [*apistos*, faithless] generation." "The qualitative overtones in 'unbelieving generation' suggest that the disciples remain indistinguishable from the unregenerate men who demand signs but are fundamentally untrue to God (Ch. 8:12, 38)."[24] He questioned them as to how long He would be able to be with them. How long could He put up with such incompetence?

> The opposition expressed between "I" and "you" in these statements is seen in its true character only when it is recognized that what God says of his relationship to faithless Israel (cf. Isa. 63:8-10), Jesus now says of his relationship to the future community of faith. It is a measure of Jesus' infinite patience that he continues to instruct the Twelve and prepare them for the day in which they will stand in his place and continue his work (Chs. 3:14f.; 9:28f.; 14:28; 16:7).[25]

23. Lane, *The Gospel of Mark*, 331.
24. Ibid., 332.
25. Ibid.

Jesus, however, was equal to the task, which He indicated by commanding, "Bring him to Me!"

9:20   That the boy was brought before Jesus may imply that he was not there in the crowd with his father but was in safekeeping not far away. The demonic spirit who possessed him recognized that he was now dealing with Jesus. Therefore the spirit "threw [the boy] into a convulsion" (*synesparazen,* aorist tense; the prefix *syn* strengthens the force of the verb, implying a violent fit), causing him to fall to the ground. There he continued "rolling about" (*ekylieto,* imperfect tense), "foaming at the mouth." "By reducing the son to complete helplessness the unclean spirit betrayed his malicious intent to destroy the child and his utter contempt for Jesus. It is evident that the Lord was deeply moved."[26]

9:21   Jesus engaged the father in conversation by asking him how long the boy had been in this condition. At the heart of Jesus' question is His compassion for people. Truly He is a sympathetic physician. Jesus obviously did not need

> this information in order to bring about recovery, but the father needs to reflect on the lengthy period of time during which his son has been in this condition, in order that he may be all the more thankful for the miracle that is about to take place. Such a reflection will also have a wholesome effect on those standing around.[27]

The sad response of the father was that the boy had been like this "from his childhood" (*paidiothen,* from *paidion,* meaning "a child").

9:22   The father added further pathetic details: the demon often had tried to throw the boy into the fire or into water in order to take his life. It was the opinion of the father that these frequent mishaps were not accidental. Lack of concern for human beings is clearly seen by the actions of this demonic spirit. The father then said to Jesus, "But if You can do anything, take pity on him and help us!" The fact that the disciples had been unable to do anything for the boy had weakened the man's faith. But "the failure of the disciples had not wholly destroyed his faith in the power of Jesus, though the conditional form (first class, assuming it to be true) does suggest doubt whether the boy can be cured at all."[28] His final cry, "Help us!" (*boētbēson*

26. Ibid.
27. Hendriksen, *Exposition of the Gospel According to Mark,* 348.
28. Robertson, *Word Pictures in the New Testament,* 1:342.

bēmin), is an aorist imperative. His words carry the force of "Do it now!"

9:23 Jesus picked up on what the man said, however, and turned it right back to him: "If You can!" Jesus said. "All things are possible to him who believes."

> The Lord repeats the father's words and places them in contrast with the spiritual facts which he had yet to learn: *'if thou canst*: for one who believes all things are possible': i.e. it is for thee rather than for Me to decide whether this thing can be done; it can be if thou believest (cf. xi.23f.).[29]

The issue was a matter of the man's personal faith in Jesus Christ. But a person must be careful not to read a blanket approval of every request one might think of in these words of the Savior.

> We are not called to 'put God to the test' by irresponsible prayer for what is our human desire but may not be His will. We are free to ask what we will, but only if it be what He wills (I Jn. v. 14). This is no mere theological quibble: it is a statement in another form of the need for the 'mind of Christ' in us. It is also a warning against taking a statement of Scripture in isolation, and basing presumptuous prayer on it.[30]

9:24 The father "immediately" (*euthys*) responded by crying out, "I do believe [*pisteuō,* present tense indicating he did still believe]; help [*boēthei,* present tense imperative asking for continuous help] my unbelief." He believed in Jesus Christ, but faith can never be perfect for sinful creatures. No matter how strongly one believes, there is always an element of unbelief.

> The ambivalence in his confession is a natural expression of anxiety and the earnest desire to see his son released, but it is also a candid plea for help at that point where his faith is ready to fail. The exchange between Jesus and the father established the personal relationship necessary for the accomplishment of the release.[31]

29. Swete, *The Gospel According to St. Mark,* 199.
30. Cole, *The Gospel According to Mark,* 147.
31. Lane, *The Gospel of Mark,* 334.

9:25   Jesus saw that the crowd was again "rapidly gathering" (*epi-syntrechei*). "A double compound here alone in the N.T. and not in the old Greek writers. *Epitrechō* occurs in the papyri, but not *episun-trechō*. The double compound vividly describes the rapid gathering of the crowd to Jesus and the epileptic boy to see the outcome."[32] With that He rebuked the demon as a being separate from the boy and gave it two commands that only Mark records. First, Jesus commanded that the "deaf [a fact noted for the first time] and dumb spirit" should "come [*exelthe,* aorist imperative implying the action should be completed] out" of the young boy. Second, He added that he should "not [never] enter him again" (*mēketi eiselthēs,* aorist subjunctive for the negative command). Truly it must have been an encouragement to the father to realize that his son was about to be set free from demonic possession and would never have to face that condition again.

9:26   The demon was not quite through with the boy, however, for in one final moment of torment it threw him into "terrible convulsions" (*sparaxas,* not the compound verb found in v. 20) as it came out.

> What a vivid description of the manner in which the boy was cured! Mark alone has all the details. He must have listened very carefully as Peter (and/or others) told the story. There was the shriek uttered by the demon who made use of the boy's vocal organs. Along with it there were those ghastly, horrible muscle spasms. And then there was rigidity.[33]

The boy was so racked by the effects of the demon's departure that he fell down as though dead. The demon did all the possible harm that it could as it left him. The conclusion of some in the crowd was that he had died (*apethanen,* aorist tense emphasizing an accomplished fact). Mark alone records this supposition.

9:27   But Jesus "took him by the hand and raised him up." This parallels the story of Jesus' raising Jairus's daughter from the dead. In both stories Jesus took the children by their hands and raised them up (cf. 5:41). Luke adds the fact that Jesus "gave him back to his father" (Luke 9:42). What a beautiful, personal touch that gives to this miracle.

9:28   Jesus and the disciples then went into a house, away from the multitudes. "The Lord went indoors, into the lodging where the party

32. Robertson, *Word Pictures in the New Testament,* 1:342-43.
33. Hendriksen, *Exposition of the Gospel According to Mark,* 350.

[was] housed . . . , to escape from the enthusiasm of the crowd, and because on such occasions further teaching was impossible."[34] It was not surprising that the disciples' first question to Him was, "Why could we not cast it out?" They must have wondered why they had failed, for the Lord had given them authority over demonic spirits (cf. 6:7), and apparently on other occasions they had been successful.

9:29 Jesus' response to His disciples was that "this kind cannot come out by anything but prayer." Some ancient manuscripts add the phrase "and fasting." Whether this was part of the original or was added by scribes to support asceticism cannot be fully resolved. Concerning the addition of this phrase, A. T. Robertson says that "it is clearly a late addition to help explain the failure. But it is needless and also untrue. Prayer is what the nine had failed to use. They were powerless because they were prayerless. Their self-complacency spelled defeat."[35]

It is also possible that by making a reference to "this kind" of spirit Jesus might have been implying that there are different kinds of demonic spirits—that some demons are more difficult to deal with than others. Or He might simply have been referring to demonic spirits in general. The point was that the exorcising of a demon was not something that the disciples could automatically assume would happen because of past performance. There must be prayerful dependence on the power of God. "[The disciples] had trusted in the quasi-magical power with which they thought themselves invested; there had been on their part no preparation of heart and spirit."[36] This, apparently, the disciples had failed to do. Were they drawing on past successes and attempting to perform the exorcism in their own strength? It was clear from the Savior's response that they were not prayerfully depending on God for His power to be exercised in this case.

INSTRUCTION CONCERNING HIS UPCOMING DEATH, 9:30-32 (cf. Matt. 17:22-23; Luke 9:43b-45)

9:30 From there Jesus and His disciples "went out and began to go through Galilee." He was leaving the region of Caesarea Philippi and coming through the region of Galilee for His last time, for He was

34. Swete, *The Gospel According to St. Mark,* 201-2.
35. Robertson, *Word Pictures in the New Testament,* 1:343.
36. Swete, *The Gospel According to St. Mark,* 202.

headed for Jerusalem where He would be betrayed. The latter part of this verse implies that He did not want (*ēthelen,* imperfect tense implying that this desire extended over a period of time) people to know where He was. For that reason Jesus and the disciples probably skirted the larger cities by traveling along the west bank of the Jordan as they headed from Caesarea Philippi toward the city of Capernaum for a final visit. Matthew's comment that "they were gathering together in Galilee" (Matt. 17:22) may imply that the disciples broke up into small parties and then mustered at certain points along the way. Perhaps this was done to avoid attracting notice. It is also true that in this period (beginning with 7:24) Jesus' primary purpose was the instruction of the Twelve.

> That was why he did not want the general public to know his whereabouts. He needed privacy, so as to have the time and the opportunity for teaching The Twelve, so that they in turn, especially after his resurrection, would be able to convey the truths concerning Jesus and his kingdom to others. Specifically, he was teaching them the lessons of the cross.[37]

9:31   As He was going, "He was teaching [*edidasken,* imperfect tense implying that the teaching continued over a period of time] His disciples" that the Son of Man was about "to be delivered into the hands of men." Jesus viewed the event as imminent and in the process of accomplishment. "The instrument of the betrayal . . . was in the company, and the Lord could see the purpose already lying as an undeveloped thought in his heart (Jo. vi.70f.)."[38] He also stated again that they would kill Him and that He would "rise [*anastēsetai,* future middle verb implying that Jesus would be involved in the process of His own resurrection] three days later." "In fulfillment of this prophecy the body of Jesus actually rested in the grave during three day-and-night periods: part of Friday, all of Saturday, and part of Sunday."[39] This was the second time Jesus made that prediction (cf. 8:31).

Though this statement was like the first one, it was a little more uncertain with regard to His being "delivered [*paradidotai,* also translated "betrayal"] into the hands of men." The word here could imply

37. Hendriksen, *Exposition of the Gospel According to Mark,* 352-53.
38. Swete, *The Gospel According to St. Mark,* 203.
39. Hendriksen, *Exposition of the Gospel According to Mark,* 353.

that both Jews and Gentiles would be involved in the carrying out of His execution. Jesus was to be delivered up to them.

> "To deliver up" or "hand over" is an important concept in the context of lawsuits and in the Jewish theology of martyrdom. More than simply the coming of an individual into another's power, the term connotes the actual fulfillment of God's will as expressed in Scripture. Particularly in martyrdom, God is the one who permits (or hinders) the handing over in fulfillment of his deeper purposes.[40]

That same word is used by Peter in Acts 2:23 to explain that the delivering up of Jesus was part of the predetermined plan of God.

9:32 The disciples again "did not understand" (*ēgnooun,* imperfect tense implying that their lack of understanding continued over a period of time) His statement. "They continued not to understand. They were agnostics on the subject of the death and resurrection even after the Transfiguration experience. As they came down from the mountain they were puzzled again over the Master's allusion to his resurrection (Mark 9:10)."[41] They were still thinking about the reigning Messiah and had a hard time comprehending how Messiah could die and yet reign. They were also "afraid to ask Him" (*ephobounto auton eperōtēsai,* also imperfect tense indicating that they continued to be afraid to ask) for further explanation. Perhaps His rebuke of Peter following the first announcement of His death (cf. 8:33), in which He called Peter a "Satan," prompted their silence at this time. "Moreover, there is a revealing clause in Luke 9:45 to the effect that there was a certain divine blinding that kept them from a full understanding of what He was telling them."[42] Whatever the reason, it is clear that Jesus' words here had a devastating effect on their hope of His being the reigning Messiah.

INSTRUCTION CONCERNING PRIDE, 9:33-37
(cf. Matt. 18:1-5; Luke 9:46-48)

9:33 Jesus and the disciples came back to Capernaum for the last time. While it is not stated that He was in Peter's home, that is probably the correct conclusion, for that was the home to which Jesus nor-

---

40. Lane, *The Gospel of Mark,* 337.
41. Robertson, *Word Pictures in the New Testament,* 1:344.
42. Howard F. Vos, *Mark* (Grand Rapids: Zondervan, 1978), 82-83.

mally came when He was in Capernaum. Another possibility is that they were in the home of Levi (cf. 2:15). As they entered into conversation, Jesus asked them an important question (*epērōta,* imperfect tense suggesting that the questioning went on over a period of time). His concern revolved around what they had been "discussing" (*dielogizesthe,* imperfect tense implying that they were discussing this issue for some time) as they traveled together. Some have tried to point out a discrepancy between the account in Mark and the same story in Matthew (cf. Matt. 18:1ff.). From Matthew's account it appears that the disciples bring the dispute to Jesus, whereas Mark implies that Jesus asked them the question first. Hendriksen proposes to solve this apparent contradiction by suggesting the following sequence of events:

> On the way to the house an argument concerning rank develops among the disciples (Luke 9:46). Indoors Jesus asks them, "What were you discussing on the road?" But they kept quiet, etc. (Mark 9:33-34). Jesus, however, knows (Luke 9:47). When they become aware of this, they ask him, "Who then *is* greatest in the kingdom of heaven?" (Matt. 18:1).—In any event the assumption of a discrepancy is unwarranted.[43]

9:34 The disciples would not answer Jesus' question. A deathly silence fell on the group, and they held their peace (*hoi de esiōpōn,* an imperfect tense indicating that silence continued to reign). They were too embarrassed to tell Him what they had been discussing, for Mark reveals that they were discussing which one of them was the greatest. When Jesus asked them His question, "they felt ashamed that the Master had discovered their jealous rivalry. It was not a mere abstract query, as they put it to Jesus, but it was a canker in their hearts."[44] Perhaps the selection of Peter, James, and John to accompany Jesus up the mountain for the Transfiguration had fueled the fires of their competitiveness. But with Jesus' enunciation of His coming death, one would think that all thoughts of status in the coming kingdom would be abandoned. Jesus did not need for them to tell Him what they had been discussing. He already knew.

9:35 Jesus sat down, as a rabbi would do, in order to teach. The fact that "He called the twelve" to Him implies that they probably had put some space between themselves and the Lord. Perhaps it was their

---

43. Hendriksen, *Exposition of the Gospel According to Mark,* 356.
44. Robertson, *Word Pictures in the New Testament,* 1:345.

sense of guilt that caused them to distance themselves. Having called them, He began to discuss with them the issue of positions of authority. Jesus' statement in this verse was repeated on other occasions (cf. 10:43ff.; Matt. 23:8ff.; Luke 22:24ff.). "If anyone wants to be first [*prōtos*], he shall be last [*eschatos*] of all, and servant [*diakonos*] of all." Positions in Jesus' kingdom are never determined by status but by a willingness to serve.

> True greatness does not consist in this, that from a towering height a person, in a self-congratulatory manner, has the right now to look down upon all others (Luke 18:9-12); but in this, that he immerses himself in the needs of others, sympathizes with them and helps them in every way possible. So, if any person—whether he be one of The Twelve or anyone else—wishes to be *first,* he *must* be *last;* that is, servant of all.[45]

9:36   To illustrate the principle He had just given, Jesus took "a child" (*paidion*) and sat him in their midst. It is possible that this child was someone from the household of Peter, perhaps even Peter's child. Jesus held the child "in His arms" (*enagkalisamenos,* literally to hold in the crook of the arm) and spoke to the disciples. "The Lord calls this little one to his side and places him 'in the midst of' all these 'big' men, perhaps in such a position that the child faced them while they were arranged in a crescent before him. The child was not afraid, for it stood by the Lord's very side (Luke 9:47)."[46]

9:37   Jesus said, "Whoever receives one child like this in My name receives Me; and whoever receives Me does not receive Me, but Him who sent Me," that is, His Father. "The action passes into a region beyond that of the visible order; to receive a lowly brother in Christ's Name is to receive Christ, and to receive Christ is to receive the Eternal Father in Whose Name He came."[47] Positions in Jesus' kingdom are not based on pride but on a willingness to serve and a willingness to accept others. The greatest marks of Jesus' servants are humility and servitude. Hendriksen summarizes this entire section well:

> Instead of asking, "Who among us is the greatest?" the followers of Jesus should learn to focus their loving attention on Christ's little ones,

45. Hendriksen, *Exposition of the Gospel According to Mark,* 357.
46. Ibid., 358-59.
47. Swete, *The Gospel According to St. Mark,* 206.

that is, on the lambs of the flock and on all those who in their condition of need and trustful dependence resemble these lambs. Such is the essence of true greatness, the greatness that reflects the same quality which in an infinite degree resides in God (Isa. 57:15).[48]

INSTRUCTION CONCERNING PARTISAN SPIRIT, 9:38-50 (cf. Matt. 18:6-14; Luke 9:49-50)

9:38 John spoke up and addressed Jesus with the term "Teacher" (*Didaskale*). This is the only comment attributed to the apostle John in the synoptic accounts. He cited something that had recently occurred, for the disciples had seen someone casting out demons in the name of Jesus. But that individual apparently was not one of the Twelve. John, probably with great pride, indicated that they "tried to hinder" (*ekōluomen,* imperfect tense indicating a repeated action) him because "he was not following" (*ouk ēkolouthei,* imperfect tense vividly picturing the action) their group. "[John] and one or more of the other disciples, probably during their recent journey through northern Galilee, had prohibited a non-disciple from using the Master's Name for the purpose of exorcising demoniacs. Ought they rather to have welcomed him as a brother?"[49]

This is a classic illustration of the narrow exclusivism of the Twelve. Perhaps this was also an attempt by John to distract his Lord's attention from the embarrassing subject of their discussion. Did Jesus' remark about receiving a child "in My name" (v. 37) bring this incident to John's mind? It is interesting that in the immediate context the disciples were unable to cast out a demon, but they were working against someone, probably a true believer, who in the name of Jesus was actually being victorious over the demonic realm. "The fact that Jesus' power was active in the man, bringing release to men who had been enslaved to demonic possession, marks him as a believer. His action was an effective witness to the imminent Kingdom of God."[50]

9:39 Jesus' response was that they should not have hindered (*mē kōlyeta,* present imperative carrying the force of "stop hindering") the individual. "Jesus opposed the narrow exclusivism of the Twelve with an open and generous spirit. The disciples' action was an abuse of

---

48. Hendriksen, *Exposition of the Gospel According to Mark,* 360.

49. Swete, *The Gospel According to St. Mark,* 207.

50. Lane, *The Gospel of Mark,* 343.

their authority, for they had presumed to speak for Jesus where they had no competence."[51] He pointed out that one cannot perform a mighty work (*dynamin*) in His name, then turn around in the next breath and speak evil of Him. J. Dwight Pentecost suggests that perhaps this man may have come to faith in Christ

> through the ministry of John [the Baptist] but continued in company with John's disciples even after John's death. An alternative explanation would be that this one had heard Jesus' words and had put faith in His person. By putting faith in His person he was doing what the disciples were not able to do while Jesus was separated from them on the Mount of Transfiguration. Either way, this man's faith was placed in the person of Christ and the works that He did were the products of that faith.[52]

9:40   Jesus' maxim "He who is not against us is for us" was here stated negatively. The positive statement of this same truth is seen in Matthew 12:30. Jesus' words show that there really are only two sides. There is no neutrality when one deals with the person of Jesus Christ. One is either for Him or against Him, and if one is for Him he certainly will not speak evil against Him. Swete says that "the man who is not a declared enemy of the Christian brotherhood may be provisionally regarded as a friend. In the present case, indeed, there was presumptive evidence of something better than neutrality, since the person in question had used the Name of Christ."[53]

9:41   But it was not only in the spectacular realm that one could work for Jesus Christ. The kind act of giving "a cup of water" to someone in His name could produce a reward. A cup of water given to quench the thirst caused by the burning Mideastern sun is clearly an act of hospitality (cf. v. 27) and also an example of humble service (cf. v. 35). It was not the act in and of itself that would give one any merit with God, but a person would perform such an act of kindness if he was a genuine follower of Jesus Christ. "[This] is the bond of universal brotherhood of the redeemed. It breaks over the lines of nation, race, class, sex, everything. No service is too small, even a cup of cold water, if done for Christ's sake."[54] The Lord sees all the actions of His

51. Ibid.
52. J. Dwight Pentecost, *The Words & Works of Jesus Christ* (Grand Rapids: Zondervan, 1981), 265.
53. Swete, *The Gospel According to St. Mark*, 208.
54. Robertson, *Word Pictures in the New Testament*, 1:346.

servants, and He will reward accordingly. "There are no distinctions between 'trivial' and 'important' tasks. There is only faith and obedience, shown in devotion to Jesus, and wherever these qualities exist they call forth the approval of God."[55]

9:42 Jesus used the statement from John to add further instruction concerning the matter of causing others to stumble or to be offended. His teaching here may be considered the negative side of v. 37. Surely the man the disciples had tried to hinder, the believer who was casting out demons in Jesus' name, was offended (*skandalisē,* aorist tense verb) by their actions. The noun *skandalon* referred to the crooked stick that would spring a trap; hence, the idea is to snare or entice. Jesus said that it would be better for one to have "a heavy millstone [*mylos onikos*] hung around his neck" and be "cast into the sea" than to cause someone to stumble.

> The millstone of which Jesus speaks is the top-stone of the two between which the grain is crushed. The reference is not to the handmill but to the much heavier stone drawn by a donkey. In the middle of the top-stone, whether of a handmill or a donkey-drawn mill, there is a hole through which grain can be fed so as to be crushed between the two stones. The presence of this hole explains the phrase "that a heavy millstone *be hung around his neck.*" With this millstone around his neck he will surely drown.[56]

It would be better to die faultless than to bring about offense.

9:43 Furthermore, if there was anything in one's life that could cause offense, one would be better off to be without that thing. "A man may place moral stumbling-blocks in his own path; the temptation may proceed not from without, but from some part of his own nature."[57] If one's hand causes one to stumble, it would be better for the individual to enter life crippled than have two hands and "go into hell [*geennan*]," that is, "into the unquenchable [*asbeston,* alpha privative, which makes the action negative, plus *sbestos* which means 'to quench,' hence, 'not able to quench'] fire."

9:44 This verse is not a part of the better manuscripts, although the statement is found in v. 48, where it appears to be authentic. Probably a scribe inserted the expression at v. 44 and also at v. 46 for emphasis.

55. Lane, *The Gospel of Mark,* 345.
56. Hendriksen, *Exposition of the Gospel According to Mark,* 365.
57. Swete, *The Gospel According to St. Mark,* 210.

9:45   The foot is also something that can cause offense. The mention of the foot naturally and logically follows that of the hand. One would be better off "to enter life" minus a foot than, having two feet, "to be cast into hell."

9:46   This verse, as mentioned above (cf. v. 44), is not part of the better manuscripts.

9:47   The eye is another possible source of stumbling. It would be better to have one's eye removed and "to enter the kingdom" with one eye than, having two eyes, "to be cast into hell." It is clear that Jesus was not teaching mutilation, for one could remove a hand, foot, or an eye and still be a terrible sinner. The source of sin does not come from portions of the body; sin originates in the heart, as Jesus taught earlier (cf. 7:18-23).

> The representation of the members [of the body] as the acting subject ("if your hand leads you to offend") belongs to the realism of Jewish thought. The radical demand that the hand or foot should be hacked off or the eye plucked out if they expose a man to the danger of final rejection juxtaposes the relative value of physical life with the absolute value of that authentic, imperishable life which is bestowed by God alone. . . . This was not a demand for physical self-mutilation, but in the strongest manner possible Jesus speaks of the costliest sacrifices. For the sake of the unconditional rule of God the members of the body must not be placed at the disposal of sinful desire. The sinful member must be renounced in order that the whole body be not cast into hell.[58]

Hell is said to be a real place. The word "hell" is the word "gehenna" (*geennan*), a transliteration of two Hebrew words that mean "the valley of Hinnom." Hinnom was an actual valley southwest of the city of Jerusalem, where King Ahaz and his son Manasseh worshiped the fire god Molech. They even sacrificed living children to this god (2 Kings 16:3; 21:6; 2 Chron. 25:3; 33:6). Later, in the reforms of King Josiah, that particular valley outside Jerusalem was pronounced unclean and became the garbage dump for the city (2 Kings 23:10).

9:48   With the understanding that the Valley of Hinnom had become a garbage dump, the statement of Jesus in this verse is easily explainable. When the refuse of a city was dumped in a specific area, it was usually burned. Those portions of the garbage dump that were not on fire were usually infested with worms. This whole imagery

58. Lane, *The Gospel of Mark*, 348.

most likely comes from Isaiah 66:24. The torment that is pictured there is both an external thing (the fire) and an internal thing (the worms). It is clear from the passage that it never ends. Thus Scripture affirms the eternal separation of the wicked from God and their eternal punishment. Although some would prefer to teach that when the wicked die they are simply annihilated, Scripture does not admit that possibility. Those who have purposefully rejected the testimony of Jesus Christ reject His love and His grace and will spend eternity apart from Him.

9:49   The words of Jesus presented here by Mark alone have been subject to much debate. In the context of the passage, it seems best to understand that Jesus was implying that those who find their way into hell will indeed be permanently "salted with fire." Salt was a preservative in that society. Jesus was using a figure they would have understood to teach that anyone who finds his way into Hinnom, or hell, will experience the permanence of God's judgment.

9:50   Salt had its good qualities. Jesus used that analogy previously to tell the disciples that they were the salt of the earth (cf. Matt. 5:13). However, if salt loses its character of being salty, what value does it have? It is impossible to make it salty again. The main source of salt in Israel was from the Dead (Salt) Sea. It was a very coarse impure variety that was subject to a deterioration that made it useless. Jesus' final word of instruction to His disciples was that they should "have salt in themselves." In other words, He was teaching them that they should be a preservative for society. "To have salt within oneself means, therefore, to have within oneself those qualities that promote truth, kindness, peace, joy, etc. within the brotherhood, and in the world at large a willingness to listen to the good tidings of salvation in Christ."[59] Furthermore, they should "be at peace with one another." This section began when Jesus asked His disciples what they were talking about (cf. 9:33). Their discussion had been an argument over which of them was the greatest. Jesus' admonition to them was indeed to be at peace with one another, rather than clamoring for position and promoting themselves.

> If within the brotherhood there is nothing but carping and quarrelling, how can those who call themselves Christians expect to win others to Christ? It is therefore not surprising that an echo of this exhortation is

---

59. Hendriksen, *Exposition of the Gospel According to Mark,* 369.

found also in the epistles of Paul (Rom. 12:18; II Cor. 13:11; I Thess. 5:13). The reward for being a man of peace and therefore a peacemaker is stated in Matt. 5:9, "Blessed [are] the peacemakers, for they shall be called sons of God." Add Gal. 5:22; James 3:18.[60]

HOMILETICAL SUGGESTIONS

The wonderful story that begins this chapter has always been a blessing to this author. The account of the Transfiguration, when the glory of Jesus Christ was revealed for the disciples to see, is a unique story. The presence of Moses and Elijah, along with the disciples, gives a perfect picture of the kingdom of Jesus Christ when it will be established on earth. All the necessary people are present with the Lord Jesus in His glory on earth.

As Jesus and the disciples descended from the mountain, however, He told them again what His immediate future would contain. The Savior would be delivered into the hands of wicked men and be killed, but on the third day He would rise again. The contrast between His words and the discussion of the disciples over greatness in the kingdom is astounding. The Savior taught these men that His disciples should not be clamoring for position. This is a wonderful word that needs to be remembered constantly today. So often, even in Christian ministry, there is a clamoring for the more glamorous places of service. The true servant of Jesus Christ simply serves, as the Lord Himself demonstrated in this gospel. The one who properly serves will never be a cause of offense. But, indeed, he will be a disciple who will be the salt of the earth, creating a thirst in the lives of other individuals.

60. Ibid.

MARK
CHAPTER
TEN

THE SERVANT'S MISSION

INSTRUCTION CONCERNING DIVORCE, 10:1-12
(cf. Matt. 19:1-12)

Hitherto, in chapters i–ix, we have had the Galilaean ministry of the Lord. Now, from x to xv, we shall have the Judaean ministry. In between the two Luke has a great mass of material, covering roughly chapters ix–xviii of his Gospel, and usually called the Lucan Travel-Narrative, of which the mission of the seventy disciples and various parables (e.g. the lost sheep, the lost coin, the lost son) are the best known features.[1]

Also much of the material from John 7–11, as well as the events in Matthew 18, fall between chapters 9 and 10 of Mark.

10:1 Jesus departed from the region of Galilee. He left the city of Capernaum where He had been with the disciples, headed southward through "the region of Judea," and crossed over the Jordan River to the eastern side. That territory was known as Perea and was under the jurisdiction of Herod Antipas.

The itinerary marks a return to the Jordan region where John the Baptist had conducted his ministry and had suffered imprisonment and martyrdom. If Jesus had been associated with John for any length of time it is possible that in coming to southern Judea and Perea he was

---

1. R. A. Cole, *The Gospel According to Mark* (Grand Rapids: Eerdmans, 1979), 154.

returning to an area and people he knew well. His reputation in these areas is attested by Ch. 3:8, although it is not clear whether it was established by direct knowledge or report.[2]

Wherever Jesus went, "crowds [*ochloi,* "multitudes"] gathered [*symporeuontai,* present tense verb picturing dramatically the action] around Him." Many pilgrims traveled these same roads on their way to Jerusalem. News of His mighty miracles and power had obviously reached this southern region. As He saw the crowds He gathered them around Him, and, following His normal custom, He "began to teach [*edidasken,* imperfect tense implying an action that continued over a period of time] them."

10:2   But "some Pharisees came" with a question that was specifically meant to test (*peirazontes,* which can mean either "to test" or "to tempt") Jesus. They chose to raise the issue of divorce, which was a widely debated point among the Jewish leaders. Jesus had taught on this issue earlier in Galilee (cf. Matt. 5:31-32), but possibly no Pharisees were present on that occasion. Their question spelled out the issue clearly, for they asked "whether it was lawful for a man to divorce [his] wife." The religious leaders were divided on that issue, based on their interpretations of the phrase "some indecency" in Deuteronomy 24:1-4. But whereas they were divided concerning the grounds for divorce, all Jews viewed the right to divorce to be a gift to them from God, which was denied to Gentiles.

There were two principal schools of thought. One school was headed by Rabbi Shammai. His conservative view taught that a man could divorce his wife only if he discovered some uncleanness in her from a premarital situation. The other school of thought was represented by Rabbi Hillel. His liberal interpretation said that a man could divorce his wife for any cause, even a trivial matter such as improperly preparing his food. The Pharisees were hoping to catch Jesus on this issue. They thought they had Him for sure. No matter what He said, someone would be unhappy with His answer.

> If the Lord sided with Shammai the Pharisees might have accused him, though not justly, of being inconsistent when he nevertheless consorted with sinners and ate with them. On the other hand, if Jesus endorsed the lax—"anything will do as ground of divorce"—interpretation, what

2. William L. Lane, *The Gospel of Mark,* NICNT (Grand Rapids: Eerdmans, 1974), 353.

would the disciples of Shammai think of him? Would not the more serious and conscientious people charge him with tolerating moral looseness? And what would the female part of the population think of him?[3]

Perhaps they hoped they could get Him to contradict Moses, who had permitted divorce, or even put Him in a position where He might incur the wrath of Herod Antipas. John the Baptist had preached strongly against Herod's divorce and that brought about his imprisonment and death. The Pharisees were probably hoping that Herod Antipas would somehow eliminate Jesus as he had done with John the Baptist. Thus, their goal of getting rid of Jesus would be accomplished, but it would not be accomplished by their own hands.

10:3 Jesus turned the question back to the Pharisees. He went to an authority they highly regarded—Moses. The Pharisees strongly believed in the Scriptures, so Jesus simply asked them, in effect, "What does your authority, Moses, command you to do in this case?" Taking them to Scripture "at once removed suspicion of heterodoxy or laxity. The Lord ever made that His function was to give a new depth of meaning to the law, not to dismiss it as meaningless (Mt. v. 17)."[4]

10:4 They knew the answer, for they said that "Moses permitted a man to write a certificate of divorce [*biblion apostasiou,* "a little book of forsaking"] and send [his wife] away." Their answer was based on Deuteronomy 24:1-4. There was a great deal involved in that process, however, for in order to write a certificate of divorce a man had to spell out specific charges over which he was divorcing his wife. Actually the provision by Moses was a gracious safeguard to protect wives from husbands who would send them away for trivial reasons. "The Mosaic provision was made for the contingency of divorce, but did not in itself determine whether that contingency was right or wrong. Its primary function was to provide a degree of protection for the woman who had been repudiated by her husband."[5]

10:5 Jesus did not deny that Moses permitted divorce, but He did point out that Moses was not the initiator of the practice. He simply was trying to put curbs on something that was prevalent among the Jewish people at that time. It was because of people's "hardness of heart" (*sklērokardian; skléros* = "hard," *kardia* = "heart") that Moses

3. William Hendriksen, *Exposition of the Gospel According to Mark* (Grand Rapids: Baker, 1975), 376.
4. Cole, *The Gospel According to Mark,* 156.
5. Lane, *The Gospel of Mark,* 354.

wrote that commandment. Men were not acting in keeping with basic morality, but they were simply sending their wives away for all kinds of reasons. It was the hardness of their hearts that produced the situation recorded in Deuteronomy 24. "The purpose of the legislation of Deut. . . . was to check this disposition, not to give it head; and for the Pharisees to shelter themselves under the temporary recognition of a necessary evil was to confess that they had not outgrown the moral stature of their fathers."[6]

10:6 But Jesus took them back even farther in history, to "the beginning of the creation," when God made man and woman. The whole concept of marriage was initiated by God. It was not simply an institution of man. "God made them male and female" (Gen. 1:27), Jesus reminded them.

> Jesus points back to the original ordinance, that is, to the way things had been "from the beginning of creation." It was then that God, even though he created Adam before Eve, at once created him as a male; hence, with a view to intimate union with Eve, who was created later on from the very body of Adam, and as a female. Each, accordingly, was made for the other, with the definite purpose of joining together *one* man to *one* woman. Those who are eager for divorce ignore this fact.[7]

10:7 "For this cause a man shall leave [*kataleipsei*] his father and his mother" (Gen. 2:24). The Greek word *kataleipsei* literally means "to leave behind" or "to forsake."

> The natural phenomenon of a man voluntarily leaving the strongest social group that he already knows (his own kith and kin) to form a new and closer link with a woman previously unknown to him would be inexplicable, were it not seen to be another instance of the outworking of this purpose of God.[8]

Many marriages end because men fail to leave their parents behind. They continue to allow their parents to have too much input into the decisions the new couple makes.

10:8 "The two shall become one flesh," Jesus replied, quoting Genesis 2:24. "They are no longer two but [become] one flesh." A

6. Henry Barclay Swete, *The Gospel According to St. Mark* (Grand Rapids: Eerdmans, 1956), 216.
7. Hendriksen, *Exposition of the Gospel According to Mark,* 377-78.
8. Cole, *The Gospel According to Mark,* 157.

physical union of oneness develops, a union that is unlike any other relationship on earth. The basis of the marriage relationship is that oneness. As God originally instituted the gracious provision of marriage, it was to be a very special relationship of oneness between a man and his wife that was to remain as long as they were alive. Only the death of one would terminate the relationship.

10:9   Jesus put a final statement on the story of creation by saying, "What therefore God has joined together, let no man separate." The act of marriage is something that God initiated, and God joins a man and a woman together. Literally the word "join" (*synezeuxen,* aorist tense indicating a completed act) means to be yoked together as animals were joined together to plow a field. A man and his wife form a team. There is a oneness, and people are not to "separate" (*chōrizetō,* present tense, "to make it a habit to be separating") what God has united. It is clear, as Jesus took the religious leaders back to the original intention of marriage, that there was to be no divorce in God's plan. Marriage was to be a lifelong commitment of one man to one woman.

> The decisive "No" to divorce provides the required safeguard against human selfishness which always threatens to destroy marriage. It also warns that the man who dissolves a union sanctioned by God inevitably stands under the divine judgment. This warning has in view the husband, rather than a judicial authority, since in Jewish practice divorce was effected by the husband himself. Behind this solemn prohibition there is a deep concern for personal relationships. Jesus does not envisage marriage as it is at times but as it can and should be—a call to fidelity, peace and love.[9]

10:10   There is no record of any discussion by Jesus with the Pharisees. His teaching was very clear: "Marriage is to be a monogamous, heterosexual, permanent one-flesh relationship."[10] But as the disciples later sat with Jesus in the house, probably in one of the villages on the road to Jerusalem, "they began questioning Him" about His teaching. It appears from the parallel passage in Matthew's gospel (Matt. 19:10) that the disciples fully understood that Jesus was saying there should be no divorce in God's plan. Their conclusion, according to Matthew's

---

9. Lane, *The Gospel of Mark,* 356-57.
10. John D. Grassmick, "Mark," in *Bible Knowledge Commentary* (Wheaton, Ill.: Victor, 1983), 149.

gospel, was that it would be better not to marry, since there would be no way to get out of a marriage. Perhaps their concern may imply that they may have favored the more liberal divorce policy of the school of Hillel.

10:11   Jesus made clear that when a man "divorces his wife and marries another" he "commits adultery [*moichatai*] against her."

> The new element in this teaching, which was totally unrecognized in the rabbinic courts, was the concept of a husband committing adultery against his former wife. According to a rabbinic law a man could commit adultery against another married man by seducing his wife (Deut. 22:13-29) and a wife could commit adultery against her husband by infidelity, but a husband could not be said to commit adultery against his wife.[11]

Some believe that Matthew 19:9 gives a possible exception if a spouse is involved in adultery.[12] Others believe from 1 Corinthians 7:15 that desertion also is possible acceptable grounds for divorce. Mark, however, mentions neither of these.

10:12   Jesus also mentioned in private to the disciples that if a woman divorced her husband and married another she too would commit adultery. Jesus did not avoid that situation, for He stated that this also was wrong. Although divorce initiated by women was not common in Jewish society, there were some who practiced it. The sister of Herod the Great, Salome, is known to have sent a document to her husband, Costobarus, dissolving their marriage. It is clear that Herodias had divorced her husband, Philip, to marry Antipas. Herodias and Philip were living in Rome at the time of the divorce; then she returned to Israel with Antipas. Is it possible that some of Mark's Roman readers might have remembered that actual historical event? For Mark's later readers this verse was a very significant statement, for divorce had become widespread among both men and women in Roman society. Wiersbe summarizes this section well:

> Mark 10:9 warns us that *man* cannot separate those who have been united in marriage, *but God can*. Since He established marriage, He has the right to lay down the rules. A divorce may be legal according to our

11. Lane, *The Gospel of Mark*, 357.
12. See my comments on Matt. 19:9 in "Matthew," in *Bible Knowledge Commentary* (Wheaton, Ill.: Victor, 1983), 63-64.

laws and yet not be right in the eyes of God. He expects married people to practice commitment to each other (v. 7) and to remain true to each other. Too many people view divorce as "an easy way out," and do not take seriously their vows of commitment to each other and to the Lord."[13]

INSTRUCTION CONCERNING FAITH, 10:13-22

FAITH AS A CHILD, 10:13-16
(cf. Matt. 19:13-15; Luke 18:15-17)

The story that follows in vv. 13-16 is an appropriate sequel to the teachings of Jesus on the sanctity of marriage.

10:13 As Jesus ministered to the disciples in the house, suddenly a number of parents showed up at the door "bringing" (*prosepheron,* imperfect tense implying repetitious action) their "children" (*paidia,* of various ages from a few days to age twelve, cf. 5:39, 42) so that Jesus "might touch them" and bless them. It was not uncommon for parents to bring their children to rabbis to receive a blessing from them. "There was, of course, no question of baptism or salvation involved, but a most natural thing to do."[14] It was also a sign of the growing reverence and respect that the people had for Jesus.

The disciples, however, "rebuked" (*epetimēsan,* aorist tense implying that their rebuke was a completed act, not a continuous one) them. This act does not imply that the disciples were mean to or angry with these people. They probably sensed that Jesus was occupied with other things. He was moving with purpose toward Jerusalem (cf. Luke 9:51), where He was going to be delivered into the hands of wicked men and crucified. Since He was spending a great deal of time with His disciples to instruct them, perhaps they felt His time could be better spent ministering to adults.

10:14 When Jesus became aware of their actions, He was moved with indignation (*ēganaktēsen,* aorist tense implying deep feelings of pain). This is the only passage in Scripture where indignation is attributed to Jesus Christ. He issued two commands to the disciples. The first was to allow the children to come to Him, and the second was to stop hindering them from doing so. He said that "the kingdom of God

---

13. Warren W. Wiersbe, *Be Diligent* (Wheaton, Ill.: Victor, 1987), 98. For further study on the subject of divorce, see Carl Laney, *The Divorce Myth* (Minneapolis: Bethany, 1986), and William A. Heth and Gordon J. Wenham, *Jesus and Divorce: The Problem with the Evangelical Consensus* (Nashville: Nelson, 1985).

14. A. T. Robertson, *Word Pictures in the New Testament* (Nashville: Broadman, 1930), 1:350.

belongs to such as these." By the term "kingdom of God," Jesus probably meant that the rule of God over a person's life applies even for children.

> The disciples' attempt to turn the children aside because they were unimportant is one more instance of a persistent tendency to think in wholly human, fallen categories which Jesus had rebuked on earlier occasions (Chs. 8:33; 9:33-37). The Kingdom of God belongs to children, and to others like them who are of no apparent importance, because God has willed to give it to them.[15]

10:15 Jesus then issued a solemn announcement: the matter of God's rule over one's life must be received like a child. Unless one receives God's rule in his life as a child, he will never be able to enter His kingdom. Jesus was implying that every individual must possess the simple faith of a child. A child is very trusting. He looks to his parents to supply all his needs, wants, and desires, and to care for his hurts.

> The little child learns to obey its parents simply and uncomplainingly. ...Jesus here presents the little child with trusting and simple and loving obedience as the model for adults in coming into the kingdom. Jesus does not here say that children are in the kingdom of God because they are children.[16]

One must recognize God's rule over his life like a child and come to Him with that kind of faith.

10:16 Jesus "took ... in His arms" (*enagkalisamenos,* as in 9:36) all the children who were brought to Him, and He blessed (*kateulogei,* imperfect tense implying that this act of blessing continued over a period of time) them. The laying on of hands was a picture often used throughout the Scriptures to communicate the idea of a transfer of blessing (cf. Gen. 48:8-20). "Jesus' action in honoring the children offered concrete illustration that the blessings of the Kingdom are freely given. In context, the bestowing of the blessing constituted a fresh reiteration of the call to true discipleship and obedience to the intention of God."[17]

---

15. Lane, *The Gospel of Mark,* 360.
16. Robertson, *Word Pictures in the New Testament,* 1:350-51.
17. Lane, *The Gospel of Mark,* 361.

FAITH FOR ETERNAL LIFE, 10:17-22
(cf. Matt. 19:16-22; Luke 18:18-23)

10:17 As Jesus was about to depart on His journey, a man came running up "and knelt before Him." The movement of the principal characters in Mark's account demonstrates clearly that this is the gospel of action. Only Mark records the running and the kneeling of this young man.

> The stranger who did this is by Matthew called *a young man* (19:20), by Luke *a ruler* (18:18), and is by all three described as *a very rich person,* one who owned much property (Matt. 19:22; Mark 10:22; Luke 18:23). Therefore the title "rich young ruler" is generally applied to him. He was probably one of the officials in charge of the local synagogue.[18]

He asked (*epērōta,* imperfect tense that continues to picture vividly what he was doing) Him a question: "Good Teacher [*didaskale agathe*], what shall I do to inherit eternal life?" He was not alone in his thinking that eternal life was something that was earned by doing. John 6:28 records that the multitude asked Jesus a similar question: "What shall we do, that we may work the works of God?" These questions contain the concept that eternal life was something that was achieved through doing.

That this man identified Jesus as "Good Teacher" is also significant. This designation "is virtually without parallel in Jewish sources and should be regarded as a sincere tribute to the impression he had made upon the man, whether 'good' be understood to signify 'kind,' 'generous,' or some other quality of goodness."[19] He was applying a word to an earthly teacher that was not normally used. Rabbis did not allow the word "good" (*agathos*) to be associated with them.

10:18 That is why Jesus responded as He did: "Why do you call Me good?" Jesus was not denying that the word should be properly applied to Him. In fact, that word truly is applicable only to God, for only He is always perfectly "good."

> Two words in the original Greek text are translated by the English word "good." The first, *agathos,* refers to what is intrinsically good. The second, *kalos,* refers to what is externally pleasing. The man used the

18. Hendriksen, *Exposition of the Gospel According to Mark,* 389.

19. Lane, *The Gospel of Mark,* 365.

word that refers to intrinsic goodness and addressed Jesus as the intrinsically good Teacher. Christ reminded him that there is only One who is intrinsically good—and that One is God. Jesus Christ had been claiming to be the Son of God. Therefore He claimed to be intrinsically good. He asked His question to see if the man would say that he addressed Him as the intrinsically good Teacher because he believed that He was the Son of God.[20]

Jesus was simply trying to help the man understand with whom he was speaking. Did the man truly come to Him recognizing Him as God? If he did, then he needed to be completely open to whatever Jesus would say to him.

10:19 Jesus turned the issue of doing good around by addressing the commandments that this young man would have known. If this young ruler was a member of the Sanhedrin, he was probably a brilliant young theological student from a wealthy merchant home, as was Saul of Tarsus. Saul discovered the futility of striving to win eternal life by law works (cf. Rom. 7:24). This young man was still trying to earn his own salvation. Jesus cited five of the commandments from the second half of the Decalogue (Ex. 20:12-16; Deut. 5:16-20), which relate to relationships with other people.

The commandments He referred to are those concerning murder, adultery, stealing, bearing false witness, and honoring one's father and mother. The one commandment that Jesus omitted from the second table was the last commandment regarding covetousness. There are some who believe that the addition Jesus made when He said, "Do not defraud," may have been a synonymous idea with covetousness. The idea is derived from passages such as Leviticus 19:13 and Deuteronomy 24:14. "When a person covets the goods belonging to another, does he not in heart and mind defraud the neighbor of that which belongs to him?"[21] Others feel that Jesus did not mention covetousness because this was the problem the young man had. He coveted his possessions, and they came between him and God. In reality he actually violated the very first commandment, for something had come between him and God.

10:20 The man's response to Jesus did not include the word "good." He simply said, "Teacher, I have kept all these things from my youth

20. J. Dwight Pentecost, *The Words & Works of Jesus Christ* (Grand Rapids: Zondervan, 1981), 360.

21. Hendriksen, *Exposition of the Gospel According to Mark,* 393.

up." He truly believed that from the day he became responsible for his own spiritual condition, the day of his bar mitzvah at age thirteen, he had kept all these commandments. "The young man is relieved by the Lord's answer. If eternal inheritance could be secured on so simple a condition as the keeping of the Decalogue, it was his already. . . . The deeper meaning and larger requirements of the Law were yet hidden from him."[22] It does appear, however, that the young man sensed that something was still missing in his life. According to Matthew 19:20 he asked Jesus, "What am I still lacking?" It appears to his way of thinking that supplying this lack was simply a matter of addition: "What else do I have to do?" Jesus' instruction in the next verse begins to show him that he does not need to do more; rather, he needs to substitute something else.

10:21   Mark alone records that, when Jesus looked at him, He "felt a love for him" (*ēgapēsen auton*).

> As the Savior allowed his gaze to rest on the rich young ruler, he loved him; that is, *a.* he admired him for not having fallen into gross outward sins and for having gone to the best possible source to obtain a solution to his problems; and *b.* he deeply, sorrowfully, ruefully pitied him, and decided to recommend to him a course of action which, if followed through, would solve his problem, and would give him the rest of soul he needed.[23]

But Jesus told him that there was one thing that he lacked, and He issued to him two commands.

He told him first to go and get rid of all of his possessions. He was to do this by selling them and giving the proceeds to the poor. "The sale and distribution of his property were the necessary preparations in his case for the complete discipleship which admits to the Divine kingdom. . . . The words are not a general counsel of perfection, but a test of obedience and faith which the Lord saw to be necessary in this particular case."[24] William Lane notes that

> the specific form of the sacrifice Jesus demanded of this man is not to be regarded as a general prescription to be applied to all men, nor yet as a demand for an expression of piety that goes beyond the require-

22. Swete, *The Gospel According to St. Mark*, 225.
23. Hendriksen, *Exposition of the Gospel According to Mark*, 395-96.
24. Swete, *The Gospel According to St. Mark*, 226.

ments of the Law. The command to sell his property and to distribute the proceeds to the poor was appropriate to this particular situation. The subsequent reduction to poverty and helplessness would dramatize the fact that man is helpless in his quest for eternal life, which must be bestowed as the gift of God.[25]

The second command was to come and follow Jesus Christ. That meant that he was to begin to follow Jesus who was heading for Jerusalem, where He was going to be crucified and on the third day rise again. In other words, Jesus was telling him that he truly needed to become His follower. "Such 'following,' to be accompanied by and to prepare for active witness-bearing, would imply that the young man must learn to 'deny himself and take up his cross,' and would therefore no longer be able to devote himself to the service of Mammon."[26]

10:22　　These words from the Savior caused the man's countenance to fall (*stygnasas,* which means "gloomy, like a lowering cloud"). "His hopes were dashed; the one thing he yet wanted was beyond his reach; the price was too great to pay even for eternal life. For the time the love of the world prevailed."[27] "He went away grieved, for he . . . owned much property." That was the thing that had come between him and his God. Although he had done everything, so he thought, to other men externally, in his heart what he treasured most was his riches and possessions. Truly that was the thing that was keeping him from God, the thing that was keeping him from faith, so that he could become a child of the kingdom.

> Here is the only man in the whole of the New Testament of whom it is said that he went away *sad* from the presence of Christ, though many were sad when they came. . . . He could not, by definition, be a disciple of Christ (Lk. xiv. 33), for this demanded a total committal, which he was not, as yet, ready to give. His reaction shows only too clearly that the Lord had laid His finger on the spot; his wealth was indeed the thing that was holding him back from the kingdom of God.[28]

25. Lane, *The Gospel of Mark,* 367.
26. Hendriksen, *Exposition of the Gospel According to Mark,* 396-97.
27. Swete, *The Gospel According to St. Mark,* 227.
28. Cole, *The Gospel According to Mark,* 163.

INSTRUCTION CONCERNING WEALTH, 10:23-31
(cf. Matt. 19:23-30; Luke 18:24-30)

10:23   As the rich young ruler walked away from Jesus Christ, the Savior turned and looked at His disciples to see what impact this event had made on them. Here is another instance recorded only by Mark that presents the "looks" of the Savior (cf. 3:5, 34). As His eyes swept the Twelve He said, "How hard it will be for those who are wealthy to enter the kingdom of God."

> As is clear from a comparison of verses 17, 23, and 26, entering that kingdom means obtaining a share in life everlasting. It means becoming saved, probably with emphasis on future salvation: becoming a partaker of ultimate bliss in the restored universe, and enjoying a foretaste of this event here and now. See also on 9:45, 47; 10:15. With what difficulty those who possess an abundance of earthly wealth and continue to cling to it will enter that kingdom. *Difficult* indeed (verses 23, 24); *impossible* even (verses 25, 27).[29]

10:24   This statement of the Savior brought amazement (*ethambounto,* imperfect passive verb indicating that they continued to be astonished) to the disciples. "This concept cut across all contemporary Judaistic thinking. After all, hadn't the Old Testament taught that wealth and substance were marks of God's favor? And it was commonly taught that the rich accumulated merit through their good works."[30] If the wealthy were not able to enter the kingdom of heaven, who could? Jesus repeated His statement: "Children [*Tekna,* a tender expression used by the Lord probably because of their confusion], how hard it is to enter the kingdom of God!" Some manuscripts repeat the idea that those who were trusting in their riches would find it hard to enter the kingdom, but those words do not appear in the oldest and best Greek manuscripts.

10:25   Jesus used a graphic hyperbole to explain what He had just said. His statement was a well-known maxim in their society: "It is easier for a camel [*kamēlon*] to go through the eye of a needle [*trymalias tēs hraphidos*] than for a rich man to enter the kingdom of God." Jesus was literally speaking about camels and needles. Luke, in Luke 18:25, actually used a technical term for a physician's needle (*be-*

---

29. Hendriksen, *Exposition of the Gospel According to Mark,* 398.
30. Howard F. Vos, *Mark* (Grand Rapids: Zondervan, 1978), 90.

lonēs). Many attempts have been made to try to explain this figure away, so that somehow the camel could pass through the needle.

> To explain what Jesus means it is useless and unwarranted to try to change "camel" into "cable,"—see Matt. 23:24, where a real camel must have been meant—or to define the "needle's eye" as the narrow gate in a city wall, a gate, so the reasoning goes, through which a camel can pass only on its knees and after its burden has been removed. Such "explanations" (?), aside from being objectionable from a linguistic point of view, strive to make possible what Jesus specifically declared to be impossible. The Lord clearly means that for a rich man in his own power to try to work or worm his way into the kingdom of God is impossible. So powerful is the hold which wealth has on the heart on a natural man! He is held fast by its bewitching charm, and is thereby prevented from obtaining the attitude of heart and mind necessary for entrance into God's kingdom.[31]

10:26 The disciples "were . . . astonished" (*exeplēssonto,* imperfect passive tense implying a continual and extensive perplexity) and said to Jesus, "Then who can be saved?" "The Twelve have not yet grasped the special difficulties of the rich, who seem from their position to have the first claim to admission into the Kingdom. If they were excluded, they ask, who can dare to hope?"[32] They understood the impossibility of the situation that Jesus was presenting.

10:27 As Jesus looked (*emblepsas,* same verb as in v. 21) at them, He reminded them that with men not all things are possible, but with God "all things are possible" (cf. Gen 18:14). If it is within the will of the Heavenly Father, He can make it come to pass. Spiritual salvation is not dependent on physical things.

> Salvation is completely beyond the sphere of human possibility; every attempt to enter the Kingdom on the basis of achievement or merit is futile. Yet even the rule of the impossibility of entrance into the Kingdom for the rich is limited by the sovereign action of God himself. The ability and the power to effect deliverance reside in God alone (cf. Rom. 8:7).[33]

31. Hendriksen, *Exposition of the Gospel According to Mark,* 399-400.
32. Swete, *The Gospel According to St. Mark,* 229.
33. Lane, *The Gospel of Mark,* 370.

10:28   At this juncture Peter spoke up and reminded the Lord that in contrast to the rich young ruler, who went away with his possessions, the disciples had "left everything" behind to follow Him. In effect, Peter was asking the Lord, "Since we have been obedient to You, what can we expect?"

> It may be that some among the apostolic band, awed by the wealth of the young man and his refusal to give all he had as the price of Christ (cf. Mt. xiii. 46), were ruefully rethinking their own initial sacrifice and sorely needed this reassurance that the Lord saw and valued. This Saying must have left a deep impression on Peter's memory, reproduced as it was in his preaching. In true humility he was always ready to preserve and retell anecdotes where he himself appeared in an unfavourable light.[34]

10:29   In another solemn affirmation ("Truly, I say to you") Jesus reminded all the disciples that "there is no one who has left" valued things behind, such as possessions and family, for the sake of the Lord Jesus Christ and the gospel who will not be cared for. "The sacrifices contemplated embrace all the material possessions included under the three heads of home, relatives, and property; the sacrifice in life is not at present in view, since none of the Twelve had been called to that as yet."[35] The expression "for My sake and for the gospel's sake" sounds very much like the previous teaching Jesus had given the disciples when He talked to them about losing one's life for His sake and for the sake of the gospel (8:35).

10:30   Those who have left everything behind shall be recompensed "a hundred times [an expression implying "many times over," cf. Luke 18:30] as much . . . in the present age." There will be other possessions and houses for them to occupy. They will find other brothers and sisters and mothers in their fellow believers in Jesus Christ. He did not repeat the expression "father" because the Father of the believer is God Himself. Mark alone adds that Jesus reminded the disciples that along with blessings there would come persecutions (*meta diōgmōn*). Those words were extremely meaningful to Mark's readers, for they were undergoing intense persecution at the hands of Roman authorities at the time of the writing of the gospel. "Paradoxically, the first part of Jesus' promise (fellowship with other believers)

---

34. Cole, *The Gospel According to Mark,* 166.
35. Swete, *The Gospel According to St. Mark,* 231.

found its deepest realization within the context of the persecution through which the Church became identified as the suffering people of God."[36] Not only will there be blessings for the present age, but Jesus reminded the apostles that there will be reward in "the age to come," the reward of "eternal life."

10:31 In a final summary statement about the nature of discipleship, Jesus reminded His hearers that whereas there are many who at the present time appear to be prominent, such as the rich young leader, they would ultimately be last. Those who appear to have the more humble positions, such as the disciples, will someday find themselves to be first. This statement appears in other contexts as well (cf. Matt. 19:30; 20:16; Luke 13:30). "Rewards in God's kingdom are not based on earthly standards such as rank, priority, or duration of time served, personal merit, or sacrifice (cf. Matt. 20:1-16), but on commitment to Jesus and following Him faithfully."[37]

INSTRUCTION CONCERNING HIS NEAR FUTURE, 10:32-34 (cf. Matt. 20:17-19; Luke 18:31-34)

10:32 It was clear now where they were heading. Jerusalem was their targeted destination, and Jesus, as a typical rabbi, "was walking on ahead" of the group. "The Lord walked in advance of the Twelve with a solemnity and determination which foreboded danger. . . . His manner struck awe into the minds of the Twelve, who were beginning at length to anticipate an impending disaster."[38] The group was both "amazed" (*ethambounto,* imperfect tense implying a continued state) and "fearful" (*ephobounto,* also imperfect tense). They were probably astonished at the purposefulness with which the Lord walked (cf. Luke 9:51). But there was a sense of foreboding because of all of the opposition that was developing. "There must have been something about the bearing of Jesus—the look in his eyes, the manner of his walk— that explains this amazement."[39] But presently He stopped, took the Twelve aside, and taught them "what was going to happen [*symbainein,* present tense infinitive carrying the idea "what was about to hap-

36. Lane, *The Gospel of Mark,* 372.
37. Grassmick, "Mark," 152.
38. Swete, *The Gospel According to St. Mark,* 233.
39. Hendriksen, *Exposition of the Gospel According to Mark,* 404.

pen"] to Him." His instruction was not meant for the crowd but only for the Twelve.

10:33   This is the third time in Mark's gospel (cf. 8:31; 9:31) that Jesus predicted He was going to die and be raised again (cf. v. 34). But this is by far the most detailed account of the events. He indicated they would be going to Jerusalem, where these things would take place. As the Son of Man (Jesus' favorite designation), He would "be delivered" (*paradothēsetai,* lit. "betrayed") into the hands of "the chief priests and the scribes." The Elders who were mentioned in 8:31 are not specified here, probably because they were the least important members of the group. But the chief priests and scribes constituted the Sanhedrin, the Jewish Supreme Court, who would condemn Jesus to death (cf. 14:55-64). Since they did not have the authority to carry out the death sentence, they would turn Jesus over (*paradōsousin,* again lit. "betrayed") to the Gentiles (cf. 15:1), who would carry out His death sentence. "Delivery to the Gentiles reveals that Jesus will be held in contempt by his own countrymen, for the Gentiles are the last people to whom the Messiah of the people of God should be handed over. The actions defining his humility are carried out by the Gentiles."[40]

10:34   In the process of carrying out that death sentence, they would mock Jesus (cf. 15:16-18), spit on Him (cf. 15:19), and scourge Him (cf. 15:15). Finally, they would kill Him (cf. 15:24, 37). Though the method of execution is not spelled out here, the well-known Roman method of capital punishment was crucifixion. But that would not be the end of the Savior, for He specifically said that three days later He would rise from the dead (cf. 16:1ff.). Hendriksen summarizes this third prediction of Jesus' death:

> The prediction, as has been shown, is far more detailed than the previous ones. The *gradual* revelation of the approaching events had a pedagogical purpose. . . . But the probability must also be granted that even in the human consciousness of our Lord, the "feel" of the approaching horror was little by little becoming more real. There was nothing static about the mind of Jesus. . . . The man of sorrows sees [His death] coming toward him. He already senses something of the perfidy, the hypocrisy, the calumny, the mockery, the pain, and the shame which like an avalanche threatens to overwhelm him. Yet, he does not retreat or even stand still. With unflinching determination he walks right into it, for he

40. Lane, *The Gospel of Mark,* 376.

knows that this is necessary in order that his people may be saved. "Having loved his own . . . he loved them to the uttermost" (John 13:1).[41]

Did the disciples understand? It is clear from an addition made in Luke's gospel (18:34) that they did not. Luke makes the additional comment that His sayings "were hidden" from them.

Why did they fail to understand such bold statements? Perhaps because of the reference to the resurrection; if they did not take that literally, then there was no clue to the other enigmas. The Bible is clear that the resurrection is *sui generis*—that, in fact, the resurrection is to be understood only in the light of the resurrection.[42]

INSTRUCTION CONCERNING POSITIONS IN THE KINGDOM, 10:35-45 (cf. Matt. 20:20-28)

10:35   Mark then explained that James and John, the sons of Zebedee, "came up" (*prosporeuontai,* dramatic present tense picturing the action of the verb "to draw near") to the Lord and asked that He would grant a request. They did not specify what it would be but simply asked the Lord to agree to grant them whatever it was they asked of Him. "Both the homage offered and the terms of the petition (cf. vi.23) suggest that the Lord is approached in the character of a King, who can gratify the desires of His subjects without limitation, as indeed in another sense He afterwards declared Himself able to do (Jo. xiv.13, 14, xv.16, xvi.23, 24)."[43]

10:36   The Lord Jesus refused to commit Himself to what in effect amounted to a blank check. It usually is not wise to make blind promises. Herod Antipas made one that resulted in the death of John the Baptist (cf. 6:22-23). Instead, Jesus asked the men to specify exactly what it was that they wanted Him to do for them.

10:37   Their request was that they be given the places of privilege at His right and His left when He sat in His glory, that is, whenever His kingdom was established, as Matthew 20:21 states it. "They are looking for a grand Jewish world empire with apocalyptic features in the eschatological culmination of the Messiah's kingdom. That dream

41. Hendriksen, *Exposition of the Gospel According to Mark,* 407.
42. Cole, *The Gospel According to Mark,* 167.
43. Swete, *The Gospel According to St. Mark,* 235.

brushed aside all the talk of Jesus about his death and resurrection as mere pessimism."[44] Had Jesus not just announced for the third time that He was going to Jerusalem to be betrayed and to die? Does their request not again bring up the issue of who was the greatest among the disciples (cf. 9:33ff.), which Jesus had already settled?

> This incident reveals that in spite of Jesus' repeated efforts since Peter's confession at Caesarea Philippi to inculcate in his disciples the spirit of self-renunciation demanded by the cross, the sons of Zebedee have understood his intention very superficially. Their ambitious request brings discredit upon them, while the indignation of the other ten disciples reflects a similar preoccupation with their own dignity.[45]

According to Matthew's gospel (Matt. 20:20-21) they were accompanied by their mother, whom most scholars believe to be a woman named Salome, the sister of Mary, the mother of Jesus (cf. 15:40; Matt. 27:56; John 19:25). If this relationship is true, their request may have been based on the fact that they were related to Jesus. Perhaps they thought this entitled them to places of privilege in Jesus' kingdom. Perhaps they thought their material prosperity placed them in a more privileged position, for their father's business was very successful (cf. 1:20). Jesus had just told the Twelve, according to Matthew (Matt. 19:28), that in the kingdom, when the Son of Man sat on His glorious throne, the disciples would have the privilege of sitting on twelve thrones judging the nation of Israel. That teaching of Jesus they had heard and believed in. In spite of what Jesus had just said about His death in Jerusalem, they believed in His kingdom reign. All these factors came into play as they came to Jesus and requested a privileged position at His right and left hands.

10:38 Jesus asked them if they truly knew what they were asking for. He asked if they would be "able to drink the cup" that He would drink and (Mark alone adds) be "baptized with the baptism" with which He would be baptized. The figure of a cup is used in the Old Testament of divine judgment on human sin and rebellion (cf. Ps. 75:8; Isa. 51:17-23; Jer. 25:15-28, 49:12, 51:7; Lam. 4:21-22; Ezek. 23:31-34; Hab. 2:16; Zech. 12:2). To share one's cup meant to share an experience in common. So Jesus was asking the disciples if they could

44. Robertson, *Word Pictures in the New Testament,* 1:354.
45. Lane, *The Gospel of Mark,* 378.

Mark 10:39   *Moody Gospel Commentary*

partake of the judgment of death (cf. 14:36; Matt. 26:39; Luke 22:41) that was about to come on Him.

> In interpreting verse 38 it is necessary to see the cup as a designation of judgment. Jesus boldly applied to himself the image of the cup used by the prophets to threaten the enemies of God with his divine vengeance. The cup which Jesus must drink has reference to divine punishment of sins which he bears in place of the guilty (cf. Chs. 10:45; 14:24).[46]

To be baptized with water meant to be overwhelmed by water and that figure also carried the idea by being overwhelmed by similar experience.

> If there is any real difference in the meaning of the two halves of Christ's question, it might well be that *drinking* the cup points rather to Christ's active [obedience]; *being baptized,* to his passive obedience. Jesus rendered both. One might even say that the two are inseparable: each views Christ's obedience from its own aspect: he *chose* to die, and he *submitted* to the blows that descended upon him.[47]

10:39   Their response to His question was, "We are able" (*Dynametha,* one word) to be associated with Him in those things. "A light-hearted and eager reply, which reveals the absence even in a disciple like John of any clear understanding of the Master's repeated warnings, and at the same time the loyalty of the men who were ready to share the Master's lot, whatever it might be."[48] Jesus' response was that they would indeed share in His experience of suffering. Church history records that James became the first of the apostles to be martyred (cf. Acts 12:2). John endured a great deal of persecution throughout his life and was finally exiled to the island of Patmos (cf. Rev. 1:9), where he received the visions of the book of Revelation.

10:40   However, the privilege of granting to individuals positions of authority in the kingdom on the right and left hand of the Savior was not His to give. Jesus indicated that was something that had evidently been prepared by His Heavenly Father, and it was not His place to usurp that authority. "Christ is indeed the appointed Distributor of

---

46. Ibid., 380.
47. Hendriksen, *Exposition of the Gospel According to Mark,* 411-12.
48. Swete, *The Gospel According to St. Mark,* 237.

all eternal rewards (2 Tim. iv. 8, Apoc. xxii. 12), but He will distribute them in accordance with the Father's dispositions."[49]

> This is a reminder that even the Son is in loving subjection to His Father; it is not even for Christ to dispense honours at His will but only at the Father's will. So, too, the last hour is hidden deep in the counsel of God (xiii. 32); and yet this is not 'Subordinationism,' for it is voluntary.[50]

10:41   When the remaining ten apostles heard about this discussion, they became "indignant [*aganaktein*] with James and John."

> The verb *aganakteō* is the same as was used (x. 14) of the Lord's reaction to the disciples when they summarily dismissed the mothers of Jerusalem. A man's character is shown by the things that provoke his strongest reactions; and so the Lord justly rebukes both the two and the ten at once, by showing to them their common ignorance of the very nature of Christian leadership.[51]

Probably the main reason the ten were angry was that they had not thought of the request first. All this led to another discussion by Jesus on the true nature of servanthood, for they had obviously not yet understood the lesson of 9:35-37. The Lord does react to them very gently, as a good shepherd who is concerned for His sheep.

10:42   Jesus then called all the disciples to Himself,

> and without referring to the circumstances, pointed out that neither ambition nor jealousy had any place in the brotherhood of the Son of Man. The tone of His words is singularly gentle; the occasion (for there had been great provocation) called for definite teaching rather than for censure.[52]

He explained to them that among the rulers of the Gentiles the thing that was enjoyed the most was the exercise of authority.

> According to Mark, Jesus described these monarchs as "*so-called* rulers." Another possible translation would be "*recognized* rulers." But in harmony with Gal. 2:2, 6, 9, the rendering "*so-called*" or "*those who are*

49. Ibid., 238.
50. Cole, *The Gospel According to Mark,* 170.
51. Ibid., 170-71.
52. Swete, *The Gospel According to St. Mark,* 239.

reputed to be" or *"are supposed to be"* is probably correct. It is very well possible, therefore, that the Master's words are here tinged with irony. If only those who are clothed with high authority would rule wisely, all would be well. But no, once they have arrived at the top, they think only of themselves.[53]

Gentile rulers loved to lord it over other people, all the while wanting those under their authority to believe they have only their best interests at heart. Probably the classic illustration of how rulers lorded it over the people was seen in the coins of the day.

> To cite only two examples, the denarius that was used for paying taxes (cf. Ch. 12:16) portrayed Tiberius as the semi-divine son of the god Augustus and the goddess Livia; the copper coins struck by Herod Philip at Caesarea Philippi showed the head of the reigning emperor (Augustus, then Tiberius) with the emperor's name and the inscription: "He who deserves adoration." There is biting irony in the reference to those who give the illusion of ruling (cf. Jn. 19:11) but simply exploit the people over whom they exercise dominion. In their struggle for rank and precedence, and the desire to exercise authority for their own advantage, the disciples were actually imitating those whom they undoubtedly despised.[54]

10:43   But Jesus declared that this was not to be the way His followers functioned. The one who truly wanted to be great needed to become (*estai,* imperative tense, "he must become") a "servant" (*diakonos*), which means a household slave. This word was used later for those who served in the church as deacons (cf. 1 Tim. 3:8ff.; Rom. 16:1).

10:44   The one who wants to be first must become a "slave" (*doulos*), the common, ordinary bond slave. Grassmick summarizes the two concepts in verses 43 and 44:

> **Whoever** aspires **to become great among you**, let him **be your** (pl.) house **servant** (*diakonos*), one who voluntarily renders useful service to others. **Whoever** aspires **to be first** (lit., "first among you") let him **be a slave** (*doulos*), one who forfeits his own rights in order to

53. Hendriksen, *Exposition of the Gospel According to Mark,* 413.
54. Lane, *The Gospel of Mark,* 382.

serve any and **all**. . . . A disciple is to serve others, not his own interests, voluntarily and sacrificially.[55]

Was it unreasonable of the Savior to demand this of His followers? **10:45**   The Lord made clear that this was the position He Himself had assumed in coming into this earth, again using that favorite expression "the Son of Man." He declared that the Son of Man, who came with His absolute deity veiled, did not come in His first advent to be a ruler. "In himself and from all eternity he is the all-glorious One. Yet he humbles himself. He becomes incarnate, and this not with the purpose of being served but of serving."[56] Indeed, He came not "to be served, but to serve" and to voluntarily give His life (cf. Isa. 53:11) as "a ransom" (*lutron*). The word *lutron* occurs only here and in Matthew 20:28. It refers to the payment of a price given to set a slave or captive free. "The ministry of the Son of Man culminates in the sacrifice of His life. He had required this supreme service from His disciples (viii. 35), and He will be the first to render it."[57] Jesus' offer to give of Himself as a ransom was for "many" (*pollōn*). The contrast is between the single life that is given and the many who benefit. The preposition "for" (*anti*) carries the idea of "in the place of." "The passage is a clear proof of Christ's substitutionary atonement."[58] The ransom was not paid to Satan, as Origen maintained; the one who held the price over the head of the sinner was God the Father (cf. Rom. 3:23-26). Clearly the price was paid for the "many." Does that imply that the death of Christ was sufficient only for those who would be the recipients of salvation, or was His death for all mankind? The fact that this passage seems to limit the effect of His death does not negate other passages that imply that the death of Jesus Christ is sufficient for the sins of the entire world (cf. John 3:16; 1 John 2:2; 2 Peter 2:1; Acts 17:30; 1 Tim. 2:4-6; 4:10; Heb. 2:9).

It appears that John ultimately understood the Lord's intention, for in later years he said, "We know by this, that He laid down His life for us; and we ought to lay down our lives for the brethren" (1 John 3:16).

55. Grassmick, "Mark," 153-54.
56. Hendriksen, *Exposition of the Gospel According to Mark,* 415.
57. Swete, *The Gospel According to St. Mark,* 240.
58. Hendriksen, *Exposition of the Gospel According to Mark,* 415.

Here in Mark 10:45 Jesus is teaching that his own willingness to humble
himself to the point of giving his life as a ransom for many must be
reflected in The Twelve and in all his followers. In his own small degree and manner every follower of Christ must, by God's grace, show
Christ's love to others.[59]

INSTRUCTION CONCERNING FAITH, 10:46-52
(cf. Matt. 20:29-34; Luke 18:35-43)

10:46   Jesus was on the eastern side of the Jordan River but was
heading for Jerusalem (v. 32). Therefore, as He crossed the Jordan
"they came" (*erchontai,* present tense picturing the story as happening) to the city that all pilgrims would encounter as they headed for
Jerusalem, the city of Jericho. At the time of Jesus there actually were
two Jerichos: the site of the ancient city, which was largely uninhabit-
ed, and the new city, built by Herod the Great, one mile to the south,
near the mouth of the Wady Kelt.

> The fertility of the climate and soil, described in glowing terms by Jos.
> *B.J.* viii.3, attracted Herod the Great and Archelaus, who adorned it with
> public buildings and a palace. Under the Procurators it seems to have
> been held by a Roman garrison (*B.J.* ii.18.6). Yet the town was not given
> over to a Hellenistic population like the cities of the Decapolis, or the
> neighbouring Phasaelis; Priests and Levites from Jerusalem found their
> way thither ([Lk.] x.31f.), and the Lord, who seems never to have entered
> Tiberius, did not hesitate to be a guest at a house in Jericho ([Lk.] xix.5).[60]

Matthew (Matt. 20:29-34) and Mark indicate that the upcoming
miracle occurred as Jesus was "going out [of] Jericho." Luke, on the
other hand (Luke 18:35-43), implies that the miracle occurred as they
were approaching Jericho. If the miracle occurred between the two
sites, both accounts are satisfied. Also Matthew states that there were
two men, but Mark and Luke mention only one. Mark is the only account that names the man, which could imply that he was known within the church, for Mark rarely records names in connection with the
incidents of healing. Perhaps the fact that Mark named the man implies that he was the more vocal of the two. The blind beggar's name
was Bartimaeus, which Mark explained as meaning "the son of Tim-

59. Ibid., 416.
60. Swete, *The Gospel According to St. Mark,* 242.

aeus." Bartimaeus was sitting beside the road. That a blind beggar would sit beside a road that was well traveled by pilgrims hoping for alms was not unusual in biblical times.

10:47   When Bartimaeus learned that the commotion and the crowd was caused by "Jesus the Nazarene" passing by, "he began to cry out." His address of Jesus as the "Son of David" is the only time in Mark's gospel that this expression is used. It should be noted that Jesus did not object to the use of this title or reject it. It truly is a Messianic title, for the Messiah must be a son of David in order to rule and reign on David's throne.

> As far as is known, in pre-Christian literature the designation "Son of David" as a title for the Messiah occurs only in the pseudepigraphical Psalms of Solomon 17:21. Though there are those who deny that Bartimaeus is using the term in the Messianic sense, the probability is that he did so intend it, for on the basis of Mark 11:9, 10; 12:35-37 . . . it is clear that during Christ's ministry on earth "Son of David" and "Messiah" had become synonyms. . . . Now the fact that Bartimaeus addressed Jesus as "Son of David" does not mean that he fully appreciated the spiritual character of Jesus' messiahship. It does, however, indicate that he was among the few who were able to give a better answer to the question, "Who do people say that the Son of Man is?" than was given by the people in general (Mark 8:28).[61]

He appealed to Jesus as the Messiah, even though the immediate context indicates that Jesus was going to Jerusalem to die. His request was that He would have mercy on him, for his condition was indeed deplorable. He truly was one on whom mercy needed to be bestowed.

10:48   Many in the crowd rebuked (*epetimōn,* imperfect tense implying that the rebukes were repeated by the crowd) Bartimaeus, "telling him to be quiet." Perhaps there was concern that the Savior did not need to be bothered at this time by a blind beggar. But the Savior was concerned for the physical needs of people. Perhaps those trying to quiet Bartimaeus were in a hurry to get to Jerusalem and did not want to be bothered with a stop. Perhaps some were concerned that the religious leaders would not appreciate the fact that Jesus was being addressed as "Son of David." Bartimaeus paid no attention to their suggestions but cried out all the more. He continued to use the title Son of David and kept asking for mercy.

61. Hendriksen, *Exposition of the Gospel According to Mark,* 419-20.

10:49   Jesus, aware of the commotion, stopped and commanded that Bartimaeus be brought forward. Those who were around Bartimaeus encouraged him to "take courage" (*Tharsei,* present tense) and to "arise" (*egeire,* present tense) because the Savior was "calling" (*phōnei,* present tense) for him. The present tense verbs all help make the words to Bartimaeus very vivid and enable the readers to picture the action as taking place before their eyes. Mark alone records these words.

10:50   Mark alone notes that with haste Bartimaeus cast aside the cloak that had probably been lying on the ground before him collecting the alms. They were not important now. He cast them aside, "jumped up" (*anapēdēsas,* another fact recorded only by Mark), and came as quickly as he possibly could to Jesus. This story is so filled with little details that one can almost see Peter telling it to Mark, who has written it down for all his readers.

10:51   Jesus asked him what he wanted Him to do. The Lord knew what he wanted Him to do, but, as in other cases, Jesus wanted the man to state what he sensed the Savior could do for him. Did he simply want alms from Jesus, as he received from others, or something more? Bartimaeus responded with a term of personal faith: "Rabboni." That title means "My Master," and the only other person in the gospels who used it was Mary when she encountered Jesus in the garden following His resurrection (cf. John 20:16). "Mark's 'Rabboni' must not be downgraded. It probably is to be interpreted as a title which, in such cases, is equivalent to Matthew's and Luke's 'Lord' (Matt. 20:33; Luke 18:41)."[62] His request was that he would "regain [his] sight" (*hina anablepsō*), which means "to recover sight (*ana-*), see again. Apparently he had once been able to see."[63] This was not an unreasonable request, for the Messiah, which the man believed Jesus to be, was supposed to be able to give sight to the blind (cf. Isa. 61:1; Luke 4:18, 7:22).

10:52   Jesus said to him, "Go your way; your faith has made you well [*sesōken,* perfect tense, indicating a completed event with a result that would continue to follow]." The Greek verb commonly meant "to save," and that may be the meaning here. As in the case of the woman with the hemorrhage of blood (cf. 5:34) and other cases, it was faith that had produced the healing and the changed spiritual condition.

62. Ibid., 421.
63. Robertson, *Word Pictures in the New Testament,* 1:356.

"Immediately" (*euthys*) Bartimaeus received his sight and began to follow (*ēkolouthei,* imperfect tense picturing his continuing along with the multitude) Jesus down the road as He headed for Jerusalem. It is possible that Bartimaeus followed Him all the way to Jerusalem, where he then would have been able to give an offering in the temple for his healing. Bartimaeus truly became a follower of Jesus Christ as Jesus had instructed His disciples earlier (cf. 8:34). His actions are in contrast to the rich young ruler, who was commanded to follow Jesus (cf. 10:21), but who went away grieved.

HOMILETICAL SUGGESTIONS

The instruction of Jesus Christ concerning the issue of divorce has been a source of many different interpretations by Bible scholars. It is clear that God never intended for divorce to occur, but Christ emphasizes the permanence of the marriage relationship. It is not easy to emphasize this teaching in contemporary American society. But one's lifestyle ought to follow the biblical pattern rather than bend the Scriptures to fit one's preferences.

Following the issue of divorce, it seems natural that Jesus would discuss the importance and significance of children. He loved children and greatly desired to have a part in their lives. His rebuke of the disciples, who were trying to keep the children away, emphasizes the importance of teaching children the truths of the Word of God that they might have their whole lives in which to serve the Savior.

As Jesus encountered the young man, who felt he had lived righteously, He came right to the heart of the matter. Anything that comes between an individual and God becomes an idol in his life, and this man's problem was his possessions. The contrast between this man and Bartimaeus at the end of the chapter is striking.

Again, Jesus told the disciples that He was going to Jerusalem to die, but the disciples were still clamoring for positions. As James and John came to Jesus asking for the most significant positions in His kingdom, it is no wonder that the other disciples felt indignant. When they learned of James and John's request, they all wanted the position, and yet none of them seemed to have learned the lesson of servanthood.

The story of Bartimaeus, however, shows one who became a true follower of Jesus Christ, for after Jesus healed him of his blindness he followed the Lord.

MARK

CHAPTER

ELEVEN

THE SERVANT'S RETURN TO JERUSALEM

THE REJECTION OF JEHOVAH'S SERVANT, 11:1–15:47

THE PRESENTATION OF THE SERVANT, 11:1-26

THE TRIUMPHAL ENTRY, 11:1-11
(cf. Matt. 21:1-11, 14-17; Luke 19:29-44; John 12:12-19)

11:1   As pilgrims came up to Jerusalem from Jericho, the first city they entered was the town of Bethany, located on the eastern slopes of the Mount of Olives. Just over the top of the Mount of Olives, which rises to about 2,680 feet above sea level, on the western side of that hill, was the little town of Bethphage. One would then go down through the Kidron Valley and finally come to the city of Jerusalem. "Although Bethany would be reached [by pilgrims from Jericho] before Bethphage, the order of mention in verse 1 is apparently dictated by the reference to Jerusalem, followed by the village which was nearer to the city."[1] From John 12:1, it appears that Jesus and His disciples came first to the city of Bethany to the home of Mary, Martha, and Lazarus. There He spent the night before the events recorded here in Mark's gospel unfolded. In fact, it is probable that Jesus spent each night of the passion week, until His arrest, in the home of these

---

1. William L. Lane, *The Gospel of Mark,* NICNT (Grand Rapids: Eerdmans, 1974), 394.

friends. As it came time for Him to enter the city, "He sent two of His disciples" on ahead.

11:2   He said to them, "Go into the village opposite you," which probably was a reference to Bethphage. There He said they would "find a colt [*pōlon*] tied . . . on which no one . . . [had] ever sat." "What kind of colt? Of a camel, a horse, a donkey? It is natural to expect 'of a donkey.' Cf. Gen. 49:11; Judg. 10:4; 12:14. Besides, from Matt. 21:5 we know that this answer is correct and in harmony with the prophecy of Zech. 9:9 (according to the Hebrew)."[2] This was also a colt on which no one had ever sat. "His choice of an animal not ridden by any before Him is another of those claims to uniqueness which contrast forcibly with His usual condescension to the circumstances of an ordinary human life."[3] They were to untie that colt and bring it to Him. Whether the Lord had made previous arrangements for this colt or this was simply something He knew because of His omniscience cannot be determined. The former suggestion seems the better alternative here.

> His precise knowledge concerning the animal and its availability suggests prearrangement with the owner (cf. Ch. 14:12-16), who may have been with Jesus at the time. While this point is not made explicit in the text, it tends to be confirmed by the fact that the message concerning the colt is not directed to the owner but to anyone who might question the disciples' action.[4]

11:3   Jesus gave the disciples a response to use in the event that someone would question what they were doing. The servants were simply to say, " 'The Lord [*kyrios*] has need of [the colt]'; and immediately he will send it back here." Some question whether the Greek word *kyrios* should be translated as "Lord" or "lord." Was Jesus claiming to be the Lord here? Some do point to the fact that the name is not applied to Jesus elsewhere in Mark or Matthew. They feel that the acceptance of Jesus as Lord is better reflected in the Gospels written later, that is, Luke and John. It seems to this writer that the normal understanding of the term *kyrios* is hard to relate to anyone other than Jesus Christ. It is an interesting point to be noted that, whereas

2. William Hendriksen, *Exposition of the Gospel According to Mark* (Grand Rapids: Baker, 1975), 432.

3. Henry Barclay Swete, *The Gospel According to St. Mark* (Grand Rapids: Eerdmans, 1956), 247.

4. Lane, *The Gospel of Mark*, 395.

Jesus had the right to claim anything for Himself, He did return those things that were borrowed.

11:4 Mark presents in greater detail than the other Gospels the expedition of those who went to find the colt. That may imply that one of the disciples who went looking for the animal was Simon Peter. The details given are that they found the colt tied outside a door, in a street, and that "they [then] untied it" (*kai lyousin auton,* a vivid present tense picturing the action). "It was the door at the end of the corridor leading from the outer court (of the house) to the outside."[5]

11:5 As they were in the process of doing this, they were challenged by "bystanders" ("owners" according to Luke 19:33) who wanted to know what they were "doing, untying the colt." This would be a natural reaction, for when two strangers show up, untie the animal, and start away, it gives every appearance of stealing.

11:6 But the two disciples spoke to them using the exact words the Savior had given them, that the Lord had need of it. With that admonition they received permission to take the animal.

> That they were satisfied with the answer . . . need cause no surprise; the Master was well known in the neighbourhood, and His disciples had been with Him before on a memorable occasion (Jo. xi.7ff.). The promise to return the animal at once could be trusted; for the present it was not required by the owners, and they might well be proud that it should be used by the Prophet.[6]

11:7 "They brought the colt" (*pherousin ton pōlon,* a vivid historical present) to Jesus, "put their [outer] garments on it" (*epiballousin autō,* another historical present for vivid action), and He sat on it. Matthew's gospel (Matt. 21:2) notes that they not only brought the colt to the Savior, but the colt's mother was brought along as well. Perhaps this had a calming influence on the younger animal.

> In riding an unbroken colt, Christ demonstrated His authority as Creator over all creation. By divine appointment (Gen. 1:26) creation was subjected to the authority of man, and that authority would be exercised by the Son of Man (Ps. 8:4-8). Now as the Son of Man Jesus was

5. Hendriksen, *Exposition of the Gospel According to Mark,* 435.
6. Swete, *The Gospel According to St. Mark,* 249.

exercising authority over creation. Matthew noted that this was a specific fulfillment of the messianic prophecies of Isaiah 62:11 and Zechariah 9:9.[7]

11:8   As they left Bethphage and began to go down the slope of the Mount of Olives, the pilgrims who were accompanying Jesus and the disciples were not to be outdone by the disciples' action. They began to remove their quadrangular wraps and spread them in the road, forming a carpeted path. Others cut down "leafy branches" (*stibadas,* "leafy boughs or branches," used only here in the New Testament) from the trees that were in the fields. Their actions should be viewed as a kind of royal salute or a gesture of respect given to a very important person. It is similar to the royal salute given to Jehu after it was announced that he was Israel's next king (2 Kings 9:11-13).

> So a Jewish conqueror should be greeted, on his triumphal ride into his capital. All had a share, however small, in the sacrifice associated with such a ride; for if one man gave the donkey, yet others sacrificed clothing; and, on this day at least, none spoke of such sacrifices as being waste. Love's extravagance in self-giving ever goes unrebuked by God, though not always by men (xiv. 4).[8]

It also appears from John's gospel (John 12:12-13) that as the commotion of the delegation was heard in Jerusalem, people from the city came out to meet them bearing palm branches. Palm branches were not native to the hills around Jerusalem and probably had been brought up from the city of Jericho.

11:9   Therefore, there was with Jesus a group of people following after Him coming from the Mount of Olives, as well as those coming out from the city who went before Him. They began crying out, "Hosanna!" This transliteration of a Hebrew word literally means "Save us now!" It was a prayer addressed to God, and it comes from Psalm 118:25-26. This psalm is part of the Hallel, the Psalms of Ascent, that were sung as the pilgrims came up to the city of Jerusalem. "'Hosanna' is properly a prayer invoking God's saving action ('save us'), but through liturgical use it came to be disassociated from its original meaning and could be used as a shout of acclamation (like 'Hallelujah') or as a greeting in addressing pilgrims or a famous rabbi."[9] Their

7. J. Dwight Pentecost, *The Words & Works of Jesus Christ* (Grand Rapids: Zondervan, 1981), 372.
8. R. A. Cole, *The Gospel According to Mark* (Grand Rapids: Eerdmans, 1979), 175.
9. Lane, *The Gospel of Mark*, 397.

cry was, "Blessed is He who comes in the name of the Lord." Literally the psalm implies, "May God be gracious to the one who comes in His name." Technically anyone who came to the city of Jerusalem for the feast days was one who came in the name of the Lord. "It was deplorable, however, that by far the most of these people did not go one step farther: they should have combined Ps. 118 with Isa. 53 and with Zech. 9:9; 13:1. Then they would have recognized in Jesus the Messiah who saves his people *from their sins* (Matt. 1:21)."[10]

11:10   A further admonition is recorded by Mark alone who notes that the crowd cried out, "Blessed is the coming kingdom of our father David." This statement truly has Messianic intent, although it is clear that this crowd was not about to attempt to overthrow the government of Rome on this day. The Roman officials did not seem to be concerned about the demonstration that occurred here. They simply regarded it as a religious act of some kind by a group of Jews. Some in the crowd only knew that this man was "the prophet Jesus," from Nazareth in Galilee (Matt. 21:11). John also notes that "these things His disciples did not understand at the first; but when Jesus was glorified, then they remembered that these things were written of Him" (John 12:16). It is clear, however, that Jesus was coming to the city of Jerusalem in fulfillment of the prophecy of Zechariah 9:9. The fact that Mark did not quote that prophecy probably is an indication of his Gentile readership rather than an omission of an important detail.

> When the people hailed Jesus as "the Son of David" (Matt. 21:9), that is, the Messiah, they were right, and those who were going to find fault with the children (Matt. 21:15) or with the disciples (Luke 19:39) for thus addressing him, were wrong and worthy of being rebuked. But when the crowds in general failed to discern the spiritual nature of his messiahship, they were wrong. Their tragic mistake was committed with tragic results for themselves. How this failure to accept Jesus for what he really was must have hurt him. It is not surprising therefore that Luke pictures a weeping King in the midst of a shouting multitude (19:39-44), nor is it strange that, a little later, when the crowds begin to understand that Jesus is not the kind of Messiah they had expected, they, at the urging of their leaders, were shouting, "Crucify (him)."[11]

11:11   As the crowd of people came into the city of Jerusalem, Jesus

10. Hendriksen, *Exposition of the Gospel According to Mark*, 438.
11. Ibid., 438-39.

entered into the courts of the temple, probably only the Court of the Gentiles, where He looked around (*periblepsamenos,* aorist participle that summarizes Jesus' visit to the temple). Mark's account omits much material that Matthew 21:10-17 and Luke 19:39-55 give.

> In recording this visit to the Temple, Mark has no intention of depicting Jesus as a pilgrim who has come to Jerusalem for the first time and has a natural desire to see "all things." The point is rather that Jesus is the Lord of the Temple, who must inspect its premises to determine whether the purpose intended by God is being fulfilled (cf. Mal. 3:1).[12]

By this time it probably was late in the day, and He was not prepared to deal with what He found there, but nothing escaped His comprehensive glance. He would deal with what He found there on the next day. Now, however, Jesus and the disciples departed, returning back over the Mount of Olives to the town of Bethany, where He spent the night in the home of His friends, Mary, Martha, and Lazarus.

> He knows that the Jewish authorities are inflamed against him, and also that his time to die has not yet arrived. So, for both of these reasons, he cannot during this night remain in Jerusalem. Also, by leaving the city he will escape the hurly-burly of the crowds, will have opportunity for prayer and meditation, and perhaps even for some moments of fellowship with his disciples.[13]

In summary of the Triumphal Entry, J. Dwight Pentecost has made these observations:

> Messiah as the Prince of Peace came on the appointed day to bring peace to the nation. This, then, was the day of Christ's *official presentation* of Himself as *Messiah to Israel.* Christ was identified before the nation as Messiah at His baptism. He was authenticated as Messiah at His temptation. His glory as Messiah was revealed at His transfiguration. But it was at His triumphal entry that Christ made an official presentation of Himself as Messiah to the nation. Such was the significance of our Lord's statement, "If you, even you, had only known on this day what would bring you peace" (Luke 19:42).[14]

12. Lane, *The Gospel of Mark,* 398.
13. Hendriksen, *Exposition of the Gospel According to Mark,* 440.
14. Pentecost, *The Words & Works of Jesus Christ,* 376.

THE JUDGMENT ANNOUNCED, 11:12-14
(cf. Matt. 21:18-19)

11:12 "On the next day," which would have been Monday in the last week of our Lord's life, He departed from the city of Bethany and headed back toward Jerusalem. In the process of the short walk, "He became hungry." Certainly Martha and Mary would have offered Jesus and the disciples something to eat before they left their home. But the reason the Savior became hungry was not stated. Henry Swete suggests,

> The Lord had not broken His fast (cf. Jo. iv.32ff.), or the morning meal had been scanty or hurried; a day of toil was before Him and it was important to recruit His strength on which the spiritual exercises of the night had perhaps drawn largely. The wayside figtree seemed to offer the necessary refreshment.[15]

11:13 At a distance He saw a fig tree that was completely covered with leaves. Mark alone records that He went to the tree to see if He could "find anything" on it. In addition Mark also notes that "it was not the season for figs." Since this was the time of Passover, the month was either late March or early April.

> In the region referred to here in Mark, the early or smaller figs, grow-ing from the sprouts of the previous year, begin to appear at the end of March and are ripe in May or June. The later and much larger figs that develop on the new or spring shoots are gathered from August to Oc-tober. It is important to point out that the earlier figs, with which we are here concerned, begin to appear simultaneously with the leaves. Sometimes, in fact, they even precede the leaves. . . . But Jesus notices that this particular tree, growing by the side of the road and thus partly in a sheltered place (Matt. 21:19), was something special. It had leaves, was most likely in full foliage, and could therefore be expected to have fruit. Yet, it had nothing but leaves! It promised much but provided nothing![16]

11:14 He spoke to the tree and said, "May no one ever eat [*phagoi*] fruit from you again!" "The verb *phagoi* is in the second aorist active optative. It is a wish for the future that in its negative form constitutes

---

15. Swete, *The Gospel According to St. Mark*, 253.
16. Hendriksen, *Exposition of the Gospel According to Mark*, 442.

a curse upon the tree."[17] Jesus' statement was later explained by Peter (v. 21) in exactly that way, as a curse on this tree. It clearly was an indication of judgment, perhaps a judgment relating to profession. The tree was covered with leaves and should have had some evidence of fruit, and yet there was none. Jesus may have been trying to show the condition of the nation of Israel, for, whereas the nation of Israel had all the trappings of religion, there was no true spiritual fruit produced by their religious system. Mark notes that the disciples heard (*ēkouon*) Jesus' comment. This verb for hearing is in the imperfect tense implying that they were listening to Him "and evidently in amazement, for, after all, it was not the fault of the poor fig tree that it had put out leaves. One often sees peach blossoms nipped by the frost when they are too precocious in the changeable weather. But Jesus offered no explanation at this time."[18]

THE CLEANSING OF THE TEMPLE, 11:15-19
(cf. Matt. 21:12-13; Luke 19:45-48)
11:15   Jesus and His disciples came into Jerusalem and "entered the temple." There Jesus "began to cast out those who were buying and selling." Jesus had cleansed the temple earlier in His ministry (cf. John 2:13-16), but the bazaar that was making a great deal of money for the priests evidently very quickly returned. Mark specifically mentions that there were those who were changing money (*kollybistōn,* from *killybos,* a small coin) and those who were selling doves in the temple area. They were probably occupying the large court of the Gentiles in order to carry out this business. It is clear that they had a very lucrative practice going.

Monies coming in from outside were of course not able to be used in the temple. Any money that was brought into the temple had to be exchanged for "clean" money, but at a price. Every Jewish man twenty years of age and older was expected to pay an annual tax for the maintenance of the temple. "This tax for the Jerusalem temple was due in the month of Adar (our March). . . . The payment had to be made in the Jewish coin, half-shekel. Hence the money-changers did a thriving business in charging a small premium for the Jewish coin, amounting to some forty-five thousand dollars a year, it is estimated."[19]

17. A. T. Robertson, *Word Pictures in the New Testament* (Nashville: Broadman, 1930), 1:359.
18. Ibid.
19. Ibid., 142

For Jesus to overturn their tables on which their piles of half-shekels stood did great damage to their business at the time of their greatest volume. Also, there was no reason for people to bring sacrifices from their homes far away to the temple, for those offerings could be provided right there at the site.

> Doves were the recognized offering of the poor, required for the purification of women (Lev. 12:6; Lk. 2:22-24), the cleansing of lepers (Lev. 14:22), and other purposes (Lev. 15:14, 29). The installation of stalls for the sale of animals and of other requirements for the sacrifice such as wine, oil and salt, had the effect of transforming the Court of the Gentiles into an oriental bazaar and a cattle mart.[20]

Of course, the price that was charged was greatly inflated. This probably grieved the Lord Jesus the most because the doves were the offerings given by the poor. To be charging exorbitant prices was certainly not in keeping with the spirit of the temple in which they were worshiping.

11:16 Mark adds a comment that none of the other gospel writers mention. Jesus also would not permit people to carry goods through the temple courts.

> By means of the gates it had become rather easy and convenient to use the temple area as a *shortcut;* for example, between the city and the Mount of Olives. The sacred place was being used for purely secular purposes. Did not even the rabbis disapprove of this? . . . What Jesus saw was that for the sake of convenience worldly-minded people were carrying all kinds of "vessels"—objects used for profane purposes—through the temple area, thereby degrading it.[21]

Jesus stopped that practice.

11:17 He taught them by quoting Isaiah 56:6-7, which says that God intended for His temple to be a house of prayer "for all the nations." It is interesting that Mark is the only gospel that mentions this fact. Jesus, however, said that they had turned it into "a robber's den" instead (cf. Jer. 7:11). The implication is that Jesus truly thought their activity was illegal. "The people as well as the temple authorities were

---

20. Lane, *The Gospel of Mark,* 405-6.
21. Hendriksen, *Exposition of the Gospel According to Mark,* 453.

guilty of graft, extortion, and desecration of the house of prayer."[22] But not only were they robbing people financially, they also were robbing them spiritually by turning the temple into a place of merchandise. When their marketplace was set up in the Court of the Gentiles, how would a Gentile feel who came to the temple to worship God? The place where he was to meditate, pray, and worship had become a noisy marketplace. The Jews were robbing him of a quiet place of prayer and worship.

> By expelling them from the forecourt Jesus freed the place where the Gentiles were allowed to worship. In view of the explicit citation of Isa. 56:7 and the allusion to Jer. 7:11, speculation that Jesus' action was aimed at reform or abolition of the Temple worship is irrelevant. He is depicted as making possible the worship of the Gentiles at the feast of the Passover which commemorated God's redemption of his people. The importance of this would not be lost upon Mark's readers and the predominantly Gentile Church of Rome.[23]

11:18   When "the chief priests and the scribes heard [*ēkousan,* aorist tense which records the fact of their hearing]" what Jesus was doing, they recognized that He was claiming great authority. This is the first time in the Synoptic Gospels that the chief priests and scribes joined together against Jesus. They understood that He was claiming authority higher than that of the high priest. "They were afraid [*ephobounto,* imperfect tense implying a continual fear) of Him" because "the multitude was astonished [*exeplēsseto,* imperfect tense implying continual astonishment] at His teaching" and loved Jesus and what He was doing. The people looked on Jesus as a hero, as the Messiah. This verse aptly describes the crisis that had come between Christ and the Sanhedrin. It was clear now that, if the chief priests and scribes were to maintain their positions, they had to figure out how they could destroy Jesus Christ ("seeking how to destroy him," *ezētoun pōs auton apolesōsin,* imperfect implying a continuous action). There was no other alternative for them.

11:19   As evening came, Jesus and the disciples went out (*exeporeuonto,* imperfect tense implying that this action was repeated each evening) of the city. Although it is not mentioned where He went, it appears that He did go back to Bethany to the home of His friends. "It

---

22. Robertson, *Word Pictures in the New Testament,* 1:360.
23. Lane, *The Gospel of Mark,* 407.

would scarcely have been safe for Him to have spent the night in the city now, with so many foes actively plotting His death; but quiet Bethany was safe, and so thither He went."[24]

THE JUDGMENT FULFILLED, 11:20-26
(cf. Matt. 21:20-22)

11:20   On the next morning, Tuesday of Jesus' last week, Jesus and His disciples were headed toward Jerusalem when they passed the same fig tree as on the previous day. Mark alone gives the detail that the tree was now "withered from the roots up" (*exērammenēn ek rizōn,* perfect passive participle indicating a condition with an effect springing from it). The fact that the tree was withered from the roots up indicates the totality of its destruction and clearly demonstrates that the words of Jesus were fulfilled, for no one would ever eat of the fruit of that tree again (cf. v. 14).

11:21   Peter, as Mark alone records, pointed out the fig tree to the Savior and said, "Rabbi, behold, the fig tree which You cursed has withered." Peter and the disciples were probably surprised at how rapidly the judgment had fallen.

> What astonished Peter—and the other disciples (Matt. 21:22)—, so that he says, "Rabbi, look!" was the fact that such a very short time, probably within twenty-four hours, the tree on which Jesus had pronounced his curse had changed from a seemingly vigorous woody perennial in full foliage, to a shrunken corpse, the ghost of its former self. Not that Peter blamed Jesus for what He had done to the tree, but, as the immediately following verse implies, he was unable to understand how it had been possible to bring about such a radical change, and that within so short a time.[25]

Perhaps the greater context of the judgment on the fig tree and the judgment on the temple bazaar by Jesus was the impending judgment about to fall on the nation of Israel. It would not be long until the Roman legions came, totally destroying the city, and driving out the Jews.

11:22   Jesus encouraged the disciples to "Have faith [*echete pistin,* present tense imperative implying something that was to be habitual] in God."

24. Cole, *The Gospel According to Mark,* 180.
25. Hendriksen, *Exposition of the Gospel According to Mark,* 457-58.

The answer is remarkable; the Lord does not explain the lesson to be learnt from the fate of the tree, but deals with the matter of more immediate importance to the Twelve, the lesson to be learnt from the prompt fulfillment of His prayer. . . . The answer is addressed not to Peter only, but to all.[26]

The object of faith is always the key, and Jesus' admonition was for them to keep their faith focused on the sovereign Lord.

11:23   It helps to remember where Jesus and the disciples were as one reads this verse. They were standing on the Mount of Olives, probably near the top. As one looks to the east from that vantage point on a clear day, one can see all the way to the Dead Sea. Therefore, the physical features of Jesus' statement were right before their eyes. This statement is a hyperbole, for Jesus was referring to the Mount of Olives and the Dead Sea when He said that the person of faith could say "to this mountain, 'Be taken up and cast into the sea.'" Jesus in effect said, "If you do not doubt [*mē diakrithē,* aorist verb that means "to be divided in judgment," from *dyo,* "two," and *krinō,* "to judge"], but believe in your heart, this can happen." A mountain was often used in the Old Testament to picture a great obstacle in one's path (cf. Zech. 4:7). Thus, Jesus was teaching the disciples that great obstacles in their lives could be removed by prayer if they would pray in keeping with the will of God. "Of course Jesus was not recommending silly prayers; He was talking about dealing with impossible situations. And though the concept is not interjected here, one cannot have absolute faith in the omnipotent power of God to accomplish something unless he has confidence that what he asks is in the will of God."[27]

11:24   Jesus, therefore, personalized the matter of prayer. He said to the disciples, "All things for which you pray and ask, believe [*pisteuete,* present tense imperative] that you have received them [*elabete,* aorist tense implying a virtual certainty], and they shall be granted you." Now this is not the only scriptural teaching on prayer. It is obvious that prayer must be in the will of God (cf. 14:36; Matt. 6:9-10; 1 John 5:14-15), and, as one prays, one must be abiding in His love (John 15:7-14). We should not

interpret Mark 11:24 to mean, "If you pray hard enough and *really believe,* God is obligated to answer your prayers, no matter what you ask."

26. Swete, *The Gospel According to St. Mark,* 259.
27. Howard F. Vos, *Mark* (Grand Rapids: Zondervan, 1978), 99-100.

That kind of faith is not faith in God; rather, it is nothing but faith in faith, or faith in feelings. True faith in God is based on His Word (Rom. 10:17; John 15:7), and His Word reveals His will to us. It has well been said that the purpose of prayer is not to get man's will done in heaven, but to get God's will done on earth.[28]

11:25   In addition, when one prays (the position for prayer in this culture was "standing," cf. Luke 18:9-14), one needs to be certain that everything in one's relationship is right with the Heavenly Father. An unforgiving spirit in one's heart is an indication that things are not right between the individual and God. When one goes to prayer, any problem with another individual should be dealt with first, and forgiveness to that individual should be expressed. "The person who prays must be willing and anxious to forgive. If he lacks this disposition he has no right to assume that his own trespasses have been forgiven."[29] However, when he forgives there is perfect fellowship between both the individual and his fellow men, and his God, his Heavenly Father, will forgive all his transgressions (cf. Matt. 6:12ff.; 18:21-35).

> Unless our Father condescends to hear and forgive, we have no hope. But, unless we forgive our fellow men freely, it shows that we have no consciousness of the grace that we ourselves have received (Mt. xviii. 32, 33), and thus we are expecting to be heard on our own merits. This would be a complete denial of the great principle of justification by faith; and so we cannot be heard.[30]

11:26   It does not appear that this verse is in the best manuscripts. It probably was repeated from Matthew 6:15 where it definitely does appear. Nevertheless, it is the logical outcome of the Lord's words in v. 25.

> Whether properly belonging here or not, the verse not only expresses a logical deduction from verse 25, but also a solemn theological truth, which is certainly to be read in the Matthean context. This is not an arbitrary refusal by God to forgive us. We in our own unforgiving spirit have made it impossible for ourselves to accept the forgiveness freely

---

28. Warren W. Wiersbe, *Be Diligent* (Wheaton, Ill.: Victor, 1987), 111.
29. Hendriksen, *Exposition of the Gospel According to Mark,* 462.
30. Cole, *The Gospel According to Mark,* 181.

offered by God since we refuse to adopt the only attitude in which it can be appropriated.[31]

THE CONTROVERSIES WITH THE SERVANT, 11:27–12:40

WITH THE RELIGIOUS LEADERS, 11:27–12:12

The Question of Authority, 11:27-33 (cf. Matt. 21:23-32; Luke 20:1-8)

11:27 When Jesus and His disciples "came" (*erchontai*, present tense for vividness) into the city of Jerusalem, the first place He went was the temple, probably to the Court of the Gentiles, the largest open area in the temple, which He had cleansed the previous day. There He was able to move about and talk with people. In the process of His conversations, suddenly Jesus was dealing with "chief priests, and scribes, and elders."

> *The chief priests* constituted a group or order consisting of the present ruling high priest, those who had formerly occupied this high office, and other dignitaries from whose ranks the high priests were generally selected. The custody of the temple had been entrusted to these people, mostly Sadducees. It is not strange that *the scribes,* mostly Pharisees, are also mentioned, for these were the men who studied, interpreted, and taught the law. Their teaching was done in both temple and synagogue. *The elders,* too, were present. In ancient Israel an elder was the head of a tribe or of a tribal division. In fact, every city or town of any importance soon had its ruling elders. With the establishment of the Sanhedrin the more prominent local elders became members of this august body. We might call them the Sanhedrin's "lay members."[32]

These men, therefore, were part of the Jewish Sanhedrin, and "this is the only instance in Mark in which the Sanhedrin approaches Jesus (apart from 14:55ff.), and this leaves no doubt that the issue of Jesus' authority was a matter of concern at the pinnacle of the religious establishment."[33] The Sanhedrin was the guardian of Israel's religious life, and they had the obligation to investigate the claims of anyone with regard to religious matters. "Clearly a large committee of the Sanhedrin including both Sadducees and Pharisees here confront

---

31. Ibid., 182.
32. Hendriksen, *Exposition of the Gospel According to Mark,* 464-65.
33. James R. Edwards, "The Authority of Jesus in the Gospel of Mark," *JETS* 37 (June 1994): 226.

Jesus in a formal attack upon his authority for cleansing the temple and teaching in it."[34]

11:28 They asked Him, "By what authority are You doing these things?" "These things" is a nebulous reference. But in light of what had just recently happened, they probably were thinking of His triumphal entry on Sunday as well as the cleansing of the temple that had occurred the day before.

> The question in itself was a reasonable one, and the men who asked it felt that they had a right to do so. The Temple was in their charge, and by forcibly ejecting the vendors whom they allowed, Jesus had laid claim to a superior jurisdiction. They now ask Him publicly to produce His credentials, to state (1) the nature of His authority, (2) the name of the person from whom He had received it.[35]

They also asked Him, "Who gave You this authority to do these things [*hina tauta poiēs,* present tense implying that He continued to do them]?" This second question "acknowledges that no one possesses such authority on his own. Thus, similar to the question of 2:7 ('Who can forgive sins but God alone?'), the issue of Jesus' divine presumption is again center stage."[36]

11:29 Jesus said, "I will ask you one question." They had asked Him two questions, but He countered with only one. This was a typical rabbinical style of teaching. In fact, today many teachers still like to answer questions with questions. "It should not be regarded as an evasion but an effort to put the question more squarely on target, an inquiry made for the sake of one's questioner."[37] He told them that, if they would answer His question, He would tell them by what authority He was doing "these things." "As on the earlier question of Sabbath observance (2:23–3:6), the counterquestion implies that Jesus stands not under the Sanhedrin but over it. His counterquestion demonstrates the authority about which he is questioned."[38]

11:30 His question was simply, "Was the baptism of John from heaven, or from men?" It should be remembered that the Jewish people had a very special reverence for the name of God. They did not

---

34. Robertson, *Word Pictures in the New Testament,* 1:362.
35. Swete, *The Gospel According to St. Mark,* 262.
36. Edwards, "The Authority of Jesus in the Gospel of Mark," 226.
37. Vos, *Mark,* 102.
38. Edwards, "The Authority of Jesus in the Gospel of Mark," 226.

use it for fear they would blaspheme. Therefore, the use of the term "heaven" came to be a euphemism for God Himself. Jesus' question basically was, "Do you believe that John's authority was from God or from men?" Jesus, by connecting Himself with John the Baptist, was in reality claiming the same authority.

> Jesus stakes his own authority entirely on that of the Baptist, and his declaration of solidarity with John is, in essence, a statement about the eschatological crisis which both knew to be at hand. John and Jesus stand in common opposition to those who disregard the will of God. The reference to John is appropriate because already in his ministry the Baptist had effected that split between the people and their leaders which characterized Jesus' ministry in the Temple (Chs. 11:18; 12:38).[39]

Mark alone records Jesus' sharp demand, "Answer Me" (*apokrithēte moi,* present tense imperative).

> If the Sanhedrin wants to know whence Jesus received authority to do "these things" it must reconsider John's baptism. A decision about John is a decision about Jesus. If John's baptism were simply of human origin, then there may be something to the Sanhedrin's accusation. But if John's baptism was of God—as the crowds believed and the Sanhedrin evidently feared—then Jesus' authority is the authority of God.[40]

11:31 The religious leaders realized that Jesus had them on the horns of a dilemma, so "they began reasoning" (*dielogizonto,* imperfect tense implying their debating among themselves went on for a period of time) together. "The alternatives are sharply presented in their secret conclave."[41] They concluded that if they were to say that John's authority was "from heaven," that is, from God, then they knew Jesus would say, "Then why did you not believe him?" That would be an embarrassing situation. If John's authority was from God, why did they reject his testimony? Why didn't they believe? "To acknowledge the Divine mission of John was to charge themselves with unbelief in having as a class rejected his baptism ([Lk.] vii.30), and to give an advantage to their Questioner which He would not be slow to use."[42]

39. Lane, *The Gospel of Mark,* 413.
40. Edwards, "The Authority of Jesus in the Gospel of Mark," 227.
41. Robertson, *Word Pictures in the New Testament,* 1:362.
42. Swete, *The Gospel According to St. Mark,* 264.

11:32   But if they were to answer that the authority of John the Baptist was from men, "they were afraid of [how] the multitude" would respond. They "considered" (*eixon,* imperfect tense showing the feeling of the people over a period of time) John to be a prophet, and certainly they had now gathered around the religious leaders as they were discussing this issue. This was an open place in the temple where many people could gather, and surely by this time a large crowd was present.

> The second conditional sentence is broken off in the middle, but the apodosis is clear from the context: if they affirm that John's authority was from men (i.e. not from God), they will discredit themselves in the eyes of the people, who could turn against them in wrath. Both John and Jesus were regarded by the people as genuine prophets, and for this reason in both instances the authorities "feared" the people (Chs. 11:18, 32; 12:12).[43]

11:33   Therefore, their response to Jesus was, "We do not know." "They saved themselves from the dilemma by a disgraceful profession of ignorance."[44] The truth of the matter was that they did know, but they were afraid to answer. Their initial inquiry was not a sincere question, for they were simply looking for ways to destroy Jesus Christ (cf. v. 18). "The root of the trouble lay not in their intellects, but in their stubborn wills. They stood self-condemned. The Lord's question was not a trap; it was yet another opportunity for them to realize and confess their blindness, and ask for sight."[45] Since they were trying to get Jesus to incriminate Himself and refused to answer His question, Jesus responded by saying He would not tell them who gave Him His authority. "Their self-imposed ignorance, refusal to take a stand about the Baptist who was the Forerunner of Christ, absolved Jesus from a categorical reply. But he has no notion of letting them off at this point."[46] He gave them a condemning parable.

43. Lane, *The Gospel of Mark,* 414.
44. Swete, *The Gospel According to St. Mark,* 265.
45. Cole, *The Gospel According to Mark,* 183.
46. Robertson, *Word Pictures in the New Testament,* 1:363.

HOMILETICAL SUGGESTIONS

Mark 11 begins to detail events in the last week of our Savior's life. The various events that take place in this week are significant, and each event should be compared with the other gospel accounts for the full details.

The Triumphal Entry is most significant, for Jesus Christ was coming in fulfillment of many Old Testament prophecies as the Messiah/King of Israel. Mark's gospel makes no reference to any of the Old Testament prophecies Jesus was fulfilling, probably because those references were unknown to his readers. But truly Jesus came in fulfillment of prophecies, perhaps even coming on the very day that Daniel had predicted He would come to complete the sixty-nine "weeks" (Dan. 9:25).

The judgment of Jesus Christ on the fig tree announced in vv. 12-14 and fulfilled in vv. 23-26 seems not to be a significant event until one realizes that it probably was picturing the nation of Israel. Israel had all the trappings of religion, and yet there was no fruit. The Savior was looking for spiritual insight from the nation in order that He might be accepted. But the nation, in spite of their religious appearance, was not interested in acknowledging Him as the true Messiah.

Jesus had cleansed the temple earlier in His ministry, as seems clear when one compares the account here with John 2:13-16. The Savior was incensed over the way the place of true worship had been turned into a den of merchandise. The actions of the Jewish merchants had robbed the Gentiles of a place for reflective worship of Jehovah. Care needs to be exerted today so that similar practices do not occur. Churches can potentially be turned into places of merchandise rather than remaining places of true worship.

Mark also gives in this chapter the beginning of the controversies that Jesus had with the religious leaders. These have always been interesting to explore. The first question Jesus dealt with was the question of authority. The way the Savior handled the religious leaders by turning the issue back to them is masterful. Since they failed to answer His question, He refused to answer theirs. The fact of the matter is that both John the Baptist and Jesus Christ worked by the same authority, the authority of His Heavenly Father.

MARK

CHAPTER
TWELVE

THE SERVANT'S REQUIREMENTS

The Parable for Instruction, 12:1-11 (cf. Matt. 21:33-43; Luke 20:9-18)
12:1   The text says that Jesus "began to speak" to the religious leaders in "parables." The phrase "began to speak" is a common idiom in
Mark. "He does not mean that this was the beginning of Christ's use of
parables (see 4:2), but simply that his teaching on this occasion took
the parabolic turn."[1] In the ensuing verses, however, only one parable
is given. Since Mark used the plural "parables," he obviously knew
that Jesus spoke more than the one story. Why he chose to record only
one of them is not explained. Matthew mentions three parables (cf.
Matt. 21:28–22:14 for the parables of the two sons and the marriage
feast of the king's son, as well as the same parable recorded by Mark).
Jesus' parable would have been a familiar story in Israel at that time.
He told of a man who planted a vineyard and did everything possible
to make that vineyard productive. A wall was put around it, a vat was
dug under the wine press to catch the juice when the grapes were
trodden, and a tower was built for protection. This imagery has many
parallels with the story in Isaiah 5:1-7, where Israel is pictured as the
vineyard of the Lord. "The vineyard had become a recognised symbol
of Israel itself, as the covenant people (Ps. lxxx.8f., Isa. v.2ff., Jer. ii.21),
and it was impossible for the members of the Sanhedrin or for the
better-taught among the crowd to mistake the drift of the parable (see

---

1. A. T. Robertson, *Word Pictures in the New Testament* (Nashville: Broadman, 1930), 1:364.

v. 12)."[2] In the parable, the owner of the vineyard rented out his vineyard to caretakers and went off on a journey. Luke notes (Luke 20:9) that the owner went away "for a long time."

> Since the whole of the upper Jordan valley and a large part of the Galilean uplands were in the hands of foreign landlords at this time, such a practice was common. A contract stipulated for the payment of rent in the form of a portion of the produce. The crucial detail is that the owner is living abroad, for the subsequent conduct of the tenants is intelligible only under the existing conditions of absentee ownership.[3]

12:2   When harvest time came, the owner sent a slave back to those caring for the vineyard in order that he might "receive some of the produce" from the field.

> The servant . . . was commissioned by the owner to collect and carry to the master's home the portion of the fruit that belonged to him. Having been delegated by him, it follows that the servant was invested with the master's authority. He made his demand or request in the owner's name. The request was altogether proper, for a definite agreement had been made and the "proper time," that is, the time of the vintage had arrived.[4]

12:3   In Jesus' story the tenants proved to be dishonest, wicked, and cruel men. They took the servant, "beat him, and sent him away empty-handed." The verb "to beat" (*derō*) in the Septuagint carried the idea of "to flay," but in the New Testament it is used only in the sense of a severe beating or a "scourging."

> The servant, instead of taking anything, is taken; sent to receive, he is sent back empty. It is difficult to decide whether the play on these words is intentional, or due to the simplicity of the style of the common tradition; in favour of the second explanation it may be noted that this feature is most noticeable in [Mark].[5]

12:4   It might be expected that the owner of the field would have responded with force to the treatment of his servant. The manner in

2. Henry Barclay Swete, *The Gospel According to St. Mark* (Grand Rapids: Eerdmans, 1956), 265.

3. William L. Lane, *The Gospel of Mark,* NICNT (Grand Rapids: Eerdmans, 1974), 417.

4. William Hendriksen, *Exposition of the Gospel According to Mark* (Grand Rapids: Eerdmans, 1975), 473.

5. Swete, *The Gospel According to St. Mark,* 268.

which the servant was treated was an insult to him as well. Instead, "he sent . . . another slave" to receive some of what he was entitled to. This time the slave was wounded in the head and treated shamefully.

12:5   A third slave was sent, but this time the slave was killed. Jesus added, "And so with many others, beating some, and killing others." The owner of the vineyard made numerous attempts to collect what was rightfully his.

> The detail . . . that the owner sent many others, was intended by Jesus to force his listeners beyond the framework of the parable to the history of Israel. In the OT the prophets are frequently designated "the servants" of God (cf. Jer. 7:25f.; 25:4; Amos 3:7; Zech. 1:6) and it is natural to find a reference to their rejection in the words "beating some, and killing others."[6]

12:6   Finally, Jesus said the owner of the field had only "one more [person] to send," in contrast with the many servants. That was his "beloved son" (*huion agapēton*). Perhaps Jesus had in mind the language the Father had spoken at the time of His baptism (cf. 1:11). "He sent him last of all [*eschaton,* used only by Mark]," thinking surely they would respect his son. "It could be expected that the son of the owner would command the respect which had been denied to the slaves who had represented him previously."[7]

12:7   But those renting the field said to one another, "This is the heir; come, let us kill him." They reasoned that the fact that the son came to collect what was due implied that the owner was dead. If they could eliminate the heir, the fields could become theirs. According to the law of the time, if a field was unclaimed, after a period of time the first person making a claim could possess it. "This provision of law explains why the tenants assumed that if they murder the son (and presumed heir), they may take unhindered possession of the vineyard. It would become 'ownerless property' which they can claim as the actual occupants of the land."[8]

12:8   Therefore, the son was taken and killed, and his body was simply discarded by throwing it over the wall of the vineyard. The parable is crystal clear.

6. Lane, *The Gospel of Mark,* 418.
7. Ibid.
8. Ibid., 419.

It was not through their failure to recognize the Son that they killed Him; that would have been pardonable. It was, as in the parable, precisely because they recognized Him for who He was that they slew Him. . . . We reject the claims of Christ not because we misunderstand them, but because we understand them only too well, in spite of all our protestations to the contrary.[9]

12:9   Jesus then addressed a question to His listeners. He asked them what they thought the owner of the vineyard would do. In Matthew's account of this parable (Matt. 21:41), it is the people who reply with the response that the owner of the vineyard would come in person and "destroy the vine-growers," and the vineyard would be given to others. "The parable at this point becomes a scarcely veiled prophecy of the Divine visitation of wrath which befell Jerusalem, the call of the Gentiles, and the fruitfulness and permanence of the . . . Church."[10]
12:10   Jesus made an immediate application from the story to Himself by turning to a Messianic psalm (Ps. 118:22). The imagery of the vineyard changed to that of a "stone which the builders rejected," but which "became the chief corner stone."

The passage refers to one of the building blocks gathered at the site of Solomon's Temple which was rejected in the construction of the Sanctuary but which proved to be the keystone of the porch. Introduced with the language of debate, the citation is intended to sharpen the application of the parable to Jesus and his immediate listeners. It confirms the identification of Jesus as the son in the parable and contrasts his despised and rejected status with the glorious exaltation to which God has appointed him.[11]

12:11   Jesus quoted from the psalm: "This came about from the Lord, and it is marvelous in our eyes." This was truly in keeping with what God had planned, and the application of this parable could not be missed. The vineyard was the nation of Israel, and those who were caring for the vineyard were the religious leaders. They had poorly treated many of the servants God had sent, some of whom they had even killed, including prophets and John the Baptist. The last thing

9. R. A. Cole, *The Gospel According to Mark* (Grand Rapids: Eerdmans, 1979), 185.
10. Swete, *The Gospel According to St. Mark*, 271.
11. Lane, *The Gospel of Mark*, 420.

they were going to do was to kill the beloved Son, the Lord Jesus
Himself.

The Leaders' Response, 12:12 (cf. Matt. 21:45-46; Luke 20:19)
12:12   The religious leaders understood exactly what Jesus was saying. They knew He had spoken this parable "against them" (*pros au-
tous*), and they would love to have seized Him and immediately
eliminated Him from their midst. But they could not do that because
they feared the multitude. Surely many of the people regarded Jesus
as a prophet. It had been only a few days before that people had been
shouting "Hosanna!" in His honor and on more than one occasion
had tried to make Him King. In addition, many had recently become
followers of Jesus because He had brought back to life Lazarus who
had been in the grave for more than four days. Truly the multitude
regarded Jesus to be at least a great hero, if not the Messiah/King. No
wonder they feared the results of their actions should they remove
Jesus from their midst. So they simply left Him and went away. Rather
than admit that they understood the parable, that was the only thing
they could do.

WITH THE PHARISEES AND HERODIANS, 12:13-17
(cf. Matt. 22:15-22; Luke 20:20-26)
12:13   The attacks on Jesus nevertheless continued, for "they sent
some of the Pharisees and Herodians" to try "to trap Him in a statement." The verb "to trap" (*agreusōsin,* found only here in the New
Testament) literally meant "to catch a fish or to ensnare a wild animal."
The joining together of Pharisees and Herodians was an interesting
match, for they were poles apart. The Pharisees were the conserva-
tives of their day, holding to all of the religious traditions. The Herodians, followers of Herod the Great, were an extremely liberal political
group. They were for all kinds of changes and had no problem what-
soever with the Roman government ruling over the Jews in the land of
Israel. These men were probably the Galilean Herodians who previously had joined forces with the Pharisees to get rid of Jesus (cf. 3:6).
They too had come from Galilee to celebrate the feast.
12:14   As these leaders came to Jesus they said some very flattering
things about Him: that He was truthful and that He deferred to no one,
for He was not partial to any. Literally the text says that He did not
look at the faces of men, which was a Hebrew expression. They affirmed that He taught the way of God in truth. "The use of the word

['truthful'] by the Pharisees is an unconscious witness to the impression which Christ's life and teaching had left even upon enemies."[12]

It is interesting that all the things they were saying about Jesus were not true of themselves. "By reminding Jesus that he was a man of integrity who paid no attention to the opinions of men but taught absolute commitment to the way of life commanded by God, his adversaries intended to force him to face squarely the issue they had decided upon."[13] Their question was, "Is it lawful to pay a poll-tax to Caesar, or not?"

> The Zealots resolutely refused to pay the tax because it acknowledged Caesar's domination over them. The Pharisees resented the humiliation implied in the tax but justified its payment, while the Herodians supported it on principle. In asking if it was allowed by the Law of God to pay the tribute money it could be assumed that the Pharisees were concerned chiefly in the moral and religious implications of the question, and the Herodians with its political or nationalistic ramifications. In point of fact the question was insincere. Its object was to force Jesus into a compromising position either theologically or politically. The form of the question ("shall we give, or shall we not give it?") was skillfully designed to thrust Jesus on the horns of a dilemma. An affirmative answer would discredit him in the eyes of the people, for whom the tax was an odious token of subjection to Rome. A negative reply would invite reprisals from the Roman authorities.[14]

12:15 Jesus knew what their true motivation was, which is why He knew them to be hypocrites. They appeared to be asking a sincere question, but they were really asking the question in order to trap Him in His words. "Their action was diabolical. While feigning innocence, they thought they had lured their enemy in a trap from which, as they saw it, he would not be able to escape."[15] He asked them why they were testing Him and then requested that they give Him a denarius to look at. The denarius was a small silver Roman coin that was used to pay the tax they were inquiring about. It was equal to the amount a laborer would earn for a day's labor.

---

12. Swete, *The Gospel According to St. Mark*, 274.
13. Lane, *The Gospel of Mark*, 422.
14. Ibid., 423.
15. Hendriksen, *Exposition of the Gospel According to Mark*, 482.

12:16   Jesus was given one of the coins, and as He held it in His hand He probably held it up for the crowd to see. He asked them, "Whose likeness and inscription is this [on the coin]?" On one side of a Roman denarius was an imprint of the current Caesar. The coin Jesus held probably had the likeness of Tiberius Caesar, who reigned from A.D. 14 to 37. Not only would his likeness have been on the coin, but there would have been an inscription that read "Tiberius Caesar Augustus, son of the divine Augustus." On the reverse side of the coin, Caesar would have been shown seated on a throne and wearing a crown, clothed as a high priest. The inscription on that side read "Highest Priest." Knowing the answer to Jesus' question, they replied that the likeness was "Caesar's."

12:17   Jesus responded by telling them they needed to pay back "to Caesar the things that [were] Caesar's." The very fact that they were using that coin showed that they had an obligation to Rome. Since that coin was circulating in their society, that implied that the Roman government had a realm of authority over them and that they were benefiting from that authority. Therefore, they should be giving back to Caesar the things that were Caesar's.

But then Jesus added one other phrase: they should be rendering "to God the things that [were] God's." The Lord was pointing out that Caesar was not God, even though the inscription on the coin implied that he was. God does have a realm in which man is held accountable, and people should render to God the things that are God's. Since God has placed within people His own image, perhaps that was what Jesus was suggesting ought to be rendered back to Him—one's very own soul.

This passage was very enlightening for Mark's Roman readers, for many at that time were accusing Christians of being contrary to the government. But Christianity is not contrary to the government. It never has been. It is no wonder that the people "were amazed [*exethaumazon,* imperfect tense implying their amazement extended over a period of time] at Him." They had never heard anything like His teaching.

> They had not expected this kind of answer. Jesus had frankly and courageously answered their question. The answer implies: Yes, the tax must be paid. There must be an adequate response to privileges enjoyed. But though the emperor must receive his due, he must not receive more than that; that is, he must not receive the divine honor he claims. At the

same time, God must receive *all* the glory and honor—In all candor, who can find fault with this answer? Certainly no one.[16]

WITH THE SADDUCEES, 12:18-27
(cf. Matt. 22:23-33; Luke 20:27-40)

12:18 The next group that "came" (*erchontai,* a present tense for dramatic effect) to debate with Jesus were the Sadducees. This is the first clear mention of the Sadducees in Mark's gospel. Mark adds the notation that the Sadducees did not believe there was a resurrection. But there is a great deal more that the Sadducees did not believe. They also failed to believe in future punishment or reward, and they doubted the existence of angels. They only believed in the written law of Moses and rigorously opposed the oral tradition of the Pharisees. Most of the people who were Sadducees were from the priestly families of Jerusalem (cf. Acts 5:17). They were the "religious aristocrats" of Judaism, whose headquarters were in Jerusalem and who thought they were better than everyone else. They too came to Jesus "questioning Him."

> It is not surprising, therefore, that the Sadducees now, in turn, attack Jesus. . . .
> In fact, it must be considered altogether probable that these men intended to strike a double blow. In exposing what they regarded as the foolishness of Christ's teaching regarding the glory awaiting himself and his followers on the other side of death, would they not at the same time triumph over the Pharisees, who likewise believed in a resurrection from the dead? If we are permitted to assume that news of the victory of Jesus over the Pharisees (and their allies) soon reached the ears of Sadducees—in view of Matt. 22:34 not an unreasonable assumption—, may we not also assume that the latter were already saying to each other, "We'll show the Pharisees that we can do better"? Were they perhaps already chuckling over the prospect of "killing two birds with one stone," that is, of exposing to ridicule both Jesus and the Pharisees?[17]

12:19 They approached Jesus by calling Him "Teacher" (*Didaskale*). "On their lips the title is purely formal; there is here no pretense of a desire to learn such as may have dictated its use by the

16. Ibid., 484.
17. Ibid., 485-86.

disciples of the Pharisees (*v.* 14)."[18] They then set up their scenario. They gave a very free rendering of the Mosaic regulation concerning levirate marriage (cf. Deut. 25:5-10). The idea was that if a man died without having a male heir, his brother or nearest male relative was to marry his widow. If they then had a male child, that child was to be given the name of the dead brother so that his name would not pass out of the family inheritance in the nation of Israel. Since this principle was Mosaic, the Sadducees were not in any sense disagreeing with it. They did, however, present an extreme illustration. Whether this principle was still being followed in the time of Christ cannot be proven conclusively.

12:20 They brought up an illustration of a family of "seven brothers." The first one "took a wife, and died, leaving no offspring."

12:21 Then the second brother took the women to be his wife, but he too died, leaving no male offspring. This also happened to the third.

12:22 In their illustration the same thing happened to all seven brothers. They all died, leaving no male heir, and then, finally, the women herself died. There are some who believe that this could have been a true story that the Sadducees were citing. Others believe that this story was adapted from the apocryphal book of Tobit, which mentions a woman who was married to seven husbands, all of whom died without an heir (Tob. 3:8). "Provided that their basic assumption—namely, that married life continues in the hereafter—was correct, two husbands would have been sufficient to prove their point. But seven makes the story more interesting and might also make belief in the resurrection seem even more absurd."[19]

12:23 Their question addressed to Jesus was that "in the resurrection, when they [would] rise again," whose wife would this woman be? All of the seven brothers had her as his wife. In other words, all seven brothers had had a sexual relationship with this woman. This was clearly meant to be a ridiculous illustration. Since the Sadducees did not believe in the resurrection, they were implying that the resurrection life is only an elevation of the greatest pleasures that men enjoy on this earth. What greater pleasure is there than the sexual relationship that a man enjoys with his beloved wife? It was as though they were implying that these poor men would not be able to enjoy

18. Swete, *The Gospel According to St. Mark,* 278.
19. Hendriksen, *Exposition of the Gospel According to Mark,* 486.

heaven because they would have to stand in line to enter into a sexual relationship with their wife. "Thus they hoped that the whole concept of the resurrection would be laughed out of court. The case they presented was a 'man of straw,' since they themselves believed in no resurrection. To present a caricature of a view, and then to demolish it, is an old pastime."[20]

12:24 Jesus told them that they were wrong (*planasthe*, "to wander away") in their understanding. He said they did not understand either "the Scriptures, or the power of God." "The Sadducees posed as men of superior intelligence and knowledge in opposition to the traditionalists among the Pharisees with their oral law. And yet on this very point they were ignorant of the Scriptures. How much error today is due to this same ignorance among the educated!"[21] They also failed to understand the power of God, for had they truly understood Him they would know that He is able to raise the dead in such a way that marriage would no longer be needed.

12:25 Jesus went on to explain that after resurrection the quality of life is going to be so different from what is known on this earth that there will no longer be need for marriage. Jesus said that in the resurrection life humans will be "like [the] angels in heaven." Jesus did not say that people would become angels, but He said that the eternal relationship of men and women would be more like the current relationship of the angels in heaven. There is no need for sexual relationships among the angels because angels do not die. In the eternal state, all humans will have glorified, resurrected bodies, and they will never again be subject to death. Therefore, there will be no need for reproduction in the heavenly sphere.

> The saved will be like the angels *in this one respect;* yes, like the angels whose very existence the Sadducees also denied (Acts 23:8), and this in spite of the fact that the Pentateuch, accepted by them, teaches their existence (Gen. 19:1, 15; 28:12; 32:1)! Does not verse 25, taken in its entirety, and in connection with what is known of the beliefs of the Sadducees, prove that these men know neither the Scriptures nor the power of God?[22]

20. Cole, *The Gospel According to Mark*, 189.
21. Robertson, *Word Pictures in the New Testament*, 1:367.
22. Hendriksen, *Exposition of the Gospel According to Mark*, 487.

12:26   Jesus took them, however, to the far more significant issue that they truly misunderstood—the concept of the resurrection. Jesus referred them to a book they should have been familiar with—the book of Exodus. They believed the writings of Moses, but somehow they had overlooked this passage. Jesus referred them to where God spoke to Moses from the burning bush (Ex. 3:6). There God said, "I am the God of Abraham, and the God of Isaac, and the God of Jacob." If Abraham, Isaac, and Jacob were dead and gone as the Sadducees believed, then God would have been wrong in saying, "I *am* the God." He should have said, "I *was* the God." But Abraham, Isaac, and Jacob were still alive, even though the words spoken to Moses occurred hundreds of years after the physical death of these individuals. "In other words, for God to say to Moses centuries after the death of the patriarchs, 'I am the God of . . . ,' requires that this fact is still true, that the patriarchs are still alive in the invisible world."[23]

12:27   Jesus summarized with His final statement: "He is not the God of the dead, but of the living."

> The concept "God of the dead" implies a blatant contradiction, especially in the context of Saducean understanding of death as extinction, without the hope of resurrection. If God has assumed the task of protecting the patriarchs from misfortune during the course of their life, but fails to deliver them from that supreme misfortune which marks the definitive and absolute check upon their hopes, his protection is of little value. But it is inconceivable that God would provide for the patriarchs some partial tokens of deliverance and leave the final word to death, of which all the misfortunes and sufferings of human existence are only a foretaste. If the death of patriarchs is the last word of their history, there has been a breach of the promises of God guaranteed by the covenant, and of which the formula "the God of Abraham, of Isaac, and of Jacob" is the symbol.[24]

He further told the Sadducees that they were "greatly mistaken" (*poly planasthe*, lit. "badly you wander"; cf. v. 24). Only Mark adds this final comment, and it shows that anyone who denies the resurrection and life after death is truly deceiving himself. He is wandering away from the established truth of the resurrection.

23. Howard F. Vos, *Mark* (Grand Rapids: Zondervan, 1978), 105.

24. Lane, *The Gospel of Mark,* 430.

There was a threefold response to Christ's proclamation of the doctrine of the resurrection. First, the crowd that heard it was "astonished at his teaching" (Matt. 22:33). This teaching was not new to them but certainly Christ's interpretation of the familiar passage in Exodus 3:6 was new. Second, some of the teachers of the law approved His teaching (Luke 20:39-40). The Pharisees felt that Jesus was supporting their doctrine of physical resurrection. In the third place, the Sadducees were silent (Matt. 22:34).[25]

WITH THE SCRIBES, 12:28-34
(cf. Matt. 22:34-40)

12:28 "One of the scribes" had been observing all that had been taking place. He heard Jesus arguing with the Sadducees and recognized that Jesus had indeed "answered them well." The scribes were the keepers of the law, and this man probably was a Pharisee.

The Pharisees, supernaturalists of the day, would have been pleased with Jesus' defense of the Resurrection and related questions about life after death. They chose one of their number, "an expert in the law," to present their question about the law to test Jesus' skill in dealing with the law. There's no apparent malice in this conversation; the lawyer was straightforward in his approach and Jesus commended him for his answer and attitude.[26]

He came to Jesus with a question: "What commandment is the foremost [or "the first," *prōtē pantōn,* first in rank and importance] of all?" There were many to choose from. The religious leaders had devised 613 individual commandments springing from the Mosaic Law, 365 negative and 248 positive. Although they had been categorized as greater and lesser commandments, many of the commandments had champions who argued for their validity as the greatest. "While they believed all were binding, they assumed a distinction between weightier and lighter statutes and often attempted to sum up the whole Law in a single unifying command."[27] Which one was the greatest of them all?

25. J. Dwight Pentecost, *The Words & Works of Jesus Christ* (Grand Rapids: Zondervan, 1981), 390.
26. Vos, *Mark,* 105.
27. John D. Grassmick, "Mark," in *Bible Knowledge Commentary* (Wheaton, Ill.: Victor, 1983), 163.

12:29   Jesus answered the scribe by saying that the foremost of all was the one that every pious Jew recited every morning and every evening. It was written on a miniature scroll and was carried in his phylactery. A longer section of the same Scripture was enclosed in every mezuzah, the metal or woolen case attached to the doorpost of every Jewish home. Mark alone reports that Jesus said that the greatest commandment was the one found in Deuteronomy 6:4: "Hear O Israel! The Lord our God is one Lord." This commandment became known as the Great Shema, because the first word in the Hebrew text is "Shema" (translated "Hear"): "The Lord our God; the Lord is one." Many synagogue services to this day begin with a recitation of the Great Shema. "It is readily understood that the Shema was and is the very foundation of monotheism. Not only that, but it stresses the fact that this one and only God wants to be loved! This is in harmony with the fact that he himself is a loving God."[28]

12:30   Because the Lord is one, a person should love the Lord with his total being: his heart, his soul, his mind, and all of his strength. With everything that he has should a person love God.

> The command to love God is an obligation which stems from his uniqueness as God and his gracious favor in extending his covenant love to Israel. It is *the Lord our God* who is to be loved with a completeness of devotion which is defined by the repeated "all." Because the whole man is the object of God's covenant love, the whole man is claimed by God for himself. To love God in the way defined by the great commandment is to seek God for his own sake, to have pleasure in him and to strive impulsively after him. Jesus demands a decision and readiness for God, and for God alone, in an unconditional manner.[29]

12:31   But Jesus added a second commandment to this, Leviticus 19:18. "In the question no reference has been made to a second commandment, but the Lord adds it in order to complete the summary of human duty."[30] A logical consequence of love for God is that "you shall love your neighbor as yourself." "If we love God, we will experience His love within and will express that love to others. We do not live by rules but by relationships, a loving relationship to God that

28. Hendriksen, *Exposition of the Gospel According to Mark,* 493.
29. Lane, *The Gospel of Mark,* 432.
30. Swete, *The Gospel According to St. Mark,* 285.

enables us to have a loving relationship with others."[31] The religious teaching of the day was that you were to love your neighbor and hate your enemy (cf. Matt. 5:43). Jesus in His teaching had clearly shown that "the neighbor" extended to anyone who was in need (cf. Luke 10:25-37). Jesus said, "There is no other commandment greater than" the understanding of love for God and love for neighbor.

> And why are these two commandments the greatest?
> First, faith and hope *take,* love *gives.* Faith appropriates the salvation that is in Christ. Hope accepts the promise of the future inheritance. Love, however, means *self-giving, self-impartation.*
> Secondly, all other virtues are included in love. See I Cor. 13. According to that chapter active, intelligent, voluntary love implies patience, kindness, and humility (verse 4), unselfishness (verse 5), faith and hope (verse 7).
> Thirdly, human love, in its noblest expression, is patterned after God, for "God is love." The all-surpassing character of love is clearly taught in Scripture (Col. 3:14; I Peter 4:8; I John 3:14; 4:8).[32]

12:32   The scribe responded to Jesus Christ, and only Mark's gospel gives his words. He said that Jesus was correct (*Kalōs,* which could be interpreted as "Right," "Excellent," or even "Beautiful"). He affirmed that God "is one; and there is no one else besides Him," quoting from Deuteronomy 4:35. Although the scribe repeated many of Jesus' exact words in this verse and the next, he did not use the sacred names for God. Instead, he substituted pronouns. He did this because of respect for the name of God that is grounded in the third commandment (cf. Ex. 20:7).

12:33   He did, however, add that to love Him with one's heart and to love one's neighbor as oneself was much more important "than all burnt offerings and sacrifices." Perhaps the fact that they were standing in the courtyard of the temple reminded him of burnt offerings and sacrifice. This idea is exactly what was taught in 1 Samuel 15:22; Psalm 51:16; Isaiah 1:10-17; Hosea 6:6; and Micah 6:6-8.

12:34   When Jesus heard the man's response, He recognized an intelligent (*nounechōs,* from *nous,* "intellect," and *echō,* "to have") answer and said to him, "You are not far from the kingdom of God."

31. Warren W. Wiersbe, *Be Diligent* (Wheaton, Ill.: Victor, 1987), 118-19.
32. Hendriksen, *Exposition of the Gospel According to Mark,* 494-95.

Jesus recognized that here was a Pharisee who truly understood the intent of the law and was close to putting his faith in Him.

> The scribe's openness and humility before God exhibited a favorable disposition, while his enthusiastic approval of Jesus' teaching revealed an attraction toward the one through whom God had brought the Kingdom near to men in an eschatological and messianic perspective. The account does not concern rabbinic discussion about the heart of the Mosaic Law, but a proclamation of the demands of the messianic Kingdom.[33]

Mark's comment, "after that, no one [*oudeis ouketi,* double negative emphasizing negation] would venture [*etolma,* imperfect tense implying no one even dared] to ask Him any more questions," is very perceptive. Jesus' opponents realized they had come close to losing one of their own, and, before they lost anyone else, they backed away and stopped asking.

> If this scribe would now, by God's grace and power, take one more step, namely, actually coming to—that is, believe in—Jesus as his Savior and Lord (Matt. 11:28-30; John 6:35), he would have advanced from a position of being "not far from" to one of being "inside" the kingdom of God. Of one thing there can be no question: by means of this very word of encouragement, "You are not far from the kingdom of God," Jesus was urging him to enter that kingdom.[34]

THE RESPONSE OF THE SERVANT, 12:35-44

The Question of Challenge, 12:35-37 (cf. Matt. 22:41-46; Luke 20:41-44)

12:35   Although they were finished asking Jesus questions, He was not through with them. Jesus took the initiative while He was in the temple courts and asked the religious leaders a question. "The question which was now asked was in fact a final answer to all opponents."[35] His question related to the person of the Messiah. He wondered how the Scribes could say that "the Christ" (the Anointed One, the Messiah) was "the son of David" (cf. Isa. 9:2-7; 11:1-9; Jer. 23:5f.; 30:9; Ezek. 34:23f.; Hos. 3:5; Amos 9:11). It was a common un-

33. Lane, *The Gospel of Mark,* 434.
34. Hendriksen, *Exposition of the Gospel According to Mark,* 496.
35. Swete, *The Gospel According to St. Mark,* 287.

derstanding among the Jews that the Messiah was to be from the line of David. This was one of the things that confused the people earlier about Jesus Christ. They thought He had come from Galilee, and yet they knew that the Messiah was to be the offspring of David from the village of Bethlehem (cf. John 7:41-42). But the title "Son of David" had been used by Bartimaeus only days before as Jesus passed through Jericho (cf. 10:47).

> Jesus' challenge was not designed to deny the word and prophecy of Scripture but to raise the crucial issue of its proper meaning. . . . [His] questions are calculated to provoke thoughtful reflection upon the character of the Messiah in the perspective of the OT witness to his lordship. What is in view is *the relationship* of the Davidic sonship to the Messiah's transcendent majesty.[36]

How could the scribes understand that the Messiah was going to be nothing more than the physical seed of King David? Actually the view concerning the Messiah had greatly degenerated in Jesus' time. Many people in the nation had simply relegated the position of Messiah to be that of a political, earthly deliverer who would come to overthrow the enemies of Israel.

12:36   The Lord, however, attempted to show the people listening to Him that the Messiah was more than simply an earthly deliverer. He took them to a psalm of David, Psalm 110, the most frequently quoted psalm in all of the New Testament. That this Psalm was understood as being Messianic is made clear by Peter (cf. Acts 2:34-35), by Paul (cf. 1 Cor. 15:25), and by the writer of the book of Hebrews (Heb. 1:13; cf. 10:13). Jesus said that David, speaking under the inspiration of the Holy Spirit, declared, "The Lord [Jehovah, Yahweh] said to My Lord [Adonai], 'Sit at My right hand until I put Thine enemies beneath Thy feet.'" Two persons are within this psalm—the Lord Jehovah and the Lord Adonai. The first person speaks to the second person and says that He is to sit at His right hand, the place of honor. At a yet appointed time He will put His enemies beneath His feet. This figure represents an enemy lying before a person in the dust so that the conqueror's feet can be placed on his neck (cf. Josh. 10:24). "Complete triumph over every foe is assured *by* 'the Lord' *to* 'the Lord.'"[37]

36. Lane, *The Gospel of Mark*, 435-36.
37. Hendriksen, *Exposition of the Gospel According to Mark*, 500.

12:37   In applying this psalm, Jesus declared that David himself was calling the Messiah "Lord," that is, God. "The point made is that David himself distinguished between his earthly, political sovereignty and the higher level of sovereignty assigned to the Messiah. The Messiah is not only 'son of David'; he is also, and especially, his Lord."[38] If He is, indeed, the Lord (God), then He must be more than simply a man who would come in the line of David and overthrow their enemies. Jesus was trying to teach this crowd that the Messiah was the God/Man, not just a man. "Behind Ch. 12:35-37 stands the same Christology affirmed in the confessional formulations of Rom. 1:3f.; II Tim. 2:8: the son of David is the exalted Lord who now reigns at God's right hand, having fulfilled the expectation of Israel according to a modality startlingly different from scribal interpretation."[39]

Mark alone adds the comment that "the great crowd" that had gathered around and was "listening" (*ēkouen,* imperfect tense implying that the hearing extended over a period of time) "enjoyed" the way Jesus was dealing with the religious leaders. It was doubtful that they understood what He was saying, but they realized that He was teaching with authority and that He was confounding their very smug religious leaders. "At the end of the 'day of questions' the Lord's popularity with the non-professional majority of His audience was unabated. Two successive days of teaching had exhausted neither His resources nor their delight."[40]

The Warning, 12:38-40 (cf. Matt. 23:1-39; Luke 20:45-47)
12:38   As Jesus continued to teach the multitudes, He warned them about the scribes—the professional teachers of Judaism, who were nearly all Pharisees—and some of their actions. Not all scribes were as Jesus described in these verses. In fact, Jesus had just dealt with a scribe whom He had said was not far from the kingdom of God (cf. v. 34). But the majority of the scribes acted as Jesus indicated in this summary sketch. (Jesus' complete indictment of the scribes is found in Matthew 23.) They loved to walk around in long, flowing white "robes" (*stolais,* the dress of dignitaries such as kings and priests) with many tassels that marked them out in a special way.

38. Lane, *The Gospel of Mark,* 437.
39. Ibid., 438.
40. Swete, *The Gospel According to St. Mark,* 289.

The scribe was distinguished by his linen robe, a long white mantel reaching to the feet and provided with a long fringe. White linen clothes were regarded as a mark of distinction, so that men of eminence (priests, Levites, scribes), or those who wished to parade their position, wore white and left bright colors to the common people.[41]

They loved to receive "respectful greetings in the market places." They loved the adulation of men. "What the men who are here rebuked were always longing for was not a mere token of friendliness but rather a demonstration of respect, a public recognition of their prominence."[42]

12:39 They wanted the "chief seats in the synagogues," that is, the bench right in front of the cabinet where the scrolls were kept. This was a prominent seat that faced the congregation, so those sitting there were clearly visible to the whole congregation. They loved "places of honor at banquets," where they would be entertained royally by the hosts. Jesus had previously warned against seeking the best seats at a banquet or a dinner (cf. Luke 14:8).

12:40 But perhaps the worse thing they did was that they took advantage of people in society who should have been cared for. Since their position did not earn them a salary, it was up to them to live off the generosity of people. Many times, as they would write up estate papers for people, they would figure out ways to make monetary gain for themselves. Widows often were taken advantage of. "The charge that the scribes 'devoured widows' houses' refers to the fact that they sponged on the hospitality of people of limited means."[43]

They also liked the pretense of great, long prayers, which made them appear to be spiritual, but all the while down in their hearts they were more concerned about position, power, and money.

The close grammatical juxtaposition of "devouring widows' houses" and "offering lengthy prayers" have led some to suggest that between these two activities there was a very close connection, the meaning being: they devour widows' houses and *to cover up their wickedness* they make long prayers. The longer they pray for the widows (or at least in their presence), the more they can prey upon them![44]

41. Lane, *The Gospel of Mark,* 439-40.
42. Hendriksen, *Exposition of the Gospel According to Mark,* 503.
43. Lane, *The Gospel of Mark,* 441.
44. Hendriksen, *Exposition of the Gospel According to Mark,* 504.

Jesus declared that they would receive a greater judgment when they stood before the Lord. "Religious teachers who use prayer as a means of securing opportunities for committing a crime, shall receive a sentence in excess of that which falls to the lot of the dishonest man who makes no pretention to piety; to the sentence on the robber will be added in their case the sentence on the hypocrite."[45] This was the last public statement Jesus gave to the crowd in the gospel of Mark. From this point on His statements were given only to the apostles. "By terminating the public ministry with this account the evangelist points to the sharp opposition between Jesus and the Jewish authorities which led inevitably to events recalled in the passion narrative."[46]

The Proper Illustration, 12:41-44 (cf. Luke 21:1-4)

12:41   Jesus went into the temple and "sat down opposite the treasury [*gazophylakiou,* a compound word from *gaza,* a Persian word for "treasure," and *phylakē,* meaning "guard"]," which was located in what was known as the "Court of the Women." This court was beyond the Court of the Gentiles, and it was the farthest point that a woman could enter in the temple. Only men were permitted beyond the Court of the Women. This court was a large area, estimated to hold as many as 15,000 people. The treasury consisted of thirteen large brass receptacles that had trumpet-shaped mouths. Each receptacle was marked with the purpose to which the offerings received would be devoted, some for the temple tribute, some for sacrifices, incense, wood, etc. Into these receptacles the Jews would place their offerings.

Jesus was watching (*etheōrei,* imperfect tense implying He watched over a period of time) as the people "were putting [*ballei,* present tense picturing the action as occurring] their money" into the receptacles. Since this was Passover season, there would have been thousands of pilgrims in the city, and Jesus was observing their stewardship. Mark specifically notes that He gave special attention to how "the rich people were putting in [*eballon,* imperfect tense indicating this happened over a period of time]" their very large sums. Earlier Jesus had warned against the practice of "sounding a trumpet" when one gave his gifts (cf. Matt. 6:2). Some individuals would take all the money they were giving and change it into small coins. The large number of coins could then be taken and thrown into the brass recep-

45. Swete, *The Gospel According to St. Mark,* 292.
46. Lane, *The Gospel of Mark,* 441.

tacle in such a way that a very loud noise would circulate throughout the entire court.

12:42   Jesus also observed "a poor widow [who] came and put [*ebalen*, aorist tense picturing a completed act) in two small copper coins." In the context Jesus had just talked about the way scribes took advantage of widows. But here was a poor widow who came and put in two small coins, two *lepta,* the smallest copper coin in circulation in Palestine, first minted during the Maccabean period. One *lepta* amounted to 1/64th of a denarius, or a laborer's wage for one day. A lepta truly was a small amount, and yet she gave two *leptas.* She easily could have kept one for herself. For his Roman readership Mark translates her gift into a coin they would be familiar with: "a cent" (*kodrantēs,* "quadrans"). It was clear that the amount was very small.

12:43   Jesus called His disciples to Him, for here was a message they should not miss. He told them that He had been observing all that had transpired in the treasury, and that this poor widow had just put in "more than all of the contributors" that He had observed. Jesus was not implying that she put in more in quantity, for many of the gifts that were brought by the rich were very large. "[The disciples] undoubtedly felt that those who were wealthy had made the significant contribution, since so much more could be accomplished with the sizable gifts they brought. . . . What was the value of two almost-worthless coins in comparison to such munificence?"[47]

12:44   Jesus pointed out that those large gifts basically had come out of the individuals' surplus, whereas this woman out of poverty had put in all that she owned. In fact, right now as she walked away, she had nothing to live on. She had nothing with which to purchase food until she was able to find some work. She had given all that she had. But she believed that God would not fail her. It is clear that the size of the gift that one gives to God is not the most significant thing to Him. What is of greater importance to Him is the commitment of heart and the sacrifice that is involved. "It is not the *portion* but the *proportion* that is important: the rich gave out of their abundance, but the poor widow gave all that she had. For the rich, their gifts were a small contribution, but for the widow, her gift was true consecration of her whole life."[48]

47. Ibid., 443.
48. Wiersbe, *Be Diligent,* 120.

HOMILETICAL SUGGESTIONS

In the previous chapter Jesus Christ did not respond to the religious leaders over the issue of His authority. But He did give them a parable which helps to properly view the religious leaders. The use of Israel as a vineyard was a figure that had been found in the Old Testament, especially in Isaiah 5. The parable clearly pictures the Old Testament prophets, John the Baptist, and Jesus Christ Himself as He would be rejected and cast out by those who were keeping the vineyard. It is clear that the religious leaders recognized themselves in this parable and were not happy with their castigation. They would have done anything to seize Jesus Christ immediately and kill Him, but since they were afraid of the multitude, they simply removed themselves.

The joining together of the Pharisees and the Herodians to trip up Jesus Christ over the issue of taxation is most revealing. The Savior's words give a classic response on the believer's responsibility to his God and to his government. Each exercises a realm of authority in one's life, and a person can be faithful in each realm.

The Sadducees brought to Jesus Christ their famous illustration of a woman who was married to seven different brothers. If indeed this was a true story, as it may well have been, the sad plight of this woman cannot be fully grasped. She truly had gone through much sorrow in her life. Jesus, however, used the story to show the reality of the issue of resurrection. Life beyond this earth is going to be so unique that all the details cannot possibly be imagined. It is clear, however, that heaven is not simply an extension of all the pleasures enjoyed on this earth.

The scribe who came to Jesus Christ asking Him to state the greatest commandment in the law gives a wonderful illustration of a man who is close to the truth. Jesus beautifully summarized the law by saying that a man should worship the true God and that he should love his neighbor. These two elements logically fit together. The scribe who came to Jesus saw that His response was true and was close to accepting Christ as his personal Savior/Messiah. Whether or not he did cannot be stated clearly from the text.

Since the religious leaders were no longer asking Jesus questions, He turned the tables on them by initiating a question of His own. His question related to their understanding that the Messiah was simply to be a physical son of David and that He would be nothing more than a political ruler. Jesus through His question was trying to help them see that the Messiah had to be more than just a man who came to overthrow the enemies of the nation of Israel. David referred to Him as "Lord," the sacred holy name of God. He had to be God as well as man in order to reign effectively on David's throne as Messiah/King.

The concluding warnings of this chapter are a beautiful contrast. Jesus spoke negatively of the religious leaders, stating that they loved to have prominent places and to be seen for their spirituality. In contrast to that Jesus pointed out the positive example of a simple widow who very quietly was placing her money into the temple treasury, worshiping her God. Worship of the Lord is not to be done so that people will see, but the Lord always notes true worship and rejoices in it.

MARK
CHAPTER
THIRTEEN

THE SERVANT'S PROPHECY

THE PREDICTIONS OF THE SERVANT, 13:1-37

THE QUESTIONS OF THE DISCIPLES, 13:1-4
(cf. Matt. 24:1-3; Luke 21:5-7)

13:1 Following His words of commendation for the widow's offering, Mark notes that Jesus departed from the temple. It was late Tuesday afternoon, and the little band started off for the town of Bethany. This may have been Jesus' final departure from the temple. Mark did not record the comments of Jesus that precipitated the disciples' response here. In Matthew's gospel, Jesus had given a long, scathing denunciation of the religious leaders of Israel for their hypocrisy. He concluded that message by saying that their house was being left desolate to them. "The word 'house' could be a reference to the city of Jerusalem, or the Jewish temple in the city, or the Davidic house to which the Jews looked for a Successor to David to deliver them and rule over them, or the nation as a whole. In any case, judgment must come."[1] He said they would not see Him again until they said, "Blessed is He who comes in the name of the Lord" (cf. Matt. 23:39).

Perhaps the reference to the house being left desolate caused one of the disciples to turn to Jesus here and say, "Teacher, behold what wonderful stones and what wonderful buildings!" Mark alone

1. J. Dwight Pentecost, *The Words & Works of Jesus Christ* (Grand Rapids: Zondervan, 1981), 394.

285

gives these precise words from that disciple. "The conjecture may be hazarded that the speaker was Peter, as on some other notable occasions (viii.29, 32, x.28, xi.21, xiii.3, xiv.29). But his name is not mentioned, since in this instance nothing turned upon his personality."[2] The temple of the Jews was truly a marvelous structure. Some consider it to have been one of the architectural wonders of the time. The renovation of the temple had been started under the administration of Herod the Great (cf. John 2:20). The temple actually was not completed until A.D. 64, but it was a marvelous structure.

> The temple was built of stones that were white and strong, and each of their length was twenty-five cubits, their height was eight, and their breadth about twelve; and the whole structure, as also the structure of the royal cloister, was on each side much lower, but the middle was much higher, till they were visible to those that dwelt in the country for a great many furlongs. . . . He laid out larger sums of money upon them than had been done before him, till it seemed that no one else had so greatly adorned the temple as he had done. (Josephus, *Antiquities* XV.11.3)

"Some of these stones at the southeastern and southwestern angles survive today and measure from twenty to forty feet long and weigh a hundred tons. Jesus had, of course, often observed them."[3]

13:2 Jesus told that disciple that these great buildings that surrounded them would not last: In fact, "not one stone shall be left upon another which will not be torn down." Jesus by the use of hyperbole was picturing a massive, total destruction that was to come on the temple, a destruction that occurred in A.D. 70. Titus and the Roman legions utterly destroyed the temple and the city of Jerusalem.

> After fire had raged through the Temple precincts Titus ordered the demolition of the Temple in the course of which buildings were leveled to the ground. Isolated fragments of the substructures and of the old city wall which had been recognized by archaeological research only confirm the degree to which Jesus' prophecy was fulfilled.[4]

2. Henry Barclay Swete, *The Gospel According to St. Mark* (Grand Rapids: Eerdmans, 1956), 295.

3. A. T. Robertson, *Word Pictures in the New Testament* (Nashville: Broadman Press, 1930), 1:373.

4. William L. Lane, *The Gospel of Mark,* NICNT (Grand Rapids: Eerdmans, 1974), 452-53.

Surely that announcement by Jesus Christ would have prompted serious reflections by the disciples.

13:3   As they left the temple area, heading toward the city of Bethany, their journey would have taken them over "the Mount of Olives" just to the east of Jerusalem. As they stopped and rested on the Mount of Olives, it was late in the day. Surely it must have been a beautiful sight as the sun was setting to the west behind the city of Jerusalem. The glorious temple, which Mark alone mentions, and the other buildings of the city would have been a spectacular sight from that vantage point. "There was the roof of the temple bathed in a sea of golden glory. There were those beautiful terraced courts and also those cloisters of snowy marble which seemed to shine and sparkle in the light of the setting sun."⁵ As they sat, Peter, James, John, and Andrew, whom Mark alone mentions and who were the first disciples Jesus called to Himself (cf. Mark 1:16-20), came to Him privately with a question.

13:4   They asked Him to explain when "these things" would occur. Their question must have been prompted by Jesus' comment that not one stone would be left upon another (cf. v. 2). In other words, they were wondering about the destruction of the temple. Furthermore, they wanted to know what would be the sign that all these things were going to be fulfilled. In their thinking, they understood from Old Testament prophecies that the destruction of the temple was the final event that would lead to the millennial kingdom of the Messiah. They did not recognize from Old Testament prophecies any break between judgment and Messiah's kingdom.

> The very form in which, according to Matthew, the question is cast seems to indicate that, as these men (spokesmen for the rest of The Twelve) interpret the Master's words, Jerusalem's fall, particularly the destruction of the temple, would mean the end of the world. In this opinion they were partly mistaken, as Jesus is about to show. A lengthy period of time would intervene between Jerusalem's fall and the culmination of the age, the second coming.⁶

It was these questions that precipitated the longest uninterrupted sermon of Jesus recorded in Mark's gospel. Matthew's recording of

5. William Hendriksen, *Exposition of the Gospel According to Mark* (Grand Rapids: Baker, 1975), 513-14.
6. Ibid., 514-15.

the sermon is even longer (cf. Matt. 24–25). The sermon is also recorded in Luke 21:5-36. The questions that were raised were related to the temple and events at the end of the age that would lead to the establishment of Messiah's kingdom. These were questions that related to Jewish events. They were not questions that related to the church. The existence of the church is not mentioned at all in Mark's gospel. The end program of the church and the end program of Israel do not necessarily coincide. Jesus was not presenting the culmination of the program of the church, but He was talking about the events that would lead to the destruction of Jerusalem and to His ultimate return in glory to establish His kingdom.

THE RESPONSE OF THE SERVANT, 13:5-37

Coming tribulation, 13:5-23 (cf. Matt. 24:4-26; Luke 21:8-26)

The first half of the Tribulation, 13:5-13

13:5 Jesus began by warning the disciples of the problem of deception. The expression literally in v. 5 is "watch out" or "take heed, be on guard," and it introduces a call to vigilance. It is very easy to be misled and to follow false teachers. "This warning against imposters is not inconsistent with the promise of the Spirit of truth (Jo. xvi.13), for the Divine Spirit is not irresistible, and the spirit of error (I Jo. iv.6) may be the stronger in individual cases."[7] The word that Jesus uses for being misled is from the verb *planasō,* the word from which we get our English word "planet," and the imagery is bold. The warning about wandering runs throughout this entire discussion.

13:6 Jesus indicated that "many will come" in His name, even declaring that they are He. Concerning the expression "I am He," William Lane says,

> As used by Jesus, these words have been generally understood to constitute a claim of dignity which finds its significance in God's own self-designation. The deceivers will claim this dignity for themselves. Thus Jesus cautions his disciples that men will emerge in the crisis who will falsely claim to have the theophanic name and power of the Messiah and they will lead many astray.[8]

7. Swete, *The Gospel According to St. Mark,* 298.
8. Lane, *The Gospel of Mark,* 457.

Of course, there were literal fulfillments enough of this in the next century; Bar-Cochba at least claimed full Messiahship. But if we follow the Old Testament analogies, to worship Christ with the wrong beliefs about Him is to worship a false Christ, by whatever name we call Him; for we, in so doing, falsely imagine Him to be other than He is, and other than He is revealed in Scripture to be.[9]

13:7   Also, there would be many "wars and rumors of wars," but these things should not upset the disciples. When Jesus spoke these words, the Roman Empire had been enjoying a long era of peace. But the return of wars will not indicate that the end of the age that leads to the kingdom has come. There will always be wars as ungodly nations rise up to fight against one another. "It would have been natural for the disciples to have seen any outbreak of conflict in the land or in the disturbances of A.D. 62–66, when rumors of revolt were common, as a sign that the end was imminent. Wars, in themselves, however, do not indicate that the consummation is at hand."[10]

13:8   "Nation will arise against nation." Kingdom will rise against kingdom (cf. Isa. 19:2). Furthermore, catastrophic disasters will take place from time to time. "There will be earthquakes," and also famines will occur.

> Vincent notes that between this prophecy by Jesus in A.D. 30 (or 29) and the destruction of Jerusalem there was an earthquake in Crete (A.D. 46 or 47), at Rome (A.D. 51), at Apamaia in Phrygia (A.D. 60), at Campania (A.D. 63). He notes also four famines during the reign of Claudius A.D. 41–54. One of them was in Judea in A.D. 44 and is alluded to in Acts 11:28.[11]

But all "these things" that Jesus had been talking about were merely the "beginning of birth pangs." "Each age brings public troubles which excite disquietude, and may at times suggest the near approach of the end. Yet the end is not reached by such vicissitudes; they are but the beginning."[12] By referring to birth pangs, Jesus was picturing the coming of the new age as being likened to the birth of a child. The events He just described were simply the preliminary birth pangs that

9. R. A. Cole, *The Gospel According to Mark* (Grand Rapids: Eerdmans, 1979), 199.

10. Lane, *The Gospel of Mark*, 458.

11. Robertson, *Word Pictures in the New Testament*, 1:375.

12. Swete, *The Gospel According to St. Mark*, 299.

would lead ultimately to the birth, but a woman's labor can last for an extended period of time before a child is actually born into the world. **13:9** Mark alone records that Jesus encouraged the disciples to "be on [their] guard." Literally Jesus said, "But take heed, you, yourselves!" He could not have put it more emphatically. The things He was about to tell them would be true for them in *their* lifetime as well as for future believers in every age as they serve Jesus Christ. They would be delivered up to "the courts" (lit. *synedria,* same word as the Sanhedrin in Jerusalem) and "be flogged in the synagogues." Jesus, by this statement, was implying that there would be religious persecution against them. "The disciples will experience rejection and abuse because of their association with Jesus. His experience will become the cruel prototype of their own."[13]

They would also "stand [*stathesesthe,* passive future tense carrying the idea of you "will be made to stand"] before governors and kings" for His sake, implying that the political authorities would be against them as well. They would be brought before these bodies because of the testimony they proclaimed for the sake of the Savior. The book of Acts contains numerous examples of such treatment by Felix, Festus, and Agrippa. "As it is presented by Mc. and Mt., the sense is that the appearance of Christians before the magistrates on a charge of loyalty to the Name of Christ would be in itself a proclamation of the Name to those who from their social position might otherwise have failed to hear it."[14]

13:10 Nevertheless, "the gospel must first be preached to all the nations."

> The force of the temporal element "first" is that the consummation cannot come until that condition has been satisfied. In itself this detail sheds no light upon the extent of the duration of the period prior to the parousia. If it is proper to understand "nations" in the sense of the Roman world, this imperative was fulfilled at least in a representative sense by A.D. 60 (cf. Rom. 1:5, 8; 10:18; 15:18-24; Col. 1:6, 23). As a necessary preliminary to the end time, however, the fulfillment of the mandate continually points to the manifestation of the Son of Man in glory at the consummation.[15]

13. Lane, *The Gospel of Mark,* 461.
14. Swete, *The Gospel According to St. Mark,* 301.
15. Lane, *The Gospel of Mark,* 462-63.

It will be the proclamation of the gospel to all the nations during the tribulation that ultimately will bring the return of Jesus Christ to earth to establish His kingdom (cf. Matt. 24:13-14). That command is not a command given to the church, although the church has been instructed to go into all the world and preach the gospel to every creature (Matt. 28:19-20).

13:11   In the process, however, of carrying the good news to all the world, believers in Jesus Christ will be arrested and delivered before various officials. The admonition of the Lord at this point was that they should "not be anxious beforehand" (*mē promerimnate,* a present imperative speaking of something habitual) about what they would need to say. "Jesus is not here referring to preaching, but to defenses made before these councils and governors. A typical example is seen in the courage and skill of Peter and John before the Sanhedrin in Acts 4."[16] The testimony needed will be given to them at the appropriate time by the Holy Spirit who will speak for them.

> There are numerous instances of extempore Christian defence in Acts. The behaviour of Peter before the Sanhedrin, acknowledged as he was by all to be an unlettered man, is but one example among many (Acts iv. 8ff.). But we may not trade on this, and 'put God to the test' (cf. Lk. iv. 12, from Dt. vi. 16). This promise is for those who are hauled unexpectedly into courts by their persecutors, not for those who have the duty of Christian instruction of others laid upon them, in set places and at set times.[17]

13:12   The persecution however will come not just from official religious bodies, but it could even be within a family or among friends. "The thought of treachery on the part of friends must have been uppermost in the Lord's mind; He was speaking in the presence of a traitor who had been a friend. What had befallen Himself must befall His followers."[18] It is possible that a "brother will deliver [his] brother, a father his child," and the children might even "rise up against [their] parents." The concept of orthodox belief is so ingrained in a Jewish family that if anyone should forsake the faith he is declared to be a heretic and is excluded from the family. "The disciples may expect to be treated with contempt by those closest to them, even as Jesus was

16. Robertson, *Word Pictures in the New Testament,* 1:376.
17. Cole, *The Gospel According to Mark,* 201.
18. Swete, *The Gospel According to St. Mark,* 303.

regarded by his brothers. . . . They can hope to be vindicated before the tribunal of God but they will not escape death at the hands of men."[19]

13:13 The persecutors might even include one's friends, for Jesus said, "You will be hated by all on account of My name." It is always possible that friendships can be stretched when the person of Jesus Christ is brought into the discussion. It is clear that the abuse heaped on the disciples is really intended for Jesus, and the persecution occurs only because of their identification with Him. Nevertheless, Jesus said that "the one who endures to the end . . . shall be saved." Jesus' comment must be understood in the context of this passage. The "end" is the end of the age, and Jesus is saying that anyone who endures to the end of the age, that is those who physically live through the Tribulation, will experience deliverance. Believers in Jesus who survive the Tribulation will be the ones who go into the kingdom as the physical subjects of the King.

It is certain that these words must have meant a great deal to Mark's Roman readers, for they were suffering great persecution. But they should not have been surprised by what was happening to them.

> The Christians in Rome were regarded as odious despisers of men whose superstitious allegiance to Jesus was worthy of exemplary punishment, and the persecution under Nero had lent a terrible reality to this prophecy. The Gospel of Mark made clear that no suffering had come to them that had not been foreseen by the Lord and experienced by him. Suffering could be born with patience when it was brought on by the community's determination to bear witness to Jesus in fulfillment of the missionary task.[20]

The second half of the Tribulation, 13:14-23

13:14 Jesus gave the identifying sign that would indicate the middle of the tribulation period, that is, the middle of the seventieth week of Daniel's prophecy (cf. Dan. 9:24-27). He identified it as "the abomination of desolation." Matthew's account of this sermon immediately identified the abomination of desolation with Daniel the prophet (cf. Matt. 24:15). An "abomination" was any object that was detestable, and usually in the Old Testament it was declared to be idolatry or sacri-

19. Lane, *The Gospel of Mark,* 464.
20. Ibid., 464-65.

lege. The abomination that Jesus was speaking about had as its end result the producing of the desolation or abandonment of the temple.

Jesus said this abomination of desolation would stand "where it should not be." In Matthew's gospel, it is clear that the abomination of desolation will take its stand in the temple of the Jews, for Matthew says that the desolation will stand in "the holy place" (Matt. 24:15). It appears from other Scriptures that the world dictator will be the one to begin this seven-year period of time by making his covenant of peace with the nation of Israel (cf. Dan. 9:27). However, in the middle of that seven-year period, he will suddenly reveal his true character and will set himself up as the object of worship, demanding that everyone worship him (cf. 2 Thess. 2:3-4). This revelation of his character will occur in the temple. That means that a Jewish temple will have to be rebuilt in Jerusalem. Whether that will occur before the rapture of the church or whether it will happen during the first part of the tribulation period cannot be determined from Scripture. Nevertheless, Jesus said that event, the abomination of desolation rising in the temple, will be the mark that indicates the midpoint of the tribulation period.

Mark adds that his readers should be careful to observe this and understand. When such an abomination occurs, those in Judea should plan to "flee to the mountains."

> The dominant note in verse 14 is the command to flee. This exhortation is developed or presupposed in each of the subsequent verses as Jesus addresses himself to the urgency for flight (verses 15-16), to circumstances which hinder flight (verses 17-18), to the reason for flight (verses 19-20), and to a final deterrent to flight (verses 21-22).[21]

13:15   If that sign should appear and one was "on the housetop" working or praying, he should not even plan to go back down into the house to take anything with him. Rooftops were usually accessible by an outside staircase that made returning into the house unnecessary. One's possessions are not to be of concern at this time, for one's life could be at stake.

13:16   Any person "in the field" working, when he became aware of the fact that the abomination of desolation had arisen, should not attempt to even retrieve his cloak. "The outer garment, designed to

21. Ibid., 467.

shut out the night chill but left upon the ground in another corner of the field, is to be abandoned rather than to risk one's life in returning for it. There is to be no deterrent to flight."[22]

13:17   "In the present passage the Lord reveals his sympathy for women who during times of great political and social distress are pregnant or are nursing babies."[23] Circumstances would be very hard, and women in those conditions would find it difficult to survive.

13:18   Jesus said they should pray that this might not happen in the wintertime, when the weather usually was bad in Israel. Many times the rains cause the usually dry riverbeds to flood, making crossings impossible. Places of safe refuge might become inaccessible. In some years Israel has even been blanketed with winter snows. It should be noted, however, that Mark did not mention one stipulation that Matthew recorded, namely, that they should also pray that their flight would not have to occur on the Sabbath (Matt. 24:30). Mark's Gentile readers would not have been concerned about that fact.

13:19   Jesus implied that those days, that is, the days following the sighting of the abomination of desolation, would bring about "a time of tribulation such as has [never] occurred since the beginning of the creation." "Verse 19 is virtually a citation of Dan. 12:1 ('And there shall be a time of trouble such as never has been since there was a nation till that time'), although the mode of expression may echo other passages which describe the day when God will visit His people in judgment."[24] Those three and a half years will entail tribulation such as the world has never seen and will never see again.

13:20   In fact, unless the Lord brings that period of time to an end, and not prolonged, no life would be saved. This verse stands in direct contrast to the statement in v. 13 that implies that there will be those who will endure to the end and experience physical deliverance. But here the idea is that if those days were allowed to continue, *everyone* would die. For the sake of the elect, that is, for the sake of the believers whom God has chosen, the days will be brought to an end. The fact that God has chosen any for salvation is a fact that is noted alone by Mark. His comment "explains the sovereign choice of God in the end by and for himself."[25]

---

22. Ibid., 470.
23. Hendriksen, *Exposition of the Gospel According to Mark,* 529.
24. Lane, *The Gospel of Mark,* 471-72.
25. Robertson, *Word Pictures in the New Testament,* 1:377.

13:21   The warning given first in v. 6 is repeated here. For even in the midst of such a precarious time there will be those who will arise, claiming to be Messiahs. Some might say that the Messiah is here or others that the Messiah is there. Jesus said, "Do not believe [them]."

13:22   There will be "false Christs and false prophets" (cf. Matt. 7:15) who will come on the scene. They might even be able to produce "signs and wonders" (cf. Deut. 13:1-3). If one is not careful, even one of the elect might be confused and led astray. It appears that the intent of the signs and wonders is to purposely lead the elect away from their belief in the true Messiah.

13:23   But Jesus gave a final warning, a word of admonition: "Take heed; behold, I have told you everything in advance." In other words, when they see these things, they have been forewarned and should be able to respond properly.

> The "all things" which Jesus has told them corresponds to the request of the disciples to know when "these things are all to be accomplished" (verse 4). From the structural perspective the response to the question of verse 4 is complete with verse 23. All that remains is to announce the final victory of the Son of Man."[26]

Coming Triumph, 13:24-27 (cf. Matt. 24:27-31; Luke 21:27-28)

Return of the King, 13:24-26

13:24   By the use of "But" (*Alla*), Jesus points out the strong contrast between the many false messiahs who will appear and His glorious triumphal return. Immediately after the just-described Tribulation, some catastrophic disturbances would affect planetary bodies—the sun, the moon, and the stars. The figures the Lord uses here come from various Old Testament prophecies, such as Isaiah 13:9ff.; Ezekiel 32:7ff.; Joel 2:1ff.; Amos 8:9; and Zephaniah 1:14-16. Some believe that this is a reference that symbolizes political and international upheaval. But it could simply be a reference to destructions that will occur in the solar system. "The sun will be darkened, and the moon" will not shine because of all of the other judgments and destruction that is taking place on the face of the earth (cf. Rev. 6:12).

13:25   The stars "falling from heaven" may very well be a reference to a hail of meteorites (cf. Rev. 6:13; 16:21). The shaking of the powers that are in the heavens could be a reference to physical forces that

26. Lane, *The Gospel of Mark*, 473.

could all be subject to new dynamics because of the natural calamities that are part of the Tribulation judgments. Another possibility is that it refers to angelic spheres, especially to demonic forces, that will be very active at this period of time (cf. Rev. 9:1ff.; 12:7-12).

13:26 This will all be followed by the return of the Son of Man as He comes "in clouds with great power and glory." The fact that Jesus comes in clouds

> probably refers not to natural clouds but to something like the "cloud of the Presence" that descended on the tabernacle in the wilderness and led the Israelites on their wilderness wanderings. Or, if one follows Wuest (p. 251), it is clouds of glorified saints and angels. Certainly in another description of this magnificent event in Revelation 19:11-16, Jesus is accompanied by innumerable hosts.[27]

The "Son of Man" is a reference to Daniel 7:13:

> The Lord had from the beginning of His Ministry assumed the title of the Son of Man (ii.10 . . .), and now at length He identifies Himself with the object of Daniel's vision; in Him the kingdom of regenerate humanity will find its Head, and His manifestation in that capacity is to be the crowning revelation of the future (cf. xiv.62 . . .).[28]

Jesus is pictured as returning in glory with power accompanied with clouds. In summarizing verses 24-26, R. A. Cole says,

> This is a typical eschatological use, and might refer just as much to toppling first-century Roman rulers as to the clash of East and West today. But verse 26, with the clear imagery of the return of Son of man to judgment (Dn. vii. 13), can refer only to one event in history, the second coming of Christ. In view of His constant use of the title 'Son of man', His disciples cannot have failed to see that He refers to Himself here, although they may well have failed to understand how such a thing could be.[29]

Regathering of believers, 13:27

13:27 As Jesus comes to the earth, "He will send forth [His] angels, and [they] will gather together His elect [*eklektous autou,* the third

27. Howard F. Vos, *Mark* (Grand Rapids: Zondervan, 1978), 115.
28. Swete, *The Gospel According to St. Mark,* 312.
29. Cole, *The Gospel According to Mark,* 204.

reference to "elect" in this context; cf. vv. 20 and 22]" from every region of the world. This regathering will include all His saints, both Jews and Gentiles, who have put their faith in Him during the tribulation period. These are those who have endured "to the end," who are to be saved (v. 13). It is the gathering of the good seed, the shining forth of the righteous into the kingdom of the Father (Matt. 13:43). It is the gathering of the good fish into containers (Matt. 13:48), the separation of the sheep from the goats (Matt. 25:31-46). This is the wedding feast into which the prepared virgins are ready to enter (Matt. 25:1-13).

Although it is not specified in Mark exactly who will be involved in the gathering, it appears that the angels will gather the living redeemed from all parts of the world. "The Greek is very brief, 'from the tip of the earth to the tip of heaven.' This precise phrase occurs nowhere else."[30] Swete says that "the phrase is perhaps colloquial rather than exact, and intended only to convey the impression that no spot on the surface of the earth where any of the elect may be will be overlooked."[31] It will also include the resurrection of Old Testament saints (Dan. 12:2,13) and the resurrection of any individual who has put his personal faith in Jesus Christ during the time of tribulation but who has been martyred for his faith. These are all gathered in order to be part of the literal, millennial, Davidic kingdom that Jesus Christ will establish on this earth.

Concluding Teaching, 13:28-37 (cf. Matt. 24:32-44; Luke 21:29-36)

The fig tree, 13:28-32

13:28   It is easy to get wrapped up in prophetic details and neglect one's service to Jesus Christ. Perhaps that is the reason Jesus concluded these marvelous predictions with two very practical parables, that is, with stories "thrown alongside" for the purpose of illustrating the truth (see the comments at 3:23). The first involved a fig tree, something that was common and understandable by all of Jesus' listeners. "The fig-tree was among the commonest products of the neighbourhood of Jerusalem; yet twice within two days it furnished Him with materials of instruction (cf. xi.13ff.)."[32] They knew that when a fig

30. Robertson, *Word Pictures in the New Testament*, 1:377.
31. Swete, *The Gospel According to St. Mark*, 313.
32. Ibid.

tree's branches became tender and the leaves appeared it would not be long at all until summer.

13:29   Jesus applied this same principle to His listeners: "Even so, you too, when you see these things happening, recognize that He is near, right at the door." The emphasis here should be on seeing all these things "happening" (*ginomena,* present participle picturing the action as occurring). It is certain that the people who heard Jesus' words did not see all the things described here. That is why the prophecies Jesus gives in these verses could not have found their complete fulfillment in the destruction of Jerusalem in A.D. 70.

13:30   With a strong admonition that demands serious attention, Jesus said that the generation that sees all these things happening is the generation that "will not pass away" until everything He predicted had been fulfilled. It is clear that Jesus was not speaking just to the generation of His time; rather, He seems to have in view a future generation. That generation will see the culmination of God's plan. Some feel that by the word "generation" Jesus meant "race," that He was saying that the Jewish race would not pass away until all these things had taken place. But in light of the context, it seems preferable to accept the idea that He spoke of that future generation that would see all these events.

13:31   Even though heaven and earth might pass away, as Jesus had just predicted, His words would never pass away.

> What Jesus here drives home is that the physical universe round about, above and beneath us—mountains, valleys, rivers, vegetation, the animal world, the sky, the soil, etc.—, *as we now see it,* no matter how firm and strong some of it may appear to be, is actually unstable, but that his own words will continue to prove their stability and worth forever and ever. The negative "will never pass away" implies a strong affirmative "will always endure."[33]

Could there be any greater emphasis on the significance of God's words? His words will accomplish their desired end.

13:32   But the exact timing of the day and hour when all of these things will come to pass was something known only to the Father. This was not a truth that had been revealed to the angels, nor did Jesus in His incarnate state, at this moment, know the precise timing. "But the time of the predestined end is one of those things which the

33. Hendriksen, *Exposition of the Gospel According to Mark,* 540.

Father has 'set within His own authority' (Acts i.7), and the Son had no knowledge of it in His human consciousness, and no power to reveal it (Jo. viii.26, 40, xiv.24, xv.15)."[34] It is amazing that some Christians today claim to know more than Jesus Christ, for many have been guilty of setting dates for His return, only to see those dates come and go. "Verse 32 contains a wise warning that, if we persist in pursuing the science of numbers, and calculate to our own satisfaction the date of the time upon which our Lord will return, we shall infallibly be wrong. This should strike caution into the most daring exponent of prophecy."[35] No one knows that time, other than the Father.

The Steward, 13:33-37

13:33   Since no one knows the time of the Lord's return, He therefore repeated again His strong admonition, "Take heed, keep on the alert." This is the fourth time that Jesus gave a strong warning (cf. vv. 5, 9, and 23). It is clear that no one knows the appointed time.

> They have been asking about the time when the Master's predictions would be fulfilled (verse 4). They should be far more concerned about the question how to spend their time profitably. They must take cognizance of the moral and spiritual dangers that are threatening (verses 21, 22), so that they can arm themselves against them and can warn others.[36]

13:34   Since that is true, Jesus gave a final parable unique to the gospel of Mark. Jesus told the story of a man who went "away on a journey," leaving his household behind. His slaves were placed in charge of various responsibilities. He expected them to carry out their duties faithfully until he returned. Therefore, if one was given the responsibility of being a doorkeeper, he had better "stay . . . alert" (*grē-gorē*, present tense implying a continual alertness or watching). "These details recall a familiar early Christian pattern of exhortation stressing vigilance and an application of the vigilance concept to the Christian ministry in terms of work and labor. The true servant will want to be actively engaged in his master's service when he returns."[37]

34. Swete, *The Gospel According to St. Mark*, 316.
35. Cole, *The Gospel According to Mark*, 206.
36. Hendriksen, *Exposition of the Gospel According to Mark*, 541-42.
37. Lane, *The Gospel of Mark*, 483.

13:35   The doorkeeper has no idea when his master might be coming; therefore, he must "be . . . alert" (*grēgoreite,* present tense imperative implying something that is habitual). He might come at any one of the watches of the night, as indicated by Roman time: "evening" (*opse*), "midnight" (*mesonyktion*), "cockcrowing" (*alektorophōnias*), or dawn (*prōi*). There were four watches in the Roman manner of telling time, only three watches according to Jewish reckoning. Whenever the master came, the doorkeeper had better be awake at the door.

13:36   It would be terrible if the master came home and found the doorkeeper asleep. Sleep would be the opposite of watchfulness. If he was a faithful steward of his responsibility, he would always be ready. "Such vigilance is the responsibility of not only the Twelve (cf. Mark 13:3) but also of every believer in every generation during this present Age. Believers should be watching and working (cf. v. 34) in light of the certainty of His return, though its time is unknown except to the Father."[38]

13:37   Jesus concluded by saying that His admonitions were given not only to the disciples but to all who might hear His words in any age. The responsibility is to "be on the alert," to be ready, to be prepared (*grēgoreite,* present tense imperative). This final admonition to be on the alert carries the force of something that is to be the continual habit of the believer's life. As Robertson puts it, believers ought to "stay awake till the Lord comes."[39]

HOMILETICAL SUGGESTIONS

The questions the disciples asked Jesus Christ as they sat on the Mount of Olives precipitated this tremendous sermon of the Savior. A much longer version of the same sermon is found in Matthew 24 and 25. It seems clear that the questions and issues raised here are all "Jewish" questions relative to the end of the age. It has never been this author's understanding that the issues in the Sermon on the Mount relate to the church, the body of Christ. To bring the issue of the Rapture into this chapter is to introduce an issue that does not relate.

38. John D. Grassmick, "Mark," in *Bible Knowledge Commentary* (Wheaton, Ill.: Victor, 1983), 173.
39. Robertson, *Word Pictures in the New Testament,* 1:378.

Jesus Christ is attempting to predict the coming period of time that is known from the Old Testament as the Seventieth Week of Daniel (Dan. 9:24-27) or the tribulation period of time. The first half of that Tribulation, as presented in vv. 5-13, is a period in which there will be wars and rumors of wars, and nations will rise against nations. However, all these things are simply introductory signs. The gospel of Jesus Christ will be carried throughout the world during the Tribulation by those who put their faith in Him following the Rapture. This could very easily include the significant ministry of the 144,000 Jews (Rev. 7:1-8), who will spread throughout the world with an evangelistic zeal like that of the apostle Paul. In the process of proclaiming the gospel, tremendous persecutions will arise. Many who come to faith in Jesus Christ in this time will become martyrs for the Savior.

The second half of the Tribulation, described in vv. 14-23, begins with the recognition of the sign that Daniel called "the abomination of desolation" (Dan. 9:27). This sign will be seen in the temple when the true character of the world dictator is seen, for he will demand that the whole world worship him. When that sign appears there will be a time of trouble such as the world has never known. Any attempt to put the church, the body of Jesus Christ, into this period of time usually minimizes the wrath of this tribulation period. The whole "week" is a period of God's wrath, as He unleashes the world dictator on the world.

However, the culmination of this period of time will end with the King's return in glory, as He comes to establish His throne on this earth. Then there will be a regathering of living believers from every region of the world. In addition to the regathering of these believers, those in glorified bodies—Old Testament saints, tribulation martyrs, and church believers—will also be present.

Jesus concludes this section with parabolic teaching concerning the fig tree and the faithful steward. When a fig tree begins to put forth its leaves, summertime is never far away. So it is with the coming of the Messiah. Those who will see "all" these signs taking place should realize that the coming of the Messiah/King will not be far away. The generation that lived in the first century did not see all the signs described in detail in this chapter. Clearly there is a future generation that will see all these signs and will experience not only the Tribulation but the coming reign of Jesus Christ. The admonition of the Savior, however, is to be faithful until He returns. All faithful stewards will keep watch as they await the return of the Lord.

MARK

CHAPTER

FOURTEEN

THE SERVANT'S TRIAL

THE PREPARATORY EVENTS
SURROUNDING THE SERVANT, 14:1-42

THE PLOT OF THE LEADERS, 14:1-2
(cf. Matt. 26:1-5; Luke 22:1-2)

14:1   The reason Jesus and the multitude of pilgrims were in the city of Jerusalem was for the observance of the Feast of Passover, followed by that of Unleavened Bread. The Feast of Passover was observed annually by Jews to commemorate their deliverance from the land of Egypt, when God "hovered" over the households of the nation of Israel, where the blood was sprinkled on the doorposts to protect from the death angel. This was one of three great feasts that the Jews observed annually. The other two were Pentecost and Tabernacles (Booths). Passover was celebrated on the 14th of Nisan, which would always occur in the current months of March or April. The Feast of Unleavened Bread commemorated the fact that no yeast was put into the bread in Egypt so that the Israelites could leave quickly and wouldn't have to wait for the bread to rise. It began on the 15th of Nisan and lasted until the 21st. It was incumbent upon every adult male to be in Jerusalem for all three of these annual feasts (cf. Ex. 23:14-17, 34:23; Deut. 16:16).

   In the midst of such a significant religious event, "the chief priests and the scribes were seeking [out]" (*ezētoun,* imperfect tense

303

implying that this was something they continually pursued) a way to seize Jesus secretly and kill Him. According to Matthew 26:3 the elders of the people were also involved in this plan.

> Mt. adds that the meeting was held in the house of Caiaphas, who for some time had advocated the policy of sacrificing Jesus to the Roman power (Jo. xi.49f.). There was no division of opinion now as to the principle, or as to the character of the means to be employed for the arrest. . . . Only the opportunity [*pōs*] was still wanting.[1]

Though the plan to kill Jesus was not new, it was probably the events of recent days, including all His debates with them, that had convinced the leaders more than ever that Jesus must be destroyed.

14:2   The conclusion of the religious leaders was that the most propitious time would not be during the festival. With so many people in Jerusalem, especially Galileans who loved Jesus and would come to His defense, it would not be wise to try to eliminate Him during the feast. It was not uncommon for the population of the city during the festival seasons to swell from about 50,000 to more than 250,000 people. However, once the festival had run its course, they could carry out their plan. "Even their objection to this judicial murder at a religious festival is not a moral objection because of its incompatibility with the nature of a religious ceremony, but purely prudential, lest a riot should break out among the excitable Passover crowds."[2]

THE ANOINTING BY MARY, 14:3-9
(cf. Matt. 26:6-13; John 12:2-8)

14:3   Mark indicated that, while Jesus was in Bethany at the home of Simon the leper, a very special moment occurred. While He was reclining at the table, a woman came with an expensive alabaster vial of perfume and anointed Him. Another anointing of Jesus by a woman in the home of a man named Simon is recorded in Luke 7:36-50. Though the account given here in Mark, as well as that in Matthew 26:6ff. and in John 26:1ff., appear to be the same, the account given in Luke is definitely not to be confused with the other three.

Whereas both anointings took place in the home of a man named Simon, the Lukan account occurred in the home of Simon the

1. Henry Barclay Swete, *The Gospel According to St. Mark* (Grand Rapids: Eerdmans, 1956), 319-20.
2. R. A. Cole, *The Gospel According to Mark* (Grand Rapids: Eerdmans, 1979), 208.

Pharisee in Galilee, and the woman who came and anointed Jesus' feet was a prostitute who had come to Him in saving faith. The account given in Mark's gospel indicated that this event took place in the home of a man named Simon of Bethany, who once was a leper but apparently was now clean (cf. 1:40-45 for a possible connection). According to the gospel of John, the woman who came and anointed Jesus was Mary, the sister of Martha and Lazarus (cf. John 12:3).

One additional fact should be noted from the account in the gospel of John. According to that record this event took place "six days before the Passover" (cf. John 12:1), that is, on the Friday before the Triumphal Entry. John's chronology is probably to be accepted, for Mark's gospel does not technically say that this event occurred at this time. Mark appears to have purposefully inserted this earlier event of Mary's act of devotion between the stories of the scribes and Pharisees and Judas as they plotted together to eliminate the Savior. "Why does Mark go back? Could it be because human nature *at its best,* because of what God in his marvelous grace did for it, stands out all the more radiantly when it is contrasted with human nature *at its worst?*"[3]

Mary's act was a gracious one, for as she broke this alabaster vial of very costly perfume, described as being "pure nard" (*nardou pistikēs*), an aromatic oil from a root native to India, she was giving an expensive gift to her Savior. "This use of *pistikos* with *nardos* occurs only here and in John 12:3. The adjective is common enough in the older Greek and appears in papyri also in the sense of genuine, unadulterated, and that is probably the idea here."[4] According to Mark's account only, she broke the narrow neck of the vial, then poured the contents over His head. The gospel of John implies that there was enough so that she also was able to anoint His feet and wipe the perfume with her hair (cf. John 12:3). With Jesus reclining on a couch as He ate His meal, it would be possible for Mary to anoint both Jesus' head and His feet.

> Anointing was a common custom at feasts (cf. Ps. 23:5; 141:5; Luke 7:46), but in this context it is clear that the woman's action expressed pure devotion to Jesus and undoubtedly thanksgiving. In association with the

3. William Hendriksen, *Exposition of the Gospel According to Mark* (Grand Rapids: Baker, 1975), 557.
4. A. T. Robertson, *Word Pictures in the New Testament* (Nashville: Broadman, 1930), 1:379-80.

banquet anointing suggested joy and festivity but Jesus found the significance of this act to be far more profound.[5]

14:4 Mark indicated that the response of some of the disciples to this anointing was indignation. According to John, the disciple who was the most vocal was Judas Iscariot (cf. John 12:4). He believed that the perfume had been wasted. "The feeling expressed aloud by Judas may have been shared by others in the Apostolic body; as men unaccustomed to luxury they might naturally resent the apparent waste."[6]

14:5 As Judas calculated the value of the perfume, he estimated it to be "over three hundred denarii." Since a denarius was the amount a worker would make in one day's labor, three hundred denarii would be the amount of money a worker would earn in an entire year. That was truly a considerable sum of money. Judas said the perfume should have been sold "and the money given to the poor." Such acts of generosity toward the poor were commonly a part of the Passover celebration (cf. John 14:20). John made clear, however, that Judas was not concerned for the poor but that, as keeper of the treasury for the disciples, he would have loved to have been in charge of that additional sum of money so that he could have pilfered some of it for himself (cf. John 12:6). As a result of his comments, others picked up on it, and they all "were scolding" (*enebrimōnto,* imperfect tense implying that they continued in their criticism) Mary. The verb used by Mark for "scolding" is used of the snorting of horses. What a picturesque word for the criticism of the disciples!

14:6 Jesus stopped them and said to leave her alone, for she had done a good deed, a very beautiful thing for Him. "He recognized in the generosity of her gift a beautiful expression of love which possessed a deeper significance than she could have possibly have understood. The woman's gift was appropriate precisely because of the approaching hour of Jesus' death."[7]

14:7 Jesus' comments in this verse contain an allusion to Deuteronomy 15:11. He said that they would always have the poor around to whom they could minister, but He would not always be with them. The contrast in the verse is not between Jesus and the poor. Rather, it is the idea of their always being able to do something for the poor

5. William L. Lane, *The Gospel of Mark,* NICNT (Grand Rapids: Eerdmans, 1974), 492-93.
6. Swete, *The Gospel According to St. Mark,* 323.
7. Lane, *The Gospel of Mark,* 493.

contrasted with the limited time for acting in His behalf, for "there would be many other opportunities to tend to the needs of the poor. On the contrary, the opportunity to show love and honor to Jesus in the state of humiliation had almost vanished. Gethsemane, Gabbatha, and Golgotha were just around the corner. What Mary had done was therefore exactly right, beautiful even."[8]

14:8   Jesus' statement, "She has done what she could," is recorded only by Mark. The meaning of this unusual expression is that "she did what she was able to do." In other words, she anointed His body beforehand for His burial. Some feel that Mary had no idea what she was doing by this act. But perhaps as Mary sat at the feet of Jesus (cf. Luke 10:39) and listened, she had gleaned the truth of what was about to happen to Him, that He was going to die. Somehow that truth escaped the detection of the disciples, but perhaps Mary understood. "Jesus declared that the woman's act was a valid but proleptic anointing of his body for burial (verse 8). This pronouncement indicates that Jesus anticipated that he would suffer a criminal's death, for only in that circumstance would there be no anointing of the body."[9]

14:9   Jesus said that wherever the gospel would be proclaimed in the whole world, the gracious act that she had performed for Him would be remembered by His followers. Truly that has occurred, for wherever this passage of Scripture is read, the truth of Mary's gracious act is recounted. But Jesus' statement about the gospel being proclaimed throughout the whole world should not be overlooked.

> "Wherever the gospel is preached in the whole world" (NASB) is a fantastic statement, viewed in this context! Apprehension is beginning to grip the hearts of the entire company of Jesus' followers. Jesus has made it abundantly clear that He is to die in Jerusalem. When it looks like the end of everything, He intimates it is only the beginning—the gospel is to be preached in the whole world.[10]

THE AGREEMENT WITH JUDAS, 14:10-11
(cf. Matt. 26:14-16; Luke 22:3-6)

14:10   Perhaps the anointing of Jesus by Mary and the waste that Judas considered it to be was still in his thinking when he "went off to the chief priests" to negotiate with them for the betrayal of the Lord.

8. Hendriksen, *Exposition of the Gospel According to Mark*, 560.
9. Lane, *The Gospel of Mark*, 494.
10. Howard F. Vos, *Mark* (Grand Rapids: Zondervan, 1978), 118.

The fact that Mark related the story of the anointing in the same context might lead to that conclusion. Clearly there was more involved in the betrayal of the Lord than that "wasteful" act, as Judas considered it to be. Luke explains that Satan entered into Judas (cf. Luke 22:3). Perhaps it was also the fact that Judas had hoped for a political kingdom, and, since it was now clear that Jesus' goals were not political but spiritual, his hopes of power were dashed. Perhaps he thought he could at least come out of this situation with some monetary gain. "In Judas' life one finds an intriguing combination of divine sovereignty and human responsibility. According to God's plan Jesus must suffer and die (Rev. 13:8); yet Judas, though not compelled to be the traitor, was held responsible for submitting to Satan's directives (cf. Mark 14:21; John 13:27)."[11]

14:11   When Judas showed up, the religious authorities "were glad . . . and promised to give him money." "No doubt the rabbis looked on the treachery of Judas as a veritable dispensation of Providence amply justifying their plots against Jesus."[12] According to Matthew 26:15, they weighed out to him thirty pieces of silver. The exact coinage that was given to him is not specified. That makes it difficult to determine the actual amount that Judas received. If he was paid in denarii, that would have been the equivalent of thirty days' worth of labor for a common man. It is possible that the amount was far more. It is also possible that the thirty pieces of silver were simply a down payment with a much greater reward coming after the betrayal was accomplished. The figure of thirty pieces occurs in two other Scriptures. Exodus 21:32 lists it as the price of a slave. In Zechariah 11:12 the rejected ministry of the shepherd was paid for with that same price.

With the price agreed on, Judas "began seeking" (cf. v. 1, where the religious leaders "were seeking") "an opportune time" to betray the Lord. Luke 22:6 states that he was looking for a time when he could betray Him apart from the multitudes. The fear of the leaders was that the many pilgrims in Jerusalem would take Jesus' side, making it impossible to betray Him during the feast days.

The Priests had transferred their anxieties to the traitor (cf. xii.12, xiv.1); it was for him now to contrive the plot. They had sought an

---

11. John D. Grassmick, "Mark," in *Bible Knowledge Commentary* (Wheaton, Ill.: Victor, 1983), 175.
12. Robertson, *Word Pictures in the New Testament,* 1:381.

opportunity of arresting an enemy; it was the business of Judas to seek an opportunity of betraying a friend. . . . The problem which presented itself to Judas was the same which had perplexed the Priests—how to elude the crowd of Galileans and other visitors at the Feast who were still with Jesus. . . . But his position in the inner circle of disciples clearly gave him an advantage in dealing with it, which the Priests did not possess.[13]

THE PASSOVER MEAL, 14:12-26

Preparation, 14:12-16 (cf. Matt. 26:17-19; Luke 22:7-13)

14:12   The statement by Mark that "on the first day of Unleavened Bread, when the Passover lamb was being sacrificed [*hote to pascha ethyon,* imperfect tense indicating the customary practice]" seems at first to be incorrect. Lambs for sacrifice were chosen on the tenth day of the month and sacrificed on the fourteenth day of the month, which was considered to be the Passover. The Feast of Unleavened Bread did not begin until the fifteenth day of the month. "There is some evidence in the rabbinical literature, however, that the day on which the paschal lambs were sacrificed (the 14th of Nisan) was sometimes loosely designated 'the first day of Unleavened Bread.'"[14] It is clear that Mark was talking about the time when the lambs were being sacrificed, that is, the fourteenth of Nisan, the Passover day.

Jesus and His disciples were apparently in the home of Mary, Martha, and Lazarus in Bethany. But the Passover lamb had to be eaten within the confines of Jerusalem. Therefore, the disciples needed to know where Jesus wanted them to go to make preparations "to eat the Passover" together.

> There are a number of positive elements in the Marcan narrative which substantiate that the Last Supper was a Passover meal. The return to Jerusalem in the evening for the meal (Ch. 14:17) is significant, for the paschal meal had to be eaten within the city walls (M. *Pesachim* VII.9). An ordinary meal was taken in the late afternoon, but a meal which begins in the evening and continues into the night reflects Passover practice (Exod. 12:8; Jubilees 49:12). The reference to reclining (Ch. 14:18) satisfies a requirement of the Passover feast in the first century when custom demanded that even the poorest man recline for the fes-

13. Swete, *The Gospel According to St. Mark,* 328.
14. Lane, *The Gospel of Mark,* 497.

tive meal (M. *Pesachim* X.1). While a normal meal began with the breaking of bread, on this occasion Jesus broke the bread during the meal and following the serving of a dish (Ch. 14:18-20, 22). The Passover meal was the one occasion when the serving of a dish preceded the breaking of bread. The use of wine was generally reserved for festive occasions and was characteristic of the Passover (M. *Pesachim* X.1). Finally, the interpretation of the elements of the meal conforms to Passover custom where the haggadah (or interpretation) is an integral part of the meal. The cumulative evidence supports the claim made in verses 12, 14 and 16 that the disciples prepared a Passover meal and that the external forms of the Passover were observed at the meal itself.[15]

14:13   Jesus "sent two of His disciples" into the city with specific instructions. According to Luke 22:8, the two that were sent were Peter and John. They were told to go to Jerusalem, and there they would meet "a man . . . carrying a pitcher [*keramion,* an earthenware jar, pitcher, or jug] of water." A man carrying a pitcher of water would be easy to spot, for men did not normally carry a pitcher of water. A man would usually carry water in a large animal skin.

The fact that a man would be carrying a pitcher of water has been thought by some to be a prearranged sign. It is entirely possible that Jesus had made arrangements in advance for the place where they would observe the Passover. It is also possible that this man was simply a servant carrying out an assigned task and Jesus by use of His supernatural knowledge was aware of the man's future movements. Whatever the explanation, the disciples were instructed to follow that man.

> The directions given [to the two disciples] are in a sense very definite; in another sense very indefinite. They are definite enough so that the two men will experience no difficulty in finding the place where the supper is to be held. Yet, they are indefinite enough for the present to conceal the name of the owner and the location of his home. Is the indefiniteness due to the fact that not until evening must Judas know where the Passover will be kept, so that Jesus may indeed observe it with his disciples, and the plan of God regarding the subsequent events may be fully carried out?[16]

15. Ibid., 497-98.
16. Hendriksen, *Exposition of the Gospel According to Mark,* 566-67.

14:14   The man carrying the pitcher of water, probably a slave, would eventually enter a home, and the disciples were to address "the owner" (*oikodespotē,* a nonclassical Greek word meaning "master of the house, the householder") of that house: "The Teacher says, 'Where is My guest room [*to katalyma mou,* still used in modern Greek for a lodging place] in which I may eat the Passover with My disciples?'" The popularity of Jesus had given Him many titles, one of which was "The Teacher." "The very simplicity of the statement, *The Master saith* (Gk. *didaskalos,* 'teacher,' i.e. Rabbi), shows both that the Lord was too well known to the man to need further identification, and that His disciples were known by sight."[17]

14:15   The owner of the home would show Peter and John "a large upper room" (*anagaion mega,* literally a large room above ground) that was "furnished and ready."

> The fact that this room was built on top of the house made it right for the present purpose. In such a room one could be relatively free from disturbance. It was a place for discussion, fellowship, meditation, and prayer. Also, it was ample: the thirteen were not crowded. And it was "furnished" and in every respect "ready" to be used for the purpose it was going to serve.[18]

The furnished room would have been equipped with the necessary tables and couches they would need in order to participate in the meal. There John and Peter were to prepare the necessary food for the supper.

14:16   "The disciples went out," entered the city, and found everything "just as [the Lord] had told them." There "they prepared the Passover." The last statement of this verse involved a great amount of work, for it meant that the Passover lamb, which presumably had been cared for by the owner of the house, had to be roasted. They would also have to secure the other elements that were used in a Passover meal—wine, bitter herbs, unleavened bread, and the sauce consisting of dried fruit spices and wine. In order to prepare all of this, many ritual customs had to be followed.

The home to which the disciples were led is not specified. There is speculation that this was the home of John Mark, the writer of this

17. Cole, *The Gospel According to Mark,* 212.
18. Hendriksen, *Exposition of the Gospel According to Mark,* 568.

311

gospel. That is a good possibility. That the home of John Mark became a center for the activity of the church following the resurrection of Jesus Christ is clearly presented in Scripture (cf. Acts 12:12). That the home was able to house the church indicates that it would have been large enough to accommodate this dinner for Jesus and His disciples. But this theory cannot be proven conclusively. Surely if this was the home of John Mark he would have been aware of it. Why then did he not mention it in his gospel account? Perhaps John Mark did not mention this so that it would not appear that he was promoting himself or his family. Their hospitality would be clear, and yet Mark did not specifically point out that it was his own family who were the hosts for this final meal of our Savior before His death.

Participation, 14:17-21 (cf. Matt. 26:20-25;
Luke 22:14-16, 21-34; John 13:21-30)
14:17   John and Peter must have finished their work and returned back to the town of Bethany, for when evening arrived Jesus "came" (*erchetai,* an historical present tense for dramatic effect) from Bethany with the Twelve and entered into the Upper Room. The Passover meal was normally eaten between 6 P.M. and midnight.

> In the verses which follow Mark concentrates all of his attention upon two incidents which mark the meal: the moment of the dipping of the bread and the bitter herbs in the bowl of stewed fruit when Jesus spoke of his betrayal (verses 18-21), and the interpretation of the bread and the third cup of wine following the meal itself (verses 22-25).[19]

14:18   It was the custom to recline at tables while they were eating. "The guests lay on their left side with their feet resting on the ground, and the couches seem to have been grouped in sets of two or three; when these were placed together, the central position was that of greatest dignity; . . . cf. Jo. xiii.23ff., from which it appears that the Lord reclined between St Peter and St John."[20] Mark does not give all the detail that John gives in his gospel, but Mark notes that as they were reclining around the table Jesus made an unbelievable announcement. He declared that one of them would betray Him, one who was in the process of eating with Him. "The explanatory words 'one who

19. Lane, *The Gospel of Mark,* 502.
20. Swete, *The Gospel According to St. Mark,* 331.

is eating with me' set the pronouncement in the context of Ps. 41:9, where the poor but righteous sufferer laments that his intimate friend whom he trusted and who ate his bread had 'lifted his heel' against him."[21]

14:19   It is amazing that each of the disciples "began to be grieved," and each one literally said, "It is not I, is it?" The way the statement was phrased in the Greek, a negative answer was expected. Apparently Judas said the same thing. But Jesus did not declare the identity of the betrayer to the group. The response Matthew records (cf. Matt. 26:25) was undoubtedly made only to Judas. Surely if the other disciples had known Judas's intentions, they never would have permitted him to leave the room (cf. John 13:27-30).

14:20   Jesus said that the betrayer would be one who had dipped with Him in the bowl. "To dip into the same dish was a token of intimacy, cf. Ruth ii.14."[22] Even this act was a fulfillment of Psalm 41:9. There David lamented the fact that his trusted friend, Ahithophel, who had shared fellowship with him around a table, had turned against him. In this culture it was the height of treachery to eat with someone and then betray that person. "Jesus' generosity in sharing this sacred meal with his intimate friend thus stands in contrast to the hypocrisy of the traitor sketched in verses 10-11 and serves to recall the mistreatment of the poor sufferer in Ps. 41."[23]

14:21   But Jesus affirmed that the Son of Man was going to carry out God's will. He would go just as it had been written of Him. But in spite of the fact that it was in the foreknowledge of God and planned from all creation that Jesus Christ would die, Judas Iscariot was considered to be a morally responsible agent. "The purpose of Jesus' poignant warning is not primarily to affirm the fate of Judas but to underscore his own assurance of vindication. Nevertheless, the betrayer is morally responsible for his action and for the horrible character of its consequences, both for Jesus and for himself."[24]

Jesus pronounced a woe on the man who betrayed him. Jesus said, "It would have been good for that man if he had not been born." This statement is quite a contrast to the earlier one that Jesus made about Mary and her gracious act of anointing His body for burial (cf.

21. Lane, *The Gospel of Mark,* 502.
22. Swete, *The Gospel According to St. Mark,* 333.
23. Lane, *The Gospel of Mark,* 503.
24. Ibid.

14:6-9). The betrayer would suffer the consequences of his own unbelief. It would be better for him if he had never existed. "What makes his guilt all the heavier is the fact that he not only planned the treachery and took the next step—volunteering to deliver Jesus to the enemy —and the next—accepting the thirty pieces of silver—but even now, in spite of Christ's impressive warnings, goes right ahead."[25] Although Mark did not record the fact, from the gospel of John (13:30) it appears that at this point Judas departed from the Upper Room and began to put into effect his plan to betray the Savior.

Initiation, 14:22-26 (cf. Matt. 26:26-30; Luke 22:17-20)

14:22   While Jesus and the eleven disciples continued to eat the Passover meal, Jesus "took some bread" from the table and after giving a blessing, "broke it; and gave it to them." "The words which the Lord used in this thanksgiving have not been revealed. To try to reconstruct them from Jewish formula prayers would serve no useful purpose. How do we even know that our Lord availed Himself of these prayers?"[26]

He said, "Take it; this is My body." It is clear that with Jesus present in the room there was no possibility that the disciples could have misconstrued His meaning. Jesus was not telling them that the bread had become His body. He was simply telling them that the bread was symbolic of His body. "This represents My body," Jesus was saying.

> In the figurative saying about the bread, Jesus was not referring to his physical body as such, but to himself. He said: "I am myself this (bread)" or "my person is this (bread)," providing a pledge of his personal presence with them that was to be recalled whenever they broke bread together. . . . As certainly as the disciples eat the bread which Jesus hands to them, so certainly will he be present with them when they gather for table-fellowship. Jesus' first gift to the disciples was the pledge of his abiding presence with them in spite of his betrayal and death. The first word thus anticipates [his] resurrection.[27]

14:23   Then "He took a cup." According to the Talmud the Passover meal contained four cups of wine that were drunk. This was probably the third cup at that dinner, which was known as the "cup of bless-

25. Hendriksen, *Exposition of the Gospel According to Mark,* 571.
26. Ibid., 573.
27. Lane, *The Gospel of Mark,* 506.

ing." Again Jesus gave thanks, "gave it to them; and they all drank from it." "By ordering 'all' his true disciples to drink this wine (Matt. 26:27), which they all did (Mark 14:23)—Judas had already left (John 13:27, 30)—the unity of all believers in Christ is stressed. Moreover, the practice of having one person, a priest, drink 'for all' is hereby condemned."[28]

14:24   He said to them, "This is My blood of the covenant, which is to be shed on behalf of many." The wine in the cup had not changed in any way. Jesus was implying that the wine represented His blood, which stood for an agreement made by one in place of the many. The word for "covenant" here is not the word that implied an agreement between two equals. Rather, the word spoke of an arrangement that was made by one party. In this case, the one party was God. Man did not in any way enter into the making of this covenant. It is simply man's obligation to either accept it or to reject it.

Jesus said that this covenant had been sealed by His blood.

> In all four accounts a relation is established between Christ's *blood* and his *covenant*. . . . The expression goes back to Exod. 24:8. See also the significant passage Lev. 17:11. And note: "Apart from the shedding of blood there is no *remission*" (Heb. 9:22; cf. Eph. 1:7); therefore also no *covenant*, no *special relation of friendship* between God and his people. Reconciliation with God always requires blood, an atoning sacrifice. And since man himself is unable to render such a sacrifice, a *substitutionary* offering, accepted by faith, is required.[29]

Just as the covenants of old were sealed with the shedding of animal blood, so now Jesus said this new covenant had been sealed with His own blood. The reference to a new covenant

> also evokes Jer. 31:31-33 where God promises to establish a new covenant with his people in the last days. That promise is now sealed through Jesus' action and the death it anticipates. The saying over the cup directs attention to Jesus as the one who fulfills the divine will to enter into covenant fellowship with his people on a new and enduring basis.[30]

28. Hendriksen, *Exposition of the Gospel According to Mark*, 574-75.

29. Ibid., 575.

30. Lane, *The Gospel of Mark*, 507.

His offer took the place of "many" having to die.

> The "many" are the redeemed community who have experienced the remission of their sins in and through Jesus' sacrifice and so are enabled to participate in the salvation provided under the new covenant. Jesus' second gift to his disciples, then, is the assurance that he will be with them as their Savior who establishes the new order through his death. He freely yields his life in order that God's will to save his people may be effected.[31]

14:25   The words of Jesus in this verse are confirmed with a solemn oath. He said that He would "never again drink of the fruit of the vine until that day" when He would drink it anew in the kingdom of God. "Jesus knew that he was about to depart from his disciples. In fact, he was going to lay down his life the very next day; or, according to Jewish time reckoning, that very day (Friday)."[32] Jesus was looking forward to that time when His kingdom would be established on this earth. When that happens there will be a time of great blessing and rejoicing, for the millennial reign of Jesus Christ will have come. Saying that He would not drink of the fruit of the vine until the kingdom was established meant that Jesus abstained from the fourth cup of wine in the Passover meal.

> The significance of this can be appreciated from the fact that the four cups of wine were interpreted in terms of the four-fold promise of redemption set forth in Exod. 6:6-7: "I will bring you out . . . I will rid you of their bondage . . . I will redeem you . . . I will take you for my people and I will be your God." (TTJ *Pesachim* X.37b). Jesus had used the third cup, associated with the promise of redemption, to refer to his atoning death on behalf of the elect community. The cup which he refused was the cup of consummation, associated with the promise that God will take his people to be with him. This is the cup which Jesus will drink with his own in the messianic banquet which inaugurates the saving age to come.[33]

14:26   As the supper came to a close, Jesus and the disciples sang the normal psalms that would have been sung at this point, Psalms 115–118. These psalms were either sung in unison or chanted antiph-

31. Ibid.
32. Hendriksen, *Exposition of the Gospel According to Mark,* 575.
33. Lane, *The Gospel of Mark,* 508-9.

onally. In view of the fact that John's gospel gives a longer discussion of the discourses Jesus gave in the Upper Room, it is probable that Jesus and the disciples did not leave immediately but remained in the home until close to midnight. They then headed down the Kidron Valley "to the Mount of Olives." This probably did not surprise the disciples. It had been their pattern to return to Bethany each night, and no provisions had been made for an all-night stay in the Upper Room. It had simply been solicited for the purposes of the Passover dinner, not for the whole night.

THE PREDICTION OF DENIAL, 14:27-31
(cf. Matt. 26:31-35; Luke 22:31-38; John 13:37-38)
14:27 Jesus announced that the disciples would "all fall away" from Him that evening. Whether Jesus actually said these words in the Upper Room as Luke and John seem to indicate or on the way to Gethsemane as Matthew and Mark imply is inconclusive. It is possible that the prediction was first made in the Upper Room but repeated when the group arrived in Gethsemane. The point is that Jesus said they would all deny Him. The word that Jesus used here (*skandalisth-ēsesthe,* future tense) "implies the desire to be disassociated from him because too close an association with Jesus invites the treatment he receives. Jesus' word emphasizes once again that every time he speaks of his passion, he provokes a crisis for the disciples (see above on Ch. 8:31f.; 9:31f.; 10:32)."[34]

To affirm this, Jesus quoted from Zechariah 13:7.

> The application of that passage to Jesus and his disciples does not present any great difficulty. It is true that in the context of Zechariah's prophecy the one who smites the shepherd is not mentioned. An order is simply issued, namely, to strike down the shepherd. On the other hand, the entire context refers repeatedly to Jehovah as being the Actor.[35]

But the death of the shepherd would not be the end of the matter. Just as Zechariah 13 ends with a promise of mercy to the tested remnant, so Jesus goes on to predict His victory.
14:28 Not only was Jesus to die, but He affirmed again the fact that He was going to be raised from the dead, after which He would go

34. Ibid., 511.
35. Hendriksen, *Exposition of the Gospel According to Mark,* 578.

before them to Galilee. It would be natural for them to return to Galilee, their homeland, following the completion of the Passover. "But on this occasion as on so many others before, the disciples were so overwhelmed with predictions of Jesus' departure or death and its consequences that they failed to notice the promise of resurrection and restoration."[36] Three days later they did not believe the first reports of the Resurrection, and an angel had to give them a special reminder to tell them to meet Jesus in Galilee (cf. 16:6-7).

14:29   Peter reacted strongly to the words of Jesus Christ. "The quotation from Zech. 13:7 made no impression on him. He was intent on showing that he was superior to 'all' the rest."[37] He could not fathom that he would forsake his Lord. He declared that even though all the others might fall away, he would never do that.

> All the Gospels show the same picture of impetuous Peter, full of false pride in his own fancied strength, and scorn for the weakness of the others; he had no difficulty in believing the Lord's words to be true of his fellow disciples. But only Luke preserves the further Saying of the Lord as to Satan's desire to winnow Peter, and the Lord's prayer for strengthening his faith (Lk. xxii.31, 32). Perhaps this was too personal a point to be included in the preaching of Peter, while the careful Luke may have culled it long after from any other of the surviving eyewitnesses (Lk. i.1-3).[38]

14:30   The Savior responded with a strong affirmation. He said that very night, "before a cock crows twice," Peter would deny Him three times. It is only Mark's gospel that mentions the cock crowing twice. The fact that it did happen (cf. 14:72) shows that this was probably a meaningful detail to Peter and that he had passed it on to Mark. Hendriksen adds that "this very rooster-crowing is also a means of bringing Peter back to repentance, for Christ's reference to it becomes firmly embedded in his mind, so that at the appropriate moment this hidden memory will suddenly pull the rope that will ring the bell of Peter's conscience. See Matt. 26:74; Mark 14:72; Luke 22:60; John 18:27."[39]

14:31   Peter, however, kept saying over and over (*ekperissōs*, adverb only in Mark, meaning "vehemently") that he would never for-

---

36. Vos, *Mark*, 122.
37. Robertson, *Word Pictures in the New Testament*, 1:210.
38. Cole, *The Gospel According to Mark*, 217.
39. Hendriksen, *Exposition of the Gospel According to Mark*, 580.

sake his Lord. "With vehemence Peter expressed his abhorrence at
such a thought and swore he was prepared to accept Jesus' fate as his
own."[40] Peter's strong words of affirmation for the Savior were picked
up and repeated by all of the other disciples as well. They could not
conceive of themselves forsaking their Lord. "Ironically, a few hours
later the disciples had fled (Ch. 14:50) and Peter summoned the same
vehemence to support his oath that he did not know the Nazarene
(Ch. 14:71). The fulfillment of Jesus' prediction concerning his faith-
lessness is precisely recorded in Ch. 14:72."[41]

THE GARDEN OF GETHSEMANE, 14:32-42
(cf. Matt. 26:36-46; Luke 22:39-46; John 18:1)

14:32   Jesus and the disciples came to a place on the Mount of Olives "named Gethsemane," a Hebrew word that literally means "an oil
press." It is natural to expect that on a hill covered with olive trees
there would be provision to press the olives to secure the oil. Olive
oil was a vital commodity in that society; it was used for cooking, for
fuel, and for medicinal purposes. This was a place that Jesus and the
disciples knew well (cf. Luke 22:39). Judas had no problem finding the
Savior at this location (cf. John 18:2). Here He left eight of His disciples and told them to remain there until He had prayed. The disciples
apparently did not sense anything strange about Jesus' actions.

14:33   Jesus "took [*paralambanei,* present tense verb to vividly picture the action] with Him Peter and James and John," and they separated themselves from the other apostles. This separation also was not
unknown to the apostolic group. These were the same individuals
who had been with Jesus when Jairus's daughter had been raised from
the dead (cf. 5:35-43) and when Jesus was transfigured on the mountain (cf. 9:2-9). In this great hour of need, Jesus desired the compan-
ionship of these three men. He "began to be very distressed [*ekthambeisthai*] and troubled [*adēmonein,* meaning 'intense discomfort']."
"Mark alone uses *ekthambeisthai* [*sic.*] (here and in 9:15). . . . The verb
thambeō occurs in Mark 10:32 for the amazement of the disciples at
the look of Jesus as he went toward Jerusalem. Now Jesus himself feels
amazement as he directly faces the struggle in the Garden of Gethsemane."[42] It is impossible to imagine what Jesus sensed at this

40. Lane, *The Gospel of Mark,* 513.
41. Ibid.
42. Robertson, *Word Pictures in the New Testament,* 1:383.

time. "Long as He had foreseen the Passion, when it came clearly into view its terrors exceeded His anticipations."[43]

14:34 He told them that His soul was "deeply grieved [or overwhelmed with sorrow] to the point of death." "The unusually strong language indicates that Mark understood Gethsemane to be the critical moment in Jesus' life when the full meaning of his submission to the Father confronted him with its immediacy."[44] The cross, which had always been in the future, was drawing closer and closer. The enormity of what it meant to bear the sin of the world was beginning to press in on Jesus Christ. "His human soul shrank from the Cross, and the fact adds to our sense of the greatness of His sacrifice."[45] He encouraged the disciples to "remain" (*meinate,* aorist tense, stating a simple fact) there and to "keep watch" (*grēgoreite,* present tense imperative, implying that the condition of keeping watch, or staying awake, was to be their habit).

14:35 "He went a little beyond them, and fell to the ground," agonizing in prayer (*proseycheto,* imperfect implying that He prayed repeatedly). Mark presents a general statement of His prayer, and in the following verse the specifics. He "began to pray that if it were possible, the hour might pass Him by." "He is in deep agony, probably, as was indicated previously, because he sees more sharply now than ever before the woes that await him. So he prays that this hour, this time of indescribably bitter pain and anguish, may pass him by."[46]

14:36 Mark quotes specifically the prayer of Jesus Christ, beginning with "Abba! Father!" Abba is a very affectionate Aramaic expression, a term that an infant would use to address his father. The closest English equivalent is probably "Da da." The use of that term by Jesus Christ showed the intimacy of His relationship with the Heavenly Father. Such intimacy with God is never found in the literature of early Palestinian Judaism. To the Jewish mind the use of such familiar household terms in prayer to God would be considered disrespectful.

Jesus acknowledged that all things were possible for the Father and asked that if possible the cup might be removed from Him. The cup was a picture of death and the judgment of God falling on Jesus Christ as He bore the sins of the world. Jesus realized that this would

43. Swete, *The Gospel According to St. Mark,* 342.
44. Lane, *The Gospel of Mark,* 516.
45. Swete, *The Gospel According to St. Mark,* 342-43.
46. Hendriksen, *Exposition of the Gospel According to Mark,* 588.

bring about a sense of separation between Himself and the Father (cf. 15:34). This prospect was not something that Jesus looked forward to with eager anticipation.

> The thought that the cup could be removed may have come from Isa. 51:17-23 where God, in a proclamation of salvation, summons Jerusalem to arouse from its drunken stupor and to recognize that "the cup of staggering" has been taken away. Yet Scripture also speaks of those who "did not deserve to drink the cup [but] must drink it" (Jer. 49:12). The tension between these alternate expressions of grace and judgment, respectively, seems to be reflected in Jesus' prayer with its confession of God's ability ("all things are possible to you"; cf. Ch. 10:27) and the firm resolve to submit to God's sovereign will. The metaphor of the cup indicates that Jesus saw himself confronted, not by a cruel destiny, but by the judgment of God.[47]

Jesus Christ did, however, submit His own will to that of the Father, for He prayed, "Not what I will, but what Thou wilt."

> The words occupy an important place in the history of the doctrine of the Person of Christ. The Church found in Christ's ["Not what I will, but what Thou Wilt"] conclusive evidence of the existence in our Lord of a true human will, distinct from the Divine Will, although even in this supreme crisis absolutely submissive to it.[48]

14:37   Jesus returned back to the inner circle of disciples and "found them sleeping." He spoke to Peter, calling him by his earthly name Simon. "The old name, not the new name, Peter. Already his boasted loyalty was failing in the hour of crisis. Jesus fully knows the weakness of human flesh."[49] All of them were asleep, but He addressed Peter, probably because he had taken the lead in pledging his loyalty to Jesus, even going so far as to boast about it (cf. v. 29). Jesus said, "Could you not keep watch for one hour?" Perhaps that was an indication of how long Jesus had been apart from the three apostles praying. Mark's statement of His prayer was obviously brief, but perhaps the Savior had been agonizing for at least an hour. "The pointed reference to [Peter's] inability to be vigilant for 'one hour' (which per-

47. Lane, *The Gospel of Mark*, 517.
48. Swete, *The Gospel According to St. Mark*, 345.
49. Robertson, *Word Pictures in the New Testament*, 1:384.

haps should be taken literally) prepares for the account of his faith-
lessness in Ch. 14:66-72, while the detail that he was asleep on three
occasions when Jesus came to him anticipates his threefold denial."[50]

14:38   He encouraged all three of the apostles to continue "watching and praying" (*grēgoreite kai proseuchesthe,* plural present tense
imperatives indicating an action that was to be constant) so that they
would not enter into temptation. "A person may be wide awake physically and may still succumb to temptation, but if he remains awake
spiritually, that is, if with heart and mind he remains 'on the alert' or
'watchful,' he will overcome temptation."[51] He had just acknowledged
that they would all forsake Him, and now He encouraged them to
continue to pray. Truly their spirit was willing, but their flesh was
weak.

> The "willing spirit" which stands in opposition to the weak flesh is not
> a better part of man but God's Spirit who strives against human weak-
> ness. The expression is borrowed from Ps. 51:12, where it stands in
> parallel with God's Holy Spirit who qualifies a man to speak with bold-
> ness before sinners. Spiritual wakefulness and prayer in full depen-
> dence upon divine help provide the only adequate provision for crisis
> (cf. Ch. 13:11). Jesus prepared for his own intense trial through vigi-
> lance and prayer, and thus gave to the disciples and to the Church the
> model for the proper resistance of eschatological temptation.[52]

14:39   He went away a second time and prayed. Mark indicated that
He basically was saying the same words over and over. "Though Jesus
did not utter exactly the same words, he did say what amounted to
substantially (though not precisely) the same *thing.*"[53] "The answer to
the first prayer seems to have been vouchsafed in a growing consciousness of the Father's Will."[54]

14:40   Then He came back and found the disciples sleeping again.
"It is absolutely remarkable that in His severe agony Jesus should have
such great concern for His disciples. In fact, Mark's focus of attention
is almost more on the sleeping disciples than on the suffering Mes-

50. Lane, *The Gospel of Mark,* 519.
51. Hendriksen, *Exposition of the Gospel According to Mark,* 589.
52. Lane, *The Gospel of Mark,* 520-21.
53. Hendriksen, *Exposition of the Gospel According to Mark,* 590.
54. Swete, *The Gospel According to St. Mark,* 347.

siah."[55] Mark adds that their eyes "were very heavy" (*katabaryno-menoi, kata* plus a present passive participle, a rare word found only here in the New Testament). It was well after midnight and certainly they were tired, especially Peter and John, who had had a very busy day making the preparations for the Passover meal. Jesus awakened them again and they did not know how to respond to Him. This uncertainty is "alone in Mark and reminds one of the like embarrassment of these same three disciples on the Mount of Transfiguration (Mark 9:6). On both occasions weakness of the flesh prevented their real sympathy with Jesus in his highest and deepest experiences."[56]

14:41 Mark does not specifically mention the details of Jesus' third period of prayer (cf. Matt. 26:44). But he does state that Jesus came a "third time" to the disciples. It is reasonable to assume that a third time of prayer intervened between the second and third appearances. When He came the third time He said to them, "Are you still sleeping and taking your rest?" This probably should be regarded as a rebuke for their continued failure to stay awake and uphold Jesus in prayer. "[His words] underscore the utter inability of the disciples to understand the significance of the moment and stress Jesus' isolation in trial."[57] The ensuing statement, "It is enough [or "It is settled"]; the hour has come," probably awakened the disciples from their sleep. Even though Jesus had prayed in v. 35 that "the hour" might pass from Him if possible, the time had come. The Son of Man, the Lord Jesus Christ, was about to be "betrayed into the hands of sinners." Concerning the use of the word "sinners," Swete says,

> In this context it would mean to the disciples 'the Gentiles,' i.e. the Roman officials; but in the Lord's own thought the Scribes and Priests were doubtless included. He had sought the company of sinners who were willing to receive Him, for He came to call them (ii.16, 17); but to be delivered to the will of sinners who refused His call was one of the bitterest ingredients of His Cup.[58]

14:42 He encouraged them to get up (*egeiresthe,* present tense plural imperative) for they needed to be going. The one who was betraying Him (cf. vv. 18-21) was just outside the garden, and they

55. Vos, *Mark,* 124.

56. Robertson, *Word Pictures in the New Testament,* 1:385.

57. Lane, *The Gospel of Mark,* 522.

58. Swete, *The Gospel According to St. Mark,* 348.

would be meeting him momentarily. "The call to 'go' ends the scene in Gethsemane, but cannot be intended to suggest flight, for the Lord had always reserved Himself for this 'hour,' and had now finally embraced the Divine Will concerning it."[59]

THE ARREST AND TRIALS OF THE SERVANT, 14:43–15:20

ARREST IN GETHSEMANE, 14:43-52
(cf. Matt. 26:47-56; Luke 22:47-53; John 18:2-12a)

14:43 "Immediately" (*euthys*), while Jesus was speaking these words to His disciples, "Judas . . . came up" accompanied by a large crowd of people. It was not necessary for Mark to identify Judas as being "one of the twelve" (cf. vv. 10, 20). The fact that he does shows how horrible Judas's deed truly was.

> Since he was "one of the twelve," it would be impossible to mention all the privileges that had been bestowed upon him during the many days, weeks, and months he had spent in Christ's immediate company. Such confidence had the other eleven reposed in this same Judas that they had even made him their treasurer. And now he was proving himself totally unworthy of all these honors and advantages, of all this trust. A shameless, disgusting quisling he had become, a wretched turncoat, one who for the paltry sum of thirty pieces of silver was delivering over to the enemy the greatest Benefactor whose feet ever trod this earth, even the Mediator, both God and man, the Lord Jesus Christ.[60]

Judas was "accompanied by a multitude" that possessed "swords and clubs." At that time Roman soldiers were the only ones allowed to legally carry swords. The clubs would have been carried by those who were part of the temple guard, who came "from the chief priests and the scribes [mentioned only by Mark] and the elders." These three groups represent all of the elements of the Sanhedrin. John 18:3 mentions that "Pharisees" were also part of the group.

> The Gospel of John also mentions "torches and lanterns." Torches and lanterns—to search for the Light of the world. And it was full moon! Swords and cudgels—to subdue the Prince of Peace. For the Man of Sorrows the very sight of this band of ruffians, which considered him

59. Ibid., 349.
60. Hendriksen, *Exposition of the Gospel According to Mark*, 594.

their quarry, meant indescribable suffering.—And to think that the men who were supposed to be leaders in Israel, highly religious and devout, chief priests and scribes and elders, together composing the Sanhedrin, had sent this force. Instead of welcoming Jesus as the long-expected Messiah, they were sending a posse to capture him, with the ultimate purpose of having him brought before the authorities that he might be sentenced to death![61]

The fact that Roman soldiers were involved in the arrest probably was precipitated by the fear of the religious leaders that either Jesus' followers, or perhaps even the multitude of pilgrims in the city, might resist the arrest. Also the Sanhedrin had learned previously that the temple police could not always be relied on. On at least one previous occasion, they had even sided with Jesus (see John 7:32, 45-49).
14:44   Judas had given "a signal" (*syssēmon*) to those accompanying Him. Robertson says that the Greek word *syssēmon* is "a common word in the ancient Greek for a concerted signal according to agreement. It is here only in the New Testament. Matt. 26:48 has *sēmeion,* sign. The signal was the kiss by Judas, a contemptible desecration of a friendly salutation."[62] It was a common practice for a pupil to greet a rabbi with a kiss (the verb is *philēō*) as he approached him. So the one he kissed was the one they should "lead . . . away under guard," or lead away securely.

> The words reveal the interest which Judas, when committed to the scheme, had learnt to take in its success. It might even now be frustrated by the escape of Jesus before there was time to arrest Him, or by a rescue on the way to the city or in the streets; hence the double direction. . . . There must be no risk of miscarriage, and Jesus had often shown a supernatural power of eluding His enemies.[63]

14:45   As Judas came into the garden, "he immediately [*euthys*] went" right to Jesus. He addressed Him by the title, "Rabbi," and kissed Him.

> Ironically, both the title "Rabbi" ("my master") and the kiss declared Judas' respect for Jesus, while his act exposed his master to gross con-

61. Ibid., 595.
62. Robertson, *Word Pictures in the New Testament,* 1:385.
63. Swete, *The Gospel According to St. Mark,* 350-51.

tempt. There is little interest in Judas in the account apart from the essential fact that Jesus was handed over to the Sanhedrin through his agency. He is not mentioned in Mark's Gospel after this point.[64]

Whether Judas's kiss was directed to Jesus' cheek or to His hand cannot be determined from this text. Both manners of greeting were practiced. The fact that the verb for "kiss" is given in the simple form in v. 44 (*phileō*) but in the compound form (*katephilēsen*) in v. 45 probably implies that the kiss that Judas gave to the Lord was fervent. It probably was not repeated, for the aorist verb tense implies a single event, but certainly the kiss was given with a great fervor.

14:46 Those who accompanied Judas "laid hands on [Jesus], and seized Him." There was no resistance on the Master's part. The plan was working perfectly. They now had Jesus Christ under their control. "John 18:3, 12 shows that the arrest was made by *a*. the soldiers and their chiliarch (commander) and *b*. the temple guards. Gentiles and Jews combine against Jesus. Cf. Acts 4:27."[65]

14:47 But "one of those who stood by drew [a] sword." From the way Mark stated "a certain one," he probably knew who that person was. The parallel accounts make clear that that person was Simon Peter (cf. John 18:10, which would not have been written until after Peter's death). The disciples had two swords with them in the garden (cf. Luke 22:38). How they came into possession of these swords is not explained.

Peter, apparently remembering his own words (that he would never deny his Lord), drew one of those swords and attempted to defend his Savior. He was probably trying to cut off the head of the person closest to him. Instead, when he struck the slave of the high priest, he cut off his right ear (cf. Luke 22:50; John 18:10). John indicates that the slave's name was Malchus (cf. John 18:10).

Since this . . . name was in common use among the Nabateans and in Syria, this man may have been a Nabatean Arab or a Syrian who attended Caiaphas as his personal servant. He seems not to have been present in Gethsemane in any official capacity, but doubtless had been charged to bring the high priest a report of the course of the action as soon as possible.[66]

64. Lane, *The Gospel of Mark*, 525.
65. Hendriksen, *Exposition of the Gospel According to Mark*, 596.
66. Lane, *The Gospel of Mark*, 526.

Jesus put an immediate stop to this defense, but Mark does not record the reaction of Jesus to this impulsive act (cf. Matt. 26:52-54). Luke states that the Savior took time to heal the ear of the servant who had been struck (Luke 22:51).

14:48   Jesus, however, did protest the manner in which He was being arrested. He asked His captors why they had "come out with swords and clubs" to arrest Him in the middle of the night as though He were a robber? He was not a hardened criminal who was guilty of an offense. "They had come out against him with an army, equipped with swords and clubs, as if he were a highwayman or, as the text can also be rendered, an insurrectionist, rebel, or revolutionary."[67]

14:49   Jesus pointed out paradoxically that every day throughout the past week or two He had been "in the temple teaching," yet they had not seized Him.

> He, a harmless teacher, had taught often in the temple. They could have taken Him there and need not have apprehended Him here like a common robber. Of course the protest would do no good and He did not intend that it should change anything. He was merely registering a point and then recognized that God was carrying out His prophetic plan, and He voluntarily put Himself in the hands of His captors.[68]

> Those who have seen secret police at work in any part of the world will appreciate this [action]. Arrests are usually made at night, for two reasons; the victims are liable to be confused and offer less resistance, and the neighbours are not likely to gather and protest. Life changes little over millennia in such matters.[69]

He understood that His arrest was "that the Scriptures might be fulfilled." The Savior may have had in mind a number of verses out of Isaiah 53 or perhaps even the passage He had quoted just hours before from Zechariah 13:7 (cf. v. 27).

14:50   Mark noted that once the Savior was taken captive, the disciples "all left Him and fled." This was exactly what He had said would happen when the shepherd was struck down (cf. v. 27). He had said that the sheep would be scattered. "Not even Peter formed an exception to the general desertion. All fled. Yet two at least recovered them-

---

67. Hendriksen, *Exposition of the Gospel According to Mark,* 598.
68. Vos, *Mark,* 125.
69. Cole, *The Gospel According to Mark,* 223.

selves so far as to follow afterwards, if at a safe distance (*v.* 54, Jo. xviii.15)."[70]

14:51 There was, however, one who did not immediately flee. "A certain young man" [*neaniskos tis*] was following Him, wearing nothing but a linen sheet over his naked body." This young man was not identified in this account, which appears only in Mark's gospel. However, most scholars believe this was probably John Mark, the author. This was his way of letting everyone know that he too was present on this occasion. If this was truly John Mark, perhaps the following scenario took place.

Jesus and His disciples had observed the Passover supper in the home of John Mark. When they left the home and went to the Mount of Olives, the household settled down for the night. Mark, a young man, went to bed covering himself with a sheet. Perhaps shortly thereafter Judas arrived at the house with a multitude looking for the Savior. This could have caused enough commotion to awaken everyone. When they left and headed for the Mount of Olives, perhaps Mark wrapped the sheet around his body and followed them. He may have even tried to get ahead of them and reach the Garden of Gethsemane in time to warn Jesus. At any rate, when they finally had arrested the Savior, John Mark "was following [*synēkolouthei,* imperfect tense picturing the process] Him" at a distance until suddenly he was detected and "seized" (*kratousin,* dramatic historical present).

> If this is correct, Mark was an eye witness to the transactions in Gethsemane. His primary purpose for including this vignette, however, appears to have been to emphasize the fact that *all* fled, leaving Jesus alone in the custody of the police. No one remained with Jesus, not even a valiant young man who intended to follow Him.[71]

14:52 "But he left the linen sheet [*sindona,* fine linen cloth often used for wrapping the dead] behind, and escaped naked" into the night. The fact that it was a linen sheet implied that the family was wealthy. That fits all the details known about John Mark's household (cf. Acts 12:12). The absence of an undergarment may suggest that he dressed rapidly in order to get to Jesus before the armed band.

70. Swete, *The Gospel According to St. Mark,* 353.
71. Lane, *The Gospel of Mark,* 527-28.

TRIAL BEFORE THE COUNCIL, 14:53-65
(cf. Matt. 26:57-68; Luke 22:54a, 63-65; John 18:24)

14:53   As soon as Jesus was arrested in the Garden of Gethsemane, He was led back through Jerusalem to the household of the high priest, Caiaphas.

> He occupied that office from A.D. 18–36, and was the son-in-law of Annas (John 18:13). He was a rude and sly manipulator, and opportunist, who did not know the meaning of fairness or justice and who was bent on having his own way "by hook or by crook" (Matt. 26:3, 4; John 11:49). He did not shrink from shedding innocent blood. What he himself ardently craved for selfish purposes, he made to look as if it were the one thing needful for the welfare of the people. In order to bring about the condemnation of Jesus, who had aroused his envy (Matt. 27:18), he was willing to use devices which were the product of clever calculation and unprecedented boldness. He was a hypocrite, as will become evident.[72]

Since all this was happening before it was morning on the fifteenth of Nisan, most of the members of the Sanhedrin had to be awakened from their sleep in order to convene the council.

In John's gospel it is noted that, while they were assembling the Sanhedrin, Jesus appeared before the former high priest, Annas (cf. John 18:12-14, 19-23), who was the father-in-law of Caiaphas. Mark only relates the trial that followed when all the chief priests, the elders, and the scribes, along with the reigning high priest, Caiaphas, gathered together. These categories of men mentioned by Mark constituted the Sanhedrin, a group of 71 men, the supreme ruling body of Israel. Mark pictures the members of the Sanhedrin as flocking to the household of Caiaphas.

> The haste with which the Sanhedrin was assembled is consonant with the deliberations reported in Ch. 14:1f., 10f. and the necessity of reaching a binding verdict before daybreak. Moreover, it was normal to try persons immediately after arrest since Jewish criminal law made no provision for detention on remand.[73]

---

72. Hendriksen, *Exposition of the Gospel According to Mark,* 604.
73. Lane, *The Gospel of Mark,* 530-31.

14:54   Mark records that Peter followed the Lord Jesus "at a distance" (*makrothen ēkolouthēsen,* aorist tense stating a completed fact). Peter's action "was probably prompted, in part, by the loud boasts he had uttered, as recorded in verses 29 and 31; in part also, by sheer curiosity, as Matt. 26:58 states, and perhaps we should add, in part by love for his Master."[74] John in his gospel reports that a disciple, probably John himself, was known to the high priest, and was able to gain entrance to the house (cf. John 18:15). It was this disciple who made it possible for Peter to enter the courtyard of the house.

> At first sight, verse 54 appears to be abruptly introduced and disruptive to the account of the proceedings before the Sanhedrin.... The reference to Peter, however, is dictated by Mark's concern to present two incidents which happened at the same time. Because the council session and the denial were concurrent events, he is not content to present them simply one after the other, but employs a literary device which is characteristic of his style. He records the hearing before the Sanhedrin prior to the account of Peter's denial, but by introducing the second incident at the beginning of the first he indicates that the episodes occur simultaneously.[75]

According to Mark, Peter came into the courtyard area and "was sitting [*sygkathēmenos,* imperfect tense indicating that this action extended over a period of time] ... warming himself by the fire" with the officers who probably had arrested Jesus. Early in the spring, the night air in Jerusalem, which is 2,500 feet above sea level, can be quite chilly. Therefore, they were all seated around the fire (lit., "he was facing the fire") so that he was quite visible. "Peter sat (Mt. Mc. Lk.) or stood (Jo.) among them, glad of the heat after his long exposure to the night air, but forgetful that the blaze lit up his features ... and exposed him to the scrutiny of enemies."[76]

14:55   "The chief priests and the whole Council" began to seek testimony so that Jesus Christ might be put to death.

> While they had long ago decided on His death for reasons good and sufficient to them, they had still to formulate a legal charge, adequate to justify the death penalty; they had no desire to assassinate Him, lest it

---

74. Hendriksen, *Exposition of the Gospel According to Mark,* 605.
75. Lane, *The Gospel of Mark,* 532.
76. Swete, *The Gospel According to St. Mark,* 355.

provoke a bloody riot and consequent Roman action. . . . But even if the high priest could find some single breach of the Torah, sufficient in Jewish eyes to warrant a death sentence, their task was still but half done. They also had to produce some political charge, sufficient in Roman eyes to warrant the carrying out of the death sentence.[77]

They did not have the authority to carry out executions (cf. John 18:31), but they could make the recommendation to the Roman officials who did have the power. However as they sought testimony that would enable them to carry out this act, "they were not finding any."
14:56   "Many were giving false testimony" (*polloi . . . epseudomartyroun,* imperfect tense implying that the false testimony was repeatedly given) concerning Jesus. The problem was that "their testimony was not consistent." In order to convict a person of a crime, the Mosaic Law required that the testimony of at least two witnesses be in complete agreement (cf. Deut. 17:6; 19:15). No man could ever be put to death on the testimony of only one witness.

The ready availability of witnesses for the prosecution suggests that they had been alerted that the arrest of Jesus could be expected momentarily and that they were to appear on call. A number were called and heard, but all that is recorded is that they failed to agree with each other and so invalidated their testimony. This detail indicates that the Sanhedrin adhered strictly to the legal standards for the hearing of witnesses. The one reproach to which the court was opened, according to Mark's record, was that they assembled together, not with the intention of reaching a just verdict, but with a firm resolve to convict Jesus of a capital crime (Ch. 14:1, 55). This violation of the purpose and spirit of the law outweighed the regard, or disregard, of external legal forms.[78]

14:57   Others "stood up and began to give false testimony" (same imperfect tense verb as in v. 56) concerning Jesus Christ. It is incredulous that a group of "religious" leaders was seeking false testimony from individuals and that all this was happening while one of their most holy festivals was taking place in their city.
14:58   This verse contains a sample of the testimony of a number of the witnesses. Some had heard Jesus say at one time in His ministry, "I will destroy this temple made with hands, and in three days I will

77. Cole, *The Gospel According to Mark*, 225.
78. Lane, *The Gospel of Mark*, 533.

build another made without hands." "The accusation was utterly serious, for throughout the Graeco-Roman world the destruction or desecration of places of worship was regarded as a capital offense."[79] The closest reference in the biblical text to this statement is the comment Jesus made after He had cleansed the temple early in His ministry (cf. John 2:19). Jesus did not say that He was going to destroy the physical building. John's editorial comment there is that Jesus actually was speaking about His own body (cf. John 2:21).

14:59   Mark alone, however, notes that even in respect to this particular testimony their words were not consistent. "Mark and Matthew do not quote the witnesses precisely alike. Perhaps they quoted Jesus differently and therein is shown part of the disagreement, for Mark adds verse 59 (not in Matthew)."[80] Not even this testimony was sufficient for the verdict to be brought against Jesus. Swete notes that "if the Lord said the words as they stand in [Mark], He said what the event has proved to be true; His death destroyed the old order, and His resurrection created the new."[81]

14:60   Finally the high priest, Caiaphas, "stood up and came forward and questioned Jesus." "For greater solemnity he arose to make up by bluster the lack of evidence. The high priest stepped out into the midst as if to attack Jesus by vehement questions."[82] He asked Jesus two questions. His first was phrased in such a way in the original text that it implied a positive answer. He said to Jesus something like this: "Surely you are going to answer these accusations, are you not?"

> Jesus was required by law to answer the accusations brought against him, and his failure to do so frustrated the council. By his steadfast silence he deprived the court of exploiting, for its purposes, the evidence that had been given against him. This brought the proceedings to a deadlock, and prompted the high priest to seek a decision by direct means.[83]

The high priest tried to get Jesus to incriminate Himself by asking Him to clarify what it was that the witnesses were testifying against Him. He

---

79. Ibid., 534.
80. Robertson, *Word Pictures in the New Testament,* 1:387.
81. Swete, *The Gospel According to St. Mark,* 357.
82. Robertson, *Word Pictures in the New Testament,* 1:387.
83. Lane, *The Gospel of Mark,* 535.

was trying to get Jesus to seal His own fate by saying something they could use to condemn Him.

14:61   Still Jesus did not respond but "kept silent" (*esiōpa*, imperfect tense implying that He was continually silent throughout all these proceedings). Actually, no charges had been leveled against Him for Him to respond to. "This was not the time for serious instruction, nor were these the men to whom it could be profitably addressed; nor could He admit the authority of an assembly which was following up an unjust arrest by the employment of perjured witnesses."[84] The high priest, therefore, continued to question Him.

In Matthew's account of this same trial, the high priest put Jesus Christ under a sacred oath by prefacing his questions with the comment "I adjure You by the living God" (Matt. 26:63). Whenever a Jew was placed under oath by the living God, he was required to answer honestly. The high priest then said to Jesus, "Are You the Christ [Messiah], the Son of the Blessed One?" The high priest was following the practice of the Jews not to refer to God by name. Instead, he used the term "Blessed One" to refer to God. But no matter what term he used he was asking Jesus, "Are You the Son of God?"

> In the Marcan account this question appears to provide the climax to the proceedings. . . . Judaism expected the Messiah to provide proof of his identity. A Messiah imprisoned, abandoned by his followers, and delivered helpless into the hands of his foes represented an impossible conception. Anyone who, in such circumstances, proclaimed himself to be the Messiah could not fail to be a blasphemer who dared to make a mockery of the promises given by God to his people.[85]

14:62   Jesus' answer to the high priest was clear and direct. He said, "I am," a statement which is "definite beyond controversy."[86] This reference surely would spark in the memory of all who heard Him the sacred holy name of God that was given when God responded to Moses at the burning bush by saying, "I am who I am" (Ex. 3:14). Jesus, however, added to His comment a prophecy that brings together Psalm 110:1 and Daniel 7:13. He said that those hearing Him, who were seeking to judge Him, would one day see Him as "the Son of Man sitting at the right hand of Power." Jesus acquiesced to their prac-

84. Swete, *The Gospel According to St. Mark,* 358.
85. Lane, *The Gospel of Mark,* 536.
86. Robertson, *Word Pictures in the New Testament,* 1:388.

tice and did not use the name of God directly. He spoke of God as being "the Power" and said that they not only would see the Son of Man sitting at the right hand of God, the place of highest honor, but they also would see Him "coming with the clouds of heaven."

"The phrase 'coming with the clouds of heaven'—see also Dan. 7:13; Joel 2:2; Zeph. 1:15; Rev. 1:7; 14:14-16—reminds us of the fact that Scripture frequently associates 'a cloud' or 'clouds' with the idea of judgment, God's coming in order to punish the wicked."[87] They were judging Him now, but one day He would judge them. "The day will come, he affirms, when those who now judge him will see him with unmistakable clarity enthroned at God's side, invested with power and majesty, and assigned the task of the eschatological Judge. He will then be unveiled in a convincing manner as the Anointed of God."[88]

14:63   When the high priest heard the words of Jesus Christ, he tore his garments. This was a gesture that any Jew would use on hearing blasphemy. But it was something specifically commanded that the high priest was never to do (cf. Lev. 10:6; 21:10). Therefore the high priest probably did not tear his high priestly garments, but he may have torn some of his undergarments as a sign that he indeed had heard blasphemy and was expressing his indignation. His rhetorical question eliminated the need for any further witnesses. "The relief of the embarrassed judge is manifest. If trustworthy evidence was not forthcoming, the necessity for it had now been superseded; the Prisoner had incriminated Himself."[89]

14:64   The high priest declared that all in the room had "heard the blasphemy." There was no need for further testimony. Jesus was guilty from His own lips. The high priest asked what they felt should be done. They all knew that the penalty for blasphemy was death (cf. Lev. 24:15-16). Therefore, they all concluded that He deserved to be put to death.

> The statement that the Sanhedrin passed a formal death sentence has frequently been disputed on linguistic and historical grounds. . . . Mark, however, unequivocally reports a death sentence, using accepted legal terminology when he says that "all condemned him as liable to death."

87. Hendriksen, *Exposition of the Gospel According to Mark,* 612.
88. Lane, *The Gospel of Mark,* 537.
89. Swete, *The Gospel According to St. Mark,* 360.

As curious as this wording may sound, it means that a formal judgment took place and that a death sentence was handed down.[90]

Since it is stated that "all condemned Him to . . . death," it is undoubtedly clear that individuals such as Joseph of Arimathea (Luke 23:51) and Nicodemus (John 7:50ff.), who were opposed to the death of Jesus, probably were not summoned to this meeting of the Sanhedrin. Every member of the Sanhedrin did not have to be present in order for the council to convene. They simply needed a quorum present to enact their business.

14:65   They began to take the law into their own hands and treated Jesus Christ as a common criminal. They "spit at Him," demonstrating their contempt for Him. They blindfolded Him and "beat Him with their fists," at the same time asking Him to prophesy. These four actions—spitting, blindfolding, beating, and asking—are all present tense infinitives. By asking Him to identify who it was that was attacking Him while blindfolded, they were trying to determine if He truly was the Messiah, the Son of God. If He were the Son of God, He would be omniscient and would know who His attackers were. Their act was partly based on their misinterpretation of Isaiah 11:2-4, where it is declared of the Messiah that He would not judge by what He saw nor make a decision by what He heard.

> The venerable(?) members of the Sanhedrin now show their real cruel, vengeanceful [sic], sadistic character. Utterly mean are they, inhuman, base, contemptible! Even if we make allowance for the possibility that the cruelty to which Jesus was now subjected was the action of the "underlings," and not directly of the priests, etc., it remains true that it was carried out with the wholehearted permission and co-operation of the members of the Sanhedrin.[91]

Jesus was then turned over to the "officers," the same group as in v. 54, those who had arrested Jesus in Gethsemane (v. 43) and who were still responsible for His security. They continued to treat Jesus in a manner that was not worthy of anyone, not even a condemned criminal. They were continually slapping Him in the face with their hands.

90. Lane, *The Gospel of Mark,* 539.
91. Hendriksen, *Exposition of the Gospel According to Mark,* 614.

"Emboldened by the conduct of their superiors, they added their own form of insult."[92]

PREDICTION OF DENIAL FULFILLED, 14:66-72
(cf. Matt. 26:69-75; Luke 22:54b-62; John 18:15-18; 25-27)
14:66   While Jesus was being interrogated in the upper room of the high priest's house, Peter was undergoing a trial of his own in the open courtyard below.

> The irony inherent in the situation is evident when the force of juxta-posing verse 65 and verses 66-72 is appreciated. At the precise time when the court attendants were heaping scorn and derision upon Je-sus' claim to be the Messiah, the prophecy that Peter would deliberately deny him was being fulfilled. The most plausible source for this tradi-tion is Peter himself, who must have authorized, if he did not actually construct, the version of the events.[93]

"One of the servant-girls of the high priest" came up to him. "[Her] first glance revealed the presence of a stranger; closer attention ena-bled her to recognize Peter. St John tells us why—she was the por-tress who at his desire had let Peter in [cf. Jo. 18:15-16]."[94] It was this contact that had enabled both John and Peter to gain access to the courtyard.
14:67   She saw Peter warming himself by the fire, for as he sat around the fire his face was illuminated by the flames. She looked at him and said, "You, too, were with Jesus the Nazarene." Her observa-tion was clearly meant to embarrass and unsettle Peter, for her identi-fication of Jesus as "the Nazarene" was certainly contemptuous. The reference to "too" perhaps implies that she was aware of the fact that John was in the house.
14:68   But Peter in a very formal, legal way stated that he did not know what she was talking about.

> The suddenness and boldness of the servant-girl's incriminating re-mark catches him off guard. In spite of all his loud and repeated prom-ises of unswerving loyalty to Jesus, promises only made a few hours earlier, he is now thoroughly frightened. One might say: he panics. Evi-

---

92. Swete, *The Gospel According to St. Mark,* 361.
93. Lane, *The Gospel of Mark,* 541.
94. Swete, *The Gospel According to St. Mark,* 362.

dently he had failed to take to heart Christ's admonition recorded in 14:38. So he tries to make the girl believe that he doesn't know or understand what she is talking about, and in his frustration he makes for the entryway, hoping that for him it will be an exit.[95]

The porch area of the courtyard away from the fire would have been much darker.

Although the NASB does not mention it here, the majority of manuscripts add "and the rooster crowed." Although the manuscripts Aleph and B do not add this comment, there is good evidence that it should be here. Whereas all the gospel accounts give the story of Peter's denial, none of the others mentions that the rooster crowed twice. Perhaps some scribe eliminated this reference from the Markan account to make it appear parallel with all the other stories. But this is Peter's account of this incident and surely he would have remembered it with the greatest clarity. He remembered that Jesus had said that "before a cock crows twice" he would deny the Savior (cf. v. 30). The fact that in v. 72 it says that a cock crowed "a second time" implies that somewhere in the story of the denial there should be another reference to a cock crowing. Since the majority text places the reference to the first crowing of the cock here in v. 68, perhaps it should be considered as genuine.

14:69   A little later the same girl saw Peter again and once more she said to those who were standing around them, "This is one of them!" It was clear in her thinking that Peter was associated with Jesus Christ. "Her remark that Peter was 'one of them' shows an awareness that Jesus had given leadership to a significant movement and had attracted a stable following of men who were nearly always with him."[96]

14:70   Again Peter denied it, and he kept on denying it, according to the imperfect tense (*ērneito*) of the verb. Perhaps it was his repetitious verbal denials that caused him to be more visible. That also opened him up to the next charge when one of the bystanders said, "Surely you are one of them, for you are a Galilean too." It was Peter's Galilean accent in his Aramaic speech that confirmed their suspicions and gave him away. Galileans pronounced some words differently from Judeans, and his speech clearly betrayed him in this courtyard of Judeans. "[Galileans] were unable to distinguish between the several

95. Hendriksen, *Exposition of the Gospel According to Mark*, 617-18.
96. Lane, *The Gospel of Mark*, 542.

guttural sounds that are so important an element in Semitic languages. Peter's speech showed him to be a Galilean and his presence among the Judeans in the courtyard invited the deduction that he was a follower of the heretic Galilean, Jesus of Nazareth."⁹⁷

14:71 Since it was clear that Peter was a Galilean, he knew he had to do something drastic. The text says that he "began to curse and swear." This does not imply that Peter used profanity. Instead, what Peter did was place himself under an oath. He in effect said, "I swear to you I am telling the truth, and if I am not telling you the truth then may the curses of God come down on my head." But in the process of doing that, he denied his Lord and lied. "He stands there invoking on himself one curse after another. And the louder this Galilean talks, the more, without realizing it, he is saying to all those standing around, 'I'm a liar.'"⁹⁸ He cleverly said he did not know "this man" they were talking about. He deliberately avoided using the term "Jesus," for that name had not come up in the most recent conversations.

14:72 Immediately following his third denial, it is said that "a cock crowed a second time." At that point "Peter remembered" the words of the Lord given to him in v. 30. As those words came back to Peter's memory, he was convicted. It is possible that at that very moment Jesus Christ was brought out of the upper room and down an outside stairway in the region of the courtyard. Luke's gospel (22:61) reveals that Jesus looked at Peter.

The combination of all these things, the look of the Savior and the conviction in his heart at the Lord's words, were more than he could handle. He ran from the area and "began to weep" (*eklaien,* an imperfect tense implying that the weeping continued over a period of time). Truly his weeping was the sorrow of genuine repentance, for Peter was restored to a position of faithful service for his Lord.

> The tradition of Peter's denial was undoubtedly included in the Gospel to provide a sober example to the Christian community in Rome.... This was of primary significance to Mark's readers, whose faith was severely tested by the measures adopted in imperial Rome to stamp out an unwanted sect. The fact of Peter's denial constituted a solemn warning that a bold affirmation of fidelity did not guarantee faithfulness. It constituted a plea to hold fast to one's confession of Jesus. But it also provided a word of encouragement that one who failed his Lord through

97. Ibid.
98. Hendriksen, *Exposition of the Gospel According to Mark,* 621.

denial could be restored, for the episode recounted in Ch. 14:66-72 remains incomplete without the promise to Peter in Ch. 16:7 that he will experience forgiveness and restoration in Galilee."[99]

HOMILETICAL SUGGESTIONS

This chapter begins with the interplay of three contrasting events. Mark presents the plot of the religious leaders to do away with Jesus Christ. On the other hand, he describes the very beautiful act of Mary as she anointed the feet of the Savior. That in turn is followed by the fact that Judas comes forward to betray his Lord. From a comparison of the other gospels it seems clear that these events did not occur in the sequence Mark presents, but he uses them thematically to portray a very graphic scene of differing attitudes toward the Savior.

The Passover meal that Jesus Christ shared with His disciples is presented in extended detail in Mark's gospel. Much of the information concerning the preparation for the meal, as well as the actual enjoyment of the meal, is given by Mark. Some of the discussions that took place around that table are presented, as well as the institution of the Lord's Supper, as Mark specifically mentions the giving of the bread and the cup. The prediction of the denial by the disciples makes a stark contrast to the events of the supper. None of the disciples was ready to admit that he would ever deny his Lord, and yet before a few hours had passed that is exactly what happened.

The prayer of Jesus Christ in the Garden of Gethsemane is given by Mark in detail as he relates the interchanges that occurred between the Savior and the three disciples. That time in prayer culminates as Judas comes forward to betray Jesus Christ so that He might be arrested and taken away. Mark mentions the act of Peter in defense of the Savior, although he does not specifically name Peter as being the one who draws the sword and cuts off the ear of the high priest's servant. In the final notes concerning the arrest of the Savior, that remarkable statement is found about a "certain young man" who was grabbed in the commotion and who fled naked into the night. What a unique way for Mark to put his signature on this book. Though it cannot be proven that this event happened to John Mark, it certainly seems most probable. This was his way of saying, "I was there, following the Savior, when others were fleeing into the night."

99. Lane, *The Gospel of Mark*, 543-44.

Mark's trial of Jesus Christ presents many of the false accusations that were brought up by various accusers. Also, the final statements of the high priest are given as he placed Jesus under oath and sought to get Him to incriminate Himself. There is a marvelous interchange showing the activity that occurred with Peter as he warmed himself by the fireside with those who had arrested the Savior. True to the Savior's word, Peter did deny his Lord and the cock crowed twice. That interesting rendition is given only in Mark's gospel and points again to the authenticity of this message as it came directly from Peter himself. The remorse and conviction in the heart of Peter did bring about his forgiveness and his restoration to a point of faithful service under his Lord.

MARK

CHAPTER

FIFTEEN

THE SERVANT'S DEATH

SECOND TRIAL BEFORE THE COUNCIL, 15:1
(cf. Matt. 27:1; Luke 22:66-71)

15:1   "Early in the morning," probably between 5 and 6 A.M., the Sanhedrin assembled once again for a consultation. Their earlier interrogation of Jesus (cf. 14:53-65) had been illegal by Rabbinic law, for no trial was to take place at night. They were out to execute Jesus, and they wanted to be sure that they did everything properly. Therefore, they waited for the sun to come up, and as soon as possible they met to formalize their conclusions so that they could quickly bring Jesus to the Roman officials to carry out His execution. Their conclusion at the night trial had been that He was guilty of blasphemy, but blasphemy was not a capital offense. The Romans would never have executed Jesus for blasphemy against Jewish laws. Somehow in the process the accusation was changed from blasphemy to treason (cf. Luke 23:2). To make their way to Pilate, they would have to travel through the streets, so to make certain that Jesus did not escape, He was bound and led away to Pilate. "The 'right of the sword' was reserved to the Roman magistrate as sole bearer of the full imperial authority (*imperium*). This was one of the most carefully guarded prerogatives of the Roman government and permitted no concessions."[1]

---

1. William L. Lane, *The Gospel of Mark,* NICNT (Grand Rapids: Eerdmans, 1974), 547.

TRIAL BEFORE PILATE, 15:2-15
(cf. Matt. 27:2, 11–26; Luke 23:1-5, 13–25; John 18:28–19:1)

15:2   Pilate was the Roman procurator of the region of Judea and Samaria. This territory had originally been given to Archelaus, a son of Herod the Great, when Herod died in 4 B.C. (cf. Matt. 2:22). Archelaus proved to be a poor ruler and was removed from his throne by Caesar. In his place, procurators ruled the region of Judea and Samaria. All procurators were appointed to their position by Caesar, although usually the appointment went to the person who paid Caesar the most money. A procurator was responsible to collect taxes, to command the Roman forces in the region, and to act as a judge in difficult cases. Pontius Pilate was the fifth procurator appointed by Caesar, beginning his reign in A.D. 26. He held his post for ten years. His place of residence normally was Caesarea on the coast, but he usually would come to Jerusalem for feast days in order that he might be there in the event of any serious uprisings.

The only accusation Pilate would be concerned with, coming from the Jews, would be one that had something to do with treason against the Roman government. Therefore, Pilate questioned Jesus concerning the matter of His being the King of the Jews. "He does not believe this [accusation] to be true, but he has to pay attention to it or be liable to charges himself of passing over a man accused of rivalry and revolution against Caesar."[2] When he asked Him directly if He was the King, Jesus answered in a way that was purposefully ambiguous. The Savior's response could be taken two ways. His answer could have been noncommittal: "It is you that say that, not I." On the other hand, it is possible that Jesus' answer was an emphatic positive similar to a slang expression that one might use: "You said it!" In all of Jesus' trials, Mark records very little of the exchanges that took place between the Savior and His accusers.

> The statement [here] is a rather guarded one, judging from the Greek text, and John 18:34-38 makes it clear that Jesus qualified His answer with an explanation of the nature of His kingdom. John also shows that Pilate's interrogation of Jesus was a private hearing after which the two went outside again to meet Jesus' accusers.[3]

2. A. T. Robertson, *Word Pictures in the New Testament* (Nashville: Broadman, 1930), 1:391.
3. Howard F. Vos, *Mark* (Grand Rapids: Zondervan, 1978), 129.

15:3 The chief priests entered into the discussion and "began to accuse [*katēgoroun,* imperfect tense implying repeated accusations] Him." They brought up as many things as they could remember concerning Jesus Christ to prove that He was guilty of treason. They may have even falsely said that He was against the paying of taxes to Caesar (cf. Luke 23:2).

> When Pilate remained unconvinced, they reintroduced their first impeachment that Jesus was stirring up the people with his teaching throughout Judea and Galilee (Lk. 23:5). Such multiple charges were common in criminal jurisdiction in the provinces during the period of the Flavian emperors. While the report of these accusations is generalized in Mark, in practice there must have been only two or three spokesmen who alleged certain facts which Pilate must adjudicate.[4]

15:4 As Pilate continued to question (*epērōta,* imperfect tense implying that the questioning went on for some time) Jesus, he was amazed that the Savior made no answer. This is reminiscent of the earlier situation with Caiaphas (cf. 14:60). Pilate encouraged Jesus to say something relative to the charges various individuals were leveling against Him. Evidently there were many accusations brought up by His accusers.

15:5 Jesus, however, did not answer even one charge. Silence was rare on the part of a condemned individual, and that may have helped convince Pilate that this man was probably innocent. "To Pilate this self-restraint was incomprehensible; he invited answers from the Prisoner, and, when He remained silent, expressed great astonishment. . . . His reserve was the more remarkable because He had answered Pilate before; but now His lips were sealed."[5] At some point in the discussion, according to the gospel of Luke, Pilate became aware that Jesus was a Galilean and that He had stirred up trouble in Galilee. Learning this, he tried to shift the responsibility of dealing with Jesus to the ruler of Galilee, Herod Antipas, who also was in town for the festival days (cf. Luke 23:6-11). Jesus did not say one word to Herod Antipas, for truly He was not accused of anything before him. Instead, Herod sent Jesus back to Pilate, where according to Mark's gospel the trial continued.

4. Lane, *The Gospel of Mark,* 551.
5. Henry Barclay Swete, *The Gospel According to St. Mark* (Grand Rapids: Eerdmans, 1956), 369.

It is clear that Mark reports only briefly on the trial of the Savior before Pilate. "It is interesting to speculate whether the reason for Mark's brevity here, where he is *kolobodaktulos* ['stump-fingered'] in style, is that Peter, his source, was not personally present at the trial before Pilate, nor that before Herod, while earlier he had been present in the high priest's hall (xiv. 66)."[6] Throughout the Markan account Jesus remained silent during His ordeal.

> From the time of his arrest until his death, he makes only two brief responses, one to Caiaphas and one to Pilate. He remains the passive one, in the conviction that the Son of Man *must* suffer and die (Ch. 8:31). Mark's reader senses in Jesus' passivity and silence that the sovereign Lord of history is accomplishing his mysterious purposes to which even the Son of Man must be submissive.[7]

15:6   Mark states that it was a custom of the Romans "to release" (*apelyen,* imperfect tense showing customary action) a prisoner during the feast whom the people "requested" (*parētounto,* imperfect tense showing something that happened habitually). The historicity of such a gracious demonstration of amnesty has been disputed primarily because Josephus makes no mention that such a custom ever existed. "There is, however, a parallel in Roman law which indicates that an imperial magistrate could pardon and acquit individual prisoners in response to the shouts of the populace."[8] This was most certainly done in an attempt to win over the Jewish people. It is clear, however, that such action did not accomplish that desired end in the eyes of the Jews.

15:7   Mark reports that there was a man named "Barabbas" (Bar Abba, i.e. "son of Abba," or "son of the father"), a well-known insurrectionist. He was "a desperate criminal, leader in the insurrection, sedition (*en tēi stasei*), or revolution against Rome, the very thing that the Jews up at Bethsaida Julias had wanted Jesus to lead (John 6:15). Barabbas was the leader of these rioters and was bound with them."[9] He had committed murder in the process of his uprising. John also states in his gospel that he was a robber (John 18:40).

6. R. A. Cole, *The Gospel According to Mark* (Grand Rapids: Eerdmans, 1979), 233-34.
7. Lane, *The Gospel of Mark,* 552.
8. Ibid., 553.
9. Robertson, *Word Pictures in the New Testament,* 1:392.

At all events, the man seems to have been a Zealot, captured after some brush with the authorities in which there had been fatalities, and whose doom was thus sealed, but whose popularity with the nationalists was also assured. The outcome of such choice was probable from the start; and the high priests made it certain, by their canvassing for Barabbas (xv. 11).[10]

15:8   As the trial of Jesus continued, some from the multitude went up to Pilate and began to ask him to release a prisoner "as he had been accustomed to do" (*kathōs epoiei,* imperfect tense showing customary action). These people may have been supporters of Jesus or of Barabbas who hoped they might be able to get their leader released.

> We are not told who were in the committee that made this request, and it is useless to guess, except to say that all or most of them must have been Pilate's own subjects. To conclude from this that all those who at this early hour were gathered in front of "the governor's palace" must have been inhabitants of Jerusalem and surroundings is deriving too much from too little.[11]

15:9   Pilate's statement expected a yes answer; it could read, "Surely you want me to release for you the King of the Jews, do you not?" "The cynicism of the Roman finds pleasure in connecting that title with this harmless dreamer, as he considers Jesus to be."[12] Pilate implied that he was planning to release Jesus of Nazareth to them. He had already declared Jesus to be innocent, and the arrival of the crowd must have been viewed by Pilate as opportune.

> He could achieve his ends by guiding the amnesty negotiations along lines he had determined. Before listening to the people he seems to have presented as his own candidate for release "the king of the Jews." His offer of generosity was doubtlessly tinged with irony, but he believed that the people would fall in line with his proposal.[13]

15:10   Pilate's motives were not completely dictated by the ideals of justice and humanity. He had seen through (*eginōsken,* imperfect

10. Cole, *The Gospel According to Mark,* 234.
11. William Hendriksen, *Exposition of the Gospel According to Mark* (Grand Rapids: Baker, 1975), 635.
12. Swete, *The Gospel According to St. Mark,* 371.
13. Lane, *The Gospel of Mark,* 554.

tense showing Pilate's growing apprehension over the conduct of the religious leaders) the ruse of the chief priests. He knew perfectly well that they had delivered up Jesus Christ not because of true charges but because of envy in their hearts.

> The pretense of loyalty to the Emperor was too flimsy to deceive a man of the world, and he detected under this guise the vulgar vice of envy. The Prophet of Galilee had earned a reputation, and gained a hold upon the conscience of the nation which the priestly rulers at Jerusalem failed to secure, and His success explained their resentment. But the people were free from the prejudices of the hierarchy, and might be trusted to demand the release of Jesus, especially when the alternative was such as Pilate proposed.[14]

15:11   Pilate, however, did not count on the ability of the chief priests to stir up (*aneseisan,* aorist tense presenting the completed process of shaking [like an earthquake]) the multitudes.

> What arguments were used to lead them to prefer Barabbas ... is a matter for conjecture; if Barabbas was a Jerusalemite, and the crowd consisted largely of his fellow-townsmen, an appeal may have been made to local prejudice; but there may have been also a lurking sympathy with the [rebels], which the Sanhedrist knew how to evoke. They would pose as advocates of Barabbas rather than as enemies of Jesus; to obtain the release of the one was to condemn the other.[15]

Instead of asking for the release of Jesus, the multitudes began to ask for the release of Barabbas, the criminal.

15:12   "Now Pilate still has Jesus on his hands. Instead of exercising the good sense or fortitude of handling the case himself, in his moment of uncertainty he put himself in the hands of the crowd and thus unwittingly in the hands of the Sanhedrin."[16] He inquired as to what they wanted him to do with their King. "If he had hoped that the populace would call for some milder form of punishment than that demanded by the chief priests he was mistaken."[17] Pilate appeared to be a weak, vacillating person in this discussion. He was not trying to do what was right. He was simply trying to do what was expedient.

14. Swete, *The Gospel According to St. Mark,* 371-72.
15. Ibid., 372.
16. Vos, *Mark,* 130.
17. Lane, *The Gospel of Mark,* 556.

When he asked, "Then what do you want me to do with the one whom you call 'the king of the Jews?'" his own immediate answer should have been, "Since he is innocent I will order his immediate and definite release." In fact, the judge should not even have asked the question at all. He knew the answer.[18]

15:13 The crowd shouted back to Pilate, "Crucify Him!" "There was a chorus and a hubbub of confused voices all demanding crucifixion for Christ. Some of the voices beyond a doubt had joined in the hallelujahs to the Son of David in the triumphal entry."[19] They encouraged Pilate to enforce the capital punishment laws of the Romans and execute Jesus Christ by crucifixion. "Both the leaders of the people and the inflamed crowd demanded not simply capital punishment, but the most ignominious form of death, crucifixion. Jesus must be declared guilty of high treason and punished with the full rigor of the law promulgated by the Emperor Augustus, the *lex Iulia maiestatis.*"[20]

15:14 Pilate, still reluctant, asked the crowd what evil it was that He had done. Pilate was not aware that Jesus had committed any crime. The other gospel accounts imply that Pilate repeatedly found no fault in Jesus. "Even when due allowance is made for parallel (duplicate) passages, the fact remains that Pilate stresses and constantly re-iterates the truth that in Jesus there is no cause of indictment. And by means of Pilate it was God himself who declared his Son's complete innocence, his perfect righteousness."[21] The crowd, however, continued to shout all the more, "Crucify Him!" "A mob has no reasons to give beyond its own will, and the only answer is a louder and wilder clamour."[22]

15:15 Pilate decided that he would "satisfy [the wishes of] the multitude" ("to content the multitude," a Latin idiom meaning "to do what is sufficient to remove one's ground of complaint"[23]). He gave in to the expedient thing and "released Barabbas [to] them." He tried one last time to placate the crowd. He delivered Jesus up for a scourging. A Roman scourging was a brutal beating that always preceded an execution, although a person could be scourged without being crucified. In a scourging the prisoner was stripped, tied to a post, and beaten

18. Hendriksen, *Exposition of the Gospel According to Mark,* 637.

19. Robertson, *Word Pictures in the New Testament,* 1:394.

20. Lane, *The Gospel of Mark,* 556.

21. Hendriksen, *Exposition of the Gospel According to Mark,* 639.

22. Swete, *The Gospel According to St. Mark,* 373.

23. Robertson, *Word Pictures in the New Testament,* 1:394.

on the back, usually by two Roman guards using leather whips studded with sharp pieces of bone, lead, or brass. There was no limit set on the number of times that a prisoner could be struck. The result of flogging was that "the flesh was at times lacerated to such an extent that deep-seated veins and arteries, sometimes even entrails and inner organs, were exposed. Such floggings, from which Roman citizens were exempt (cf. Acts 16:37), often resulted in death."[24] That still did not please the crowd, so Pilate delivered Jesus up to be crucified.

> The statement that Pilate "delivered him to be crucified" may have been formulated to call to mind Isa. 53:6, 12 LXX, where the expression "delivered" is used in reference to the sufferings and death of the servant of the Lord. The early Christians were less interested in the question whether the decision of the prefect was a legal sentence than in the fact that his action marked the fulfillment of OT prophecy.[25]

MOCKING BEFORE THE ROMAN SOLDIERS, 15:16-20
(cf. Matt. 27:27-31; John 19:2-3, 16b-17)
15:16 "The soldiers took [Jesus] away into the palace," which Mark identifies by the Latin term "Praetorium," which meant the governor's official residence. Scholars debate whether this was Herod's palace in Jerusalem or whether it was the fortress of Antonia, the large Roman area on the northwestern edge of the temple mount. Hendriksen summarizes the argument:

> The language used in Luke 23:7, the fact that according to Mark 15:8 those who wanted to see Pilate had to *ascend* in order to do so, the mention of "the stone platform" in John 19:13, and the fact that Pilate was not a friend of Herod (Luke 23:12) make it well-nigh impossible to believe that the meaning of Mark 15:1 would be that Jesus was brought to Herod's palace. The reference must be to the fortress of Antonia at the northwest corner of the temple area. Pilate had rooms in this fortress in close proximity to the garrison (Mark 15:16), though his main residence was in Caesarea.[26]

When the soldiers brought Jesus into that place, they called together the whole "cohort." This term implies a group of soldiers normally

24. Hendriksen, *Exposition of the Gospel According to Mark,* 640.
25. Lane, *The Gospel of Mark,* 557-58.
26. Hendriksen, *Exposition of the Gospel According to Mark,* 628.

amounting to about six hundred. However, because of the festival days and the fact that Pilate probably had been accompanied by a large contingent of soldiers from Caesarea, the number could have been far greater.

15:17   If Jesus was, indeed, the King of the Jews, He should be dressed as such. Therefore, the soldiers proceeded to make a mockery of Him.

> Mark's description suggests a kind of grotesque vaudeville: Jesus, bruised and bleeding, is pushed among the coarse soldiers who gathered in the expectation of a few moments of entertainment. From their point of view the condemned man represented a welcome diversion from the tension that always mounted in Jerusalem during the festival season.[27]

They dressed Him in purple, probably an old, faded cloak of a Roman soldier, and they wove a crown of thorns, which they placed on His head.

> With fiendish cruelty the soldiers, having made "a crown" out of these thorny twigs, press it down upon Christ's head. It represented not an imperial wreath but a crown such as would be appropriate for a "king of the Jews." Those who were engaged in this bit of fun wanted to mock Jesus. They also wanted to torture him. The crown of thorns satisfied both purposes.[28]

Matthew states that they also gave Him a staff, which was to serve as a mock scepter (Matt. 27:29).

15:18   They took turns mockingly acclaiming Jesus with statements such as, "Hail, King of the Jews!" Such a statement probably was very close to what they were used to shouting in amphitheaters: "Hail, Caesar."

15:19   They beat Jesus about His head "with a reed."

> Before any of these mockers vacated his position in front of Jesus, he would remove the stick from the hand of the victim and strike him on the head with it, as if to say, "What a king you are! One that gets hit over

---

27. Lane, *The Gospel of Mark,* 559.
28. Hendriksen, *Exposition of the Gospel According to Mark,* 644.

the head with his own scepter!" And as the fiend hits Jesus, the thorny spikes are driven deeper into the flesh.[29]

As a sign of indignity they spat on Him. "The act of spitting at him may be interpreted as a parody on the kiss of homage which was customary in the East."[30] They continually knelt and bowed before Him. The imperfect tenses of all these verbs imply that these actions continued over a period of time. They truly were mocking the King of the Jews not only because of His claim to kingship but because of their hatred for these people whose land they were occupying.

15:20 After they had mocked Him for a period of time, they finally removed the purple cloak from Him, put His own garments on Him, and "led Him out" (*exagousin auton,* historical present giving vivid detail after the imperfect tense verbs of v. 19) to be crucified. Their actions were terrible, but something far worse was yet ahead. The execution squad that was going to carry out this dastardly deed probably consisted of four soldiers (cf. John 19:23) headed up by a centurion. In light of the fact that it was the festival time with multitudes of people in the city, it may very well have been that a larger group of Roman soldiers accompanied this small group to make sure that the crucifixion would be carried out. Although Mark does not record the fact, it appears from John 19:4f. that Pilate again entered the picture. He brought Jesus before the crowd and uttered those famous words, "Behold the man!" The crowd, however, would have none of it, and their cries of "Crucify!" came once again. Pilate, therefore, washed his hands (Matt. 27:24) of the whole affair and sent Jesus out to be crucified.

THE CRUCIFIXION OF THE SERVANT, 15:21-32
(cf. Matt. 27:32-44; Luke 23:27-43; John 19:17-27)

The story of Christ's crucifixion is told by all four evangelists in some detail. Mark's account is the shortest. Slightly longer is Matthew's. Luke's report is almost twice the length of Mark's. John's is about as much longer than Matthew's as it is shorter than Luke's. If we assign the convenient figure of 10 to the length of Matthew's account of the crucifixion, Mark's would be 9, Luke's 17 and John's 13½.[31]

29. Ibid.
30. Lane, *The Gospel of Mark,* 560.
31. Hendriksen, *Exposition of the Gospel According to Mark,* 646.

15:21 It was customary for a condemned prisoner to carry his own cross, or at least the crosspiece, to the place of execution, which was always outside the city. When one considers all that Jesus had been through, with probably little or no sleep, as well as the intense beatings that He suffered, it is not surprising that Jesus was unable to bear His own cross. So the Roman soldiers "pressed into service" (*aggareuousin*, "to compel," dramatic present tense verb) a man by the name of Simon of Cyrene. Cyrene was a city in north Africa, in modern-day Libya, that had a large Jewish population. Whether Simon had moved back to Jerusalem or simply was in Jerusalem for the Passover festival is not clear. It is noteworthy that Mark alone makes the notation that Simon was "the father of Alexander and Rufus." Clearly Alexander and Rufus were individuals known to the readers of this gospel. If Mark's readers were primarily located near or around the city of Rome, it should be noted that the apostle Paul sent greetings to a man named Rufus in the city of Rome when he wrote his letter to that city (cf. Rom. 16:13). There is no way of knowing for certain if these two men are one and the same, but that could very well be the case. Why else would Mark have mentioned the children of Simon of Cyrene?

15:22 Jesus was "brought" (*pherousin*, historical present tense) outside the walls of the city (cf. Heb. 13:12) to a place that was apparently well known to the Jews. In Aramaic it was "Golgotha." Mark translates that Aramaic expression for his Roman readers, informing them that Golgotha meant "Place of a Skull." Probably just outside the wall of the city (John 14:20), there was a slight rise, although no Scripture calls it a hill. But there must have been something about the locality that impressed the people with the resemblance to a skull. Perhaps the rise had a smooth, rounded top devoid of vegetation that reminded the people of a bald head or skull. The English word "calvary" is basically a translation of the Latin word for skull, calvaria. Some have tried to read into the idea "a place of skulls," that is, that this area was a cemetery. That would not be in keeping with a proper understanding of the word, nor in keeping with the burial customs of that time.

> Though today it may well be impossible to point out the exact spot where Jesus was crucified, the Church of the Holy Sepulchre has tradition on its side. Not too much can be made of this, however, for the "tradition" is rather late (fourth century A.D.). Within the large space covered by this church there is room for the site of the crosses and also

351

for that of the tomb in which Joseph of Arimathea laid Jesus' body. The place of execution and the tomb were very close to each other (John 19:41, 42).[32]

15:23   Before they crucified Jesus, they offered (*edidoun,* imperfect tense implying that the wine was repeatedly offered) Him a wine mixture that had myrrh in it.

> The myrrh gave the sour wine a better flavour and like the bitter gall [Matt. 27:34] had a narcotic and stupefying effect. Both elements [myrrh and gall] may have been in the drink which Jesus tasted and refused to drink. Women provided the drink to deaden the sense of pain and the soldiers may have added the gall to make it disagreeable.[33]

Certainly the experience before Jesus would have been horrible, and anything that could help with the pain would be beneficial. Jesus, however, refused to take the mixture of wine and myrrh. "The Lord tasted the mixture (Mt. [27:34]), but declined to drink it; He had need of the full use of His human faculties, and the pain which was before Him belonged to the cup which the Father's Will had appointed (xiv.36ff.), of which He would abate nothing."[34]

15:24   With a very simple statement, Mark indicates that Jesus Christ was "crucified" (*staurousin,* vivid historic present tense) by the Roman soldiers. No details of the event are given. No details would have been needed by the Roman people reading or hearing these words. They had all witnessed many crucifixions and knew exactly how it was carried out. Normally the victim was stripped of all clothing and then his outstretched arms were either tied with cords or nailed to the crosspiece, usually with the nails being driven through the wrists. That crosspiece was then lifted and either fitted onto a post or tied to a post that was already permanently embedded in the ground. Sometimes there was a peg sticking out from the upright post that gave a man a place to sit. Often the feet were then nailed to the upright post through the ankles. It was a horrible way to die.

> Among the horrors which one suffered while thus suspended . . . were the following: severe inflammation, the swelling of the wounds in the

32. Ibid., 649-50.
33. Robertson, *Word Pictures in the New Testament,* 1:231.
34. Swete, *The Gospel According to St. Mark,* 380.

region of the nails, unbearable pain from torn tendons, fearful discomfort from the strained position of the body, throbbing headache, and burning thirst (John 19:28).[35]

Death usually came as the result of either dehydration or from asphyxiation as a man would no longer be able to hold himself upright and his chest would cave in. When he was no longer able to breathe, death would follow. It could take days for a man to die while hanging on a cross. Sometimes in order to hasten the death, the victim's thigh bones would be broken (cf. John 19:31-33). The breaking of the bones would cause excruciating pain, and the man also would no longer be able to hold himself upright, thus hastening his death by suffocation. "The height of the cross varied. Normally it was not much higher than the stature of a man, so that the feet of the crucified nearly touched the ground. A high cross seems to have been used when there was the desire to make the victim visible for as wide a radius as possible."[36]

Those involved in the crucifixion of Jesus "divided up His garments among themselves, casting lots" to determine what each would take. They did not realize they were fulfilling Scripture as they did so (cf. Ps. 22:18). The only possessions Jesus had that the soldiers went away with were His outer garments, a belt, sandals, and perhaps a head covering.

15:25   Mark alone records that it was the third hour when Jesus was crucified. The rendering of time here in Mark's gospel follows the Jewish custom rather than the normal Roman method he usually presented. This would be the third hour following sunrise, or about 9:00 A.M. John, writing his gospel at a much later time, used the Roman methodology of telling time. "Thus [John] put Jesus' trial before Pilate at 'about the sixth hour,' that is, approximately 6 A.M. The interval between 6 and 9 A.M. was filled with the soldiers' mockery (cf. Mark 15:16-20), Pilate's verdict on the two robbers (cf. 15:27), and preparations for the crucifixions."[37]

15:26   Every individual who was crucified had a placard (*epigraphē*, the English word is "epigraph") placed on his cross that listed the crime for which he was being executed. These charges were normally carried before the condemned man as he walked to his place of exe-

35. Hendriksen, *Exposition of the Gospel According to Mark,* 650-51.

36. Lane, *The Gospel of Mark,* 565.

37. John D. Grassmick, "Mark," in *Bible Knowledge Commentary* (Wheaton, Ill.: Victor, 1983), 188.

cution. Each gospel mentions the inscription on Jesus' cross with slight variations. John's gospel indicates that the inscription was written in three different languages: Hebrew, Latin, and Greek (John 19:20). Perhaps the complete inscription was the combination of the words from all the accounts: "This is Jesus of Nazareth, the King of the Jews."

Pilate, in effect, was explaining why this man was dying—because He was the King of the Jews. John stated that the inscription offended the religious leaders, but Pilate refused to change one word of it (John 19:21-22). There are many suggestions given as to why Pilate worded the epigraph above Jesus' cross as he did. William Hendriksen suggests that

> Pilate hated the Jews, especially their leaders. He was keenly aware that just now they had won a victory over him; for, as he probably saw it, they had forced him to sentence Jesus to be crucified. So now he is mocking them. By means of the superscription he is saying, "Here is Jesus, the King of the Jews, the only king they have been able to produce, a king crucified at their own urgent request!"[38]

15:27 As Jesus was crucified two others were crucified with Him, "one on His right and one on His left." They were described as being "robbers" or "thieves." Being a robber or a thief was not a capital offense. Probably these individuals were insurrectionists who may have been associated with Barabbas, who was also called a robber. Perhaps the cross in the middle had been meant for Barabbas.

> By causing Jesus to be crucified between these two culprits did Pilate intend to insult the Jews even more? Did he intend to say, "Such is your king, O Jews, one who is not any better than a bandit, and therefore deserves to be crucified between two of them"? However that may have been, one thing is certain, the prophecy of Isa. 53:12—"He was reckoned with the transgressors"—was here being fulfilled.[39]

15:28 The better manuscripts do not include v. 28 at this point. Mark rarely quotes from the Old Testament Scriptures because those Scriptures did not have the same significance to his readers as they did to Jews. Probably this verse was added by a scribe to show what

38. Hendriksen, *Exposition of the Gospel According to Mark,* 653.
39. Ibid., 654.

Old Testament prophecy was fulfilled as Jesus was crucified between the two thieves.

> Whether or no it should be read in the text here is not of great moment, for it corresponds to a great theological truth, to which allusion is also made in xiv. 48. He was treated by the authorities as an evil-doer, it is true; but this was also an outward picture of the deeper truth that He was treated as an evil-doer by God upon the cross for our sakes (2 Cor. v. 21).[40]

15:29   Those who passed by on this public road going to and from the city picked up on the accusations and verbal abuse against Jesus Christ.

> If, as some believe, Calvary even then was located at the conjunction of roads—cf. The Church of the Holy Sepulchre—then the expression "the bypassers" begins to make real sense. Not everyone belonged to the multitudes (Luke 23:48) that were going *to* Calvary that day, to watch everything that happened there from beginning to end. There were also those who merely "passed by." On their way elsewhere they stop long enough to take in the scene.[41]

They too cried out against Him, blaspheming Him, making fun of Him. The fact that He had at one point said that He was "going to destroy the temple and rebuild it in three days" was probably circulated among the crowd. That was one of the accusations brought against Jesus as they were looking for testimonials against Him (cf. 14:58-59). Jesus, of course, had never said that He was going to destroy the temple building in Jerusalem.

15:30   Their challenges to Him were that He ought to attempt to save Himself. He could do that if He would just come down from His cross. By suggesting that He "come down" from His cross, the implication is that His cross must have been a fairly high one, rather than simply one where the condemned man was almost at ground level. But no one had ever come down from his cross. Humanly speaking, that would have been impossible. "The jest was the harder to endure

40. Cole, *The Gospel According to Mark*, 240.
41. Hendriksen, *Exposition of the Gospel According to Mark*, 654.

since it appealed to a consciousness of power held back only by the self-restraint of a sacrificed will."[42]

15:31   The religious leaders of the day, those members of the Sanhedrin who had condemned Him to death, actually took the time to come out of the city to make sure that the execution was carried out. They stood by His cross and mocked Him among themselves. They were reminding themselves of the fact that this Man had supposedly saved others but He could not save Himself.

> When they refer to others he had "saved" they undoubtedly think of Jesus' healing ministry, but Mark intends his readers to understand these words in their full Christian sense. Paradoxically, the scornful words of verse 31b expressed a profound truth. If Jesus was to fulfill his mission on behalf of men he could not save himself from the sufferings appointed by God (Ch. 8:31).[43]

They were actually capsulizing the truth of the gospel at this point. Jesus Christ did save others, but the only way He could save others was for He Himself to die. If He had saved Himself from death on the cross, then all of mankind would have been lost. "Hence, to descend from the cross was not indeed a physical impossibility, but a moral and spiritual impossibility for the Messiah. If He did so, He would cease to be God's Christ, treading God's path of Messiahship; instead, He would become a mere human Christ."[44]

15:32   They addressed Him as "this Christ, the King of Israel." That was a slight variation from the epigraph that hung on the cross above His head. Since Pilate refused to change the wording of that sign, they gave to it their own interpretation. They said, let Him "now come down from the cross, so that we may see and believe!" "There is cruel sarcasm in the challenge 'come down now,' which seeks to throw into bold relief Jesus' helplessness, while the addition 'that we may see and believe' clothes their taunt in the garb of piety."[45]

Would they indeed have believed in Him if Jesus had wrought some miraculous miracle and had come down from the cross? It is highly unlikely.

42. Swete, *The Gospel According to St. Mark*, 383.
43. Lane, *The Gospel of Mark*, 569-70.
44. Cole, *The Gospel According to Mark*, 241.
45. Lane, *The Gospel of Mark*, 570.

> If healing all kinds of diseases, restoring sight to those born blind, cleansing lepers, and even raising the dead, if these works of power and grace, all of them performed in the fulfillment of prophecy!, did not cause them to believe in Jesus, but rather hardened their hearts so that they hated him for it, would a descent from the cross have caused them to accept him as their Lord and Savior? Of course not![46]

Their minds had been made up for some time that this Man was unworthy of their worship, and they did everything they possibly could do to eliminate Him.

The men who were crucified on either side of Jesus also picked up on the insults and reproached (*ōneidizon,* imperfect tense implying that their reproaches were repeated) Him. It is clear, however, from Luke's gospel that at a later point in time one of those two asked the Lord to remember him when He came into His kingdom (Luke 23:39-43). Jesus' response to that condemned man was, "Truly I say to you, today you shall be with Me in Paradise" (Luke 23:43). "Is it not possible—probable even—that this calm and majestic behavior of our Lord, coupled with the prayer, 'Father, forgive them, for they do not know what they are doing' (Luke 23:34), was used by God as a means to lead one of these two robbers to repentance?"[47]

THE DEATH OF THE SERVANT, 15:33-41
(cf. Matt. 27:45-56; Luke 23:44-49; John 19:28-30)

15:33   Mark presents a second time reference (cf. v. 25) when he declares that from the sixth hour until the ninth "darkness fell over the whole land." Using the Jewish scheme of rendering time, as was discussed earlier, this would mean that from 12:00 noon until 3:00 in the afternoon the land of Israel became dark. This could not have been a natural phenomenon, for the Passover of the Jews always occurred at the time of the full moon. It would be impossible for an eclipse to darken the sun, and no eclipse ever lasts for three hours. The darkness was an indication of the judgment of God: "the judgment of God upon our sins, his wrath as it were burning itself out in the very heart of Jesus, so that he, as our Substitute, suffered most intense agony, indescribable woe, terrible isolation or forsakenness."[48]

46. Hendriksen, *Exposition of the Gospel According to Mark,* 656-57.
47. Ibid., 658.
48. Ibid., 660.

15:34 It was finally at the ninth hour that Mark records his only saying of Jesus from the cross: "Eloi, Eloi, lama sabachthani?" This Aramaic expression is translated by Mark so that his readers would understand exactly what Jesus had said. Those words, taken directly from Psalm 22:1, meant, "My God, My God, why hast Thou forsaken Me?" This saying actually helps one to understand the darkness that had been going on for three hours. It was in that three-hour period of darkness that Jesus Christ became the sin offering for the world. As the sin offering of the world, God was not able to look on His Son. Jesus was abandoned in a judicial sense, not of course in any kind of a relational sense. Jesus never ceased being the Son of God, but He sensed the abandonment. In the Garden of Gethsemane He had struggled under the load of that anticipated separation (cf. 14:33-34).

> Now on the cross he who had lived wholly for the Father experienced the full alienation from God which the judgment he had assumed entailed. His cry expresses the profound horror of separation from God. "Cursed is everyone who hangs upon a cross" was a statement with which Jesus had long been familiar, and in the manner of his death Jesus was cut off from the Father (Deut. 21:23; Gal. 3:13; II Cor. 5:21). The darkness declared the same truth. The cry of dereliction expressed the same unfathomable pain of real abandonment by the Father. The sinless Son of God died the sinner's death and experienced the bitterness of desolation. This was the cost of providing "a ransom for the many" (Ch. 10:45). The cry has a ruthless authenticity which provides the assurance that the price of sin has been paid in full.[49]

Jesus Christ knew, however, that He had not been separated completely from His Father, which is why He cried out to Him as "My God, My God." Jesus was anticipating a glorious restoration of fellowship with His Father after bearing the sins of the world.

15:35 When some of the bystanders heard Him cry out, they said, "Behold, He is calling for Elijah." Whether they had misunderstood His cry and actually thought that He was calling out to Elijah or whether they simply were continuing to antagonize Jesus Christ is unknown.

> But the resemblance between either the Hebrew "Eli" or the Aramaic "Eloi" and the name of the Old Testament prophet was probably close enough so that *perverted minds and lips* could turn that similarity into a

49. Lane, *The Gospel of Mark*, 573.

coarse joke. Moreover, was it not a Jewish belief that Elijah would introduce the Messiah and live beside Him for a while as his assistant and the rescuer of those who were about to perish?[50]

Perhaps they were saying, "Let's see if Elijah will come to help Him."

15:36 Someone, therefore, ran, "filled a sponge with sour wine," and placed it on a reed to lift it up to Jesus to drink. "A sour wine vinegar is mentioned in the OT as a refreshing drink (Num. 6:3; Ruth 2:14), and in Greek and Roman literature as well it is a common beverage appreciated by laborers and soldiers because it relieved thirst more effectively than water and was inexpensive."[51] Those around the cross were probably hoping to extend His life so they could see if Elijah would come to take Him down from the cross.

15:37 Mark then declares that Jesus "uttered a loud cry, and breathed His last." That loud cry was probably the one word cry that was recorded in John 19:30, "Testelestai." That one word is translated, "It is finished!" Jesus knew that the work of man's redemption had been accomplished; therefore, He breathed His last breath (*exepneusen,* aorist tense signifying an accomplished fact). With His last breath He also issued a statement as He committed His spirit into the hands of His Father (cf. Luke 23:46). Clearly the relationship of Jesus Christ and the Father was not broken permanently by the fact that He bore the sin of the world. It is clear also that "the Death of the Lord was a voluntary surrender, not a submission to physical necessity."[52] Jesus was in control through this entire process. "The strength of the cry indicates that he did not die the ordinary death of those crucified, who normally suffered long periods of complete exhaustion and unconsciousness before dying."[53]

15:38 When Jesus died, Mark adds that there was an accompanying sign: "the veil of the temple was torn in two from top to bottom." The tense of the verb is passive, implying that the tearing was not done by men. That would, in fact, have been impossible, since the tear occurred from the top to the bottom and because of the thickness of the temple curtains. This veil was probably the veil that separated the holy place from the most holy place in the temple. This rending of the veil "must be regarded as a miracle. Any secondary means that may have

50. Hendriksen, *Exposition of the Gospel According to Mark,* 663.
51. Lane, *The Gospel of Mark,* 573.
52. Swete, *The Gospel According to St. Mark,* 387.
53. Lane, *The Gospel of Mark,* 574.

been used to effect it are not mentioned, and it would be futile to speculate."[54]

This event occurred at the very moment that a priest was in the holy place preparing for afternoon prayer. That priest probably thought his life was over as the veil was rent and the way into the holy of holies was there for him to see. He was, of course, in no danger, for the glory of the Lord representing His presence had departed from the first temple before its destruction by the Babylonians in 586 B.C. (see Ezek. 10:18-19; 11:22-25). The glory of the Lord will not return to the temple until it is again built in the millennial age (see Ezek. 43:1ff.). The significance of this sign is stated by the writer of the book of Hebrews (Heb. 10:19-20). It is clear that Jesus Christ has inaugurated for all mankind access into the very presence of a holy God through His blood that He offered on Calvary's cross.

15:39   Mark also states that "the centurion" (*kentyriōn,* from *centurio,* a Latin word used only here and in v. 44) was standing at the cross observing all that had taken place. This comment made by Mark alone implies that the centurion was carefully watching Jesus and observing the scene. He is recorded as making a very interesting comment as he saw the way that Jesus died: "Truly this Man was the Son of God!" There technically is no article in the text before the expression "Son of God"; however, with proper nouns and titles, forms without articles can still be definite. Whether or not this centurion truly believed that Jesus Christ was "the" Son of God or whether he was simply acknowledging the fact that Jesus Christ was an extraordinary divine person probably cannot be determined simply from the text.

> The conduct and sayings of Jesus, so unique in his experience of crucifixions, culminating in the supernatural strength of the last cry, the phenomena which attended the Passion—the darkness, the earthquake, perhaps also the report of the event in the Temple, impressed the Roman officer with the sense of a presence of more than human greatness.[55]

However, it is certain that Mark regarded his statement as a clear acknowledgment of the person of Jesus Christ as God's Son. He saw far more in the centurion's words than the centurion himself realized.

54. Hendriksen, *Exposition of the Gospel According to Mark,* 666.
55. Swete, *The Gospel According to St. Mark,* 389.

This is clearly seen as one compares his statement to all of the others around the cross who were mocking Him and bringing all kinds of accusations against Him. In the midst of that scene, a Roman centurion spoke up and said, "This Man was the Son of God." Surely that would have brought encouragement and joy to Mark's Roman readers.

> In contemporary practice the designation "Son of God" had been arrogated for the Roman ruler, who was worshipped in the state cult. Most effectively, therefore, Mark reports that the centurion proclaimed that the crucified Jesus (and not the emperor) is the Son of God. His words provide a discerning Gentile response to the death of Jesus.[56]

15:40   Mark also notes that some of the last witnesses of the death of Jesus Christ on the cross were women. They were "looking on from a [long] distance," "where they could be safe from the ribaldry of the crowd, and yet watch the Figure on the cross—not the 'daughters of Jerusalem' who had bewailed Jesus on the way to Golgotha, but followers from Galilee."[57] Three women are named by Mark, although it is clear that His mother, Mary, had also been there earlier (cf. John 19:26-27). Still present at the time of the Savior's death were Mary Magdalene, Mary the mother of James and Joses, and Salome.

Mary Magdalene was a woman from the village of Magdala on the western shore of the Sea of Galilee, from whom Jesus had cast seven demons (cf. Luke 8:2). The second Mary is simply identified as a woman who was known for her two sons, James the less, who was an apostle (cf. 3:18) and Joses. Finally, there was Salome. The name "Salome" appears only here in the gospel of Mark, but it is thought that she probably was the wife of Zebedee and therefore the mother of the apostles James and John (cf. Matt. 27:56).

15:41   These women had been extremely helpful to Jesus and to His disciples while He was ministering in Galilee. They "used to follow Him and minister to Him" (*ēkolouthoun autō kai diēkonoun autō*, both imperfect tense verbs implying long ministries) on many different occasions so that He was able to carry out His work (cf. Luke 8:1-3). In addition to these women, Mark notes that there were other women who also had come up with Jesus and His disciples to Jerusalem. The assistance of these women enabled Jesus to minister without

56. Lane, *The Gospel of Mark*, 576.
57. Swete, *The Gospel According to St. Mark*, 389.

having to be concerned about the normal routines and activities of life.

> The significance of the presence of these women to Mark is that they were eyewitnesses to the primary events proclaimed in the gospel, the death (verses 40-41), burial (verse 47) and resurrection (Ch. 16:1) of Jesus. The details of what took place could be substantiated by their testimony.[58]

THE BURIAL OF THE SERVANT, 15:42-47
(cf. Matt. 27:57-61; Luke 23:50-56; John 19:38-42)

15:42   Since Jesus died at about 3:00 in the afternoon, the concluding events had to move rapidly. Mark indicated that evening had already come. The late part of the afternoon from about 3:00 P.M. until sundown was what was in view in this text. Mark indicates that the day when Jesus died was "the preparation day" (*paraskeuē*). That Greek word is the modern-day word for Friday. The next day would be the Sabbath. Since no work could be done on the Sabbath, it was necessary that the dead body of Jesus be removed from the cross and placed into a tomb. The law specifically required a proper burial for all bodies, even those of criminals. Deuteronomy 21:22-23 specifically says that a man hanged on a tree must be taken down and buried before sunset. But who was going to take care of this? The disciples had fled (Matt. 26:56). John had been present at the crucifixion, but Jesus had entrusted to him the care of His mother (John 19:27). If someone had not come forward, Jesus' body would have been placed in a common grave provided for criminals.

15:43   Joseph of Arimathea came forward at this time. He was from a village located about twenty miles northwest of Jerusalem but probably in recent years had made his home in the city of Jerusalem. He was "a prominent member of the Council" (*euschēmōn bouleutēs*, a high ranking member of the Sanhedrin), and he himself "was waiting [*prosdechomenos*, imperfect tense implying something that had extended over a period of time] for the kingdom of God." John says that he was a disciple of Jesus Christ, although he was a "secret one" (John 19:38), and Luke notes that he had not agreed with the council's vote concerning Jesus (Luke 23:51).

58. Lane, *The Gospel of Mark*, 577.

The events of the day had brought about the end of his secrecy, for he boldly (*tolmēsas,* aorist participle, "becoming bold") went before Pilate to ask for the body of Jesus. That was a very unusual thing for him to do, for first of all he was not a member of the family. Mary, however, was exhausted by the events of the day and in no condition to request the body. There is no evidence that any of Jesus' brothers or sisters were in the city. Second, since Jesus was a condemned criminal the chances were not good that Pilate would grant his request. Third, it would very clearly mark him out as a disciple of Jesus Christ. He would no longer be able to hide that fact before his friends on the council, the Sanhedrin.

> Here was real courage, for a man of his position to risk an association with a leader already fallen and thus apparently incapable of benefiting him further. . . . But Pilate would have almost certainly refused to grant the body to such humble disciples, for it was the property of the Roman Government, as that of any condemned and executed criminal was; but to a responsible man like Joseph, he was prepared to grant it. Like Esther (Est. iv. 14), Joseph had been prepared for a time like this.[59]

15:44   When Joseph came to Pilate, Mark alone records that Pilate wondered if Jesus had already died. Normally a man who was crucified could linger for days before dying. Mark did not record the request of the Jews that the legs of the three men might be broken to hasten their deaths, nor the carrying out of the request on the two criminals (cf. John 19:31-33). Therefore, Pilate summoned the centurion, probably the one who had been on duty at Jesus' cross. He questioned him as to whether or not Jesus Christ was truly dead, a fact reported only by Mark.

15:45   He determined from the centurion that indeed Jesus was dead. Mark's reference to the centurion's testimony, the only reference in the gospel accounts, shows that the death of the Savior was clearly attested by a Roman official. When he found out that Jesus was dead, Pilate "granted the body [*ptōma,* "cadaver, corpse," the only instance where this word is used of Jesus' body] to Joseph."

Why he did this is not clearly stated. Perhaps this was his final attempt to get back at the Jews by allowing the body to be taken and

---

59. Cole, *The Gospel According to Mark,* 249.

properly buried, rather than indiscriminately buried in an unmarked grave.

> The release of the body of one condemned of high treason, and especially to one who was not an immediate relative, was wholly unusual and confirms the tenor of the Gospel account of the Roman trial (Ch. 15:1-15). Only if Pilate had no reservations concerning Jesus' innocence of the charge of *lèse majesté,* but had pronounced sentence begrudgingly to placate the irate mob, would he have granted the request of the councillor.[60]

15:46 Joseph, being a wealthy man, would have been able to quickly purchase the necessary items as well as secure the necessary help to prepare the body of Jesus for burial. According to the gospel of John (John 19:39-40), he was assisted in this process by Nicodemus, who also was a silent disciple of Jesus but who now declared his loyalty to the Savior. They, along with servants of Joseph, took the body of Jesus, washed it, wrapped it in a linen cloth using the one hundred pounds of spices brought by Nicodemus (cf. John 19:39), and laid it "in a tomb which had been hewn out [of] the rock."

> This detail indicates that the body of Jesus was accorded an honorable burial. While none of the Gospels speaks of the washing of the body, this was considered so important in Jewish practice that it was a permitted action on the Sabbath. . . . It is unlikely that Joseph took time to secure the linen cloth and yet left the corpse bloody. The statement that Jesus was buried according to the Jewish tradition (Jn. 19:40) furnishes presumptive evidence that the body was washed before it was wrapped tightly with linen.[61]

According to Matthew 27:60, a tomb that Joseph had purchased for his own use was the burial place for the Savior. It had been hewn out of the rock, and no body had ever been placed in it. Mark indicated that, with the task of caring for the body accomplished, a stone was rolled against the entrance of the tomb. Such stones were quite large and would probably take several men to move. The purpose of the stone was to keep out wild animals as well as possible grave robbers.

60. Lane, *The Gospel of Mark,* 579.
61. Ibid., 580.

If the tomb was an exceptionally fine one, it may have had an elaborate disc-shaped stone, about a yard in diameter, like a millstone, which was placed in a wide slot cut into the rock. Since the groove into which the stone fitted sloped toward the doorway, it could be easily rolled into place; but to roll the stone aside would require the strength of several men. Only a few tombs with such rolling stones are known in Palestine, but all of them date from the period of Jesus.[62]

15:47   Mark finally notes that Mary Magdalene and Mary, the mother of Joses, remained to the very end. They were watching (*etheōroun,* imperfect tense implying that their observation continued over a period of time) what Joseph, Nicodemus, and the others were doing. They saw where the body of Jesus Christ was placed, and "hence they knew where it was laid and saw that it remained there (*tetheitai,* perfect passive indicative, state of completion)."[63] When the first day of the week came, they would be able to return to this same location and look once again at the tomb where Jesus had been buried.

Homiletical Suggestions

With a very brief statement of the official deliberations of the Sanhedrin condemning Jesus Christ, He is then brought before the Roman Governor Pilate for His "official" trial. It appears from Mark's gospel that Pilate clearly saw through the ruse of the chief priests as they were delivering to him an innocent man. Yet Pilate does not appear to be a strong ruler in Mark's account. He simply acquiesces to the crowd and does that which is expedient. Not only is Jesus dealt with improperly by the Roman officials, but Mark also reveals that the Roman soldiers treated Jesus Christ in a way that was not befitting any prisoner, as they beat Him and mocked Him.

The details of the crucifixion that Mark gives are minimal. The reason for that probably was the fact that his audience was well aware of the process of crucifixion. It needed no explanation. Notations are made concerning the timing of the crucifixion and of the Savior's death. There is very little in Mark concerning the statements the Savior made as He hung on the cross. Yet there is much made of the continual taunting that took place by those who passed Him by. The

62. Ibid., 581.
63. Robertson, *Word Pictures in the New Testament,* 1:398.

Savior's death occurred much more quickly than the normal death of a person by crucifixion. Yet when the Savior died, a Roman official clearly attested to the unusual circumstances surrounding the death, for the centurion spoke up, saying, "This Man was the Son of God."

With the notation that there were a number of women present observing the events of the Savior's death, Mark records that Joseph of Arimathea came forward to request the body of Jesus so that it could be buried properly in a grave. Normally a criminal's body was simply taken and buried in an unmarked grave. That, of course, could not have happened to the Savior, for then there would have been no way to verify His resurrection. Joseph was obviously a man prepared by God to carry out this special act of burial. The Savior's body was prepared, wrapped, and placed in the tomb.

MARK

CHAPTER

SIXTEEN

THE SERVANT'S RESURRECTION

THE RESURRECTION OF JEHOVAH'S SERVANT, 16:1-20

THE REVELATION OF THE WOMEN, 16:1-8
(cf. Matt. 28:1-8; Luke 24:1-8; John 20:1)

16:1 The Sabbath of the Jews was a time of inactivity. As soon as the body of Jesus was placed in the tomb, as seen in the previous section, all the participants headed for their homes to observe the Sabbath, which included Friday evening and all day Saturday until sunset. But as soon as the Sabbath was over, Mary Magdalene, Mary the mother of James and Joses, and Salome went out from their homes to buy spices. The spices they went to purchase were aromatic oils. These oils were prepared in a mixture that was poured over the grave wrappings surrounding the body of a dead person in order to counteract the effects of decaying human flesh. These women did not plan to embalm or mummify the body. That custom was not known among the Jews. They simply wanted to visit the grave of Jesus and use the aromatic spices to counteract the effects of the decaying flesh.

> It is not uncommon to find in Palestinian tombs dating to the first century such funerary objects as perfume bottles, ointment jars and other vessels of clay and glass designed to contain aromatic oils. . . . The preparations for returning to the tomb in performance of an act of piety

show that the women had no expectation of an immediate resurrection of Jesus. Since in the climate of Jerusalem deterioration would occur rapidly, the visit of the women with the intention of ministering to the corpse after two nights and a day must be viewed as an expression of intense devotion.[1]

16:2 "Very early on the first day of the week," which would have been Sunday, Nisan 16, three women left the place where they were staying, which most probably was Bethany.

> Some people are greatly disturbed over the fact that Jesus did not remain in the grave a full seventy-two hours. But he repeatedly said that he would rise on the third day and that is precisely what happened. He was buried on Friday afternoon. He was risen on Sunday morning. If he had really remained in the tomb [a] full three days and then had risen after that, it would have been on the fourth day, not on the third day.[2]

John 20:1 says that they left while it was still dark and presumably arrived at the tomb shortly after sunrise.

> It is true that these women should have paid more attention to the Lord's repeated prediction that he would rise again on the third day. On the other hand, while we may criticize their lack of sufficient faith—a lack which they shared with the male disciples—let us not overlook their exceptional love and loyalty. They were at Calvary when Jesus died, in Joseph's garden when their Master was buried, and now very early in the morning, here they are once more, in order to anoint the body. Meanwhile, where were the eleven?[3]

16:3 The fact that there were no men with them became a concern for the women as they remembered that a large stone had been rolled in front of the opening of the tomb. It had been rolled there because Joseph "feared common tomb-robbers, at whom so many tomb-imprecations of early centuries are directed. A hundred pounds of spices was worth a king's ransom, if stolen; and there were numerous cases of tombs being re-used by others for a second 'private' burial, after

1. William L. Lane, *The Gospel of Mark*, NICNT (Grand Rapids: Eerdmans, 1974), 585.
2. A. T. Robertson, *Word Pictures in the New Testament* (Nashville: Broadman, 1930), 1:400.
3. William Hendriksen, *Exposition of the Gospel According to Mark* (Grand Rapids: Baker, 1975), 678.

the expulsion of the first body or bones."⁴ The three women began to discuss (*elegon,* imperfect tense implying that this was discussed as they walked along together) this issue, and their question was, "Who will roll away the stone for us from the entrance of the tomb?" Mark alone records this concern. They probably were unaware of the extra precautions of a guard that had been taken by the Jewish leaders, as well as the sealing of the tomb (cf. Matt. 27:62-66).

16:4   When they arrived at the tomb, they were surprised to discover (*theōrousin,* "to behold," a dramatic present tense verb) that the stone that had previously been in front of the door "had been rolled away" (*anakekylistai,* perfect passive verb implying that the stone had been rolled back and remained there to leave the tomb open). Although Mark gives no indication of how the stone was removed, Matthew "attributes the removal of the stone to the descent of an Angel, accompanied by an earthquake; the Angel sits upon the stone which he has rolled away, and is there apparently when the women arrive [Matt. 28:2-5]."⁵

The surprise of the women related primarily to the "extremely large" size of this stone. The size of the covering of the tomb opening implies surely that this tomb was very large, possibly allowing visitors to stand erect after they entered. Nevertheless, they found the tomb open, and they were able to enter.

16:5   Tombs in the time of Jesus normally consisted of at least one entry room beyond which there could be other chambers for the placing of bodies. Into that first room, families often came to visit the remains of their loved ones. As the women entered into this first room, they were surprised to see "a young man [*neaniskon,* same word as in 14:51] sitting at the right, wearing a white robe." According to Luke's and John's accounts of the resurrection, there were two angels present, whereas Matthew and Mark mention only the more prominent one. According to Matthew, the person who greeted the women was declared to be an angel (Matt. 28:2-5). "The very diversity of the accounts strengthens the probability that the story rests upon a basis of truth; the impressions of the witnesses differed, but they were agreed upon the main facts."⁶

---

4. R. A. Cole, *The Gospel According to Mark* (Grand Rapids: Eerdmans, 1979), 253.

5. Henry Barclay Swete, *The Gospel According to St. Mark* (Grand Rapids: Eerdmans, 1956), 396.

6. Ibid, 397.

The angel had moved the stone away from the door, not to allow the Lord Jesus to leave the tomb but to permit the women and others to come and enter the tomb. The women were utterly "amazed" (*exethambēthēsan,* aorist verb, a strong word for great amazement including a note of dread, used only by Mark in the New Testament) at what they saw.

16:6   The angel sensed their state of confusion and told them not to be amazed (*Mē ekthambeisthe,* present tense imperative, "Stop being amazed!"). He said that he knew they were looking for Jesus the Nazarene, a designation found only in Mark, who had been crucified. But the One who had been crucified now had been raised (*ēgerthē,* aorist passive verb implying that the resurrection of Jesus Christ was accomplished by the power of the Father). "The resurrection presupposes the death and burial of Jesus, and both of these events are specified in the angel's declaration."[7]

"He is not here," the angel said. But he identified the place where the body had been laid. John 20:6-7 states that the grave clothes that had been wrapped around the body of Jesus were still there in the tomb. The resurrected Savior's body had passed through the grave clothes, leaving them in the same state in which they had been wrapped around His body.

The fact that women were the first to receive the announcement of the resurrection is significant in view of contemporary attitudes. Jewish law pronounced women ineligible as witnesses. Early Christian tradition confirms that the reports of the women concerning the empty tomb and Jesus' resurrection were disregarded or considered embarrassing (cf. Lk. 24:11, 22–24; Mk. 16:11). That the news had first been delivered by women was inconvenient and troublesome to the Church, for their testimony lacked value as evidence. The primitive Community would not have invented this detail, which can be explained only on the ground that it was factual.[8]

16:7   The angel told the women that they were to be the first witnesses of the resurrection. The women were instructed to go and "tell His disciples and Peter." Mark is the only Gospel that makes a special mention of Peter, and it is the first mention of Peter since his denial (cf. 14:66-72). It should be remembered that Peter had strongly testi-

7. Lane, *The Gospel of Mark,* 588.
8. Ibid., 589.

fied that he would never denounce his Lord, and yet he had denied the Lord three times. Perhaps Peter felt that this disqualified him from being an apostle. The angel's words obviously reassured Peter that, although he had denied his Lord, the Lord had forgiven him. He was still considered to be a vital part of the apostolic band. Technically all of the disciples had fled from the garden and only John appears to be around at the crucifixion. Nevertheless, they were all still "His disciples."

The message to the disciples was that Jesus would be "going before you [*proagei,* historic present tense giving vivid action] into Galilee," where they would see Him just as He had said. This surely would have brought back to their minds the statement that Jesus had made to them as they were walking toward the Mount of Olives (14:28).

> The reminder is necessary, for the words of Christ would be forgotten . . . in the excitement of the great events which had occurred. It is more difficult to understand why the matter should have been so urgent if a week at least was to intervene before the Risen Christ left Jerusalem (Jo. xx.26). Perhaps it was important to dispel at the outset any expectations of an immediate setting up of the Kingdom of God in a visible form at Jerusalem (cf. Acts i.6).[9]

16:8   The women, however, "fled from the tomb," and both "trembling and astonishment had gripped them [*eichen gar autas,* imperfect tense implying that their fear extended over a period of time]." For awhile "they said nothing to anyone, for they were afraid [*ephobounto,* imperfect tense]." The full ramification of the announcement that had been given to them was not understood.

> And it was because of this inner disposition, this mental state, that they not only fled away from the tomb, but also did not stop along the way to relate the cause of their fright to anyone. They had been rendered speechless. It is true that they were also filled with joy, but it is not Mark who mentions this. It is also true that when they had somewhat recovered from their mental terror they ran to deliver to the apostles the message that had been entrusted to them. But again it was not Mark who says this [cf. Matt. 28:8].[10]

9. Swete, *The Gospel According to St. Mark,* 398.
10. Hendriksen, *Exposition of the Gospel According to Mark,* 681.

THE APPEARANCES OF THE SERVANT, 16:9-14

There is widespread disagreement among Bible scholars as to the ending of the gospel of Mark. Verses 9-20 are not found in two of the most trustworthy manuscripts of the New Testament, according to some scholars. The verses, however, are found in the majority of the manuscripts. It is thought by many that if Mark's gospel ended at v. 8 that the ending would be very abrupt. Instead of ending triumphantly with the resurrection, the gospel of Mark would end with a group of fearful women doing nothing about the resurrection.

Lane has an excellent comment on this, quoted at length in the Introduction on page 26. He suggests that the ending of the gospel of Mark at v. 8 with a group of fearful women is "thoroughly consistent with the motifs of astonishment and fear developed throughout the Gospel."[11] Some manuscripts also add a conclusion to the gospel of Mark that reads, "And they promptly reported all these instructions to Peter and his companions. And after that, Jesus Himself sent out through them from east to west the sacred and imperishable proclamation of eternal salvation." There is no clear manuscript evidence to support the inclusion of these words to Mark's gospel.

The issue probably will never be settled. The reader is encouraged to look again at the introductory material in this book where the subject is discussed in greater detail. Since these verses are disputed, it certainly seems that one would not be wise to base any matter of doctrine or experience on a verse that was found only in this section. However, these verses will be analyzed and possible suggestions given to the various problems.

TO MARY, 16:9-11

(cf. John 20:11-18)

16:9 Mark declares that, after Jesus had arisen early on the first day of the week, "He first appeared [*ephanē prōton,* aorist passive verb indicating a completed event] to Mary Magdalene." Mary Magdalene had been mentioned several times previously in the gospel of Mark, even in the immediate context (cf. 16:1), but now it is stated that this was the Mary from whom Jesus "had cast out [*ekbeblēkei,* past perfect tense indicating the act had occurred with an abiding result of demonic freedom] seven demons."

11. Lane, *The Gospel of Mark,* 591-92.

She is introduced to the reader, as if she had not been named before
... alone of the three she sees the Lord, and announces the Resurrection
to the Eleven, and no explanation is given of this unexpected turn in the
events. Lastly, the paragraph has evidently been detached from some document in which the Lord has been the subject of the preceding sentence.[12]

The details of the appearing of Jesus to her are not presented in
this text, but they are found in John 20. There it was stated that after
she saw the angel at the tomb, Mary ran and told Simon Peter and
John about the Resurrection. They ran out to the tomb, saw that it was
empty, and departed back to the city. But Mary, according to John
20:11ff., remained in the area of the tomb weeping. There she had the
privilege of meeting her risen Savior, thus being the first person to
encounter the risen Lord.

16:10   After she had met with Jesus, "she went and reported" to the
disciples, rendered here as "those who had been with Him," that she
had been with Jesus. This designation for the disciples, which appears
only here in Mark, may imply that there were more people to whom
Mary reported than just the eleven remaining disciples. This group of
people were still "mourning and weeping" (*penthousi kai klaiousin,*
present active participles indicating that the process was continuing)
over the loss of their Savior.

16:11   When they heard that Jesus was alive and that Mary had seen
Him, "they refused to believe" (*ēpistēsan*) her. A. T. Robertson says
that this verb *ēpistēsan* "is common in ancient Greek, but rare in the
N.T. and here again in verse 16 and nowhere else in Mark."[13] It could
very well be that this was a reflection on the Jewish culture, for the
testimony of women was not considered to be of great value. "As in
John xx. 18, love's feet were swift to bear the news; but as Luke xxiv.
11 and 22–24 makes plain, the disciples regarded all such women's
talk as *lēros,* 'rubbish.' There is nothing more tragic than the refusal of
natural man to receive such Christian witness (I Jn. v. 9, 10)."[14]

TO TWO DISCIPLES, 16:12-13
(cf. Luke 24:13-32)
16:12   "After that" (*Meta de tauta,* only found here in Mark)—that
is, after Mary's testimony to the disciples—Jesus "appeared in a differ-

12. Swete, *The Gospel According to St. Mark,* 399.
13. Robertson, *Word Pictures in the New Testament,* 1:404.
14. Cole, *The Gospel According to Mark,* 259.

ent form [*en hetera morphē,* different from His normal appearance] to two" of those who had heard the testimony from Mary. They were walking along the road "on their way to the country." This is evidently the same story that Luke records with greater detail, when Jesus appeared to two disciples who were heading back to the town of Emmaus (Luke 24:13-35) on the same day as the Resurrection. Mark's comment that He appeared in "a different form" could mean "different from the one in which He had appeared to Mary." Though that is possible, it might be better to understand that the form in which Jesus appeared to the two disciples was simply not the normal form in which they were used to seeing Him. Luke 24:16 states that their eyes were prevented from recognizing Him. Mark's account, in other words, was indicating that they did not recognize Him when He first appeared to them as they walked along the road. "There was clearly nothing in the Lord's appearance to distinguish Him from any other wayfaring man."[15] It was not until He was breaking bread with them in their house that they recognized that it was the Lord.

16:13 When the two disciples returned back to the city of Jerusalem and reported to the rest of the disciples that the Lord had appeared to them, they too were met with unbelief. The disciples refused to believe that Jesus had appeared to them, just as they had refused the testimony that He had appeared to Mary.

> But Luke's report of the two on the way to Emmaus is to the effect that they met a hearty welcome by them in Jerusalem (Luke 24:33-35). This shows the independence of the two narratives on this point. There was probably an element who still discredited all the resurrection stories as was true on the mountain in Galilee later when "some doubted" (Matt. 28:17).[16]

It seems that the idea of the resurrection of Jesus Christ, of which He had spoken on many occasions, still had not worked its way into every disciple's heart.

> The emphasis in Mark 16:9-14 is on the unbelief of the disciples who were mourning and weeping instead of rejoicing at the good news. Was it because they were prejudiced against the witness of the women? Perhaps, for the testimony of women was not accepted in a Jewish court.

15. Swete, *The Gospel According to St. Mark,* 402.
16. Robertson, *Word Pictures in the New Testament,* 1:404.

But even when the two Emmaus disciples gave their witness, not every-body believed.... Apparently there was division in the Upper Room until Jesus Himself appeared.[17]

TO THE ELEVEN, 16:14
(cf. Luke 24:36-43; John 20:19-25)
16:14   Mark finally records that Jesus "appeared to the eleven . . . as they were reclining at the table." The reference to "the eleven" was probably a reference to the apostolic group without an attempt to ac-tually count the number present. If this was the appearance of Jesus to the apostolic band on the day of His resurrection, then only ten of the men were present, for Thomas was not with them (cf. John 20:19-25). However, eight days following the Resurrection, Jesus appeared to the disciples again, and this time Thomas was present (cf. John 20:26ff).

The paragraph which follows seems to be a summary of the various narratives within the writer's knowledge which spoke of appearances to [the eleven]. It is without note of time or place, and *v.* 19 suggests that it is intended to cover the whole period between the evening of the Resurrection-day and the Ascension.[18]

When Jesus appeared to the disciples, "He reproached them for their unbelief and hardness of heart [*sklērokardian,* literally "hard-heartedness"]." Why had they failed to believe those who had given a firsthand report of the Resurrection? Had not the Savior said He would rise from the dead? Surely they should have believed the re-ports, especially when they came from some of their own followers in the faith. "The [Savior's] words are harsher than any which the Lord is elsewhere reported to have used towards His disciples, although it is possible, as has been suggested, that a peculiarly drastic treatment was necessary at this moment."[19] However, it is clear that the disciples by hearing of the Lord's resurrection before actually seeing Him would understand in their hearts what it meant to believe the testimony of another that Jesus had been raised from the dead. The message they were going to go out to proclaim was that the Savior was alive. They were going to ask people to believe. They now understood firsthand what that message truly meant.

17. Warren W. Wiersbe, *Be Diligent* (Wheaton, Ill.: Victor, 1987), 153.
18. Swete, *The Gospel According to St. Mark,* 402-3.
19. Ibid., 403.

THE COMMISSION OF THE SERVANT, 16:15-18
(cf. Matt. 28:16-20)

16:15   The command of Jesus in this verse need not automatically be connected with the previous appearance to the disciples. It is possible that some time later Jesus said to His disciples, "Go into all the world [*kosmon hapanta,* the "whole (emphatic form) world"] and preach the gospel to all creation." This commission is roughly the same as the one given in Matthew 28:19-20, which clearly occurred later and in Galilee. The commission is to take the gospel to the ends of the earth, not bypassing any region or settling down in any region to the exclusion of others.

16:16   In response to the preaching of the gospel, many individuals will believe. It was the view of the early church that belief in Jesus Christ should immediately be followed by baptism. The two ideas in this verse are linked together by a single Greek article. Believing and being baptized showed a combination of an inward, efficacious act that occurred in the heart of a person followed by an outward public expression of the faith that was internal. It certainly appears that the New Testament writers assumed the idea that under normal circumstances every believer in Jesus would be baptized. But that baptism is not a requirement for salvation is evidenced by the fact that the second half of the verse declares that it is only the one who disbelieves who is condemned. "Baptism is not mentioned because unbelief precludes one's giving a confession of faith while being baptized by water. Thus the only requirement for personally appropriating God's salvation is faith in Him (cf. Rom. 3:21-28; Eph. 2:8-10)."[20]

16:17   Jesus said that certain signs would "accompany those who [had] believed." As the disciples went out and proclaimed the gospel of Jesus Christ, they could expect that certain things would happen to demonstrate their authenticity.

First, in His name they would be able to "cast out demons." This was something that the disciples had already done, for they had been sent out with that authority in 6:7ff. The same authority was given to the seventy when they were sent out (cf. Luke 10:1-20). Authority over demons demonstrated that the messenger had greater power and authority than Satan.

---

20. John D. Grassmick, "Mark," in *Bible Knowledge Commentary* (Wheaton, Ill.: Victor, 1983), 196.

Second, Jesus said they would be able to "speak with new tongues." This was evidenced most clearly within just a few days as the gift of the ability to speak in a language not previously learned was given on the Day of Pentecost (cf. Acts 2:1-12). This same ability was also demonstrated later on in the history of the early church (cf. Acts 10:46, 19:6; 1 Cor. 12:10).

16:18   The third and fourth signs that Jesus said would accompany the disciples have caused some difficulties. It is probably best to view the first two clauses in this verse as conditional clauses. Therefore, these signs should probably be understood in this manner: If anyone is compelled to pick up serpents, or if anyone is required to drink any deadly poison, he shall not be hurt. There are no illustrations of either of these signs happening in the pages of the New Testament. The poisonous snake that crawled out of the firewood and bit Paul's hand on the Island of Malta (cf. Acts 28:3-5) was not an intentional handling of a snake.

These two signs should be understood as something that might be forced on a follower of Jesus Christ. "The great doubt concerning the genuineness of these verses (fairly conclusive proof against them in my opinion) renders it unwise to take these verses as the foundation for doctrine or practice unless supported by other and genuine portions of the N.T."[21] Warren Wiersbe summarizes these ideas:

> The person who takes up serpents just to prove his or her faith is yielding to the very temptation Satan presented to Jesus on the pinnacle of the temple (Matt. 4:5-7): "Cast Yourself down and see if God will take care of You," Satan said in effect. He wants us to "show off" our faith and to force God to perform unnecessary miracles. Jesus refused to tempt God, and we should follow His example. Yes, God cares for His children when, in His will, they are in dangerous places; but He is not obligated to care for us when we foolishly get out of His will. We are called to live by faith, not by chance, and to trust God, not tempt Him.[22]

The final authenticating sign was that they would "lay [their] hands on the sick," and they would recover. There are a number of healings recorded in the book of Acts (cf. Acts 9:12; 28:8) and in some of the epistles (cf. James 5:14).

21. Robertson, *Word Pictures in the New Testament,* 1:405.
22. Wiersbe, *Be Diligent,* 155.

Whether or no such evidential manifestations were intended to be continuous in the life of the Church, or restricted to this period, or sporadic, must be considered in the light of the rest of the New Testament; in view of the uncertain textual evidence for this longer Conclusion, no dogmatic assumption should be made from it alone. Paul's cautious words (I Cor. xii and xiii) are a wise guide to follow.[23]

THE ASCENSION OF THE SERVANT, 16:19-20
(cf. Luke 24:50-53)

16:19   Mark reports that when the Lord Jesus had finished His post-resurrection ministry, "He was received up into heaven" (*anelēmphthē eis ton ouranon,* aorist passive indicating the accomplishment of the event). That much the disciples were able to see, for they stood on the Mount of Olives and watched as He went up from the earth into the heavens (cf. Luke 24:50-51; Acts 1:9). The second half of Mark's statement must be accepted by faith, for it is declared that He "sat down at the right hand of God." By the use of this expression the author

> passes beyond the field of history into that of Christian theology. The belief that the risen and ascended Christ stands or sits at the Right Hand of God is one of the earliest and most cherished of Christian ideas . . . based on the Lord's own use of Ps. cx.1 (xii.36, xiv.62), and it is not unlikely that the writer has adopted here a primitive formula, or echoes a creed-like hymn.[24]

The ascension was in fulfillment of promises made in Psalm 110:1, which the Lord Himself had referred to in His discussion with the religious leaders in the last week of His life (cf. 12:13, 36). Peter also in his sermon on the Day of Pentecost picked up that same psalm and proclaimed that Jesus Christ had now been exalted to the right hand of the Father in heaven (cf. Acts 2:33-36). When Jesus stood in the midst of His accusers at the trial of the Sanhedrin, He said that the Son of Man would be seated at the right hand of God (14:62). Therefore, it is not surprising that when Jesus ascended into heaven He sat down at the right hand of God, the place of privilege, the place of

23. Cole, *The Gospel According to Mark,* 262.
24. Swete, *The Gospel According to St. Mark,* 407.

authority. It is from this position that Jesus has entered into a new work in heaven, for His personal work on earth has been concluded.

16:20 However, He still works on earth through His followers whom He has left behind. Mark says that the followers of Jesus Christ "went out and preached everywhere." "Another rapid summary. The writer passes over without mention the return to Jerusalem, and the founding of the Palestinian Churches, and hurries on to the fulfillment of the Catholic mission confided to the Eleven after the Resurrection (v. 15)."[25] The Lord continued to work with them and confirmed their testimony "by the signs that followed." In the immediate context, the signs of vv. 17 and 18 must be what the author has in mind. Those signs were very prevalent in the early days of the church, but as time moved on the signs increasingly diminished (cf. Hebrews 2:3-4).

Although the spectacular signs seem to have grown less frequent, the testimony nevertheless has continued throughout the world.

> The whole of the Acts of the Apostles is covered here in this single twentieth verse; and it may be more than an accident that the style of this last verse is much more the style of Acts than that of Mark. There can be no going back to the old; the Church must move forwards, with her Lord—we as well as they.[26]

That is why the gospel of Jesus Christ continues to be preached everywhere and men continue to put their faith in the precious Servant of Jehovah, the One who came not to be served but to serve and to give His life a ransom for many.

HOMILETICAL SUGGESTIONS

The glorious message that Jesus Christ had proclaimed on previous occasions is revealed in this chapter. The Savior had said that He was going to Jerusalem, that He would be turned over into the hands of wicked men, and that He would be crucified. But on the third day He would rise again. As the women came to the tomb on Sunday following the Sabbath, they found the stone rolled away from the entrance to the tomb and the Savior gone. An announcement was made

25. Ibid., 408.
26. Cole, *The Gospel According to Mark*, 263.

by an angel that Jesus had been raised from the dead. They were to go and proclaim this message to His disciples and to Peter, and let them know that the Lord would meet them in Galilee. The women, however, were fearful and fled from the tomb trembling and astonished. Although Mark's gospel does not record the fact that they went and told the disciples, the other Gospels make it clear that after a period of time they did indeed do this.

The addition to the gospel of Mark, while probably not a part of Mark's inspired text, nevertheless gives stories that are found in other Gospels. If one is preaching through Mark, one probably should bring a message on the whole chapter. The appearances of the Savior to Mary, to the disciples on the road Emmaus, and to the eleven disciples are all found in other gospel accounts.

The chapter concludes with the Lord Jesus commissioning the disciples to go into all the world and preach the gospel to every creature. That message is indeed proclaimed at the conclusion of Matthew's gospel as well as in the opening chapters of the book of Acts. The authenticating signs that Jesus said would accompany the disciples did indeed follow, especially in the early days of the church. But Mark's gospel concludes with the fact that Jesus ascended back to the right hand of the Father where He is involved in His current ministries to believers in the body of Jesus Christ, the church. It is the privilege of the church to continue to proclaim the glorious message of the Servant, who came into this world to die, thus giving His life a ransom for many.

SELECTED BIBLIOGRAPHY:
FOR FURTHER STUDY

Alexander, Joseph Addison. *The Gospel According to Mark*. New York: Scribner & Sons, 1858. Reprint. Minneapolis: Klock & Klock, 1980.

Barclay, William. *The Gospel of Mark*. Edinburgh: Saint Andrew, 1954.

Barnhouse, Donald Grey. *Mark: The Servant Gospel*. Wheaton, Ill.: Victor, 1988.

Blaiklock, Edward Musgrave. *Mark: The Man and His Message*. Chicago: Moody, 1965.

———. *The Young Man Mark*. Exeter, Decon, U.K.: Paternoster, 1965.

Blaising, Craig A., and Darrell L. Bock, eds. *Dispensationalism, Israel and the Church*. Grand Rapids: Zondervan, 1992.

Brooks, James A. *Mark*. New American Commentary. Nashville: Broadman, 1991.

Cole, R. Alan. *The Gospel According to Mark*. Tyndale New Testament Commentary. Leicester, U.K.: InterVarsity, 1989.

Dyer, Charles H. "Do the Synoptics Depend on Each Other?" *Bibliotheca Sacra* 138 (July–September 1981): 230-45.

Earle, Ralph. *The Gospel of Mark*. Grand Rapids: Baker, 1961.

———. *Mark: The Gospel of Action*. Chicago: Moody, 1970.

Edwards, James R. "The Authority of Jesus in the Gospel of Mark." *JETS* 37 (June 1994): 217-33.

English, Donald. *The Message of Mark*. Leicester, U.K.: Inter-Varsity, 1992.

English, E. Schuyler. *Studies in the Gospel According to Mark*. New York: Publication Office "Our Hope," 1943.

Enns, Paul. *Moody Handbook of Theology*. Chicago: Moody, 1989.

Erdman, Charles R. *The Gospel of Mark*. Philadelphia: Westminster, 1917.

Framer, William R. *The Last Twelve Verses of Mark*. London: Cambridge Univ. Press, 1974.

Fuller, David Otis, ed. *Counterfeit or Genuine? Mark 16? John 8?* Grand Rapids: Grand Rapids International Pubns., 1975.

Geisler, Norman B., and Kent Nix. *A General Introduction to the Bible*. Chicago: Moody, 1968.

Grassmick, John D. "Mark," in *Bible Knowledge Commentary*. Edited by John F. Walvoord and Roy B. Zuck. Wheaton, Ill.: Victor, 1983.

Gundry, Robert H. *A Survey of the New Testament*. Grand Rapids: Zondervan, 1970.

Henriksen, William. *Exposition of the Gospel According to Mark*. Grand Rapids: Baker, 1975.

Hiebert, D. Edmond. *Mark: A Portrait of the Servant*. Chicago: Moody, 1974.

Hobbs, Herschel. *The Gospel of Mark*. Grand Rapids: Baker, 1971.

Hughes, R. Kent. *Mark*. 2 vols. Westchester, Ill.: Crossway, 1989.

Hunter, A. M. *The Gospel According to Saint Mark*. London: SCM, 1962.

Hurtado, Larry W. *Mark*. Good News Commentary. San Francisco: Harper & Row, 1983.

Ironside, H. A. *Expository Notes on the Gospel of Mark*. Neptune, N.J.: Loizeaux Bros., 1948.

Kelly, William. *An Exposition of the Gospel of Mark*. Reprint. Sunbury, Pa.: Believershelf, 1971.

Lagrange, M. J. *The Gospel According to St. Mark*. London: Burns Oates & Nashbourne, 1930.

Lane, William L. *The Gospel of Mark*. NICNT. Grand Rapids: Eerdmans, 1974.

Lenski, R. C. H. *The Interpretation of St. Mark's Gospel*. Columbus, Ohio: Wartburg, 1946.

Maclaren, Alexander. *The God Who Serves*. Reprint. Old Tappan, N.J.: Revell, 1987.

Mann, C. S. *Mark.* Vol. 27 of the Anchor Bible. Garden City, N.Y.: Doubleday, 1986.

Martin, Ralph. *Mark: Evangelist and Theologian.* Grand Rapids: Zondervan, 1973.

McClain, Alva J. *The Greatness of the Kingdom.* Grand Rapids: Zondervan, 1959.

Morgan, G. Campbell. *The Gospel According to Mark.* Old Tappan, N.J.: Revell, 1927.

Morison, James. *A Practical Commentary on the Gospel According to St. Mark.* London: Hodder & Stoughton, 1887.

Moule, C. F. D. *The Gospel According to Mark.* Cambridge: Cambridge Univ. Press, 1965.

Pentecost, J. Dwight. *The Words and Works of Jesus Christ.* Grand Rapids: Zondervan, 1981.

————. *Things to Come.* Findlay, Ohio: Dunham, 1958.

Plummer, Alfred. *The Gospel According to St. Mark.* Cambridge: University Press, 1915.

Plumptre, E. H. *The Gospel According to Mark.* Grand Rapids: Zondervan, 1957.

Robertson, A. T. *Studies in Mark's Gospel.* New York: MacMillan, 1919.

————. *Word Pictures in the New Testament.* 8 vols. Nashville: Broadman, 1930.

Robinson, Charles S. *Studies in Mark's Gospel.* New York: Century, 1888.

Ryle, John Charles. *Expository Thoughts on the Gospels: St. Mark.* Reprint. Greenwood, S.C.: The Attic, 1973.

Ryrie, Charles C. *Basic Theology.* Wheaton, Ill.: Victor, 1986.

Scroggie, W. Graham. *The Gospel of Mark.* Grand Rapids: Zondervan, 1979.

Stedman, Ray C. *The Ruler Who Serves.* Waco, Tex.: Word, 1976.

————. *The Servant Who Rules.* Waco, Tex.: Word, 1976.

Stuart, C. E. *Sketches from the Gospel of Mark.* New York: Loizeaux Bros., Bible Truth Depot, n.d.

Swete, Henry Barclay. *The Gospel According to St. Mark.* Grand Rapids: Eerdmans, 1956. Reprinted as *Commentary on Mark.* Grand Rapids: Kregel, 1977.

Taylor, Vincent. *The Gospel According to St. Mark.* London: MacMillan, 1963.

Tenney, Merrill C. *New Testament Survey.* Grand Rapids: Eerdmans, 1961.

Thiessen, Henry C. *Introduction to the New Testament.* Grand Rapids: Eerdmans, 1943.

Thomas, John Christopher. "A Reconsideration of the Ending of Mark." *JETS* 26 (December 1983): 407-19.

Vos, Howard F. *Mark: A Study Guide Commentary.* Grand Rapids: Zondervan, 1978.

Wiersbe, Warren W. *Be Diligent.* Wheaton, Ill.: Victor, 1987.

Willis, Wesley R., and John R. Master, eds. *Issues in Dispensationalism.* Chicago: Moody, 1984.

Wuest, Kenneth S. *Mark in the Greek New Testament.* Grand Rapids: Eerdmans, 1950.

INDEX OF SUBJECTS

authorship, 11-12
characteristics of, 23-24
date, 19-20
ending of, 24-28, 372
occasion of writing, 21-22
outline, 28-31
place of writing, 22-23
relationship to Matthew and
Luke, 16-19
Mark. *See* John Mark
Marriage, 220-21
Mary (James the Less's mother),
361, 365, 367
Mary (Jesus' mother), 92
Mary Magdalene, 361, 365, 367,
372-73
Matthew, 65-66, 84
Messiah, 186-87
Mourning, 128-29
Mystery, 98

Nathaniel, 84
New covenant, 315-16
Nicodemus, 364

Olivet Discourse, 288-300

Papias, 11, 13
Parable
of the doorkeeper, 299-300
of the fig tree, 297-98
of the lamp, 102
of the mustard seed, 105-6
of the patched garment, 69-70
of the seed, 103-4
of the sower, 96-98, 100-102
of the tenants, 263-67
of the wineskins, 70
Parabolic teaching, 89, 95-96, 98-
99, 106, 110-11

Passover, 303, 309-10, 311, 312
Persecution, 291-92
Peter, 51, 82-83
death of, 20
denial of Christ, 318, 336-39,
370-71
relationship with Mark, 12-14
Pharisees, 78, 267
Philip, 83, 84
Pontius Pilate, 342
Prayer, 53, 256-58, 320-22
Progressive dispensationalism, 44

Raising the dead, 127-31
Ransom, 239
Repentance, 36, 44-45, 139
Resurrection
of Christ, 367-71
doctrine of, 272-74
Rich young ruler, 225-28

Sabbath, 70-73, 76
Sadducees, 270
Salome (Herodias's daughter),
142, 143-45
Salome (Mary's sister), 47
Salome (Zebedee's wife), 361,
367
Sanhedrin, 258, 329
Satan, 42, 89-90, 100
Scourging, 347-48
Scribes, 61-62, 157-58, 258, 279-
81
Sea of Galilee, 45, 108
Second Coming, 191, 295-97
Sermon on the Mount, 86
Shema, 275
Sign of Jonah, 179
Signs, 376-78, 379
Simon of Cyrene, 351

INDEX OF AUTHORS

INDEX OF SCRIPTURE
AND ANCIENT WRITINGS

391

23:8	272	3:13	358	Hebrews	
28:3-5	377	4:4	43	1:1-2	198
28:8	377	5:22	216	1:6	49
28:30-31	19	5:22-23	101	1:13	278
				1:14	42
Romans		Ephesians		2:3-4	379
1:3	279	1:7	315	2:9	239
1:5	290	1:10	43	2:11	191
1:8	290	2:8-10	376	9:22	315
1:16	168	6:11-12	49	10:13	278
2:9	168			10:19-20	360
3:21-28	376	Philippians		13:12	351
3:23-26	239	1:23	101	13:15	101
7:2-3	142	2:12	106		
7:4	101	2:13	106	James	
7:24	226			1:19	197
8:7	230	Colossians		2:19	49
10:17	257	1:6	101	3:17-18	101
10:18	290	1:6	250	3:18	216
12:18	216	1:23	250	5:14	139, 377
15:18-24	290	3:14	276	5:17	178
16:1	238	4:10	15	5:18	178
16:13	22, 351				
		1 Thessalonians		1 Peter	
1 Corinthians		4:13-18	198	4:8	276
7:10	18	5:13	216	5:13	13, 15
7:15	222				
9:5	51	2 Thessalonians		2 Peter	
12:10	377	2:3-4	293	1:13-15	13, 22
13	276			1:16-18	198
14:33	149	1 Timothy		1:21	20
14:40	149	2:4-6	239	2:1	239
15:25	278	3:8	238		
		4:10	239	1 John	
2 Corinthians				2:2	239
5:21	49, 355, 358	2 Timothy		3:14	276
13:11	216	2:8	279	3:16	239
		4:8	237	4:6	288
Galatians		4:11	15	4:8	276
2:2	237			5:9	373
2:6	237	Philemon		5:10	373
2:9	237	24	15	5:14	204
				5:14-15	256